Thomas Paine

A Lifetime of Radicalism

Thomas Paine

A Lifetime of Radicalism

David Benner

 Life & Liberty Publishing Group
Nashville, TN 37011

www.davebenner.com

ISBN-13: 978-0578273402

"If, to expose the fraud and imposition of monarchy, and every species of hereditary government; to lessen the oppression of taxes; to propose plans for the education of helpless infancy, and the comfortable support of the aged and distressed; to endeavor to conciliate nations to each other; to extirpate the horrid practice of war; to promote universal peace, civilization, and commerce; and to break the chains of political superstition, and raise degraded man to his proper rank—if these things be libelous, let me live the life of a libeller, and let the name of libeller be engraved upon my tomb."

-Thomas Paine, 1792

Contents

A Note from the Author

In Paine's time, authors exercised great stylistic license, and did not adhere to rigid spelling, grammar, or capitalization standards. In some cases, I have adapted period text to modern convention for the sake of sentence flow, but have generally left words spelled as their writers did. For longer passages, I have left words and style completely unmodified.

Introduction

As the harmony between Britain and the American colonies began to unravel, an unknown and undignified penman concluded a concise but direct pamphlet with the declaration that Americans could "begin the world over again." Rather than merely endorse patriot resistance against Britain, the writer advocated a governmental transformation that would rip asunder the traditional connections between the colonies and the British Empire. With his paradoxical claim that independence was "the only bond that can tie and keep us together," he courageously professed that the "birthday of a new world is at hand."[1] Undoubtedly, it was this voracious temperament that came to frame the writer's life.

Although he has been called "The Father of the American Revolution," Thomas Paine was perhaps the most unlikely man in the world to carry the torch of American independence. An Englishman who was once employed by the same king he grew to despise, Paine had been a failure in almost every aspect of life. His first wife died in labor, and his short-lived marriage to his second wife ended in separation within just three years. His attempt to petition Parliament for better compensation and working conditions for himself and his fellow tax collectors fell on deaf ears, and he accumulated immense personal debt. Bouncing frequently between professions and failing businesses, he struggled to find his way in life. That was, of course, until he picked up the pen.

Among those promoting a revolutionary break from the British Empire, Paine was an atypical patriot agitator. He owned little wealth, had few social connections, and called for absolute abolition of monarchy during an epoch when such an idea was virtually unimaginable. Connecting more with the everyday tradesman than the moneyed lawyer, he successfully transformed the colonial struggle for independence into a populist uprising. As 19th-century biographer Moncure Conway wrote, he was an "authentic commoner, representing English freedom in the new world."[2] At a time when many demanded reconciliation with the mother country, Paine believed total severance from the same was the only viable path to liberty and prosperity.

Paine was a true enigma of his time, and the story of his life reads much like an unpredictable and elaborate novel. From meager beginnings as a working-class laborer, he became well-regarded among the world's intellectual giants in both America and Europe. As an incendiary pamphleteer, he made friends of some of the most important people of his era—only to die broken, unpopular, and friendless. A one-time tax collector of the British crown, he achieved fame mostly through his persuasive ambush on Parliament for levying taxes against the American colonies. His first published essay was a gigantic flop, but his most famous works were best-sellers that captivated the minds of nearly every literate American and European. He chastised hereditary monarchy in no uncertain terms, but desperately pleaded for the life of the deposed King Louis XVI at the height of the French Revolution. His friends perceived him as a brilliant purveyor of wisdom, while his enemies condemned him as a heretical charlatan. His words served as catalysts for two revolutions on the world stage, yet he came from a tiny, unremarkable village. Through it all, he was the most notorious radical of his age.

While he is recognized most as the author of *Common Sense*, the most influential tract calling for American independence, Paine's entire life was a tenure of political zealotry—during which he had a hand in virtually every momentous event of his time. His compelling defense of natural rights, constitutional government, hard money, the absolute separation of church and state, universal suffrage, and the power to alter or abolish one's government made him the scourge of two continents. His political writings both vaulted him to the height of popularity, and lowered him into the deepest valley of disgrace. Throughout his life, Paine thought and lived by the conviction that being candid was more important than being popular.

As soon as *Common Sense* was released, Paine's ideas won the immediate endorsement of America's most distinguished revolutionaries. Continental Army general Charles Lee wrote that his work was a "masterly irresistible performance" that revealed the "transcendent folly and wickedness" of the British ministry. In the words of Philadelphian political writer Samuel Bryan, Paine "not only laid the foundation of liberty in our own country, but the good of mankind through the world." Revered Virginian statesman Richard Henry Lee, who drafted the resolution calling for the separation of the colonies from Britain, called him "fearless in the expression of his opinion." Samuel Adams, the agitator who ignited the flame of colonial resistance in Massachusetts, remarked that Paine's pamphlet had "unquestionably awakened the public mind" in America's transition toward independence and republicanism. Thomas Jefferson, author of the Declaration of Independence and the wordsmith's lifelong friend, opined that "no writer has exceeded Paine in ease and familiarity of style, and perspicuity of expression, happiness of elucidation, and in simple and unassuming language." Patriot physician Benjamin Rush, who encouraged the man to write *Common Sense*, observed that Paine's words "were sudden and extensive upon the American mind." Benjamin Franklin, the legendary character who first endorsed Paine's passage to America, called the well-known penman an "ingenious, honest man" whose work had "great effect on the minds of the people."[3]

Despite Paine's clarion call for independence, republicanism, and unrestricted liberty, not everyone was interested in remaking the world. Even among those who came to favor independence from Britain, Paine attracted enemies who considered his diatribes hyperbolic and impractical. His political enemies accused him of encouraging mob-rule democracy, which they claimed would dismantle the cornerstones of Western civilization. To the Tories who viewed American independence as an unscrupulous and illegitimate rebellion, he was the vilest creature imaginable. A writer calling himself "Cato" denounced his tract as "common nonsense," warning that it would serve as a blueprint for "bloodshed and desolation" in America.[4] Notorious French Jacobin Jean-Paul Marat denounced him as an incompetent fool who could not be trusted.[5] Another detractor called Paine "a crack-brained zealot for democracy," condemning his famous pamphlet as "an outrageous insult on the common sense of Americans, an insidious attempt to poison their minds and seduce them from their loyalty and truest interest."[6]

Those connected to church establishments deemed him irreverent and godless, even though he was one of the most resolute supporters of freedom of religious expression the world had to offer. Aristocrats often mocked him as a corrupt scoundrel, intent on fame and notoriety rather than the successful actualization of liberty. Many political philosophers considered him reckless and uncouth, and even as the source of bloodshed and political instability. Nearly all Paine's adversaries warned that his ideas would undermine enlightenment principles rather than reinforce them, and exacerbate political miseries rather than solve them.

During the Deane Affair, for instance, Paine found himself at the center of a political crucible. When it became apparent that an American agent in France, Silas Deane, had engaged in war profiteering, Paine first revealed the scheme to the public by way of his writings. As he divulged the information in a candid attempt to preserve republican virtue and guard against corruption, Paine drew the ire American politicians who accused him of compromising the fortitude of America's geopolitical alliances and undermining the War for Independence itself. Even after it became clear that Deane was indeed every bit the scoundrel Paine declared him to be, the author never regained the standing he once had in the United States, and was forced out of his civil position for his commitment to transparency in government.

As the American states secured their independence from Britain, Paine celebrated in earnest, but still considered the quest for republicanism incomplete. To the contrary, he thought the cause brought to fruition in America was but the first step in an undertaking applicable to every corner of the world. "The cause of America is in a great measure the cause of mankind," he asserted. The circumstances that liberated America were "not local, but universal...through which the principles of all lovers of mankind are affected."[7] Undoubtedly, Paine believed that individual liberty was a sacred and immutable part of humanity that should be embraced by all civilized peoples. Though many railed against him for such a position, he declared that the aims of other anti-monarchical revolutions were inextricably linked with the precedent-setting struggle for American independence.

In perhaps the most uncelebrated angle of Paine's life, the illustrious essayist displayed considerable ability in the physical and natural sciences. As one of the first men in world history to promote modern bridgebuilding techniques, he helped open a new frontier in engineering. Though his dream of constructing his own permanent iron bridge in America or Europe was never fulfilled, his designs won the praises of leading inventors and architects, and his trailblazing architectural ideas are now on full display in every part of the modern world. Furthermore, he demonstrated aptitude in astronomy and epidemiology, and was a natural academic. If he had devoted more of his life to these pursuits, it is likely we would today recognize him more for his scientific talents than for his political writings.

Despite the admiration Paine received in his lifetime, his candid and direct outbursts also did much damage to his reputation. He found a special knack for alienating several former friends, including the venerable George Washington, whom Paine eventually accused of ambition, dishonesty, and personal betrayal. His writings on such topics as monarchy and religion often advocated ideas that were unprecedented and unpopular. Regardless, Paine maintained the tenacity to express his thoughts in a manner that was unfiltered and uninhibited by social or political constraints. As he wrote, "he who dares not offend cannot be honest."[8]

If Paine's life had ended at the culmination of American independence, he and his work would still be worthy of modern attention and scholarly study. Nevertheless, the remainder of his undertakings remain undeniably prescient, and solidified his importance in world history. Indeed, his call for the complete severance of established religion from government was unique in his time, but today Americans live with the advantages of that reality. In addition, Paine's promotion of the French Revolution and musings on an ideal framework for government catapulted him to enormous fame in France, and his feud with legendary member of Parliament Edmund Burke stands as the most timeless philosophical debate between classical conservatism and classical liberalism. Undeniably, his continual yearnings for an egalitarian society echoed throughout the course of Western civilization and helped build the world in which we now live.

As the bloodiest stage of the French Revolution unfolded before his eyes, it was ironically Paine—the notorious radical—who attempted to temper the period's far-reaching excesses. He fought ever as vigorously to oppose attempts by French politicians to abolish universal suffrage and institute public executions—all while defending the idea of the revolution. Just as Maximilien Robespierre rose to power in an atmosphere of revolutionary fervor, Paine aligned himself with the rival Girondins and devoted his energies to political reform. When the National Convention suspended the French Constitution of 1793 and established the Committee of Public Safety to seize all governmental authority, Paine's indignation was raised to newfound heights. His volley of defiance quickly put himself in the crosshairs of the Jacobins, who sought first to undermine him, then execute him as a counterrevolutionary traitor.

Long before many of his contemporaries, Paine came to view slavery as an abject evil. He brought this opinion with him to France, where the question of emancipation was soon of pressing importance. When he returned to the United States, he reiterated his position and promoted anti-slavery efforts until the end of his life. An uncompromising abolitionist, Paine considered slavery a malevolent affront to natural rights, and as an inevitable source of future conflict between political factions. At the forefront of a movement to eliminate slavery from the new American states, Paine was quick to link the cause of independence to such a cause.[9] He planted the first seeds of abolition in America, and inspired Western civilization's first widespread manumission effort. In this case, too, his stance proved groundbreaking and prescient.

Although his detractors often accused him of atheism—an outlook held by virtually no one in his era—Paine clearly believed in a singular, divine, benevolent creator. However, as can be seen in *The Age of Reason*, his most controversial tome, his conception of God was that of a clockmaker creator who formed the world, then left it to develop naturally without intervening afterward. Denying the miraculous aspects of the Bible, but regarding the moral teachings of Jesus as matters of supreme importance nonetheless, Paine came to believe that religious institutions had corrupted humanity's conception of God, creating doctrine to encourage the defilement of liberty and to justify violent acts. The Bible was merely "a book of lies and contradictions, and a history of bad times and bad men," he wrote.[10] While critics charged him with seeking to undermine God, Paine ironically viewed his work as a defense of the deity's true quintessence.

Regardless of his controversial theistic opinions, his insistence on the absolute separation of church and state also made him an innovator in an era where state and religion were inseparable.

For much of his life, Paine lived on a spectrum between absolute poverty and modest prosperity. His personal experiences and genuine pursuit of egalitarianism undoubtedly led him to relate to and sympathize with the poor to a degree that his peers did not. Indeed, his desire to "raise degraded man to his proper rank" became an important part of his platform.[11] The essayist called for state programs to aid the impoverished and elderly, which were to be funded by a progressive income tax. In addition, he recommended the creation of a tax on cultivated land to support the redistribution of revenue from its proceeds. The program was a forerunner to modern universal basic income measures, where each citizen within a society would receive a periodic stipend from the government. Both proposals were groundbreaking for their time, and utterly ignored by his day's political class.

Among its defining characteristics, the 18th century was noteworthy for the emergence of several vying philosophical outlooks, one of which included radicalism, a term derived from the Latin root word "radix," literally translated as "root." After the word was adopted into common language in England, it was given a political context and applied to those who sought to identify and eradicate a problem at its source. Political radicals then, were those devoted to striking at the root of an underlying problem rather than proposing mere reforms to lessen its consequences. In his age, no one exemplified such a definition more than Paine, a man who challenged almost every conventional political norm of his day, and popularized republicanism for the first time since the fall of the Roman Republic.

If nothing else, Paine was the prototypical contrarian of his time. A truth-teller in an age before true freedom of the press, he often made himself into a public enemy in the eyes of government censors. Even so, he never ceased his volley of criticism against tyranny and injustice, even after receiving a death sentence from two governments. For every man who reviled him, though, another was stirred to defend his ideas merely after reading his works. The polemicist bounced among professions almost aimlessly, overcame personal tragedies, endured frequent professional set-backs, and narrowly avoided death seven times. He was both the hero and the menace of two continents.

Paine's blunt style made it impossible to misconstrue his position on any given political issue of his day. Nevertheless, those of nearly every modern political persuasion have sung his praises. Modern conservatives recognize him as one of America's founding fathers, a vigilant advocate for rights and military opposition to the British. All the same, Paine is ad-mired by today's progressives for supporting universal suffrage and devel-oping a proposal for a social welfare system long before such an idea was fashionable. Libertarians view Paine, a true thorn in the side of govern-mental tyranny, as an 18th-century forefather of their own philosophy. Alt-hough each of these branches of contemporary political thought would de-test certain facets of Paine's work or life, they all claim him as their own.

It is unsurprising, then, that so many commentators of various profes-sional, geographical, and political stripes have given Paine such thoughtful praise. Eminent historian Gordon Wood wrote that he "spoke with a rage that few writers before him had ever expressed," and successfully con-nected with "ordinary people about issues of government and religion as no one in history ever had." Journalist and social critic Christopher Hitch-ens remarked that in a time where "both rights and reason are under several kinds of open and covert attack, the life and writing of Thomas Paine will always be part of the arsenal on which we shall need to depend." Accord-ing to biographer Craig Nelson, he should be "ranked among the brightest and most undeviating luminaries in the age in which he has lived." Re-nowned American inventor Thomas Edison wrote that no man "helped to lay the foundations of our liberty—who stepped forth as the champion of so difficult a cause" as Paine did.[12]

Despite Paine's public downfall late in his life, it is impossible to over-look his mark upon the contemporary world. In nearly every way, the ex-tent of his influence has been so monumental that it is taken entirely for granted today. His energetic defense of meritocracy over aristocracy, citi-zens over subjects, and representatives over lords are all preferences that have become hallmarks of Western civilization. Our age should thank him whenever a figure ascends to public office without being forced to adhere to a particular religious creed. When one publishes a sincere but unpopular political opinion, his idioms are ever apparent. Any time citizens engage themselves in the political process, or yearn for representative government, his sensibilities are resurrected once again. Whenever the inclination to criticize one's government is portrayed as the most patriotic stance imaginable, his presence is felt as well.

In the winter of 1790–1791, Paine kept to his upper room in London's Angel Inn and drafted *The Rights of Man*, his groundbreaking political treatise, when his thoughts were most clear and without the bustle of the city center to distract him. Over several years, I have written this work while holding to the same tradition, in candid research of Paine's life and with the utmost admiration for the vision he promoted with such unparalleled skill. This project represents my best effort to emulate Paine's incredible aptitude for propagating "unanswerable truths, with principles of the purest morality and benevolence, and with arguments not to be controverted."[13] If this book exhibits a thousandth of the ability my subject did with the pen and quill, I will consider it an undeniable success.

Rather than focusing heavily on an analysis of all details of Paine's life, this narrative emphasizes his revolutionary ideas. I do include substantial biographical information, but tried to do so with the intention of providing context that explains why his assertions were often made at the risk of his own life. I think my subject would have appreciated this approach, as he eschewed personal experiences and anecdotes in favor of principles and purpose. If the reader walks away from this text looking upon Paine as the man who ignited the fire of revolutionary passion, the fearless penman of individual rights, and the most important radical of his age, this writer will consider his objectives fulfilled.

Chapter 1

Humble Beginnings

At any early period, little more than sixteen years of age, raw and adventurous, and heated with the false heroism of a master who had served in a man of war, I began the carver of my own fortune, and entered on board the Terrible, Privateer, Capt. Death. From this adventure I was happily prevented by the affectionate and moral remonstrance of a good father.

-The Rights of Man

On February 9, 1737, the penman who incited revolution on two continents was born in the small town of Thetford, England, to a family without riches or social standing. Thomas Paine was raised under modest and quiet circumstances, apart from the splendor and commotion of life in London. In those days, Thetford was the downriver port of King's Lynn and a market town that gave rise to specialized artisanry. The town predated the Norman Conquest of 1066, and consisted of farmers, servants, apprentices, craftsmen, and a miniscule population of wealthier gentry. By chance, world's most infamous radical was born into working-class obscurity in an unremarkable village.

Paine grew up as an only child, his only sister dying shortly after birth. We know little of his mother, Frances, apart from the fact she was the daughter of a rich Anglican lawyer—whose upbringing contrasted greatly with that of his Quaker father, Joseph. Anglicanism, as the official established religion of England, was by far the country's most prevalent religious doctrine. Conversely, Quakers faced continual persecution in England, even after the Toleration Act of 1689 granted freedom of worship to Christian nonconformists. Although baptized into the Church of England, Paine was immersed in Quaker doctrine for most of his youth.[14] The contrasting influences of his parents' incompatible sects likely had a profound influence on his perception of religion—a subject which came to dominate much of his attention later in life.

In a rare moment of reflection upon his religious upbringing, Paine wrote of his bewilderment regarding Christianity at the age of eight. God's decision to allow his own son to die for the redemption of humanity caused him a moment of "serious reflection," he remarked. Believing "God was too good to do such an action, and also too almighty to be under any necessity of doing it," Paine began to doubt the legitimacy of such a creed. His cynicism had also extended to his father's denominational preferences. Had God consulted Quakers at the creation, he wrote later in life, "what a silent and drab-colored creation it would have been!"[15] In the end, neither Quakerism nor Anglicanism won Paine's heart.

As the maker of stays for women's corsets, Joseph Paine was master of an unremarkable trade. Designed to stiffen the structure of the corset and provide support for the posture of the woman wearing them, stays were fashioned from whalebone, shaped with a knife or other carving instrument, and inserted into the corset. Though the trade required incredible patience, attention to detail, and a steady hand, and was comparable to many artisanal professions of the day, Paine's political adversaries would in the future routinely bring up his family profession in their attempts to mock him.

As was typical, especially of those who were the sole child in their family, Paine was expected to follow his father's work as an apprentice after a menial education in reading, writing, arithmetic, and Latin. After his poor father received a loan from a wealthier relative, Paine was enrolled in Thetford Grammar School, which still operates today and boasts of its seventh-century origins.[16] One of the few remaining scraps of Paine's childhood is a poem written at the age of eight in honor of a dead crow:

Here lies the body of John Crow,
Who once was high, but now is low;
Ye brother Crows take warning all,
For as you rise, so must you fall.[17]

As a schoolboy, "the natural bent of my mind was to science," he recalled.
He also confessed that the thought "of seeing the western side of the Atlantic" never left him after he read a book on the history of Virginia. However, Paine drew away from both inclinations, and began to take up his
father's craft at age 13. Although he admitted this decision provided "the
value of moral instruction," he soon came to loathe the stay-making profession, complaining of boredom and yearning for an alternative.[18]

After he bought his father's business and left home, Paine began to
dabble in a vastly different trade—privateering. As a privateer, he helped
crews of independently-owned warships loot commercial vessels that
sailed under the flag of enemy countries, a practice actively encouraged
by British foreign policy. Now virtually unknown to the world, privateering was once a world-spanning activity. The practice was a highly capri-
cious trade—with notable spikes during times of war and lulls during
peacetime. Privateering was a popular profession in wartime because it
provided lucrative revenue streams for merchants that funded expeditions,
and was perceived as less wasteful than conventional warfare that often
culminated in the complete destruction of ships.

For much of his time as a privateer, the kingdom was engaged in the
Seven Years' War, a global conflict that involved the world's greatest
powers. Ironically, the source of the conflict largely resulted from the
deeds of a man who was then an unknown major in the Virginia militia,
Paine's future friend George Washington. The struggle between Britain
and France brought about a new opportunity for Paine, who considered it
the perfect avenue to escape the destiny of his father's trade.

Fate narrowly saved Paine from an early demise when he chose not to
embark upon a privateering stint on Captain William Death's *Terrible*.
Soon after the *Terrible* launched into the English Channel, it was oblite-
rated in a three-hour battle by the *Vengeance*, a French privateer. Only 17
of the ship's original crew survived, and more than 150—including all of

its officers and Captain Death himself—perished. Decades later, Paine recounted that his father's intervention had delivered him from the abject tragedy:

> At any early period, little more than sixteen years of age, raw and adventurous, and heated with the false heroism of a master who had served in a man of war, I began the carver of my own fortune, and entered on board the Terrible, Privateer, Capt. Death. From this adventure I was happily prevented by the affectionate and moral remonstrance of a good father.

However, Joseph Paine could not keep his son away from privateering for long. Within weeks of the departure of the *Terrible*, Paine was recruited by Captain Edward Menzies for a stint on his ship, the *King of Prussia*.[19] For several painstaking years, Paine helped crewmen loot the ships of French vessels with success. The *King of Prussia* captured eight ships within a half year, an impressive feat, and Paine returned to London to collect a lucrative commission. Ironically, it was through privateering that Paine assisted Britain, the government he later condemned, and pillaged France, the nation he later helped to nurture.

After his stint on the *King of Prussia*, Paine became disillusioned with the profession, but admitted it encouraged within him "a perseverance undismayed by difficulties" and "a disinterestedness that compelled respect."[20] After returning from his voyages, Paine seemed ready to pursue other endeavors. It appears that Paine was encouraged in this direction through his discovery of London in 1757, which was then the cultural epicenter of the universe. Indeed, London offered everything Thetford lacked—a cosmopolitan environment, the latest fashions, and the chance to exchange ideas with the world's leading theorists. In the Western world, its magnificence was rivaled only by Paris. To Paine, it was a true marvel.

By his own account, Paine's intellectual awakening began in London. Suddenly exposed to Western science and political theory, he devoted much of his time in the city to the discovery of new ideas and entered an obsessive period of self-directed study. Although Paine rarely cited the books he read or his ideological influences, he later reflected upon this period of his intellectual journey:

As soon as I was able I purchased a pair of globes, and attended the philosophical lectures of Martin and Ferguson, and became afterwards acquainted with Dr. Bevis, of the society called the Royal Society, then living in the Temple, and an excellent astronomer.[21]

Hastily absorbing the greatest minds of his day, he began to frequent clubs where important ideas were openly discussed. Paine came to view the city as the zenith of the Age of Enlightenment, where modern science and philosophy could be debated, embraced, or disregarded. These two subjects, more than any others, were to Paine of the utmost importance in the context of Western civilization, and thus framed the entirety of his renowned future.

London of the 1750s was a world of commerce, discovery, intrigue, and famous personalities. Thousands of carts transported wares from place to place, as horses filled the streets and bustling markets offered food, tobacco, oil, clothing, knives—and almost everything else Europe had to offer. Westminster Bridge was opened in 1750, linking Westminster with Lambeth. It was a true engineering marvel that encouraged housing development and aided in the exchange of goods. *A Dictionary of the English Language* by Samuel Johnson, perhaps the most influential dictionary in the history of the world, was released in 1755. Legendary parliamentarian Edmund Burke, with whom Paine would come to spar in the future, published his first works on philosophical and religious theory and began to write a history of England. He too was a rising star that would come to influence the world.

Though Paine was enthralled by his first encounter with England's greatest city, he struggled to make a living there. During his first two years there, he made a small salary through an apprenticeship to a London staymaker, but by doing so inhibited his prospect to earn a better living by striking out on his own. In 1758, he finally chose to do so. Deciding to become a staymaker after all, he left London, though its allure would draw him back more than once.

By all accounts, Paine's experience in Sandwich from 1758–1760 was a dark and peculiar period of his life. He first found work in Dover as a staymaker, but soon began a stay-making business of his own in the small town of Sandwich through a loan secured through his employer. It was there in 1759 that he took a wife, Mary Lambert, the maid of a wool draper's wife. Shortly thereafter, Paine's business suffered profusely, and Mary became pregnant. The couple migrated to the nearby coastal town of Margate, where Mary and her child died in labor—an extremely common occurrence for the time. At the age of only 23, Paine was now a widower. Evidently, the tragic combination of his wife's death and his failing practice persuaded him to abandon stay-making for good, and to explore new economic frontiers once again.

Early readers of his seminal future pamphlet *Common Sense* would likely have been shocked to discover that its sharp condemnation of British taxation had been composed by a former tax collector for the crown—but such a profession took hold of Paine's life for the next decade. Specifically, Paine hoped to become an excise officer. After studying all aspects of the profession for several months in London, he returned to Thetford, then gained work gauging brewers' casks in Grantham. Sitting along the River Witham in the county of Lincolnshire, Grantham was where Isaac Newton, perhaps the most acclaimed Englishman of his time, received his formal education a century earlier. After about two years of work in Grantham for which there is little record of Paine's activities, he was appointed to collect taxes in the nearby town of Alford.

In those days, tax collection was a hazardous profession. Excisemen who uncovered acts of smuggling received special payments for their efforts, but they risked their life to do so. This was because the collection of taxes always had the potential to spark violent outbursts, and Paine's situation was especially dangerous, as the advent of alcoholic gin stimulated rampant smuggling along England's coast. Britain's Gin Act of 1751, designed to drastically reduce the consumption of spirits, placed a burdensome tax thereon, and in 1757, Parliament went to even greater lengths to suppress the production of gin. The act was repealed in 1760, but Parliament slapped crippling taxes on the gin at the same time. Ultimately, these laws did more to encourage smuggling than they did to lessen consumption, and Dutch traders routinely sidestepped the law to get untaxed gin into England.[22]

English tax collection was also steeped in corruption, where tax collectors could often be bribed to look the other way while goods were smuggled in front of their eyes. Because excise taxes were exceedingly unpopular with merchants, and perceived as generally odious to British subjects, smuggling was not seen as morally suspect. In some parts of the British Empire, the crown found it nearly impossible to secure convictions for smuggling because juries could rarely be fielded to do such a thing.[23] Also, because of the occupation's meager earnings, tax collectors would often cut corners by accepting the word of a merchant rather than engaging in an actual inspection of his goods—a practice known as "stamping."

At the age of 28, after serving his post at Alford for just over a year, Paine was charged with doing just that. In a 1765 incident, Paine failed to make a routine inspection of goods, though his journal recorded that such an inspection had been made nonetheless. After an investigation of the matter, the local Board of Excise dismissed Paine:

> Thomas Paine, officer of Alford (Lincolnshire), Grantham collection, having on July 11th stamped the whole ride, as appears by the specimens not being signed in any part thereof, though proper entry was shown in journal, and the victualler's stocks drawn down in his books as if the same had been surveyed that day, as by William Swallow, Supervisor's letter of 3rd instant, and the collector's report thereon, also by the said Paine's own confession of the 13th instant, ordered to be discharged.[24]

Though practice was relatively commonplace, it was an official breech of protocol for which Paine was ejected from his station.

Apologizing for the oversight, Paine petitioned to be reinstated the next summer. "Though the nature of the report and my own confession cut off all expectations of enjoying your honors favor then," he wrote, "I humbly hope it has not finally excluded me therefrom, upon which hope I humbly presume to entreat your honors to restore me."[25] He also attempted to reinforce his repute, adding that no other complaint of dishonesty had been recorded against him during his year of service as a tax collector in Alford. His restoration was granted, but he begrudgingly travelled southeast to Diss in Norfolk County, where he returned to stay-making once again.

Paine was still waiting for a new assignment from the Board of Excise at the beginning of 1767, so he left stay-making in Diss to take a series of low-paying jobs as an English teacher in London. During his foray into teaching, Paine accumulated a large amount of knowledge, and believed such a benefit helped allay his impoverished circumstances. It was only in mid-1767 that Paine was offered his new assignment as an excise officer in Grampound, a village on the southwestern tip of England. Geographically, it was far from everything he knew, so he turned appointment down to await another vacancy. Early in the next year, he was presented a similar opportunity in Lewes, a market town in Sussex County. The town had a population of about 5,000, and a long history that dated back to the Anglo-Saxon period, when it contained a mint. After the Norman Conquest of 1066, William the Conqueror awarded Lewes to a subordinate who had helped him win the Battle of Hastings.

The county of Sussex adopted a notable pro-republican streak during the English Civil Wars of the 17th century. Algernon Sidney, perhaps the most radical republican theorist and member of the Long Parliament, was appointed as a military governor of the region in 1645, and the county remained under control by Parliament during most of the period. It was Sidney's seminal political treatise *Discourses Concerning Government*, that influenced America's upcoming rift with Britain to an extent that was surpassed only by the works of John Locke. The region also produced William Cawley, elected to Parliament in 1647, who became a regicide—one of the signers of King Charles I's death warrant.

In Lewes, Paine took residence in the second floor of Bull House, a tobacco shop owned by Samuel Ollive and Esther Ollive. The building, which still stands and is now the headquarters of the Sussex Archaeological Society, bears the following inscription: "1768–1774, IN THIS HOUSE LIVED THOMAS PAINE, WRITER AND REVOLUTIONARY." Lewes today still celebrates the life of Paine. In 2009, an annual 10-day celebration of his life commenced, where visitors can attend serious intellectual seminars, folk dancing, and stage performances. The following year, the town also unveiled a statue of his likeness outside of the town library.[26]

While he resided in Lewes, a friend's account noted that Paine had already developed into a political Whig—then at odds in England with the much more conservative Tories. Even at this stage, it seemed Paine's radical leanings were simmering. He was "tenacious of his opinions, which were bold, acute, and independent, and which he maintained with ardor, elegance, and argument." Paine's character had come to be defined by "perseverance in a good cause and obstinacy in a bad one."[27] The future would prove this observation uncanny in its accuracy.

During this period, Paine also rediscovered the art of debate, which he had first encountered in London. Lewes was home to the Headstrong Club, an organization that held community dinners at the White Hart Inn, where food was followed by rigorous debate on the politics of the day. Though there are few records of the topics discussed, it is certain that he was exposed to radical Whig ideas, which quickly took root in his mind. According to Paine scholar Craig Nelson, it was here where Paine first unleashed his rhetorical wit and intellectual mind.[28] Paine seemed to thrive in such an atmosphere, where his mind was wholly calibrated to the pressing issues of the day.

Paine's proprietor Samuel Ollive died in 1769, leaving behind his wife Esther and daughter Elizabeth. Paine's friendly relationship with the Ollives remained even after he lived elsewhere and led him to assist the widowed Esther Ollive with the tobacco company. Through this endeavor, he also became more familiar with Elizabeth. On March 26, 1771, Paine married her in St. Michael's Church in Lewes. Like Thomas, Elizabeth had been raised a Quaker, but was ten years younger than he. At the time, it seemed a fitting match that would finally add steadiness to his life. While strain would soon come to define their marriage, Paine could not have known it at the time. He now had a stable income, a new bride, and jovial relations with the inhabitants of Lewes.

The next tangent of Paine's life would unexpectedly bring him into the political arena for the first time. In 1772, a class of British excisemen began to gripe about the typical grievances of their occupation. The group of tax collectors intended to bring their complaints to Parliament in hopes of producing a remedy for the monotony and lackluster working conditions of the profession. Needing a spokesman to articulate their concerns, they turned to Paine. In 1772, he prepared an official argument in the form of a

pamphlet, *The Case of the Officers of Excise; With Remarks on the Qual-*
ifications of Officers; and of the Numerous Evils Arising to the Revenue,
from the Insufficiency of the Present Salary.

The petition complained that the salaries of excisemen were paltry. "To
point out particularly the impossibility of an excise officer supporting himself and family, with any proper degree of credit and reputation, on so
scanty a pittance, is altogether unnecessary," he wrote. The tract also protested that excisemen near the sea could benefit from awards given from
the seizure of contraband goods, for which their inland counterparts would
have no such opportunities. Additionally, frequent removals—shifts in a
tax collector's geographical assignment—often made it impossible to
maintain ties to one's family and friends, Paine declared.[29]

His argument on behalf of his peers made an unmistakable emotional
assault against economic insufficiency, a theme that Paine would revisit in
the future. "Poverty," he wrote, "begets a degree of meanness that will
stoop to almost nothing." To make matters worse for the government, the
meager earnings of the trade only exacerbated "negligence and indifference" in the crown's duties, while "the revenue suffers, and the officer is
discharged." To provide a proper remedy, the petition urged Parliament to
take the labor and fatigue of the excisemen into account, and raise their
salaries accordingly. This solution would strengthen the consistency of tax
collecting as "laws and instructions receive new force," secure the excisemen "from the temptations of poverty," and "out-root the present corruptions."[30]

The writing was first printed in 1772, but it was not until 1773 that
4,000 copies were published in pamphlet form. The supplementary publication was only made possible only through the donations of Paine's fellow excise officers, wholly impressed with the product of the penman's
hand. During this time, Paine attempted to lobby individual members of
Parliament to side with his cause. Calling himself "the principal promoter
of a plan for applying to Parliament this session for an increase of salary,"
he asked for the petition to be considered in the House of Commons.
Though the tract was officially submitted to Parliament and circulated
elsewhere, it was never sold.[31] Paine was able to win some support for the
composition from those who sided with the gripes of the excisemen—a
wildly unpopular cause indeed—but Parliament never acted on the matter.

Just weeks after the publication of the petition, on April 8, 1774, Paine was again discharged from the excise board. The official reasoning for this was that Paine had "quitted his business, without obtaining the Board's Leave for so doing, and being gone off on account of debts which he hath contracted."[32] In his quest to seek redress for qualms of his peers and profession, Paine had indeed contracted debt and was unable to fulfill the duties of his post—which included surveys in Lewes and Brighton. The government announced an immediate liquidation of his assets, which included household furniture and materials for cutting and grinding tobacco. Paine was also at risk of arrest and confinement to debtor's prison, a commonplace institution of his time.

Once again, he attempted to petition the Board of Excise for reinstatement. This time he was unsuccessful, though his superior had argued energetically on his behalf. Unable to work as tobacconist, homeless, and exiled from his primary trade, Paine's misery was now compounded by separation from Elizabeth after just three years. The reason for the severance is unclear, but it may be surmised that economic hardships and personal turmoil had come to affect the couple's marriage, which, according to the account of one of Paine's friends, was unconsummated.[33] For reasons unknown to history, the couple never formally divorced and thus remained officially married throughout the rest of their long lives. The couple also remained on friendly terms in the next decades. After he had achieved some prominence and fortune, Paine sent Elizabeth money anonymously, and she refused to help the British authorities undermine him over the publication of his work.[34] Entirely in line with his typical propensity to omit personal details from his writings, Paine never expounded upon the course his marriage took, even in letters to friends.

Impoverished and yearning for purpose in life, Paine left for London once more. This time, fate led him to a relationship that guided the course of the rest of his life. By circumstance, he became acquainted with Benjamin Franklin, who was likely the most popular man in the world at the time. As the schism widened between Britain and their North American colonies in the 1760s, the famed Pennsylvanian was the American that Britons most trusted. Prior to his eventual commitment to independence, Franklin was a cordial voice of mediation in a hostile environment. His writings were well known, as was his charm—and he made friends wherever he ventured.

That year, serving on behalf of several colonies, Franklin beseeched Parliament to end the concerted oppression against British subjects in North America. The undertaking came in response to the Boston Tea Party—or "the Destruction of the Tea" as it was then called—after which British Parliament levied a series of crippling laws to penalize Massachusetts colony. Parliament referred to the set of laws as the Coercive Acts, and their implementation generated instantaneous vexation in the American colonies.

The Massachusetts Government Act, calculated to reform the colonial government to prevent patriot misbehavior, rescinded the colonial charter of Massachusetts and replaced it with an arbitrary framework under which members of the colony's executive council would now be appointed directly by the crown rather than elected by the colonists themselves. In addition, virtually all civil offices within the colony, including those of the attorney general, judges, and sheriffs, were also to be filled through the king's prerogative. Lastly, the law greatly circumscribed the primary crux of political agitation in Boston—the town meetings—restricting such gatherings to one per year.

Perhaps most egregious to those in Massachusetts was the Boston Port Act, which completely shut down the port of Boston to foreign trade until the colony reimbursed the East India Company for the destroyed tea. The law had sweeping effects upon the maritime economy of New England. Mercy Otis Warren, a contemporary observer and historian, recounted that the port bill cut off "many thousands of the best and most loyal subjects" from their means of sustenance. "Poverty started in the face of affluence, and a long train of evils threatened every rank," she wrote, and "multitudes must have inevitably perished."[35] Most controversially, the law was deliberately crafted to punish the region as a whole rather than those responsible for the tea's destruction. With "no other alternative than to stay and starve, or turn out to beg," Paine would later describe Bostonians as "prisoners without the hope of redemption."[36]

Patriot agitators such as Samuel Adams and Joseph Warren responded in kind, launching public campaigns opposing repayment to the firm. This effort resulted in the Solemn League and Covenant, a formal pledge to end

the importation of British goods after August 31 and visit commercial retribution against those who chose to continue doing business with the British. As historian Murray Rothbard wrote, the radical Bostonians "firmly
declared that they would see Boston burned before paying a farthing to the
East India Company."[37]

Through the Administration of Justice Act, Parliament drastically expanded the judicial power of the British crown, allowing the king's agents
to transfer the trials of British officials to other jurisdictions within the
British Empire, including Britain itself. Counting on juries that were sure
to be more sympathetic in comparison to their counterparts in North America, the law was designed to ensure favorable verdicts for accused British
agents. Here too, rather than quell animosities between agents of the
crowns and colonial Whigs, the law was met with unambiguous resentment. George Washington called it an "attack upon the liberty and property of the people of Boston," and professed that the act warranted putting
patriot "virtue and fortitude to the severest test."[38]

The Quartering Act empowered the royal governor of Massachusetts to
furnish accommodations for British soldiers in "houses, outhouses, barns,
or other buildings as he shall think necessary to be taken." The measure
was widely panned, rousing the indignation of virtually all economic and
political classes in the colony. Bostonian Whigs also pointed out that the
law contravened the British constitution, which, through the 1628 Petition
of Right, prohibited the billeting of soldiers in peacetime. Indeed, no law
but the Quartering Act could have been more calculated to arouse the ap-
prehensions of the colonists.[39]

Those who championed the passage of the Coercive Acts insisted that
the program was the crown's only recourse to the belligerent rabble-rous-
ers in New England. As Prime Minister Lord North put it, "the Americans
have tarred and feathered your subjects, plundered your merchants, burnt
your ships, denied all obedience to your laws and authority." With the latest circumstances inducing Parliament "to take a different course," North
made clear that British retaliation to the Destruction of the Tea would represent a sharp contrast to the polices of repeal and remediation that characterized the Rockingham administration. Through the Coercive Acts,
Parliament's chief objective was to isolate Massachusetts and persuade
those in the other colonies not to emulate the deeds of the Boston agitators.

"Whatever the consequences," the Prime Minister professed, "we must risk something; if not we do not, all is over."[40]

Parliament's earnest attempt to convince the other colonies to abandon their radical sympathies could not have failed more spectacularly. Rather than inhibiting colonial resistance to British taxation, the Coercive Acts led to an outpour of continental support for the plight of Massachusetts. Charitable donations poured in from every corner of British North America, and many of those previously maintaining a neutral streak in the polarizing political climate were now brought firmly into the patriot camp. The laws gained notoriety as instruments of tyranny, and were quickly dubbed the "Intolerable Acts."

For much of his role as an arbitrator during the Imperial Crisis between Britain and the American colonies, Franklin adopted a moderate approach and urged reconciliation. However, the esteemed Pennsylvanian's stance gradually shifted in favor of patriot sentiment. Franklin considered the harsh policies an inflammatory overreaction on the part of the British government, and began to doubt that a peaceful settlement between the colonies and crown was possible. Franklin's change in attitude was encouraged by Parliament's propensity to treat him as a scapegoat for American belligerence, and by the crown's decision to dismiss him as postmaster general for the colonies.

Paine was introduced to Franklin through George Lewis Scott, a brilliant mathematician who built personal and professional relationships with many of the great minds of his day. Their first interaction was likely the result of Franklin's belief in meritocracy, an idea spread throughout Europe during the Age of Enlightenment. Franklin's willingness to meet with Paine, despite his low stature, also appears to have resulted from the commoner's interest of the Pennsylvanian's electrical experiments.[41]

The timing of Franklin's shift in sensibilities could not have better for Paine, who was about to arrive at the riskiest decision of his life—but one that would propel him to fame and political prominence. Evidence suggests that Franklin was impressed by Paine's quest for knowledge, and provided sound advice to his young admirer. If Paine sought kindred supporters of great ideas, Franklin suggested he should look westward, across the vast ocean.

He therefore handed Paine a letter of recommendation to be delivered to William Franklin, the royal governor of New Jersey—who was the elder Franklin's son:

> The bearer, Mr. Thomas Paine, is very well recommended to me, as an ingenious, worthy young man. He goes to Pennsylvania with a view of settling there. I request you to give him your best advice and countenance, as he is quite a stranger there. If you can put him in a way of obtaining employment as a clerk, or assistant tutor in a school, or assistant surveyor, (of all which I think him very capable,) so that he may procure a subsistence at least, till he can make acquaintance and obtain a knowledge of the country, you will do well, and much oblige your affectionate father. My love to Sally and the boys.[42]

A few months later, Paine made the most consequential choice of his life when he boarded a ship to Philadelphia. For a time, it seemed as if the decision was a disastrous one. Along with many others, Paine contracted typhoid fever from the ship's contaminated water supply. Several of the crew did not make it through the journey, and Paine became so sick and disheveled that he had to be carried in a blanket from the docks of Philadelphia by John Kearsley, Franklin's doctor. His health recovered only after an agonizing six weeks at Kearley's residence.

By the standards of the day, Philadelphia was an incredibly advanced city. With a population of 30,000, it was the biggest in the new world, and possessed one of the continent's three largest ports. The streets were paved with cobblestones, the ports were open for trade, and the city was the epicenter of the American press. Philadelphia was also a haven of religious freedom from its earliest days, when William Penn, the Quaker founder of the colony, cultivated a bastion of religious tolerance at a time where few such regions existed in the world. The city had several firefighting companies—including one founded by Benjamin Franklin all the way back in 1736, which still serves as the primary model for modern volunteer firefighting forces.

Such a modern city was also becoming a hotbed for political radicalism, as evidenced by an incident that occurred less than a year before Paine's arrival. A British ship, the *Polly*, docked in Philadelphia with tea from the East India Company. Unlike the antecedent Boston Tea Party—where tea was unloaded into the harbor by those taking on Indian garb—a group of agitators in Philadelphia instead issued thinly-veiled threats against the ship's captain:

> You are sent out on a diabolical Service; and if you are so foolish and obstinate as to complete your Voyage, by bringing your Ship to Anchor in this Port, you may run such a Gauntlet as will induce you, in your last Moments, most heartily to curse those who have made you the Dupe of their Avarice and Ambition. What think you, Captain, of a Halter around your Neck—ten Gallons of liquid Tar decanted on your Pate—with the Feathers of a dozen wild Geese laid over that to enliven your Appearance? Only think seriously of this—and fly to the Place from whence you came—fly without Hesitation—without the Formality of a Protest—and above all, Captain Ayres, let us advise you to fly without the wild Geese Feathers.[43]

Sardonically calling themselves the "Committee for Tarring and Feathering," those who authored the note were not universally supported in their methods, but they certainly reflected the indignation of the city. The Tea Act of 1773, which lowered the taxes on British tea, ignited controversy because it granted a legal monopoly on the sale of tea to the East India Company, squelching local competition. It also confirmed suspicions that the British intended to enforce the remaining Townshend duties, crafted not to regulate trade as through the traditional Navigation Acts, but to generate revenue from the American colonies.[44] Persuaded by the threat, the captain of the ship sailed back to Britain with its controversial cargo. "The Philadelphia Tea Party," as it has since been called, was another in the growing list of incidents resulting from the radical trends in colonial sentiment.

The beginning of life in America was tumultuous for Paine, but he did happen upon "many friends and much reputation." In an early letter, he thanked Franklin for sponsoring his transatlantic voyage, and noted that he had earned a living through teaching. Paine also mentioned a more consequential detail—that he had been tapped to assist in the publication of a growing newspaper in Philadelphia, the *Pennsylvania Magazine*. He was recruited to the task by the wealthy Robert Aitken, who had interest in starting a newspaper but had no aptitude or interest in writing.[45] For such a skillset he turned to Paine, who had both experience in professional writing and the enthusiasm to bring about Aitken's vision. It would be the springboard of his career.

As the editor of the *Pennsylvania Magazine*—also known as the *American Monthly Museum*—Paine made regular contributions touching on the subjects of science, politics, philosophy, and advice. A defining feature of the publication was its periodic focus on English inventions that had little exposure in the North American colonies. According to eminent Paine biographer Moncure Conway, it was these pieces that first piqued the interest of local politicians, such as George Clymer, Benjamin Rush, and Peter Muhlenberg. Although various pseudonyms were used to give the appearance that many contributed to the publication, it was Paine who authored most of its articles. By all accounts, he executed this task with great precision and ability, and the subscription base increased under his tutelage. In its heyday, the magazine had 1,500 subscribers, making it the most popular periodical in the New World.[46]

The timing of Paine's professional ascension, and the evolution of his political sensibilities, could not have provided better fuel to his philosophical fire. In 1774, a young, unknown lawyer named Thomas Jefferson released *A Summary View of the Rights of British America*, originally a list of recommendations to Virginia's delegates to the First Continental Congress. The tract characterized Parliament's intervention in the internal affairs of the colonies as an egregious violation of traditional English rights. According to Jefferson, the rights of mankind were "derived from the laws of nature" rather than by "the gift of their chief magistrate." The pamphlet conceived of the British Empire as a federally-oriented framework, where the common connection to the colonies was not a shared legislature, but the king as the common executive. "Let no act be passed by any one legislature which may infringe on the rights and liberties of another," he implored.

Jefferson's view stood in stark contrast to the common Tory conception of parliamentary sovereignty—the idea that Parliament held the legitimate power to legislate for all parts of the British Empire. This view was predicated on the culmination of the Glorious Revolution of 1688, after which the Parliament declared itself supreme under the new joint monarchy of William and Mary. Unpersuaded by such a doctrine, Jefferson implored the king to hear the grievances of the colonists and intercede on their behalf by vetoing the controversial acts of Parliament. "Let not the name of George the third be a blot in the page of history," he cautioned. To those who warned against provoking the wrath of the crown through radical action, Jefferson countered, "Let those flatter who fear; it is not an American art."[47]

The same year, a legal prodigy in North Carolina, James Iredell, penned *To the Inhabitants of Great Britain*. The work set out to refute the doctrine of parliamentary sovereignty and justify the common American perception that Britain had engaged in unconstitutional transgressions against the colonies, especially in the case of Massachusetts. "A free government can only subsist by the general confidence of the people," Iredell wrote, making recent British wrongdoings "totally destructive of this universal right." In addition, he argued that in "an empire divided into several different and distinct states," such as the British system was, each region should be consulted on such important matters, lest those areas outnumbered be subjected "to chance, or the very certain, whimsical caprice, or mean rapacity of the others."[48] To those who argued that taxation was only just when it was imposed by the local representatives of the people and complained that the colonies lacked a place in Parliament, this argument struck a nerve. After Iredell published the pamphlet at the mere age of 23, it became a sensation in North Carolina.

While the radical outlook he would come to adopt was gaining influence in the colonies, Paine seemed a world removed from such men. He had no training in law, no connections to high society, and few strokes of earnest luck. He lacked the credentials and fortune of either Jefferson or Iredell, but he assumed a similar perspective nonetheless. By this time, he had developed into a full-fledged patriot with the advantage of an outlet to spread his political views at his disposal.

As editor of the *Pennsylvania Magazine*, Paine released his first piece of revolutionary satire in January of 1775. "A Dialogue between General Wolfe and General Gage in a Wood Near Boston," as it was called, referred to two famous generals of the British Army, and was filled with contemporary allusions to the rift between Britain and the colonies. In the article, General James Wolfe, known as the "Hero of Quebec" for his role in the French and Indian War, serves as one character; General Thomas Gage, who had recently been sent to Massachusetts to implement and enforce the Intolerable Acts, is his counterpart. Consisting of contrived discussion between the two men, the article adopted a clever and hyperbolic tone—which quickly become a trademark of Paine's writing.

Just as Gage announces his intention to execute the orders of the king, "a prince of unbounded wisdom and goodness," Wolfe chides him for endeavoring to deprive his "fellow subjects of their liberty." Though Gage characterizes Parliament as the epicenter of "wisdom and liberty," Wolfe warns that the "wisest assemblies of men" were "as liable as individuals, to corruption and error." Gage portrayed Bostonians as unruly ruffians engaging in "open rebellion," while Wolfe declared the same "entitled to all the privileges of British subjects," defending their resistance as the natural product of British tyranny. The inhabitants of Massachusetts Bay were "once a brave and loyal people," said Wolfe, who had become disaffected only because the king's ministers had "sent counterfeit impressions of his royal virtues to govern them." British Parliament had enacted a "system of despotism."[49]

Depicting Wolfe as a British Whig with pro-liberty sensibilities, and Gage as a ruthless tool of an oppressive king, the tract captured the spirit of the times. It was not the last time Paine unleashed his anti-royal perspective. A subsequent article signed "Vox Populi," Latin for "voice of the people," levied an attack against titles of nobility and the propensity for monarchical systems to social standing through birthright rather than through merit:

> WHEN I reflect on the pompous titles bestowed on unworthy men, I feel an indignity that instructs me to despise the absurdity. The *Honourable* plunderer of his country, or the *Right Honourable* murderer of mankind, create such a contrast of ideas as exhibit a monster rather than a man. Virtue is inflamed at the violation, and sober reason calls it nonsense.

In contrast to those who judge a man's character by his royal distinctions, Paine wrote that "the reasonable freeman sees through the magic of a title, and examines the man before he approves him." He added that modesty forbids men from assuming titles, lest they betray their own character on face value. Calling the public "the fountain of true honor," Rather than governmental endowments, Paine viewed individuals as the true source of their own worth.[50]

In response to a pamphlet circulating in Philadelphia, Paine also commented upon the practice of dueling, which had become a popular method to settle attacks upon one's reputation. Entitled *Cursory Reflections*, the tract proposed a legal alternative to dueling, whereby both parties would summon a group of peers, engage in a joint discussion concerning the merits of the dispute, and submit secret ballots regarding which party's position was more odious—along with a recommendation for concession. Amusingly, the writer proposed that "all this be done, if possible, free from the embarrassing intervention of lawyers." Paine thought the remedy impracticable, given that quarrelling parties would hardly be prone to referring their private matter to a "court of honor." Nonetheless, he did express a notable legal void when it came to laws that discouraged dueling, and added that the great Swedish King Gustavus Adolphus had brought dueling to an end by threatening to execute the winner of any duels. Paine scoffed at the notion that duelists were honorably settling personal disputes, claiming rather that they reeked of hypocrisy. This was, as he wrote, because duels were especially prevalent in countries with established religions, revealing "how little mankind are, in reality, influenced by the principles of the religion by which they profess to be guided."[51]

The March 8, 1775 issue of the *Pennsylvania Magazine* contained a brazen attack on slavery, one of the first of its type in North America. The article, "African Slavery in America," was published by Paine and began with a direct moral indictment against the practice:

> Our Traders in MEN (*an unnatural commodity!*) must know the wickedness of that SLAVE-TRADE, if they attend to reasoning, or the dictates of their own hearts; and such as shun and stifle all these, wilfully sacrifice Conscience, and the character of integrity to that golden Idol.[52]

According to the writer, "such wicked and inhuman" inclinations encouraged the English to enslave thousands, conscripting many for use in war.

Beyond that, the writer alleged that England even waged war for that express purpose. The piece criticized the supposition that slavery was sanctioned by the Bible, instead maintaining that enslavement as an "outrage against humanity and justice" practiced only by "pretended Christians." Its writer unambiguously condemned slavery as an affront to God. Continuing the practice in America was a cruel injustice, declared the writer, because slaves "have still a natural, perfect right" to freedom.[53]

The article also blamed slavery for the separation of family members, inspiring barbarity and lewd behavior, and even for "opening the way" to adultery and incest between slaves and slave owners. All these things, the author wrote, were those "of which the guilty masters must answer to the final judge." To avoid acting "contrary to the natural dictates of conscience," the author recommended providing legislative relief to slave owners, such that slaves could be employed or receive charity from sympathizers. If such an abolitionist plan was impossible, the essay suggested the formation of frontier settlements for former slaves. Warning that slavery "has been pursued in the opposition of the redeemer's cause," the author signed the article "JUSTICE AND HUMANITY."[54]

It was a wildly radical pitch, even in Pennsylvania. At the time, slavery existed in every North American colony, though it was much less prevalent in some regions. In 1775, there were about 6,000 slaves in Pennsylvania, and while many of the state's prominent figures considered the institution an injustice, there were few who had gone so far as to endorse outright abolition. In fact, as a publisher Paine was the first to do so in the North American colonies. During the War of Independence, several states would pass gradual manumission laws that aimed to set slavery on the path to extinction—while failing to free those already in slavery.[55] It is impossible to exaggerate the revolutionary nature of Paine's call for abolition.

While the essay was published by Paine, there remains some question over the authorship of the essay, and even uncertainty regarding when it was written.[56] Whether or not Paine composed the essay, his opposition to slavery and the slave trade was unmistakable from his earliest days as an editor. In another article, he complained that Americans had engaged "in the most horrid of all traffics, that of human flesh." Consequently, slavery had "ravaged the hapless shores of Africa, robbing it of its unoffending inhabitants to cultivate her stolen dominions in the West." He yearned for

God to bless the Americas through legislation "which shall put a stop to the importation of negroes for sale, soften the hard fate of those already here, and in time procure their freedom."[57] At a time where the slave trade was a lucrative venture among merchants in Philadelphia and other major ports, this was a groundbreaking sentiment in the same vein as "African Slavery in America."

Paine also criticized British policy in East Asia, slamming the crown for its mistreatment of Indians. Instead of providing "Christian examples to the Indians," he opined that cruel practitioners had "basely tampered with their passions, imposed upon their ignorance, and made them tools of treachery and murder." According to Paine, the mistreatment was due to intentional malevolence rather than negligence:

> When I reflect on the horrid cruelties exercised by Britain in the East Indies—How thousands perished by artificial famine—How religion and every manly principle of honour and honesty were sacrificed to luxury and pride—When I read of the wretched natives being blown away, for no other crime than because, sickened with the miserable scene, they refused to fight—When I reflect on these and a thousand instances of similar barbarity, I firmly believe that the Almighty, in compassion to mankind, will curtail the power of Britain.[58]

Here Paine made reference to the Great Bengal Famine of 1770, exacerbated by the exorbitant taxes and extreme regulations imposed by the British government upon colonial India. In the end, the famine caused mass starvation, and resulted in about 10 million deaths.[59] Paine considered the disaster a desperate moment that dehumanized the empire and called for divine intervention.[60]

Paine's also wrote about many other subjects, including the utility of items found within the earth, in particular metals and fossils. Those who could properly harness either, he thought, provided inimitable benefits to humanity: One by "scientifically examining their structure and composition," and "the others, by industry and commerce, are transmuting them to gold." The earth yielded matchless value, and it was up to humanity to take hold of its "happy advantages." As he wrote, "every man's landed property extends to the [center] of the earth."[61]

In his most peculiar subject matter, Paine tackled the social anxieties of women. He observed that history was evidence that man, despite his interests of exerting power, always managed to fall for the allure of women. "He has been at once their tyrant and their slave," he wrote. Nonetheless, he commiserated that women had been "continually surrounded with griefs and fears" as a result of earthly repression. Paine believed women suffered most in uncivilized nations:

> Society, instead of alleviating their condition, is to them the source of new miseries. More than one half of the globe is covered with savages; and among all these people women are completely wretched. Man, in a state of barbarity, equally cruel and indolent, active by necessity, but naturally inclined to repose, is acquainted with little more than the physical effects of love; and, having none of those moral ideas which only can soften the empire of force, he is led to consider it as his supreme law, subjecting to his despotism those whom reason had made his equal, but whose imbecility betrayed them to his strength.[62]

The remedy to these troubles, Paine wrote, was to be found in avoiding "the cold and deliberate oppression of pride" and "the violent and terrible tyranny of jealousy." He added that losses of life in warfare, while appearing to penalize men more than women, were actually of greater distress to the latter. Men "can only die in the field of battle," but women "have the misfortune to survive those whom we love most." Paine urged women to make an assertive stand in the hopes of making men more empathetic to their common plight, while admitting that all men "have not been equally unjust to their fair companions."[63]

The publicist also tackled the subject of unhappy marriages, an ironic subject given the separation from his own wife in England. According to the penman, martial severance was the result of "the young, the rash and amorous, whose hearts are ever glowing with desire," and those who cling to "the first amiable image that chance throws in their way." Tellingly, though, Paine admitted that "as extasy abates, coolness succeeds, which often makes way for indifference, and that for neglect"—a description that seemed to echo his own circumstances.[64] Though never disclosing the specifics of his own marriage, it appeared as if Paine's personal life leaked from his pen for the virtually the only time in his writing career.

More than all other subjects, though, Paine's political pontifications would earn him the most recognition. Under his oversight, the *Pennsylvania Magazine* became a true fountainhead of American radicalism. As Paine addressed the most controversial matters of his day—such as slavery, relations with Britain, and hereditary privilege—he helped nurture the essence of the American psyche on the eve of independence. As seminal Paine biographer Moncure Conway put it, the writer shrewdly "scattered the seeds of great reforms ripening with the progress of civilization."[65] As editor of the city's most successful periodical, Paine had finally discovered his calling. He lacked social pedigree and national notoriety, but possessed all the eagerness in the world.

Chapter 2

Beginning the World Over Again

Should an independancy be brought about…we have every opportunity and every encouragement before us, to form the noblest purest constitution on the face of the earth. We have it in our power to begin the world over again. A situation, similar to the present, hath not happened since the days of Noah until now.

- Common Sense

As Paine's radical political outlook hardened, the state of colonial affairs only ensured that his sensibilities found a place in the New World. Indeed, the fallout of the Intolerable Acts left relations between Britain and her American colonies in an irreparable state. However, the laws attracted an outpouring of financial aid for Massachusetts. The program led many previously dispassionate North Americans to side with the Bostonians. Furthermore, the turmoil in New England provided the catalyst for increased political involvement from the other colonies. Once viewed as a matter confined to Boston, the Intolerable Acts transformed the imperial dilemma into a continental affair.

In quick response to the circumstances, Maryland's legislature passed a set of resolutions addressing the plight of Massachusetts in May of 1774, adding that any colony that refused to join the nonimportation association with Massachusetts should face boycotts as well. Around the same time, Rhode Island expressed interest in supporting such a joint boycott. Despite warnings from the royal governor of North Carolina, Josiah Martin, a six-county meeting not only pledged to abide by nonimportation, but recommended a blanket nonexportation decree as well.[66]

In July, the Commonwealth of Virginia passed the Fairfax Resolves, denouncing the British government for violating the constitutional charters and traditional rights of the colonists. The Resolves also challenged the doctrine of parliamentary sovereignty, pledged to continue boycotts on British goods, and urged the formation of a general Congress of all colonies to determine a response to the situation in Massachusetts. According to the resolutions, the Intolerable Acts had created an "iniquitous system" designed to strip the colonies of their political autonomy over local matters. By September of the same year, twelve colonies of British North America heeded the call to form a general assembly of delegates from each colony. The First Continental Congress, as it came to be known, was tasked with developing a concerted response to the incendiary British posture. Convening at Carpenter's Hall in Philadelphia, each colony's delegation carried instructions from their respective regions, and each delegation had an equal say in proceedings.

The same month, the Massachusetts county of Suffolk organized a convention that resulted in the issuance of the Suffolk Resolves, a set of policies aiming to obstruct the provocative British laws. The resolves imposed a widespread nonimportation obligation, rejected the attempts to reform the Massachusetts government and close the port in Boston, demanded resignations from those appointed under the new crown-oriented government, articulated a refusal to pay taxes until the colonial legislature was restored, promised the establishment of a new republican government to displace its royal counterpart, and urged the other colonies to begin raising and mustering militia forces.

Throwing the Massachusetts Government Act to the wayside, patriots within Boston quickly formed a shadow government, the Massachusetts Provisional Congress. The new republican assembly proceeded to assume all political power over the colony, categorically ignoring the British mandates. The new administration elected John Hancock as its president, and began preparations for armed conflict. Under guidance of the provisional government, Paul Revere was sent on horseback to Philadelphia, where the First Continental Congress had assembled. There, he presented a copy of the Suffolk Resolves, requesting that they be adopted in the common cause of the colonies. After some debate, the assembly gave its assent to the Resolves on September 17. "This day," wrote John Adams, "convinced me that America will support Massachusetts or perish with her."[67]

The chief policy accomplishment of the First Continental Congress was the Continental Association, a framework for a multi-colonial trade boycott against Great Britain. The plan put an absolute ban on goods from Britain, Ireland, and the British West Indies, and promised a more radical export ban on goods emanating from the member colonies if the Intolerable Acts were not repealed by September 10, 1775. The Association condemned the king's agents for fostering "a ruinous system of colony administration…evidently calculated for enslaving these colonies." Because the Congress lacked any means to do so, enforcement of the boycotts was to be carried out by special committees within each colonial government. As months passed, the boycott proved extraordinarily effective. Though merchant price-fixing also hurt American colonists, imports from Great Britain fell from £2.6 million in 1774 to about £200,000 in 1775.[68]

Nonetheless, the rigidity of the boycott apparatus and outpouring of support for the Massachusetts militias was paralleled by an equally ambitious plan of enforcement by the British government. As patriot sentiment grew, Thomas Gage—then the royal governor of Massachusetts colony—groveled before Parliament for military support to assure compliance with the controversial laws. When news of the Continental Congress' endorsement of the Suffolk Resolves reached London, it was met with considerable alarm, and high-ranking figures within the British ministry predicted imminent military conflict. In the end, Britain's ministry came to believe that militarized enforcement of the controversial Intolerable Acts was the only feasible recourse. Redcoats would therefore be used to close Massachusetts fisheries and end the lucrative maritime trade that sustained the New England economy. Paine's future philosophical foe Edmund Burke despised the plan to treat Massachusetts so harshly, and labored to rally a Parliamentary faction to obstruct the punitive response.[69]

With troops now at his disposal, Gage spent the fall and winter taking proactive steps to avoid future patriot uprisings. Eliminating such threats, he thought, required the removal of gunpowder from storage houses near Boston. Gage endeavored to conduct the seizures in secret and during early morning hours so that word of his plans would not spread. On September 1, 1774, an event that became known as the "Powder Alarm"—a successful mission to remove armaments from the gunpowder magazine supply in Somerville—produced a rumor that the British expedition had fired upon patriot Whigs. Even though the rumor was false, the allegation spread like wildfire, and attracted the immediate attention of nearby patriot militias that were displaced only after reaching the outskirts of Boston. Ultimately, the event served as a "dry run" mobilization effort that the local militias would emulate in the future.

Gage ordered an expedition of redcoats to seize gunpowder stores from Concord in April of 1775, sparking a series of events that changed everything for Britain's North American colonies. While marching toward Concord, about 77 militiamen from Massachusetts confronted 400 of Gage's British regulars at Lexington. Shots began to ring out at sunrise. Eight patriot militiamen were killed in the skirmish, while the British suffered only a single casualty. Failing to reach their objective in Concord, British regulars were outnumbered by patriot forces that stood in their way, and retreated back to Boston after a short engagement. Along the way, additional militiamen converged on the route and fired upon the redcoats.

Widely perceived as an incendiary offense against the rights of Englishmen, the clashes at Lexington and Concord forced everyone to choose sides. From Mount Vernon, future head of the Continental Army George Washington condemned Gage for setting out to "destroy private property," and professed that "once-happy and peaceful plains of America are either to be drenched in blood or inhabited by slaves." Joseph Warren, one of the leading patriot agitators in Boston, pledged retribution against the king. "To the persecution and tyranny of his cruel ministry we will not tamely submit," he wrote. Undoubtedly, Warren believed the crisis had reached a boiling point: "Appealing to Heaven for the justice of our cause, we determine to die or be free." Paine called the event the "Massacre at Lexington," and wrote that when he learned of the tragedy, he "rejected the hardened, sullen tempered Pharaoh of England forever."[70] Paine now believed that political separation from Britain was both necessary and inevitable.

Conversely, the British government made clear that the rebellion in Massachusetts would not be tolerated. The crown sent an army of 4,500 reinforcements under three of its finest commanders—William Howe, Henry Clinton, and John Burgoyne—to assist Gage. This deployment of experienced military commanders backed by a surge of troops signaled to all that Britain was committing to its most forceful approach yet in order to compel American compliance with Parliamentary law.

One month after the battles of Lexington and Concord, the North Carolina county of Mecklenburg adopted a series of radical resolutions that condemned Britain for its hostile treatment of the patriots in Massachusetts and its abridgement of traditional colonial liberties. One resolution held that "all laws and commissions confirmed by, or derived from the authority of the king or Parliament, are annulled and vacated." Rhode Island followed suit in July, unilaterally declaring independence from Great Britain through an act of renunciation. Devised by Jonathan Arnold, the act condemned the king for "forgetting his dignity" and charged him with "endeavoring to destroy people of this Colony, and of all the United Colonies, by sending fleets and armies to America, to confiscate our property, and spread fire, sword and desolation, throughout our country, in order to compel us to submit to the most debasing and detestable tyranny." Accordingly, the act stripped the king of all governing authority over the colony.[71]

In Virginia, Patrick Henry urged his peers to devote formal military support to Massachusetts. Deeming the events in Boston as "nothing less than a question of freedom or slavery," the delegate warned that the "clanking" of patriot chains "may be heard on the plains of Boston!" Maintaining that Virginia's role in the crisis was unavoidable, Henry delivered what became the most memorable oratory in American history:

It is in vain, sir, to extenuate the matter. Gentlemen may cry, Peace, Peace but there is no peace. The war is actually begun! The next gale that sweeps from the north will bring to our ears the clash of resounding arms! Our brethren are already in the field! Why stand we here idle? What is it that gentlemen wish? What would they have? Is life so dear, or peace so sweet, as to be purchased at the price of chains and slavery?

Forbid it, Almighty God! I know not what course others may take; but as for me, give me liberty or give me death![72]

Among those in the crowd were George Washington, Thomas Jefferson, and St. George Tucker. One soldier, Colonel Edward Carrington, was so moved by the speech that he asked to be buried at the exact spot from which he heard it, near a window outside of St. John's Church in Richmond—a request that was fulfilled in 1810. Henry's passionate dialogue captivated his audience, and persuaded a divided Virginian aristocracy to commit military forces to the patriot cause.

Notwithstanding the rush of colonial solidarity, many viewed the turmoil in Massachusetts as a localized catastrophe that should not concern the other colonies at all. Among this contingent were many who sympathized with the plight of Bostonians, but believed that such conditions were not enough to justify either open defiance against Parliament's laws or military support for Massachusetts. Loyalist sentiment was so strong in Georgia, for instance, that the conservative faction successfully thwarted attempts to send delegates to the First Continental Congress and sign onto the Continental Association. In addition, loyalist devotees were convinced that those engaging in such anti-British resistance were merely unruly ruffians that would only draw the anger of the crown—such that their own regions would be treated as harshly as Massachusetts.

On June 17, 1775, militia from Massachusetts, Connecticut, New Hampshire, and Rhode Island squared off again against the British at the Battle of Bunker Hill in Charlestown, Massachusetts, just north of Boston. There, as the redcoats endeavored to secure heights surrounding Boston, Colonel William Prescott's men met them from a redoubt on Breed's Hill. After several frontal assaults, the British occupied the hill, sending the colonial militia on retreat to Cambridge. The British Army suffered two times the casualties of the patriots, but was able to establish a stranglehold on Boston. The illustrious Joseph Warren—the Whig foreman who penned the Suffolk Resolves—perished in battle, shot through the head. Days later, British soldiers beheaded the corpse and "committed every act of violence upon his body" until it was beyond recognition.[73]

In an earnest attempt to quell lingering enmity, Congress moved to produce a formal, written explanation for the bloodshed in Massachusetts.

Without condemning the king or British soldiers directly, the Declaration of Causes and Necessity of Taking Up Arms purported that the patriot response at Lexington and Concord was the result of "an unprovoked assault on the inhabitants" of Massachusetts colony. Though it was necessary "to repel this cruel aggression," said the letter to the king, the document patently denied the Americans intended to sever the colonies from Britain. "We have not raised armies with ambitious designs of separating from Great Britain, and establishing independent states," the letter stated.

At roughly the same time, Congress finalized the Olive Branch Petition. Primarily the work of Pennsylvanian John Dickinson, it adopted a much more conciliatory tone and asked that King George III's "royal authority and influence may be graciously interposed to procure us relief from our afflicting fears and jealousies." Lauding the monarch, the appeal communicated the desire to remain "connected with Great Britain by the strongest ties that can unite societies," and promised to preserve "the former harmony between her and these colonies." The king read neither letter, refusing to officially receive them and arguing that the Continental Congress was not a legitimate assembly. Save for a few outlying characters, the colonists still overwhelmingly hoped for and anticipated a peaceful end to strife with Britain.

As all of these events were unfolding, Paine remained editor of the *Pennsylvania Magazine*. He realized the magnitude of the so-called Imperial Crisis, and his loyalties were firmly with the most ardent Whig opponents of the crown. Of all the matters that caught his attention, the clamor for resistance on one side and reconciliation on the other captured Paine's attention most. While many Whigs called for agitation until the liberties of Englishmen were restored, most stopped short of calling for independence outright—thinking it either too radical a prospect or impossible to achieve. Nevertheless, Paine considered overt severance from the mother country the only true solution to America's troubles—and set out to make such a case in writing. He therefore spent the fall of 1775 working on what was to become the most influential political pamphlet in American history.

In Paine's day, pamphlets of fewer than 100 pages of text were the most common medium used to disseminate and debate political ideas. They were cheap and accessible to the common man, and could be purchased for a fraction of the cost of a hardbound book. The prevalence of pamphlets reached a high point in 17th and 18th centuries. Though intended for a general audience, they were usually written by lawyers and filled with legalese that inhibited their popularity. Paine was to emphatically change that dynamic with *Common Sense*.

Throughout the second half of 1775, a rift between Paine and the owner of the *Pennsylvania Magazine* began to widen. Though information on feud's origins is sparse, the relationship between Paine and Robert Aitken eventually reached the point that Paine's friends attempted to mediate. At one point, the same group even offered to bankroll the establishment of a new publication under Paine's independent control, but the editor declined for unknown reasons. According to biographer Craig Nelson, this may have been because *Common Sense* was consuming most of his time.[74]

The project for which Paine was to receive such notoriety was initially planned as a series of letters to be published at different times. However, as his writings grew lengthy, Paine realized it would be best suited for pamphlet form. He completed his work at the very end of 1775, and set out to find a publisher. In Philadelphia, Paine's friend and philosophical ally Benjamin Rush persuaded him to seek out Robert Bell, someone who, according to one account, was known to publish a variety of works regardless of their incendiary and radical nature.

Despite Bell's reputation as a like-minded republican, he demanded very specific terms from Paine before agreeing to print the pamphlet. Under the proposal, Paine was to be liable for printing costs if the work stood to be unprofitable, receive half of any profits made, and agree to sell the pamphlet for two shillings—a steep price at a time when most similarly sized works were sold for a single shilling. Paine originally intended the pamphlet to be called "Plain Truth," but Rush ultimately convinced the penman to change the title to *Common Sense*.[75] Paine's eagerness to release his work in a timely fashion led him to accept Bell's terms.

At the time, political writers were generally reluctant to put their own name on their work. Instead, they typically published writings anonymously or under pseudonyms. This tendency was commonplace in the 18th century for a few reasons. First, doing so led the reader to focus on the quality of the arguments rather than the individual making them. Second, putting one's name on his work would be deemed haughty and elitist—especially among patriot Whigs who shunned such an inclination in favor of humility and public virtue. Lastly, adopting the pseudonym of famous historical figures—almost always Greek or Roman—allowed authors to connect themes within their writings to well-respected people.

The first version of *Common Sense* consequently lacked Paine's name, and noted only that it was written by "an Englishman." The first 1,000 copies were printed and released on January 10, 1776. The pamphlet was divided into four parts. The first focused on social compact theory, natural law, and related both subjects to England's constitutional framework. The pamphlet's second section contained Paine's direct assault on hereditary monarchy. In the third part, Paine responded to the current state of affairs between Britain and the colonies. The last section suggested a remedy to the contemporary political crisis.

Common Sense began with the assertion that "a long and violent abuse of power" naturally called the moral legitimacy of such a practice into question. The people of North America, wrote Paine, had been "grievously oppressed by the combination" of the King of England and Parliament. The goal of his pamphlet, therefore, would be to "inquire into the pretensions of both," and "reject the usurpation of either." To do so, he earnestly believed, was to the benefit of all humanity:

> The cause of America is in a great measure the cause of all mankind. Many circumstances hath, and will arise, which are not local, but universal, and through which the principles of all Lovers of Mankind are affected, and in the Event of which, their Affections are interested. The laying a Country desolate with Fire and Sword, declaring War against the natural rights of all Mankind, and extirpating the Defenders thereof from the Face of the Earth, is the Concern of every Man to whom Nature hath given the Power of feeling.

Still, Paine admitted that this incendiary idea was not yet a popular one. "Perhaps the sentiments contained in the following pages, are not *yet* sufficiently fashionable to procure them general favor," he wrote.[76] By all accounts, this would soon change.

Paine's pamphlet contended that society should not be conflated with government. "Society is produced by our wants, and government by our wickedness," he wrote, "the former promotes our happiness positively by uniting our affections, the latter negatively by restraining our vices." Because the interests and of government and mankind were often distinct, thought Paine, the two terms should not be considered as interchangeable. In one of the pamphlet's most famous declarations, he suggested that "society in every state is a blessing, but government even in its best state is but a necessary evil; in its worst state an intolerable one." According to the author, this was because of the Whig view that man "finds it necessary to surrender up a part of his property to furnish means for the protection of the rest."[77] In his seminal *Second Treatise of Civil Government*, John Locke explained that such an aim was the moral basis for the creation of any government—and all Whig political philosophy hinged upon it.

Paine explained that man originally accumulated property by extracting it from the state of nature—a pre-political society in which no organized society existed. Individuals would then be inclined to foster beneficial relationships with each other in order to survive and find social belonging. "His mind so unfitted for perpetual solitude, that he is soon obliged to seek assistance and relief of another, who in his turn requires the same." This state of being was to Paine "the first parliament of every man," where natural right was paramount and all disputes would be settled by small communities.[78]

According to the writer, the expansion of communities and development of trade led naturally to the inception of government. As property became more susceptible to damage and thievery, and it became too inconvenient for all members of a community to convene to make decisions, a contract between all members of society would be entered into. Under such an arrangement, communities would be divided into "convenient parts," each of which would elect delegates to defend the property of their electors. Government would thus be "rendered necessary by the inability of moral virtue to govern the world," and provide freedom and security where individuals could not do so by themselves.[79] As with the natural law precepts Paine adopted, these concepts too were based on Lockean social compact theory.

Paine declared that the English constitutional framework was the product of the "base remains of two ancient tyrannies" combined with some "new republican materials." Accordingly, he considered the first tyranny was evident in the "person of the king," and the second "in the persons of the peers"—or the English House of Lords. These two institutions, "by being hereditary," wrote Paine, "are independent of the people; wherefore in a *constitutional sense* they contribute nothing towards the freedom of the state." The prevalent idea that the House of Commons could sufficiently check the power of the monarch, he wrote, was "farcical" because the authority to obstruct the king's taxes could be defeated by the king's own prerogative to exercise a negative—or veto—on other bills. This constitutional apparatus, Paine commented, was indicative of "of a house divided against itself."[80]

Within the first few paragraphs, Paine's assertions were sure to raise the indignation of Tories. Pro-British patriotic sentiment in North America—especially in the wake of the French and Indian War—was at its zenith. The British system offered much more individual freedom than other nations, many suggested, and it was foolish to disregard or criticize such a scheme when so many in the world were in greater bondage. When it came to this viewpoint, Paine had little sympathy:

> Individuals are undoubtedly safer in England than in some other countries, but the *will* of the king is as much the *law* of the land in Britain as in France, with this difference, that instead of proceeding directly from his mouth, it is handed to the people under the more formidable shape of an act of parliament. For the fate of Charles the first, hath only made kings more subtle—not more just.

Such praise for England's constitutional model, he remarked, "arises as much or more from national pride than reason."[81] To the author it was therefore the virtue of the people, rather than the benevolence of the government, that kept the country free.

Before addressing the specifics of the feud between Britain and her North American colonies, Paine challenged readers to question the legitimacy and efficacy of monarchy itself. In doing so, he was determined to make a moral and historical case against the most prevalent form of government on the planet—an incredibly novel pursuit at the time.

According to Paine, monarchy "was the most prosperous invention the Devil ever set on foot for the promotion of idolatry." To support his argument, he sought to refute the idea that God had endorsed monarchy through the experience of the ancient Israelites—a common argument among Tories at the time. To the contrary, wrote Paine, "the will of the Almighty" had expressly condemned monarchy, and "all anti-monarchical parts of scripture have been very smoothly glossed over in monarchical governments."[82]

From the outset, Paine wrote that the Jews had clamored for a king under "a national delusion." Under a primitive form of republic, he contended, the Israelites first acknowledged God as the only king worthy of devotion. It was only when they broke from this piousness, though, that they demanded an earthly king as their heathen neighbors had—and God was displeased at such a shift. Quoting from the King James Version of the Old Testament, Paine reminded his audience that God through Samuel had warned his people that such a request would be a foolish one:

> This shall be the manner of the king that shall reign over you; he will take your sons and appoint them for himself, for his chariots, and to be his horsemen…he will take your fields and your olive yards, even the best of them, and give them to his servants…and he will take the tenth of your sheep, and ye shall be his servants, and ye shall cry out in that day because of your king which ye shall have chosen, AND THE LORD WILL NOT HEAR YOU IN THAT DAY.

God responded by giving his people their wish, along with thunder and lightning, and the Israelites admitted the sinfulness for their request. "That the Almighty hath here entered his protest against monarchical government is true, or the scripture is false," Paine concluded.[83]

From the beginning, Paine wrote, England had suffered under the treachery of kings who had no moral prerogative to rule. William the Conqueror—who successfully overthrew the country's reigning dynasty and established Norman rule in 1066—was merely a "a French bastard landing with an armed banditti," a usurper of the highest degree who assumed power only through armed force.[84] The royal line contemporary to Paine's time was as such illegitimate, and therefore could not be so easily distinguished from the hordes of Asia or Africa. George III, then, was simply the contemporary beneficiary of a brutish despot.

One of monarchy's most hideous features, Paine explained, was its hereditary nature. Such a framework for succession unnecessarily subjected men to the whims of fortune, he thought. England, he commented, "hath known some few good monarchs, but groaned beneath a much larger number of bad ones." Accordingly, one needed only to glance back a few generations to acknowledge the malignance of Charles I and James II. "Men who look upon themselves born to reign, and others to obey, soon grow insolent," Paine wrote, and such kings would inevitably become ignorant of their subjects' interests. These factors convinced him that nature disapproved of hereditary monarchy entirely. Otherwise, Paine contended, "she would not so frequently turn it into ridicule by giving mankind an ass for a lion."[85]

A second reason the lifelong, hereditary characteristic of the monarchy was destined for failure, he wrote, was its propensity to lodge an immense amount of power in infantile and geriatric men—both of which were unsuitable to rule. If a kingdom should befall a national tragedy, where a monarch's guidance is most needed, "the public becomes a prey to every miscreant, who can tamper successfully with the follies either of age or infancy." To the Tory belief that monarchy was necessary to make peace and stave off bloody warfare, Paine scoffed. Since the Norman conquest, he claimed, there had been no less than eight civil wars and nineteen rebellions. Several disputes between ruling families—such as the Wars of the Roses of the 15th century—had resulted in prolonged carnage and exposed the follies of hereditary succession. Hereditary monarchy had bathed the world in "blood and ashes," he wrote, and was "a form of government which the word of God bears testimony against."[86]

Countering the notion that humanity could not thrive without kings, Paine invoked several episodes from history that demonstrated otherwise:

In the early ages of the world, according to the scripture chronology, there were no kings; the consequence of which was there were no wars; it is the pride of kings which throw mankind into confusion. Holland without a king hath enjoyed more peace for this last century than any of the monarchial governments in Europe. Antiquity favors the same remark; for the quiet and rural lives of the first patriarchs hath a happy something in them, which vanishes away when we come to the history of Jewish royalty.[87]

If trajectories in history were cyclical, as virtually all Whigs believed, he reasoned that monarchy was hardly a societal imperative. If countries could thrive for centuries without monarchy, then nature did not preclude a return to non-monarchical systems; therefore, pursuing such a course was a virtuous quest and the controversy with Britain for a unique opportunity.

Common Sense proposed a civic alternative—republicanism—that would inherently curb the flaws of royalism. "The nearer any government approaches to a republic," he wrote, "the less business there is for a king." By this he meant that most political issues should be dealt with locally by representatives of the people rather than by a far-off monarch. Even though the North American colonies possessed a king, he thought, the Parliamentary system that characterized Britain—though actually a hereditary monarchy—was at least semi-republican in orientation. Calling the English House of Commons the "republican part in the constitution," Paine declared that the "monarchy hath poisoned the republic."[88]

While Paine was not technically accurate in regard to the British governmental system, Britain did seem much more republican than many of its counterparts. This was especially true after the Glorious Revolution of 1688, a pivotal event that ejected the Stuart monarch Charles II from the English throne at the directive of Parliament. In the aftermath, Parliament proclaimed itself sovereign over the power of the king, and the new joint monarchs, William and Mary, were forced to acknowledge that the monarchy was to become a subordinated institution. Even today, the principle of parliamentary sovereignty—through which Parliament remains dominant over the king and legislates throughout the United Kingdom—stands as the cornerstone of the English constitutional system.

In 1776, China was ruled by a unified imperial dynasty where the emperor held virtually limitless power. The empires of Russia, Germany, and the Middle East were governed by monarchies that wielded boundless political power. Japan was controlled by the Tokugawa shogunate—a feudal system where local lords were appointed by a military dictator and representation was nowhere to be seen. In France, the Bourbon kings held much more power than their English counterparts, and often ruled alone for decades at a time without any legislative assembly whatsoever. In fact, when King Louis XVI summoned the Estates General in 1789, it was the first time the body had convened in over a century and a half. The British political system, even for all of its faults Paine was to articulate, was more representative in nature than all of these—and this could especially be seen in the North American colonies.

Paine's opposition to the English crown—and monarchy in general—put him at odds with some Whigs. This was because many of the same wholeheartedly believed in traditional English liberty, but not at the expense of what was then deemed to be one of the most critical institutions of Western civilization. The greatest swath of patriots who opposed and obstructed the controversial laws of Parliament, after all, did not reject the colonial connection with Britain's king. To these Whigs, the Imperial Crisis represented a conservative battle for traditional liberty rather than a radical departure from orthodox institutions. To oppose the monarchy, as Paine so eloquently did, was to adopt a position that was utterly different and radical.

During the English Revolution of the 1640s and 1650s, England had, after all, fought a series of civil wars, put to death the tyrannical Stuart king, Charles I, abolished the monarchy entirely, established a republic, then restored the monarchy yet again after a period of just over a decade. The Cromwellian Interregnum, as it came to be known, had settled for many the question of whether a republic was a feasible course for Western civilization. Even Algernon Sidney and Cato—prominent republican martyrs of ages past—could not halt the collapse of their respective governments. For all of its follies, most came to believe that monarchy was an absolute necessity. Thus, Paine's views on monarchy were utterly inconceivable to most living within the British Empire, making him an obvious outlier even in early 1776.

In less than two short years since moving to North America, Paine had witnessed the ideological battle over the proper course for the colonies, and his home colony of Pennsylvania became a microcosm of this divide. There, political strife between radicals and conservative aristocrats, and religious squabbles between Quakers and other sects, underscored the ideological schisms present in all other colonies. Despite the ensuing public debate, Paine thought any hope of remediation was but a fantasy, especially following the scuffle at Lexington and Concord. "The period of debate is closed," he cautioned. A peaceful settlement with Britain was but "an agreeable dream" that "passed away and left us as we were."[89]

Adamant in his zeal for American independence, Paine used the next section of *Common Sense* to warn that the most pressing question had already been decided. "Arms, as the last resource, decide the contest," he professed. Such an assertion was deemed a presumptuous fallacy by Tories who vehemently opposed militarism against Britain, but radicals such as Paine iterated that no other options remained. Military recourse "was the choice of the king," Paine wrote, "and the continent hath accepted the challenge."

When it came to the looming War of Independence, Paine preached that "the sun never shined on a cause of greater worth." Making an appeal to the happiness of posterity, he claimed that those born generations from now in America would reap the benefits from those who sacrificed now:

'Tis not the affair of a city, a country, a province, or a kingdom, but of a continent—of at least one eighth part of the habitable globe. 'Tis not the concern of a day, a year, or an age; posterity are virtually involved in the contest, and will be more or less affected, even to the end of time, by the proceedings now. Now is the seed time of continental union, faith and honor. The least fracture now will be like a name engraved with the point of a pin on the tender rind of a young oak; the wound will enlarge with the tree, and posterity read it in full grown characters.[90]

Rather than preserve English liberty, the American crisis was to Paine a rare opportunity to create a more perfect world. The considerable risk involved in such an undertaking would be matched with immeasurable reward, he thought, and everyone on the continent was involved in the struggle whether they desired to be or not. This generation-spanning, universal call to action was a theme he would revisit many times.

Complaisant acceptance of rule by the British crown, wrote Paine, was an immoral posture. This was because, he wrote, posterity was to suffer most by the calculated inaction of the present generation. "As parents, we can have no joy, knowing that *this government* is not sufficiently lasting to ensure anything which we may bequeath to posterity," Paine lamented. "As we are running the next generation into debt," he continued, "we ought to do the work of it, otherwise we use them meanly and pitifully." Even if the American colonies remained attached to the mother country, he warned the association would be "forced and unnatural," and would "in a little time fall into a relapse more wretched than the first." Any delay, he cautioned, would result in "bringing ruin upon posterity." In contrast, those urging to accept the demands of Parliament possessed "the heart of a coward, and the spirit of a sycophant."[91]

Common Sense purported that Britain's constitutional system was unviable and undesirable for the American colonies. To support this view, Paine pointed to several defects. Besides allowing hereditary privilege to determine both the monarch and the members of of the House of Lords, he argued that the counterbalance of the House of Commons was insufficient to restrain the power of the king. This was because, as Paine wrote, the king's absolute veto over acts of Parliament diminished the lower house's inclination to reject his calls for taxation.

Paine also ranted that the British constitution was simply too nebulous and arbitrarily applied. The application of Parliament's statutes, for instance, was often subject to discretion by the kingdom's law enforcement apparatus or by the king's courts, and often spared the noble class from penalties imposed on commoners. Squabbles between the king and Parliament often resulted in the concoction of two divergent and complex legal positions—both of which claimed to be constitutionally sound. Such clashes often became constitutional crises from which no bloodless resolution followed. To Paine, these episodes made the system "subject to convulsions, and incapable of producing what it seems to promise." Britain's constitution was "so exceedingly complex," Paine wrote, "that the nation may suffer for years together without being able to discover in which part the fault lies."[92]

The constitution of Britain was not a written document, but a collection of customs, procedural guidelines, legal precedents, checks upon the king, and major pieces of legislation that underscored Britain's history. Notwithstanding traditional divisions of power between government entities and guarantees of individual liberty, there were few limitations on the extent of Parliament's power—the body's mandate to pass law on virtually any subject was the direct result of the Glorious Revolution of 1688. To Paine, this made it too difficult to objectively determine when constitutional usurpations were made. A simpler system, he preached, would be less liable to be destroyed by precedent and ambiguity.[93]

Although Paine accepted that separation from Britain was inevitable, he devoted many pages in *Common Sense* to pitch such a case to the masses. In doing so, he made both moral and utilitarian arguments, and carefully assessed the military, economic, and cultural considerations that concerned the average American. Even so, Paine realized that American opposition to independence was fiercely popular and persuasive—so he crafted the tract in such a way that it would answer the prevalent arguments of his detractors.

Of all the woes expressed by Americans, perhaps the most pervasive was the objection that Parliament could not justifiably impose its will upon Americans because the colonies lacked proportional representation in Parliament. According to American Whigs, this constitutional precept had been long-established, standing as a hallmark of the British constitution since the Magna Carta in 1215. That year, England's rebel barons imposed a charter upon King John that, among other things, restricted his ability to engage in arbitrary taxation without baronial consent. Recognizing this antecedent, in combination with King Charles I's arbitrary taxing schemes in the runup to the English Civil Wars, American Whigs held that British taxation without the consent of the people's local representatives was a flagrant constitutional violation.

If Americans were simply provided representation in Parliament, some argued, most of the anxieties arising from the crisis with the mother country would soon be quelled. Taking such a suggestion to heart, Edmund Burke, the famous parliamentarian who sympathized with the plight of the beleaguered Americans, had even proposed such a plan to Parliament. In a famous 1775 speech, Burke recommended ending the strife with the colonies through a plan to provide adequate representation in the assembly:

> My idea, therefore, without considering whether we yield as matter of right, or grant as matter of favor, is to admit the people of our Colonies

into an interest in the Constitution, and, by recording that admission in the journals of Parliament, to give them as strong an assurance as the nature of the thing will admit, that we mean for ever to adhere to that solemn declaration of systematic indulgence.

Admitting American representation to Parliament, he remarked, would restore "the general character and situation" of the American colonists.[94] However, Burke's proposal failed to gain traction. This was largely because it was only weeks after his oratory that the confrontation at Lexington and Concord took place in Massachusetts, dissipating any political capital amassed by Burke and his allies in Parliament who wished to reconcile with the Americans.

Despite the sincerity of Burke's representation proposal, *Common Sense* scoffed at the idea. One critical problem with such a scheme, thought American Whigs, was the sheer distance between London and the North American colonies. Even if virtuous delegates were selected to fulfill such a task, communication and travel barriers would soon weaken their attachments to their constituents. Unable to respond quickly to the concerns of colonial legislatures, propose bills of timely importance, or understand the present condition of their homelands, they were destined to become ineffectual middle-men at best.

Paine sincerely believed these logistical hurdles were acute and made Burke's proposal unfeasible. Britain was, after all, "so distant from us, and so very ignorant of us; for if they cannot conquer us, they cannot govern us." Reponses to the redress of grievances, he noted, would take four to five months to answer, with five or six more required to provide possible recompense. In the end, such a lengthy and impracticable process would be "looked upon as folly and childishness."[95] The only moral solution to this geographical impediment, he believed, could be found in the absolute independence of the colonies.

Common Sense also cast doubt upon the value of the cultural fondness Americans had for Britain. In fact, he alleged the crown's guardianship over the colonies cast greater moral doubt upon its recent treatment of them. "But Britain is the parent country, say some. Then the more shame upon her conduct. Even brutes do not devour their young, nor savages make war upon their families," he wrote. Rather than protect the colonies from foreign danger for their own sake, Paine declared that Britain had done so for its own benefit—for "the sake of trade and dominion." In addition, he claimed that military hostility in North America had only materialized because of the colonial attachment to Britain in the first place. As an "an open enemy," Britain therefore "extinguishes every other name and title" to the colonies.[96]

Even if independence was possible, Tories and American conservatives had long argued that America's military weakness relative to Britain would prove fruitless in any armed conflict, but Paine cast aside such a claim. America's strength was in its potential for unity, he argued. While no single colony could expel the British military, "the whole, when united, can accomplish the matter, and either more, or less than this, might be fatal in its effects."[97] On the surface, this seemed an exaggerated and boastful claim. In 1776, Britain's army was the world's best, with experienced commanders, the ability to project force on a global scale, and the capacity to mobilize quickly.

Any future protection that Britain could provide to the colonies, Paine thought, would also pose an incredible challenge. "A navy three or four thousand miles off can be of little use, and on sudden emergencies, none at all," he averred. Naturally, Paine suggested that the colonies protect themselves by creating their own navies or by paying premiums to privateers—privately held ships that could be commissioned by governments in times of necessity. In this suggestion, he must have tapped into his own experiences as a young privateer. With the continent's immense supply of tar, timber, iron, and cordage, Paine reasoned that no other country was "so internally capable of raising a fleet as America."[98]

To supplement locally-controlled naval forces, he claimed the colonies could skillfully prepare their own war supplies:

In almost every article of defense we abound. Hemp flourishes even to rankness, so that we need not want cordage. Our iron is superior to that of other countries. Our small arms equal to any in the world. Cannon we can cast at pleasure. Saltpetre and gunpowder we are every day producing. Our knowledge is hourly improving. Resolution is our inherent character, and courage hath never yet forsaken us.

Accordingly, the colonies could train, support, and arm their own militia forces, which would be much more responsive to immediate threats. Moreover, militia companies would be much more familiar with the local terrain and other environmental considerations. The North American continent, he wrote, possessed "the largest body of armed and disciplined men of any power under heaven."[99]

Unwilling to stop at merely criticizing the British crown and lambasting monarchism in general, Paine proposed an alternative to the status quo—severance from the current system, and the creation a republican form of government under a written constitution. This recommendation, so novel for its time, became the pamphlet's most defining pitch, and offered the prospect of a new Roman-style republic favored by almost all Whigs. "A government of our own," Paine professed, "is our natural right."[100]

Paine's ideal governmental model called for a centralized American assembly to meet annually—similar to the Continental Congress—with a president to guide proceedings but without the power of a British monarch. The assembly would be apportioned based on colonial populations, but with at least 30 delegates from each colony and at least 390 delegates in total. Paine thought this increase in the ratio of population to delegate would make such an assembly much more representative and closely connected to the interests of the people. The institution would use a rotational system whereby the president would come from a different colony each year. In addition, the passage of law would require the assent of three-fifths of the delegates present.[101]

To supplement the proposed assembly, Paine thought a subcommittee of all colonies should be summoned for the sole purpose of framing a "Continental Charter"—or written constitution—for the new system of government. As he envisioned, the chief tasks of the convention would be to determine apportionment in Congress, secure "freedom and property to all men," provide safeguards for freedom of religious worship, and delineate powers between the continental and provisional entities. Paine characterized the potential framework as "a bond of solemn obligation, which the whole enters into, to support the right of every separate part." By suggesting greater relative power for the new continental assembly, Paine let slip his penchant for a stronger, more cohesive central government. "Our strength is continental, not provincial," he noted.[102]

Paine recommended that the conference be populated by two delegates from each colony to be selected by each colonial legislature, in addition to five representatives for each colony chosen by voters as a whole within that colony. According to Paine, this would assure the delegations to be filled with "able and useful counsellors" with "experience in national concerns." Paine expressed the conference should dissolve immediately after drafting the new republican charter and fulfilling these tasks.[103] Soliciting the opinions of both the colonial governments and inhabitants of said polities as separate demographics, he thought, would provide the proper balance in a new continental system.

Absolute freedom of religious expression was a paramount component of Paine's system. "I hold it to be the indispensable duty of all government to protect all conscientious professors thereof," he wrote.[104] Although he would not flesh out of his opinions on government and religion until his later writings, *Common Sense* first articulated Paine's lifelong desire to disentangle government from religious institutions and practices—a tall order in a world where government and religion were intimately connected. Even in America, where unorthodox religious practices were often protected to an extent that far surpassed most of the world, most of the colonial governments featured established churches, religious oaths as a requirement to hold civil offices, and subsidies for particular sects.

Governmental suspicion toward religious dissidents, Paine opined, was "the companion of mean souls, and the bane of all good society."[105] Novel for the time, his ideas represented a threat to the long-held notion that government-backed religion was an integral element of Western civilization. Such an inclination only emboldened Paine to defend those persecuted for their religious convictions, even—perhaps especially—when those beliefs differed from his own. Indeed, Paine considered religious liberty of the utmost importance through the rest of his life, devoting many pages of his future writings to this theme.

To those unsure that American could stand on a republican footing, Paine insisted that the colonies had long ago laid the groundwork for such a transition. The distance from Britain gave rise to relative political autonomy, he argued, and established the law as supreme over all other political institutions and officeholders. America's king, he wrote, "reigns above, and doth not make havoc of mankind like the royal brute of Britain." Such a pointed verbal assault on the king himself, rather than his subordinates, was virtually unprecedented at the time. In plain contrast to the English monarchy, Paine proclaimed that "in America THE LAW IS KING." Every inhabitant thereof, then, was subject to its impositions, regardless of political class or hereditary status. Conversely, every occupant was also entitled to all the rights that had been traditionally enjoyed by Englishmen. Whereas in absolute monarchies "the king is law," in free countries—like Paine's vision for the American colonies—"the law ought to be king; and there ought to be no other."[106] Such a distinctive characteristic, he claimed, was the foundation of republicanism.

By the time he drafted his pamphlet, Paine carped that all American efforts to make amends with the mother country—of which there were several—had run their course. "Every quiet method for peace hath been ineffectual," he explained. "Our prayers have been rejected with disdain," he continued, and "only tended to convince us, that nothing flatters vanity, or confirms obstinacy in kings more than repeated petitioning."[107] *Common Sense* thus portrayed secession—an absolute embrace of political self-determination—as the only clear-cut solution to America's maladies. As the near future would prove, however, delegates from the colonies would soon make additional attempts to petition George III for a redress of grievances.

If the failure to secure reparation from the crown was not enough to nudge fence-sitters into supporting independence, Paine alleged that even the laws of science and geography cast doubt upon Britain's rule over North America. "But there is something very absurd, in supposing a continent to be perpetually governed by an island," he declared. Beyond these immutable laws of nature, Paine grounded his support for political severance on a universal interest in the future of humanity:

> I am not induced by motives of pride, party, or resentment to espouse the doctrine of separation and independence; I am clearly, positively, and conscientiously persuaded that it is the true interest of this continent to be so; that every thing short of *that* is mere patchwork, that it

can afford no lasting felicity,—that it is leaving the sword to our children, and shrinking back at a time, when, a little more, a little farther, would have rendered this continent the glory of the earth.

For "God's sake," he wrote, "let us come to a final separation, and not leave the next generation to be cutting throats, under the violated unmeaning names of parent and child." In Paine's mind, there was no turning back from this course. All human wisdom could not, "at this time, compass a plan short of separation, which can promise the continent even a year's security." Any hope of intercession had passed the point of no return. "Reconciliation is now a fallacious dream," he declared.[108]

In its conclusion, *Common Sense* also stressed the importance of foreign relations in the struggle for American independence. Alliances to support American autonomy, he supposed, were only possible if Americans renounced their status as subjects of Britain. Until then, his countrymen "must, in the eye of foreign nations, be considered as rebels." Paine explained that neutral nations inclined to support the colonial quest for independence, such as France and Spain, would only go to such lengths if it could be assured that their enemy—the British monarchy—was made to suffer.

As a last step, Paine proposed that the colonies collated their grievances, along with a record of attempts to seek resolution with Britain, in a written work that encapsulated the Whig position for complete political dissolution from Britain:

Were a manifesto to be published, and despatched to foreign courts, setting forth the miseries we have endured, and the peaceable methods we have ineffectually used for redress; declaring, at the same time, that not being able, any longer, to live happily or safely under the cruel disposition of the British court, we had been driven to the necessity of breaking off all connections with her; at the same time, assuring all such courts of our peaceable disposition towards them, and of our desire of entering into trade with them.

Foreshadowing the Declaration of Independence, such document would convey the American case for independence to the world. "Such a memorial would produce more good effects to this continent," Paine wrote, "than if a ship were freighted with petitions to Britain."[109]

Despite the pamphlet's clarion call for immediate severance from Britain and the creation of new republican system of government—both radical political ideas—Paine did not seek a complete societal overhaul. Without calling for a dramatic shift in the economic system, serious reform of the colonial assemblies, or a dissolution of traditional institutions, Paine merely argued that the only way to preserve traditional liberty was through political disaffiliation from Britain. This was made possible, he argued, by harnessing the archetypal American spirit. In every case, *Common Sense* depicted Americans as capable and industrious, with every advantage at their disposal to forge a new world for themselves and their posterity.

Paine went to great lengths to ensure his readership would extend beyond the landed, politically-connected aristocracy. Unlike the standard audience for political pamphlets, which were primarily written for and marketed to lawyers and wealthy merchants, *Common Sense* was intentionally crafted with the common man in mind. It used direct verbiage, made familiar cultural references, and avoided complex legal jargon. In its trademark vitriol, it appealed especially to artisans, farmers, and businessmen. It was "vulgar" in its prose, and was even priced and structured in such a way that it was easily accessible to all.

Paine did not attach his name to *Common Sense*, a practice that was relatively common, though not universal, for political works at the time. The primary reason for this, he explained within its pages, was to bring attention to "the doctrine itself, not the man." The first publication of the tract denoted only that it was "written by an Englishman." Uninterested in making profit from the endeavor, Paine intended to donate his share of earnings from the pamphlet to clothing for Washington's troops in Massachusetts.[110]

The pamphlet's publication date came at a propitious time for Paine, occurring the same day a copy of a speech by King George III to Parliament, which overtly declared that some within the colonies had engaged in a "rebellious war" against the crown, reached Philadelphia. By one account, Paine and his publisher, Robert Bell, had deliberately set the pamphlet's release date to coincide with the dissemination of the king's speech.[111] Whether or not this was orchestrated, the publication's timing undoubtedly propelled the popularity of the work to a degree that would not have been achieved otherwise.

All 1,000 copies of the first batch were sold in the following days at a price of two shillings each. Shortly thereafter, a squabble over royalties materialized between Paine and Bell. When Paine sought his initial share of earnings, Bell claimed that there were no profits to speak of. Paine was incensed by this claim, and quickly took the manuscript to a rival Philadelphia publisher with the intent of a second printing. In February of 1776, William and Thomas Bradford answered the call and created 7,000 new copies—priced at a single shilling each—for the pamphlet's second run. Bitter in his own right, Bell claimed that Paine had breached their original publication agreement, and printed his own second version—which was completely overshadowed by the Bradford counterpart.[112]

No publicity or marketing campaign accompanied the release of the 47-page *Common Sense*. As Paine himself wrote, "no plan was formed to support it," and the work "was turned upon the world like an orphan to shift for itself." In truth, the pamphlet's instant success came as a complete shock, not only to Bell and Paine, but also those who knew both men. While arguing against a political opponent a few months later, Paine boasted that "there never was a pamphlet, since the use of letters were known, about which so little pains were taken, and of which so great a number went off in a short time."[113]

In the Bradford printing, Paine also included an addendum to the pamphlet that refuted prevailing Quaker criticisms that had arisen in the first weeks of its release. The crux of their opposition was the notion that taking up arms against Britain would violate Quaker religious principles, and exacerbate domestic hardships. Paine retorted that "our plan is peace forever," and contended there was to be no real end to strife with Britain "but in a final separation." Rather than fight for revenge, conquest, pride, passion, or plunder, Paine proposed that Quakers take up arms to avert bloodier and more costly battles that would inevitably result from ignoring British offenses against the colonists.[114]

Even in its initial run, *Common Sense* became a smash hit, and the sheer influence of the pamphlet was immeasurable. With its widespread popularity and rapid propagation throughout patriot circles, Paine's arguments became unavoidable. Segments of the work were reprinted in American newspapers in and outside of Pennsylvania, and nearly every literate American home soon became acquainted with the pamphlet.[115] As copies were consumed so swiftly, it became harder and harder for fence-sitters to maintain a course of neutrality between patriots on one hand and Tories on the other.

The tract's explosive popularity was such that the political aristocracy of each colony were forced to consider the merits of the arguments found within. *Common Sense* therefore found its way into the hands of colonial legislators, governors, militia commanders, and delegates sent by each colony to the Second Continental Congress, assembled at the nearby Pennsylvania State House. Not everyone in attendance, however, was ready to embrace the pamphlet's radical tenets and discard all hope of reconciliation with Britain.

The number of copies sold is still a subject of great debate among scholars. Almost three months after the pamphlet's release, Paine boasted that *Common Sense* had sold 120,000 copies. Given the work's sudden popularity and the colonial population in 1776, the figure seems plausible at first glance. However, there are two reasons to question Paine's approximation. First, because the penman received no royalties from the first version of the work—and had quickly severed relations with publisher Robert Bell—it is quite unlikely that he had access to any sales records that established such a number. Moreover, Paine gave two other estimations for the number of copies sold at later points, one of which contradicted his earlier claim. In early 1779, he told South Carolinian aristocrat Henry Laurens that the work had sold 150,000 copies; later, in 1791's *The Rights of Man,* he claimed that it had sold 100,000 copies.[116] If the pamphlet not achieved the latter figure until 1791, it could not have sold 120,000 merely three months after its release in 1776. This series of inconsistencies—rather than an accurate reflection of sales through the years—strongly suggests that no one, including Paine, ever knew the true number of copies sold.

In 1892, eminent Paine biographer Moncure Conway estimated that 500,000 copies were sold "in the end," a figure repeated by many modern academics. In 1776, there were approximately 2.5 million inhabitants in all of North America.[117] Consequently, this would have meant that one of every five individuals owned a copy of *Common Sense*. Given that literacy was by no means universal in North America, and that distribution of any printed work save the Bible was scattershot, the 500,000 number represents a highly unrealistic figure.

In reality, it is nearly impossible to determine exactly the number of copies sold. Conway gave no citation for how he arrived at such a number, and provided no explanation for what he meant by "in the end." Due to the propaganda war in the press and the lack of authoritative sales records, most of the figures were based on anecdotal evidence that does not withstand basic scrutiny. Nonetheless, the pamphlet's sheer influence—both to those that treasured and those that reviled it—was profound.

Mere weeks after the pamphlet was unveiled to the colonies, a writer assuming the pseudonym "Cato" published a series of letters to the *Pennsylvania Gazette* that challenged its premises and portrayed the writer of *Common Sense* as a reckless, ignorant lunatic. Far from yearning for everlasting piece, Cato wrote, the author and his adherents would simply widen the rift between the colonies and the crown. The counter-agitator also lambasted Paine for brushing aside the benefits of a colonial connection to Great Britain. Trade advantages, military protection, and cultural similarities were also reason to keep such ties close, he contended. Cato also blasted *Common Sense* for its hasty call for independence:

> If we mean to change this ground, and reject all propositions of peace, from that moment we are deserted by every advocate of our cause in Great Britain; we falsify every declaration which Congress hath heretofore held forth in our behalf; we abandon all prospect of preserving our importance by trade and agriculture—the ancient, sure, and experienced road to wealth and happiness.

Abandoning reconciliation was an invitation for "bloodshed and desolation," Paine's adversary admonished. The author of *Common Sense*, wrote Cato, was simply peddling "mischievous tenets and palpable absurdities." He quipped, "is this common sense or common nonsense?"[118]

In addition to Cato, another opponent called Paine a "crack-brained zealot for democracy," countering that a declaration of independence was a "scheme which must infallibly prove ruinous," and warned that all complicit with such an endeavor would be treated ruthlessly as rebels. "Civis" scoffed that Paine's work only encouraged "the dark and untrodden way of independence and republicanism." Yet another of Paine's foes published a pamphlet that condemned Paine's assault on the English constitution, which the writer described as "the pride and envy of mankind," and argued that the author of *Common Sense* was purely consumed by "ambitious purposes." Even John Adams, famous agitator for independence in the Continental Congress, expressed that he "dreaded the effect" of the pamphlet, which he said "so democratical, without even an attempt at any equilibrium or counterpoise, that it must produce confusion and every evil work." Adams thus pledged to do all in his power to counteract the radical impact of *Common Sense*.[119]

Paine decided to answer his fiercest critics in the press—particularly Cato—through a series of responses under the pseudonym "The Forester." Within, he countered Cato's allegation that British ministers were merely "ambassadors of peace." The recent experience of the colonies, wrote Paine, proved instead that British officials in the colonies were nefarious "distributors of pardons, mischief, and insult." To Cato's supposition that the king could use his authority to relieve tensions hastily, Paine replied that even the king could not repeal the contentious acts of Parliament. In reply to Cato's assertion that the First Continental Congress gave no sanction to the doctrine of independence, Paine responded that "times and things are altered," and that "the true character of the king was but little known" a year before. "Cato's royal sovereign," Paine declared, was now "a royal savage."[120]

Cato warned that breaking off from Britain would endanger cross-continental trade and naval protection of cargo, but Paine denied that such a system was purely advantageous for the American colonies. This was, he harangued, because remaining connected with Britain made the colonies inherit all of Britain's enemies, most of whom would otherwise have no quarrel with Americans or their merchandise. In another letter, Cato humorously alleged that Paine's acolytes would invite foreign mercenaries to aid in the war, which would engage in "bloody massacres" and "unrelenting persecutions." In rejoinder, Paine mocked the writer as a lunatic, and wrote that it would be impossible for Cato's imaginary mercenaries "to exceed, or even equal, the cruelties practiced by the British army."[121]

While some of his adversaries garnered the respect of Tories in the presses, none of their works had nearly the effect on the public discourse as Paine's work did. The volley of oppositional pamphlets served only to drive *Common Sense* to the forefront of public dialogue, and even exacerbated radical behavior. At one point, a mob of Whigs seized 1,500 copies of a pamphlet that intended to refute Paine's tract and burned them in a giant pyre on New York Commons.[122]

While Paine's work was catching fire in political circles, the Continental Army languished. Desertions, lack of supplies, communicable diseases, and poor morale plagued the forces during the winter of 1775–1776. While British soldiers enjoyed the shelter of Boston, General Washington lamented that a "dirty, mercenary spirit" swept through his army, and begged the Continental Congress for additional funds. As John Adams scrambled to obtain additional aid for the troops, several colonial delegations balked at the mere appearance of support for a rebellious American force. With his army at about half the size in January of 1776 as it was in mid-1775, Washington told a subordinate that he would not be surprised "at any disaster that may happen."[123]

By the beginning of April, however, the commander had noted that morale had improved in the Continental Army. *Common Sense*, which had reached Washington's hands, was "working a powerful change…in the minds of many men." The general went so far as to have the pamphlet read to his troops, who became exposed to Paine's radical ideas for the first time. "The sound doctrine and unanswerable reasoning contained in the pamphlet" he gushed, made "the propriety of separation" undeniable.[124] Washington's change in temperament entirely reflected the state of the Continental Army. What could have gone down as an obscure rebellion in the chronicles of British history had become a full-fledged struggle for independence—and *Common Sense* was instrumental in the transformation. Even as the Continental Congress attempted to maintain a moderate tone, the newfound outlook of the soldiers in the field was tangible.

The Virginian general was hardly alone—virtually every recognizable figure from the era discussed *Common Sense* and its effect on the American mindset. From Philadelphia, the venerable Benjamin Franklin wrote that the pamphlet "has made great impression." Massachusetts Superior Court Judge William Cushing wrote that the work encouraged unanimity "on the grand subject of independence" in Boston. Future signer to the Declaration of Independence William Whipple professed that "Common Sense has made all the southern colonies his friend...it's my opinion under the rose that the salvation of America depends on him." General Charles Lee, one of the highest-ranking commanders in the Continental Army, was completely enamored with the pamphlet. *Common Sense* exposed "the folly and wickedness of the ministry," he alleged, and would "give the coup de grâce to Great Britain."[125]

As word spread, newspapers throughout the colonies published a torrent of praise for *Common Sense* and its author. According to the *New York Journal*, the pamphlet's creator had "given liberty to every individual to contribute materials for that great building, the grand charter of American liberty." The editor of Connecticut's *New-London Gazette* extolled the writer for expressing the "sentiments of millions," and boasted of the pamphlet's power to convert naysayers. "We were blind, but on reading these enlightening works the scales have fallen from our eyes," he wrote. The *Pennsylvania Evening Post* professed that the penman "has done wonders and worked miracles...His style is plain and nervous; his facts are true; his reasoning just and conclusive."[126]

Readers of the pamphlet were now petitioning their colonial legislatures—directly and indirectly—to address the concerns contained within the pamphlet. Applauding its merits, Professor John Winthrop of Harvard College urged Congress to adopt the prescription found in the tract. A town hall meeting in Canterbury, Connecticut declared that it had "unanimously adopted the principles of independence contained in *Common Sense*," and pressured the colonial legislature to allow for direct election of delegates to the Continental Congress. One petition to John Adams carried such a message: "What in the name of *Common Sense* are you gentlemen of the Continental Congress about?"[127] Certainly, many Americans now expected their representatives to embrace Paine's ideas.

Before *Common Sense*, the American aristocracy generally favored making amends with Britain in a candid way. The passage of the Olive Branch Petition represented the most calculated attempt to bring such a reconciliation to fruition, but the new stir of independence—largely at the behest of Paine—squandered the effort. As King George rejected American overtures of appeasement, so too did the growing masses of American onlookers.

On the surface, Paine appeared the most unlikely man to carry the torch for American independence. He was, after all, a native Englishman—and one that had only recently immigrated to the continent. He was uncouth, low-born, and without civil office. Outside of a few nascent friendships, he had few ties to the political aristocracy of his day. He had little wealth, and expected to earn nothing from his pamphlet. Nonetheless, he possessed an uncanny ability to communicate to and connect with the common American—a crucial skill during a time of momentous debate.

According to his friend and ideological collaborator Benjamin Rush, the pamphlet came at "a point of time full of critical danger to America." *Common Sense*, Rush added, was responsible for "changing the sentiments of the people from dependence to Independence and from the monarchial to the republican form of government." In the words of historian Joseph Ellis, the work "swept through the colonies like a firestorm, destroying any final vestige of loyalty to the British crown."[128]

Paine's work, then, changed the entire context of the rift between the American colonies and Britain. After *Common Sense*, the debate was less about moderation and reconciliation than separation and independence. The pamphlet would quickly raise Paine's notoriety to its zenith, but it was not all he had to offer the world. In order to aid his fellow patriots in their struggle with Britain, Paine would have to fight—quite literally—for the principles he espoused.

Chapter 3

The Crisis

THESE are the times that try men's souls. The summer soldier and the sunshine patriot will, in this crisis, shrink from the service of their country; but he that stands by it now, deserves the love and thanks of man and woman. Tyranny, like hell, is not easily conquered; yet we have this consolation with us, that the harder the conflict, the more glorious the triumph.

- The Crisis

Rampant speculation over the authorship of *Common Sense* began almost immediately after the work was published. At first, some attributed the pamphlet to this or that prominent aristocrat known to support independence. "Some say Doctor Franklin had a hand in it," observed Joseph Hewes, merchant from North Carolina and eventual signer of the Declaration of Independence. At roughly the same time, wealthy Bostonian William Tudor wrote that some credited the same work to John Adams.[129]

Though Paine deliberately concealed it, his authorship of *Common Sense* was revealed to all in a matter of weeks. By February of 1776, John Adams revealed his knowledge of the author to General Charles Lee, who was enamored with the pamphlet. In a letter to James Warren, president of the Massachusetts Provincial Congress, Adams described the author as "a keen writer, but very ignorant on the science of government."[130] The second edition of the work, published February 14, 1776, featured a cover that revealed Paine's authorship.

A firestorm of controversy consumed all parties involved in the publication. Original publicist Robert Bell criticized the Bradford edition as a sub-par knock-off of the first edition. Paine and the Bradford brothers, now trusted by the author with continued publication, lambasted Bell for depriving Washington's Continental Army of cold-weather mittens. It was Paine, after all, who wished to devote all proceeds from the pamphlet to such a cause. In the next weeks, the author purposely renounced any claim to a copyright for *Common Sense*, thereby allowing any interested printer to offer his own version of the work to the market.[131]

Paine's decision to release *Common Sense* into the public domain was largely responsible for the immense success of the work. Repudiating his copyright assured that the pamphlet would be printed and distributed not only throughout all of the colonies—including those yet to receive sufficient supply—but also throughout the Western world. Where those interested in the pamphlet once had to rely upon delayed correspondence with friends to receive it, now the work was available to customers of any printer who wished to offer it. The new distribution also assured that travelers brought the tract to Europe, where new editions were also printed, though many were highly censored, omitting passages such as Paine's tirade against monarchy and hereditary privilege.[132]

In March of 1776, Paine's written fount of inspiration was augmented by the first notable patriot success on the battlefield. Through the master stroke of military prodigy Henry Knox, heavy artillery pieces that had been seized from Fort Ticonderoga were rapidly transported in brutal winter weather to Boston, where Washington had them placed on Dorchester Heights. Seeing the position as indefensible, General William Howe withdrew his entire army to Halifax, Nova Scotia, and Washington marched triumphantly into the city as a liberator.[133] By all accounts, it was one of the most stunning military exploits of the entire conflict. Few may have guessed that Britain would never regain control of Boston.

As the cause of independence grew more popular, the Continental Congress became more concerned with European affairs, and in March began to court foreign powers as allies. With the hope of bolstering the financial and strategic condition of the beleaguered American colonies, the body concentrated first on England's longtime military rival, France, which was known to contain many sympathizers of the patriot cause. The newly-formed Committee of Secret Correspondence employed Silas Deane of Connecticut as a clandestine envoy to Paris. Once there, the well-connected merchant began a surreptitious money laundering scheme with famous playwright Pierre-Augustine Caron de Beaumarchais, a zealous advocate for American independence. The operation led to mass shipments of weaponry to aid the colonies in the war, a critical source of support. The operation would continue unabated, in secret, for more than two years.

Paine spent most of 1776 as a public celebrity, a development that was entirely foreign to him. Praise for his writing poured in from all corners of British America, and the penman rose from obscurity to distinction. As the Continental Congress convened in Philadelphia, he was given his first true opportunity to mingle with America's leading aristocrats. Though he was not elected to any civil office, Paine's ideological influence over the more radical delegates was plainly evident throughout the marked political transition that was soon to unfold in Pennsylvania.

In mid-1776, radicals in the state organized the Pennsylvania Provincial Conference, a quasi-legal assembly that condemned the ruling colonial government and issued a resolution calling for a constitutional convention for the state. "The present assembly of the colony is not competent to the exigencies of affairs," the resolution held, an overt attack upon conservative ranks.

Even though the question of independence had yet to be settled within the colony, the new body quickly supplanted the existing colonial government and established the Pennsylvania Council of Safety to govern until a republican constitution was drafted and ratified. Benjamin Franklin presided over the convention, but primarily acted as a figurehead and did not intend to influence the specifics of the new framework.[134] True power in Pennsylvania was now in the hands of Paine's radical allies, and they intended to make serious reforms to the government.

The same month, delegates of the Continental Congress took recess, and a committee was formed to draft a document that articulated the reasons for which the American colonies would withdraw from Britain. While such a drastic decision had yet to be made, the intention was to lay the groundwork for one should the political trends continue in the direction of independence. The chairman of the committee, John Adams, was then the most vocal advocate for independence in the body. Also selected to the group were Benjamin Franklin, Thomas Jefferson, Robert Livingston, and Roger Sherman.

Had it not been for more pressing political concerns, Adams may have chosen to write the document himself. Instead, the eminent Bostonian lawyer delegated the task to Jefferson, not only because of the young Virginian's aptitude with the pen, but also for the political advantage of placing someone from that influential colony at the forefront of the crusade for independence. Adams also perceived that Jefferson was more likable in the eyes of fellow delegates to the Continental Congress than he was.[135]

Acquiescing to Adams' plan, Jefferson stayed behind in Philadelphia to take the primary role in writing the first draft of what was to become America's most famous document. While he did so, he devoted most of his attention to Virginia, where he worked on a proposal for the state's first republican constitution.[136] Nevertheless, the first version of the Declaration of Independence was produced in mere days, and the committee made adjustments in due time. After 17 days of writing and revision, Jefferson's draft was presented to the Continental Congress on June 28, 1776.

The question of independence, even though actual war had been raging with Britain, was one of immense magnitude. Even by this time, some still viewed the conflict as reconcilable, favored the strategic establishment of military alliances prior to any declaration of independence, and expressed trepidation over the prospect of the war expanding into colonies that had made their military intentions less clear. Even so, the eminent Virginian statesman Richard Henry Lee proposed a resolution that called for an immediate severance between the colonies and the mother country. Holding that "these united colonies are, and of right ought to be, free and independent States," the resolution declared that the colonies "are absolved from all allegiance to the British crown, and that all political connection between them and the State of Great Britain is, and ought to be, totally dissolved."

In the run-up to a vote of all delegations on July 2, it seemed uncertain as to how some delegations would vote. The youthful Edward Rutledge of South Carolina opposed independence, but made clear that unanimity among all delegations could sway his delegation to support the resolution.

The Delaware delegation was split on the question, but the arrival of Caesar Rodney on the same day broke the tie between Thomas McKean and George Read to carry the colony's vote in the affirmative. In Pennsylvania, John Dickinson and Robert Morris both abstained from voting on the resolution—the former being the most vocal opponent against independence in the entire body—allowing the three remaining delegates to vote in favor. The entire New York delegation abstained, having lacked expressed instructions to do so by the provincial government of the state. After the Lee Resolution passed on July 2, the Declaration of Independence itself, after heavy editing by the assembly, was adopted on July 4.[137]

Invoking the same Lockean credo that Paine accentuated in *Common Sense,* the document held that man was endowed by his creator with "unalienable rights," stressed that government's only legitimate function was to secure such rights, and declared that government derived the entirety of its authority from the consent of the governed. Should any government violate these boundaries, it ceased to merit compliance, and it was therefore the right of the people to "alter or abolish it," and in despotic conditions, to "throw off such government" and "provide new guards for their future security." According to Jefferson biographer Joseph Ellis, the document assured that the new American republic was imbued with radical romanticism.[138] This was, of course, the same style Paine cherished and espoused.

With the majority of the draft dedicated to the "train of abuses and usurpations" of the British government, the Declaration blamed the king himself—as the head of the British state—for the severance. Among other grievances, the charges condemned the king for irrationally dissolving the colonial legislatures, sending "swarms of officers" to harass Americans and seize their property, keeping standing armies in the colonies in times of peace, imposing taxes without colonial consent, cutting off American trade with all parts of the world, and denying the right of trial by jury. In totality, the document reproved "a history of repeated injuries and usurpations, all having in direct object the establishment of an absolute tyranny over these states."

The original draft of the Declaration contained a scathing denunciation of the king for prolonging the international slave trade in the colonies:

He has waged cruel war against human nature itself, violating its most sacred rights of life and liberty in the persons of a distant people who never offended him, captivating & carrying them into slavery in another hemisphere or to incur miserable death in their transportation thither. This piratical warfare, the opprobrium of infidel powers, is the warfare of the Christian King of Great Britain. Determined to keep open a market where Men should be bought & sold, he has prostituted his negative for suppressing every legislative attempt to prohibit or restrain this execrable commerce.

The accusation also made reference to Britain's attempt to offer freedom for slaves willing leave their masters and fight against the patriots on behalf of the British military—an endeavor tried by the royal authority in Jefferson's home state of Virginia. "He is now exciting those very people to rise in arms among us," it read, "and to purchase that liberty of which he has deprived them, by murdering the people on whom he has obtruded them." By the end of deliberations, the entire passage was removed from the document by the Continental Congress after the protests of Georgia, South Carolina, and northern delegates representing merchants that stood to benefit financially from the practice.[139]

In several ways, the attack on the foreign slave trade was eerily reminiscent of Paine's written condemnation of the same. Biographer Moncure Conway even argued that the similarities between this clause and Paine's written castigation of slavery were so striking that the anti-slavery clause was authored by Paine himself.[140] While there are similar refrains in both passages, Jefferson was known to detest the foreign slave trade at the same point in time, and there is no written record to suggest Paine's authorship or collaboration with the Virginian. Nonetheless, the clause perfectly echoed Paine's abolitionist outlook.

Rather than homogenize the colonies into a unitary nation—as is sometimes supposed—the Declaration of Independence pronounced that each of the former American colonies were now autonomous, independent, sovereign states. Like the "state of Great Britain," as the document iterated, each of the fledgling polities were thereby "absolved from all allegiance to the British crown," and thus possessed "full power to levy war, conclude

peace, contract alliances, establish commerce," and all other powers belonging to a self-determining nation. Beyond liberating the American
states from their former warden, the Declaration expressed that each remained completely independent of each other.

Even though independence had already been declared by several states
prior to this point—such as Rhode Island and Virginia—the adoption of
the Declaration was a momentous event. No longer would the struggle
against Britain be the isolated affair of a single region, or an abstract debate over political philosophy. The document was widely publicized and
read in every corner of the former colonies—now states—and its implications led to immediate commotion. This "expression of the American
mind," as Jefferson later put it, was the consummation of Paine's radical
quest for American independence.[141]

After liberating Boston in March, Washington moved his army to New
York, making camp in Manhattan. On July 9, after the commander-in-
chief and several brigades of the army listened to a public recitation of the
document, a mob of unruly commoners swarmed to the southern tip of the
island, where a giant statue of King George III had been erected in 1770.
The crowd pulled the statue down with ropes, removed its head, and
shipped the remainder to Connecticut where it was melted into musket
balls to be hurled at the same monarch's forces.[142]

By early August, a gargantuan fleet of 400 British ships occupied the
strategically vital New York Harbor. Later that month, General William
Howe launched an unimpeded land invasion of Long Island. To the complete horror of the Continental Army, his forces quickly overwhelmed and
outflanked Washington's on August 27, and the Virginian was forced to
abandon the position and retreat through Pennsylvania and New Jersey.[143]
A calamity in every way for the Americans, Washington's entire army was
nearly captured, and the British war ministry occupied the city for the remainder of the war. The recent celebration of the Declaration of Independence, then, was quickly subdued by such a momentous defeat.

While Paine spent the summer of 1776 lobbying the conservative-leaning Pennsylvania Assembly in Philadelphia to embrace independence, he
likely crossed paths with Jefferson. As kindred ideological spirits, the two
unlikely peers held nearly identical views on law, philosophy, and political
strategy. Moreover, the two shared the belief that the common man could

be trusted to dictate his own affairs without the encumbrance of magistrates. In a friendship that spanned the entirety of his life, Paine would often cross paths with Jefferson at critical junctures, and the latter would often defend Paine when he came under attack. For the time being, though, the two remained on remarkably divergent paths.

As the Declaration of Independence was signed in August by the delegates of the Continental Congress, Paine decided to take up arms. He resigned from the *Pennsylvania Magazine*, his employer for a year, and enlisted in a Pennsylvania militia company. The "Flying Camp," as the unit came to be called, was assigned to Amboy, New Jersey, where it was thought British forces were soon to swarm. The suspected invasion never came to pass, however, and the unit soon disbanded.[144] Consequently, Paine still lacked real experience in a militia, unlike many of those who fought on the patriot side of the war.

With his earnest desire to aid the patriots unfulfilled, Paine enlisted in the Continental Army and travelled to Fort Lee, an outpost along the Hudson River. The fort was named for Paine's most zealous supporter in the army, General Charles Lee, who considered *Common Sense* the work of a genius. With immense experience in Europe as a mercenary, Lee was at that time viewed by many as the most talented soldier on the American side. Fort Lee was at that point commanded by General Nathanael Greene, a gifted officer that had helped Washington liberate Boston in March of 1776. At the time of Paine's arrival, about 2,000 soldiers were responsible for defending the fort.

Just after Paine's departure for the Continental Army, Pennsylvania was placing the finishing touches on its first republican constitution. The convention tasked with drafting the document was populated largely by Paine's radical political allies, who were determined to create a revolutionary, egalitarian document that reflected many of features laid out in *Common Sense*. Among those most influential in its formulation were James Cannon, David Rittenhouse, and Timothy Matlack. Additionally, radicals such as Thomas Young, George Bryan, and Paine himself shrewdly worked behind the scenes to influence the product of the convention.[145] From the outset, these men aspired to invent the "simple" government Paine proposed, drastically expand voting enfranchisement, and to transform Pennsylvania into a totally egalitarian society. The document unveiled on September 28, 1776, was truly a radical instrument without parallel in Western civilization.

Stunningly, Pennsylvania's 1776 constitution entitled virtually all males to vote. Under the new framework, suffrage was restricted only to those who were non-freemen, those under 21 years of age, those who had not achieved one year of residency, and non-landowners who had not paid state taxes. Most of the other colonies featured far stricter guidelines for voting, disqualifying prospective voters for lack of property and the failure to profess allegiance to established state churches. Furthermore, many of the other fledgling states imposed rigid residency requirements. The sweeping extension of voting rights was designed to inhibit power held by virtue of profession or birthright, and echoed the Whig prerogative to establish a meritocracy in which the common people are entrusted with the reins of government.

The Pennsylvania constitution created a single-house legislature, the House of Representatives. Forgoing an aristocratic upper house entirely, the unicameral legislature held all power to create law without the impediment of supplementary legislative checks. Representatives were limited to a single term of two years, and could not run again for three years after leaving office. Officeholders were also prohibited from reelection until after three years had passed. To make its proceedings visible, the doors of the legislature were to be made open to the public. The unitary entity was intended to ensure that public policy would be the unfiltered byproduct of the electorate.

To prevent the legislature from making policy against the interests of the people, the new constitution also required that all law take effect only at the time of the next session of the assembly, rather than immediately. This check was intended to give the people a chance to assess the necessity of each law, and to arm them with the ability to overturn unpopular policies before long-term legal precedents were set.

Rather than a powerful executive, the convention opted for a rotational executive council of twelve members, each of whom were subject to removal by the legislature at any point. The president would be elected to preside over the body by the council at large, but the institution would possess no veto power and little political authority at all. In contrast, South

Carolina's 1776 constitution granted to its executive plenary power to execute war, enter into treaties with foreign governments, and even dissolve
the legislature. In the hopes of impeding executive abuse, the state's executive council was to be strictly subordinate to the legislature, and the passive executive council was indicative of the anti-monarchical slant of the
new state's radicals.

Pennsylvania's 1776 constitution included a declaration of rights that
pushed individual freedom further than the world had ever seen. In a provision that was germane to Paine and his profession, the right to freedom
of expression and publication was guaranteed in explicit terms. "The people have a right to freedom of speech and of writing," the document read,
"therefore the freedom of the press ought not to be restrained." Another
trailblazing facet was the explicit assurance of firearm rights, which had
been assumed under English common law but was never codified. "The
people have a right to bear arms for the defense of themselves and the
state," the declaration established.

The framework also iterated the right of individuals to maintain "their
houses, papers, and possessions free from search and seizure," notwithstanding a judicial warrant. This safeguard was a deliberate response to
the general writs—also known as writs of assistance—which had given
British officials arbitrary and unlimited authority search the belongings of
colonists. In 1761, Bostonian Whig agitator James Otis took the case of a
group of merchants who had been subjected to the writs. During "Paxton's
Case," Otis exploded into a provocative oratory that condemned the British for violating the privacy rights of the colonists. The persuasive power
of Otis' argument, which John Adams cited as having kickstarted the
American independence movement, undoubtedly inspired the drafters of
the Pennsylvania constitution.[146]

Among other protections, the document safeguarded the right to legal
counsel in all criminal cases, the ability to petition government for redress
of grievances, the guarantee of a trial by jury in both criminal cases and
civil suits, and even the power to travel to unsettled territories in North
America to establish new states. Short of abolishing slavery in Pennsylvania outright, the text also drew influence from the Declaration of Independence in acknowledging that "all men are born equally free and independently, and have certain natural, inherent and inalienable rights."

The convention was also concerned with religious freedom, and therefore included several clauses to guarantee widespread religious liberalization. The document declared that "all men have a natural and unalienable right to worship Almighty God, according to the dictates of their own consciences and understanding," and guaranteed that no man could be "deprived or abridged of any civil right as a citizen" as a result of their religious preferences. While a novel concept in relation to much of the Western world, this guarantee reflected and built upon the longstanding tradition of religious acceptance in Pennsylvania.

In spite of the common allegation that Paine played a critical role in the inception of Pennsylvania's 1776 constitution, the subject himself admitted that he "held no correspondence with either party, for, or against" the document, and that he "had no hand in forming any part of it, nor knew anything of its contents" until the document received widespread publication.[147] Even so, Paine's political ideals were intimately woven into the framework despite his lack of direct influence on it. Universal suffrage, the presence of a unicameral legislature, the lack of a strong executive, and the guarantee of free religious exercise were all measures the provocateur championed. While it was preceded by several other colonial constitutions, Pennsylvania's version contained all the hallmarks of the radical Whigs, and created the most democratic constitutional system in the world. Far from mere political reform or a changing of the guard, it was a revolutionary alteration. Its ratification represented a marked shift from landed aristocracy to radical republicanism, a transition that echoed many of Paine's musings.

Still, the Pennsylvania revolutionaries attracted their share of detractors. Eminent Pennsylvanians such as John Dickinson, Thomas Mifflin, Robert Morris, and James Wilson were deeply opposed to the new model, viewing it as an instrument that would eliminate political stability, threaten the patrician class, eradicate checks and balances, and undermine traditional governmental offices that had remained in Pennsylvania since the colonial charter of 1701. In a joint letter, Mifflin and Wilson lambasted the document as "one of the most detestable that was ever formed." Even Benjamin Rush, Paine's friend and collaborator, professed that the new constitution "substituted a mob government to one of the happiest governments in the world." Had the new framework "been lodged in the hands of one man," he continued, "it would have been less dangerous to the safety and liberties of the community."[148]

After arriving at Fort Lee in September, Greene appointed Paine as one of his aides-de-camp. Typical duties included handling and organizing the general's personal correspondence, copying his orders for dissemination to subordinates, and, at times, gathering intelligence on the movement of enemy forces. The role was well-suited to Paine, who was then known to all for his aptitude for writing. Most notably, the position gave him access to some of the most important figures of the war.

Paine's first true military assignment ended in abject disaster. Fort Lee was strategically integral to the British invasion of New Jersey, where Howe ordered Lord Charles Cornwallis to use the navigable waters to uproot resistance and capture the undermanned patriot forts before the winter weather set in. After successfully capturing nearby Fort Washington mere days earlier, Cornwallis ferried more than 4,000 redcoats across the Hudson River on November 19. With just enough time, Greene evacuated Fort Lee. The supply depots were seized and ransacked, and the Hudson River was now completely indefensible. The Continental Army narrowly escaped into New Jersey, where it eventually regrouped in Newark.

The situation was desperate yet again for the Continental Army, and Washington warned the Continental Congress that Philadelphia was the next logical British target. Stunned by the losses, some within the assembly pondered replacing Washington with Lee, who had begun a secret writing campaign to undermine his superior. Rumors of Philadelphia's capture flew wildly through the presses. In Paine's own words, it was "the blackest stage of affairs." Believing his army was in a desperate condition, even Washington himself revealed to his brother that "the game is pretty near up."[149] It was in these desperate circumstances that Washington turned to the now-distinguished penman.

To Paine, Washington seemed something of a gallant messiah—an invaluable hero in a troubling time. Reciprocating this was the general's appreciation of Paine, with whose work he was already familiar. The two formed a close friendship of mutual respect, with both viewing each other as utterly indispensable to the overarching dream of independence. It was during this critical point for the army that Washington asked Paine to compose new material, this time in the hopes of inspiring the languishing troops.

Refusing to let his exemplar down, Paine began work on *The Crisis*, a new series of essays that appeared periodically until the war concluded in 1783. Eventually, there would be 13 total entries—one for each of the new American states, and each designed to be much shorter than *Common Sense*. The first five were later collated and published under the title *The American Crisis*. Paine may have found secondary motivation for the project in a London periodical entitled *Crisis Extraordinary*, a series of 92 writings that supported American independence.[150]

For several entries in his new series, Paine spent his evenings writing while performing the duties of his military post during the daytime. As the army faced brutally cold conditions in Hackettstown, the first offering was signed by his now well-known moniker, "Common Sense," and hastily distributed to Paine's editorial contacts. The *Pennsylvania Journal* published it to the masses on December 19. Immediately, Philadelphia printers engaged in a colossal effort that replicated that which had followed the publication of *Common Sense*. In time, periodicals all throughout the colonies ran the article.

"These are the times that try men's souls," the first essay began. "The summer soldier, and the sunshine patriot will, in times of crisis, shrink from the service of his country," Paine lamented, "but he that stands it now, deserves the love and thanks of man and woman." In what is now one of the most recognizable pieces of 18th-century prose, the English firebrand challenged those who shared his aims to stay the course. "Tyranny, like hell, is not easily conquered," he warned, but added the assurance that "we have this consolation with us, that the harder the conflict, the more glorious the triumph."[151] These words, of course, were an implicit plea to both homebodies and soldiers in the field to sacrifice their own personal comfort and aspirations for the prospect of independence—and ultimately human liberty. As the next years demonstrated, this was a challenge that proved nearly insurmountable. Washington's Army often faced suffering, desertion, and the frustrating lack of re-enlistments.

In eloquent fashion, Paine reminded readers that the patriot cause was a valorous and moral quest. To articulate his case, he stressed the tyrannical nature of the British government. Using language lifted from the 1766 Declaratory Act, he professed that the authority to "bind us in all cases whatsoever" was tantamount to abject despotism. "If being bound in that manner is not slavery," the introduction read, "then there is not such a thing as slavery upon earth." The assumption of a government with such "unlimited a power," Paine asserted, "can belong only to God."[152]

In acknowledgement of the Continental Army's recent retreat into New Jersey—a subject fresh in the mind of onlookers—Paine sought to ease panic. The evacuations of Fort Lee and Long Island were carried out "with a manly and martial spirit," he assured readers. Refuting the prevalent allegation that independence was declared too early, Paine opined that the decision should have been made sooner, such that the previous winter could have been used better strategically. Nonetheless, he said the Continental ranks were now in good hands, showering praises upon Washington. "God hath blest him with uninterrupted health, and gives him a mind that can even flourish upon care," he wrote.[153]

Continued Tory resistance against patriot efforts, Paine cautioned, were but "an invitation to the enemy," and would only allow the British to exploit a schism that should be ended. Paine assured Tories and neutral observers alike that those willing to drop their acrimony with the patriots and take up the cause of independence would be welcomed with open arms. Everyone in the new states shared the same fate, "the evil or the blessing," argued Paine, regardless of their current profession, political faction, or wartime association.[154]

Paine portrayed the conflict as a defensive struggle—a concerted response to British aggression and oppression that should not be suffered:

Not all the treasures of the world, is far as I believe, could have induced me to support an offensive war, for I think it murder; But if a thief break into my house, burn and destroy my property, and kill or threaten to kill me, or those that are in it, and to "bind me in all cases whatsoever," to his absolute will, am I to suffer it?

A direct refutation of the common Tory refrain that the Americans had in fact been the aggressors, the passage portrayed the patriot cause as a more virtuous and noble one. "I love the man that can smile in trouble, that can gather strength from distress, and grow brave by reflection," he added. Those who failed to heed such a call—and in Paine's eyes abandon their posterity—were the betrayers of virtue. "The heart that feels not now is dead" he scorned, and "the blood of his children will curse his cowardice, who shrinks back at a time when a little might have saved the whole, and made them happy." It was "the business of little minds to shrink," Paine cautioned, but "he whose heart is firm, and whose conscience approves his conduct, will pursue his principles unto death."[155]

Howe's victory in Long Island gave fervent Tories new ammunition to lambast the Americans as traitors, undermine the American war effort, and promote George III as the rightful sovereign once again. "Let them call me rebel and welcome, I feel no concern from it," Paine countered, "but I should suffer the misery of devils, were I to make a whore of my soul by swearing allegiance to one whose character is that of a sottish, stupid, stubborn, worthless, brutish man." Far from a rightful ruler, Paine repeated that the king was unfit to govern the affairs of America. Accordingly, his henchmen were no different, and sought only to inflict oppression. "Howe's first object is," he wrote, "to terrify or seduce the people to deliver up their arms and receive mercy ... a peace that would be the immediate forerunner of a worse ruin than any we have yet thought of." Paine therefore urged his now-home state of Pennsylvania to galvanize behind the war effort, and resist Howe's imminent disarmament campaign.[156]

The conclusion of the essay promised that the new Continental Army was growing despite the hardships, and prepared for a new campaign against the British. "By perseverance and fortitude we have the prospect of a glorious issue," he averred. In reality, the Continental Army remained in a desolate condition. Just as Paine's spirited writing was released to the masses, a vast portion of Washington's army was set to be lost at the end of the year due to expiring enlistments.[157] Without a swift military triumph of some kind, the failing war effort may have been irreversible.

Still, Washington was determined to strike while he had a chance, and Paine's new project was part of his formula for success. On December 23, Washington ordered Paine's essay read aloud to the Continental Army. If the essay was truly as inspirational as it has since been characterized, this timing could not have been more consequential. Washington gave the signal—the password "Victory or Death"—for a daring foray into Trenton on Christmas day. His forces would cross the Delaware River in the dead of night in order to execute a bold strike upon the Hessians encamped there. The task involved calculated military intelligence, inclement weather, and the coordination of multiple moving units.

The 1,500-man Hessian unit was caught by complete surprise. After a brief but violent scuffle, the Hessian force was completely overwhelmed and the commander was mortally wounded. Outflanked, the Hessians agreed to terms of surrender after nominal patriot losses. About two-thirds of the unit was captured, and Washington's men impounded weaponry and other supplies from the camp.[158] The small but important victory catapulted patriot morale, and led to the extension of enlistments in the Continental Army. Likely, they salvaged the entire undertaking of American independence.

Shortly after the new year, Washington followed his astonishing feat in Trenton with another in Princeton, where he defeated an outnumbered force of British regulars under Lieutenant Colonel Charles Mawhood, a subordinate of Cornwallis. Inspired by American successes in Trenton and Princeton, Paine addressed the next essay in *The Crisis* to General Howe himself. Published in January of 1777, the new offering declared that "he that rebels against reason is a real rebel, but he that in defense of reason rebels against tyranny has a better title to "Defender of the Faith," than George the Third." With this highly incendiary assertion, Paine boasted of the recent patriot exploits in New Jersey, and insulted the character of the British commander-in-chief.[159]

Paine charged Howe with underestimating the fortitude of the patriots. America was "too extensive to sleep all at once, and too watchful, even in its slumbers, not to startle at the unhallowed foot of an invader." American patriots would "grow rich by the ill policy of Lord Howe," he avowed, "and the generous defection of the Tories." Paine suggested that the British cause was now crippled by the inferiority of its moral illegitimacy—a "hellish and damnable" cause that under which "every thinking man's heart must fail him." Where the redcoats may triumph at times on the battlefield of bloodshed, he purported that they would ultimately suffer on the battlefield of ideas.[160]

Though Britain appeared as a benevolent actor on the world stage, Paine wrote that the empire's pursuit of conquest and political control was at the epicenter of its malevolence:

> Britain, as a nation, is, in my inmost belief, the greatest and most ungrateful offender against God on the face of the whole earth. Blessed with all the commerce she could wish for, and furnished, by a vast extension of dominion, with the means of civilizing both the eastern and western world, she has made no other use of both than proudly to idolize her own "thunder," and rip up the bowels of whole countries for what she could get.

Citing British antecedents to the American struggle for independence, such as the subjugation of India and the exploitation of the island of Saint Vincent, Paine denounced the crown for pursuing yet another unjust war. The American states would pose a more insurmountable challenge, the penman cautioned, as crafty reactionaries. "Like a game of darts," Paine reasoned that the patriots could "move out of one square to let you come in, in order that we may afterwards take two or three for one...we can always prevent a total defeat."[161]

Any attempt to take Philadelphia, he claimed, would simply rile new animosities against the British, and motivate neutral observers to take up arms in defense of their homes. Rather than greet the redcoats as liberators, the conquered would necessarily develop "a very contemptible opinion" of the British war machine and its imposition of political policy. In addition, Paine wrote that the continent's expansive geography, hardly the "little country" that the British invaders had been accustomed to, made conquest a near impossibility. British advances would be made even more difficult by the country's precarious financial situation, he added, which ironically was the original impetus for Parliament to tax the internal commerce of the colonists. In the first published use of the phrase, Paine wrote that "The United States of America" would soon achieve as much notoriety in world history as "the kingdom of Great Britain."[162]

While the Continental Army was in winter quarters, Paine remained on Greene's staff but was instructed to return to Philadelphia where his talents could best be put to use. His station on Second Street put him in close proximity to Philadelphia's leading society of Quakers, who deemed him an absolute demagogue. One of the Quaker figureheads, John Pemberton, published a testimony late in 1776 that declared allegiance to the British government. Because the Quakers condemned the American patriots for bearing arms, while failing to criticize the redcoats for the same offense, Paine assaulted the publication as a hypocritical farce. "These men are continually harping on the great sin of our bearing arms," he wrote, "but the king of Britain may lay waste the world in blood and famine, and they, poor fallen souls, have nothing to say." Nonetheless, Paine never gave up on attempting to convince Quakers to join the patriot cause, and implied that there were likely those within the society that were sympathetic to the patriots.[163]

Howe spent the beginning of 1777 attempting to lure the Continental Army into battle in northern New Jersey. A total victory in the North, he believed, would disrupt patriot morale and allow British forces to march directly to Philadelphia and take what he believed to be the most important American city. However, after the British were forced to flee from the banks of the Delaware, bands of Tories that intended to assist them were often left stranded and without support, and New Jersey was torn by ferocious guerilla warfare.[164] The British war ministry, disturbed by recent military endeavors, were forced to consider a new strategy with which to confront Washington's army and the patriot militias.

From January until March of 1777, Paine was appointed by the Continental Congress to a temporary commission to finalize treaties with Iroquois in Eaton, Pennsylvania. In the process, he conversed with Last Night, the leader of a local Iroquois tribe, about the war. In one anecdote, the chief likened King George III to a fish that "can wag his tail" when in water, but "lays down on his side" when on land. In his trademark sardonic fashion, Paine commented several decades later that "the English government had but half the sense this Indian had."[165]

In April of the same year, the Continental Congress rebranded its Committee of Secret Correspondence—which worked covertly to encourage sympathetic Europeans to support American independence—into the

Committee of Foreign Affairs. The gargantuan task of solidifying European alliances brought about new responsibilities for the board, and the Continental Congress looked to Paine to assist the new committee. In an unprecedented move, the assembly appointed Paine—who had no experience in civil service—as the secretary of the committee. In this role, he worked to assist Benjamin Franklin, Arthur Lee, and Silas Deane, who were already working with overseas agents to bring military and financial support to the fledgling states.

It was around this time that Paine drafted the lengthy third entry of *The Crisis* in Philadelphia. Within the essay, Paine ridiculed the Tories for representing American victories on the battlefield as abject losses. By such a tendency, Paine wrote, these manipulators "converted a retreat into a defeat; mistook generalship for error; while every little advantage purposely given the enemy." Such a scheme would backfire, he continued, because the Tories had only "promoted the cause they designed to injure, and injured that which they intended to promote." The British had abandoned the battlefield, the tract alleged, to fight the war in the press alone. "The enemy have long lain idle, and amused themselves with carrying on the war by proclamations only," Paine heckled. "Like a wounded, disabled whale," he continued, the British military floundered while the strength of the patriots increased.[166]

After refuting the prevailing Tory narrative, Paine also reminded readers of the war's true cause. Quoting the 1766 Declaratory Act, Paine derided British Parliament for assuming the power to "bind the colonies in all cases whatsoever," calling such a gesture "the loftiest stretch of arbitrary power that ever one set of men or one country claimed over another." The colonies, to their merit, denied the right of Parliament to levy internal taxes upon the colonies, boycotted British goods, and petitioned the crown for redress of grievances. It was only after all of these candid methods had failed, and when America was invaded by an army, that colonists had properly asserted their "right of self-protection," wrote Paine. After their feeble plots, Britain was now a "gamester nearly ruined," having put "all her losses into one bet" and "playing a desperate game for the total."[167]

In the summer of 1776, the British war ministry adopted a fundamentally new plan that altered the course of the war. Upon the advice of "Gen-

tleman Johnny" Burgoyne, the British general who had fought successfully in Canada under Guy Carleton, Lord George Germaine approved
plans for a three-pronged strike that aimed to capture Albany, New York,
and isolate New England from the other colonies. To achieve this, Burgoyne's army of about 8,000 would move south from Montreal through
the Hudson River Valley to Albany, where it would link up with a smaller
force under Lieutenant Colonel Barry St. Leger. At the same time, Howe's
army was to advance northward from New York City to Albany.[168] Because it relied upon multiple moving armies and favorable weather conditions operating under the constraints of 18th-century communication barriers, the plan was decidedly bold. However, whether due to insubordination or a breakdown in communication, Howe failed to move his army
northward at all, and instead set his sights on Philadelphia.

Pushing southward, General Burgoyne scored his first victory when his
army vastly overwhelmed patriot general Arthur St. Clair at Fort Ticonderoga. Having arrived to take command of the fort only a few weeks earlier, St. Clair wisely developed plans for a retreat in anticipation of a British offensive. As Burgoyne occupied the high ground around the Fort, St.
Clair's force of 3,000 regulars and militia loaded the fort's supplies onto
boats. The majority of the troops travelled southeast and reached Castle-
ton, which was then part of the New Hampshire Grants—the precursor to
the independent republic of Vermont.

To the American patriots, the loss was met with considerable lamentation. The capture of Fort Ticonderoga—which until that point had stood
as a rare symbol of American success—demonstrated that the war was far
from over, despite Paine's optimistic writings. The impediment was also
reminiscent of the losses of Fort Washington and Fort Lee, both of which
forced similar American retreats and allowed Howe to go on the offensive.
Pervasive outcry over the abandonment of Fort Ticonderoga led to an official congressional investigation of both St. Clair and the head of the
Northern Department of the Continental Army, Philip Schuyler. Though
clearing both men of wrongdoing, Schuyler was forced to step down from
command in favor of the British-born Horatio Gates.[169]

On September 11, 1777, Washington's cause suffered a major loss at
the Battle of Brandywine in southeastern Pennsylvania. That summer,
Howe brought his forces from occupied New York City to the northern tip

of the Chesapeake Bay, landed his troops in Maryland, and marched northward. Blocking his path to Philadelphia was Washington's Continental Army, which had assembled on the east side of Brandywine Creek. Due to a blunder in intelligence, Howe's forces were not detected until he had outflanked the patriot army and nearly encircled it.

Breaking through Washington's line, Howe's army and its Hessian conscripts inflicted serious damage to both the left and right flanks of the patriot line. Forced to order a mass retreat, Washington himself was threatened as Howe's column pushed eastward. The fraught commander deployed Nathanael Greene's brigade to delay the enemy, and the troubled army fled to the northeast after suffering about 1,000 casualties. The British victory left the seat of the Continental Congress, Philadelphia, uniquely vulnerable to attack and occupation. Immediately upon hearing news of the battle's outcome, the delegates fled the city and reorganized in Lancaster, then in York, Pennsylvania.[170]

The day after the battle, Paine published the fourth installment of *The Crisis*. "Those who expect to reap the blessings of freedom," he began his essay, "must, like men, undergo the fatigues of supporting it. Though addressing the losses, he wrote that the Battle of Brandywine was "one of those kind of alarms which is just sufficient to rouse us to duty, without being of consequence enough to depress our fortitude." Taking to damage control, Paine characterized the occasion as a minor loss that left the Continental Army intact to fight again. "But the dejection lasts only for a moment," he contended, and the renewed patriot forces, with "the glow of hope, courage and fortitude" would "kindle the whole heart into heroism."[171]

The threat to Philadelphia could be turned into "a real advantage," Paine claimed, by serving as the source of inspiration for those who had not yet chosen a side. With the city the target of Howe's campaign of "plunder and destruction," the indisposed were now the bystanders of their city's salvation or demise. Such men "ought not to think an hour upon the matter," but "spring to action at once." Paine concluded the essay with one of his classic philosophical outbursts:

We are not moved by the gloomy smile of a worthless king, but by the ardent glow of generous patriotism. We fight not to enslave, but to set a country free, and to make room upon the earth for honest men to live in. In such a case we are sure that we are right; and we leave to you the despairing reflection of being the tool of a miserable tyrant.[172]

The radiant portrayal of the patriot cause also took a jab at Tories who prepared to assist in the capture of the most important American city. Perhaps the most detested of these was Joseph Galloway, Pennsylvania delegate of the First Continental Congress, who was now advising Howe.

Whatever semblance of good news Paine brought through *The Crisis* soon dissipated. Two weeks after the publication of the latest essay, Howe's 20,000-man army marched into Philadelphia unopposed. The city's Tories greeted the redcoats as liberators, and jubilant celebrations swept through the city. However, a mixed reception followed the British entry into what was then the largest and most important American city. Anticipating Howe's arrival, many radical Whigs had fled Philadelphia, and the ones who remained adopted an apprehensive posture. The city's significant Quaker populace, still wishing to remain neutral, failed to respond in a concerted way—though their silence was to Paine implicit support for the redcoats.

By 18th-century standards, the capture of city of Philadelphia's importance often guaranteed complete capitulation. In America's case, however, this was not so. The Committees of Correspondence that arose in the years prior to the war proved to Americans the value of mobility, and many republicans with civil and military responsibilities had grown accustomed to answering imminent danger with rapid movement and reorganization. Faced with this spirit of persistence, Howe was never able to force Washington's army and the patriot militias to lay down their arms. Anticipating the capture of Philadelphia, the Continental Congress continued to direct the war from York. In the years to come, the body would continually relocate to new locations when faced with the danger of British capture.

Despite the fall of Philadelphia, Washington was determined to strike. In an elaborate maneuver, he planned to send four columns of Continental forces to greet Howe somewhere outside the city. Striking at nighttime, each column was to approach from different directions and entrap the greater portion of the British army. Similar to his exploits in Trenton and

Princeton, the plan relied heavily on military intelligence, complex logistics, and the element of surprise. Knowing Howe would be obliged to leave part of his army behind in Philadelphia to solidify the occupation, Washington reasoned that he had no choice but to attack before Howe could be aided by the addition of Burgoyne's army.

In perhaps his boldest operation in the entire war, Washington's forces clashed with those of Howe in Germantown, just outside of Philadelphia. From the outset, weather plagued the ambitious scheme. Fog crept onto the battlefield, delaying advances, obscuring terrain, and leading ultimately to friendly fire between patriot units. After a series of fruitless assaults and tactical blunders, the Continental Army was forced to withdraw. Washington considered an additional frontal assault, but was dissuaded from such an idea in favor of a retreat to Valley Forge, Pennsylvania. Though casualties were roughly even on each side, Howe captured several hundred Continental troops and the engagement failed to produce the result Washington desired. Still, Howe was censured by the London press for not seizing the moment to destroy the Continental Army for good.[173]

Though he missed the battle itself, Paine reached the Continental Army on the same day, arriving from Philadelphia. As he rejoined Washington after the general had suffered his recent losses, Paine must have come under the realization, once more, that his uncompromising dream of independence had become imperiled once again. From virtually all accounts, indeed, the battles of Brandywine and Germantown were significant losses that led many to question whether Washington or his subordinates could ever score another victory. However, they also proved that the Continental Army had evolved beyond its original ragtag form into a professional fighting force. Washington's attacks may have appeared as acts of desperation, but he had in fact prevented Howe from providing support to Burgoyne and gave the British commander-in-chief an inflated sense of confidence.[174]

As Washington was suffering losses in Germantown, the most miraculous patriot triumph of the war unfolded in New York. As General Burgoyne was marching southward, General Horatio Gates met him at Saratoga on September 19. That afternoon, an elite force of patriot riflemen under the command of Daniel Morgan, aided by repeated assaults from

General Benedict Arnold's men, inflicted serious damage upon Burgoyne's advancing army. Burgoyne then paused to regroup and await the arrival of General Henry Clinton's army, then situated in New York City.

Clinton's reinforcements never arrived, and a second scuffle erupted on October 7. By this point, Arnold had been officially relieved from duty by Gates, who accused him of insubordination and refused to credit him for the successes of the September 19 battle. Nevertheless, Arnold defied these orders, effectively took command of the army in the battle, and made several daring charges into the British lines. Gates sent a subordinate after him with orders to return, but he was not reached until after the battle was over. Burgoyne retreated, but Gates calmly sent his forces to surround the British Army and seize their boats rather than engage in additional assaults. Ultimately, Burgoyne realized his army's situation was precarious and agreed to terms of surrender. More than 5,000 of Burgoyne's men then laid down their arms.[175]

Burgoyne's capitulation produced an outburst of elation in all patriot circles. Terminating the British advance through New York, Saratoga proved that Americans still possessed a fighting chance against the British military. Indeed, the communication breakdown in the British high command was exploited to great effect, and showed that superior tactics could make up for relative lack of training and supplies. However, some believed even Saratoga—as monumental as it was—would prove a double-edged sword in regard to geopolitics. Paine himself, for instance, was specifically concerned that one of the terms of Burgoyne's surrender—which allowed his soldiers to return to England unmolested—would frustrate potential European allies and likely prevent them from entering the war on the side of the Americans.[176]

Contrary to Paine's concerns, though, Saratoga was an unambiguous catastrophe for Britain, and Gates' victory ultimately led to a pivotal military alliance with France. John Alden, renowned historian of the war, wrote that news of Burgoyne's surrender "shocked the British nation and shook the North ministry."[177] While the groundwork for such a companionship had already been laid by Silas Deane, Arthur Lee, and Benjamin Franklin, the battle's conclusion emboldened the French agitators for war against Britain and succeeded in convincing King Louis XVI that his country shared a mutual interest in dislodging its classic rival from North America entirely.

Howe's troops spent the winter of 1777–1778 in Philadelphia's most comfortable houses, enjoying the best supplies imaginable. In contrast, Washington's 12,000-man army shivered in the cold, undersupplied and malnourished, and shortages of clothing, food, and shelter were the norm. Frostbite, hunger, and raised agitations resulted from the harsh combination of hindrances. In late December, Washington warned Henry Laurens, then the president of the Continental Congress, of the possibility of a "dangerous mutiny." If the situation persisted much longer, he wrote, the army would "starve, dissolve, or disperse." Conditions were so bad that Washington felt compelled to stress that his words were "not an exaggerated picture" of their predicament.[178]

As men suffered in Valley Forge, and Gates claimed triumph in the North, a group of officers within the Continental Army began to disparage Washington and challenged his fitness for leadership. The "Conway Cabal," as it came to be called, sought to undermine Washington and replace him with Gates, whom the participants argued had been much more effective in the field. A combination of factors bolstered the claims of the commander-in-chief's detractors. For one, Washington could lay claim to few victories, and his successes at Trenton and Princeton were dismissed by some as anomalous outliers that obfuscated the general's true lack of ability. Additionally, the Virginian was blamed for losing Philadelphia, and for unwisely engaging Howe in several disastrous clashes in 1777.

The instigator of the undertaking, General Thomas Conway, eventually articulated his criticisms in letters that were forwarded to the Continental Congress. Within the body, certainly, were delegates critical of Washington. Richard Henry Lee, Samuel Adams, and even the man responsible for elevating Washington to his position—John Adams—had grown skeptical of the commander-in-chief's capacity to overcome the British. Washington's correspondence reflects that he was generally aware of a plot to subvert him, but no such plan came to fruition. The general's political allies quickly mobilized to squash any effort to make such a significant substitution. In the end, Gates and Conway both apologized to Washington, and the latter resigned from the Continental Army.[179]

Paine was with the Continental Army at Valley Forge when he received a special request from the Pennsylvania Assembly to provide regular intelligence on Washington and the army. At the same time, he was engaged in regular correspondence, as part of his duties as secretary to the Committee of Foreign Affairs, with delegates in the Continental Congress.[180] This division of duties made Paine uniquely qualified to comment on both military and political activity, and he used his free time to continue his stirring chronicle of the war, *The Crisis*. However, the next entry in the series of essays would not appear until the next year.

As they learned of the Continental Army's condition, delegates to the Continental Congress were horrified. Among them was John Adams, who had done much to secure Washington's position at the head of the army, and now served on the body's Board of War. In early 1778, the body sent a five-man delegation to observe the condition of Washington's army. The result of this was the implementation of numerous reforms, including the replacement of Quartermaster General Thomas Mifflin with Nathanael Greene. A brilliant commander and former superior of Paine, Greene capably supplied the army such that it survived the brutal winter. In addition, popular New York Governor George Clinton made speedy arrangements to send 100 head of cattle and 150 barrels of salt pork directly to Valley Forge. He assured Washington of his desire to provide "the most vigorous exertions" of food, and made additional preparations for more food to be sent a week later.[181] If not for these indispensable provisions, Washington's Continental Army—and with it, the prospect of American independence—likely would have foundered.

As 1778 arrived, the formal alliance between France and the United States — cemented by two separate treaties, the Treaty of Alliance and the Treaty of Amity and Commerce — began to bear fruit for the Continental Army. Under the first arrangement, France and the United States would aid each other while at war with Britain, and all parties promised never to negotiate a separate peace with Britain under any circumstances. In addition, France explicitly named the complete independence of the American states as one of its objectives for the war. Through the Treaty of Amity and Commerce, trade relations between the two countries were amplified through a reduction in tariffs, and all powers agreed to guarantee mutual protection of cargo vessels. Furthermore, the pact also guaranteed safe harbor to allied ships, the right of French subjects and American citizens to own property in each other's territory, and the prerogative of both parties to trade with enemy nations of the other.

By all accounts, the new Franco-American alliance was a stunning diplomatic setback for London. Britain was now forced to divide its naval forces between North America and Europe, which greatly hindered its ability to implement blockades. It also forced the British to abandon an aggressive strategy in North America in favor of a defensive one that relied on concentrating troops in occupied cities. In addition to the significant military ramifications, the new Franco-American pact led to a shakeup in the British government. With their newfound political capital, Charles James Fox and his Whig associates unveiled a new plan to recognize the independence of the United States, leading Lord North to contemplate resigning as prime minister.[182] What was once a near-hopeless, far-flung clash between a ragtag army and the greatest military on the planet was now effectively a critical trans-Atlantic clash between the two strongest European powers.

Paine's fifth essay in *The Crisis* was perhaps his most brazen yet. Authored in Lancaster, the tract was addressed to Howe, whom Paine harangued yet again. "To argue with a man who has renounced the use and authority of reason, and whose philosophy consists in holding humanity in contempt," Paine declared, "is like administering medicine to the dead, or endeavoring to convert an atheist by scripture." The enemy general had been guilty of "indolence and inability," and had been "the patron of low and vulgar frauds" in his position at the head of the army. The essay also boasted of France's entry into the war on the side of the United States, which would encourage Britain to "take her endless farewell not only of all America but all of the West Indies."[183]

In his signature radical style, Paine portrayed the crown's deeds in North America as an unprecedented campaign of oppression:

> Never did a nation invite destruction upon itself with the eagerness and the ignorance with which Britain has done. Bent upon the ruin of a young and unoffending country, she has drawn the sword that has wounded herself to the heart, and in the agony of her resentment has

applied a poison for a cure. Her conduct towards America is a compound of rage and lunacy; she aims at the government of it, yet preserves neither dignity nor character in her methods to obtain it.

Britain's deeds were tantamount to "every species of villainy which the lowest wretches on earth could practice or invent." In its quest to topple the state governments and subjugate Americans to Parliament's absolute will, Paine wrote that the British government was guilty of unleashing a malignant system of tyranny upon the fledgling states. "If there is a sin superior to every other," Paine continued, "it is that of willful and offensive war." Britain's cruel methods in North America, he explained, would actually be counterintuitive to the empire. The king's war effort "lets loose the whole contagion of hell, and opens a vein that bleeds a nation to death."[184]

After Howe submitted his resignation as commander-in-chief for all British forces for North America, and as the Franco-American alliance was christened, Clinton was promoted to replace Howe. The new commander planned to march his army from occupied Philadelphia to New York, concentrating British forces in a defensive position where they would be less vulnerable. Meanwhile General Charles Lee, a strong supporter of Paine's work, was released in a prisoner exchange and rejoined the Continental Army in May of 1778. As a skilled and experienced officer, Lee had been highly critical of Washington's calamity on Long Island but was still trusted by his superior all the same.

While on the march to Sandy Hook, New Jersey, where Clinton hoped to ferry his men to New York, the general engaged Washington's army for the first time at the Battle of Monmouth on June 28, 1778. There, Washington committed about 5,000 men—then about a third of his army—to attack Clinton's forces. As a prelude to battle, Lee was to command a band of about 600—including some of the best trained soldiers in the Continental Army—to disrupt Clinton's army before it arrived at Sandy Hook. At Monmouth, Lee found himself overwhelmed by Clinton's superior numbers and forced to order his men to retreat to Englishtown, where Washington had remained.

Believing Lee's decision to be an extreme act of insubordination, Washington dressed his fellow general down in a manner rarely before seen, denouncing him in front of the army. He then halted the retreat, and ordered renewed attacks designed to hinder the British general from actualizing his objective, and the stalemate allowed Clinton to ferry his troops to New York several days later.

After the battle, Lee vociferously defended his decision to retreat, accusing Washington of "an act of cruel injustice" for having treated him in such a way. Without "some reparation for the injury committed," Lee wrote that he would resign from the army after the current campaign. At Washington's urging, the Continental Congress would court-martial Lee in August and relieve him from command for a full year. This decision caused Lee to lash out at the decision, and as a result, the body terminated his service with the army. Although Lee continued to seek vindication by publishing written justifications for his deed at Monmouth, his reputation never recovered.[185] With his exit from the military—and later the world stage in general—one of Paine's first and most significant admirers was absent from public life.

As Clinton made his way to New York, Paine became embroiled in a controversy that drastically affected his standing in America's aristocratic circles. The hullaballoo materialized around the actions of Silas Deane, the agent who had been funneling critically-needed arms from France to the American patriots while France remained technically neutral.

However, one of Deane's American colleagues in Paris, Arthur Lee, discovered that Deane had improperly collected personal commissions for the clandestine arms deals. Deane had claimed that the Continental Congress was obliged to repay Pierre Beaumarchais, an acclaimed Parisian writer who secretly directed the effort from the French side, a gigantic sum of 4.5 million livres for his services. However, Paine revealed that his cursory examination of Lee's correspondence with French officials established that covert funds from Beaumarchais were actually intended as a gift that required no repayment. Indeed, in March of 1778, the American commissioners—including Deane himself—authored a letter assuring the Continental Congress "that no repayment will ever be required from us for what has already been given us either in money or military stores."[186]

Lee's accusations of corrupt dealings by Deane and his congressional backers led to an investigation into Deane's transactions. As secretary to the Committee of Foreign Affairs, Paine was quick to support Lee, a kindred radical Whig. As the political scuffle played out in the Continental Congress and in the press, Paine acted as the unofficial spokesman for the congressional faction that admonished Deane for financial wrongdoing, and portrayed the agent's financial scheme as an unethical affront to the American treasury and republicanism in general. Deane claimed that he had left his financial records behind in Paris, and failed to provide information to Congress in regard to where they were located. "There is something in this concealment of papers that looks like an embezzlement," Paine wrote.

Deane's assertion that he had left his records in France, wrote Paine, was a puzzling reply that raised more questions than it answered. "No apology can be made for Mr. Deane," he contended, until the records could be located. According to Paine, Deane had also engaged in a "barbarous, unmanly, and unsupported attack" on those reporting his misdeeds in the press, and for deflecting, rather than answering, the accusations against him. In this view, he was hardly alone. Fellow radicals Samuel Adams and Richard Henry Lee lambasted Deane for mixing his personal and private business. Even Paine's ideological foe John Adams supposed that the circumstances would culminate either in "the ruin of Mr. Deane, or the ruin of his country." The New Englander considered Deane's doings that of "a wild boar, that ought to be hunted down for the benefit of mankind."[187]

Perhaps Paine's most controversial angle was his implication that Robert Morris—then the superintendent of finance for the Continental Congress—was involved in Deane's financial misconduct. This could be supported, he wrote, by the fact that Deane established a commercial relationship with Morris. The eminent Pennsylvanian financier was notorious for his propensity to keep his commercial activities secret from the government, raising the suspicions of some.

Admitting his reluctance to do so, Morris released records of his business dealings with Deane, declared that such behavior was not expressly prohibited by his home state, and maintained that none of his transactions with the man were improper. Nevertheless, Paine scolded Morris merely for engaging in mercantile relationships while in his civil position. "Such a connection unfits the Delegate for his duty in Congress," he wrote, and "tempts him to an undue freedom with public money and public credit."

As the following decades would prove, the imbroglio foreshadowed a series of conflicts between those who favored a mercantilist, aristocratic government and those who believed republican virtue proscribed such a system.[188]

Despite Paine's earnest attempt to expose the improprieties of the "Deane Affair," as it came to be known, the revelations endangered the diplomatic bond between France and the United States. Substantiating this was French foreign minister Conrad Alexandre Gérard's immediate demand that Paine withdraw his accusations in the press. Never one to reverse a controversial opinion, Paine instead published new information on the subject that, rather than take back his earlier claims, added new information in regard to France's covert aid and Deane's role in the program. This decision added fuel to the fire of a controversy that was already blazing, and emboldened the pro-Deane congressional faction that sought to punish the secretary.

Gouverneur Morris, the esteemed delegate from New York and ardent foe of Paine, derided the radical penman as "a mere adventurer from England, without fortune, without family connections, ignorant even of grammar." The campaign against Paine, however, was not limited to denunciations from within the Continental Congress. At least twice, Paine was beaten by partisans in the streets of Philadelphia.[189] This combination of adversarial incidents must have been rude awakenings to the now-polarizing figure, who earnestly believed he was doing a service to all Americans by revealing corruption in the government. Even while all parties realized that Paine's charges were accurate, the Continental Congress was wholly split on whether or not he should be reprimanded.

Nonetheless, Paine's detractors ultimately succeeded in issuing a formal request to purge Paine as secretary to the Committee of Foreign Affairs. The writer was called before the Continental Congress, where he was asked directly by the president of the body, John Jay, whether he had penned all tracts in question that were signed by his famous pseudonym "Common Sense." Without hesitation, Paine answered in the affirmative, resulting in his dismissal while the delegates mulled a rejoinder.

Apparently surprised that he had been summoned to answer such a question, Paine wrote to the assembly to inquire upon which aspects of his writings were considered improper or provocative. "If any gentleman has presented any memorial to this house which contains any charge against me," he wrote, "I request, as a servant under your authority, an attested copy of the charge, and in my present character as a freeman of this country, I demand it." Now assuming a defensive bearing, Paine avowed that he could not "submit to be censured unheard." Whatever the issue against him, Paine reiterated that the respect he had earned and the evidence he possessed would vindicate him.[190] To Paine, transparency was an essential element of republicanism—a maxim he had eagerly preserved by revealing Deane's dishonesty to the public.

The attempt to oust Paine from his position resulted in a series of tie votes in the Continental Congress, with two divergent factions split on the issue. Having discovered that his plea to the body had not been entered into the journal the previous day, Paine resigned as secretary to the Committee of Foreign Affairs on January 8, 1779. In his resignation letter, he described the chagrin he felt at the "expressions of suspicions and degradation" levied against him, and defended his published writings on the Deane Affair:

> My wish and my intentions in all my late publications were to preserve the public from error and imposition, to support as far as laid in my power the just authority of the Representatives of the People, and to cordialize and cement the Union that has so happily taken place between this country and France. I have betrayed no Trust because I have constantly employed that Trust to the public good. I have revealed no secrets because I have told nothing that was, or I conceive ought to be a secret. I have convicted Mr. Deane of error, and in so doing I hope I have done my duty.

In unapologetic fashion, Paine denied that he had engaged in wrongdoing by exposing the follies of officials who sought personal benefit from their civil station. Despite his own downfall, Paine professed that "the People should know that before America had any agent in Europe," French supporters "were her warm friends." To that end, he felt wholeheartedly justified by his assertions. "I have the pleasure of saying and reflecting that as I came into the office an honest man, I go out of it with the same character," the letter concluded.[191]

John Adams was soon selected to replace Deane as emissary to France, a position that seemed ill-suited for someone without command of the French language and notorious for his hot-tempered disposition. In 1780, the Continental Congress ultimately allowed Deane to return to France to retrieve his records, but the revelations of Arthur Lee and Paine, in tandem with Deane's own unsatisfactory response to the charges, made him a villain to nearly everyone. According to Samuel Adams, Deane's activities had encouraged "divisions and parties," and threatened the new states' nascent relationship with France. Only deceitful, "interested men" that were "united in politics and commercial combinations are and must be his advocates," he wrote.[192]

The Deane Affair was yet another entry in the long list of occasions where Paine maintained a controversial and unpopular outlook despite the steep political penalties for doing so. By any assessment, fallout from the Deane Affair turned some in the aristocratic class against him forever—even though many realized he had only promulgated truth. Though he suffered greatly for it, Paine's role in exposing the Deane Affair made him one of America's first whistle-blowers. Centuries before Edward Snowden, Paine divulged government records intended to be kept secret from the public—at great personal risk to himself.

Several years later, Paine received partial vindication for his crusade against Deane. In 1781, the former agent began composing and distributing essays that disavowed American independence and advocated for renewing political ties with the crown. He was soon branded a traitor, even by former political allies. In time, even some of Deane's most partisan defenders came to realize the extent of his duplicity, but this did not stop Paine from suffering damage to his reputation for the moment. By any measure, the ejection from his position was a particularly harsh consequence for a man who had so successfully marketed the patriot cause, fought in the conflict against Britain directly, and worked on behalf of the American people to expose malfeasance in government. Decades later, a review of royal correspondence proved that Silas Deane had, in fact, served as a British informant for the entirety of the war, and had been every bit the scoundrel that Paine castigated him for.[193]

After being ejected from his secretarial office, Paine turned his attention back to his writing. In July of 1779, he began a public campaign in support of the right of the states to retain fisheries along the Eastern Sea-board—specifically those along the banks of Newfoundland. In Paine's eyes, the entry of France meant the twilight of the war with Britain, and a forthcoming peace treaty with Britain. Any settlement, he believed, should retain American rights to the fisheries, and ambassadors should resist the urge to use the resources as a bargaining chip to secure peace. That one "should become an advocate for the exclusive right of Britain to the fish-eries," he wrote, "is something very extraordinary."[194]

When a critic writing under the pseudonym "Americanus" had argued that the states had no right to the fisheries because such a privilege had not been mentioned in any of the colonial charters, Paine rejected his premises. "Had it been mentioned, it might have been contended that the right in America was only derivative; and been given as an argument that the orig-inal right lay in Britain," he answered. Paine insisted instead that Britain's claim to the fisheries was wholly dependent upon its association with America—a bond that was now broken. "Wedded to the continent," he wrote, "she inherited its fortunes of islands and fisheries, but divorced therefrom, she ceases her pretentions."[195]

Furthermore, Paine argued that its new ally, France, would certainly object to the American surrender of a profitable trade because of the obvi-ous benefit it would provide the crown. Were this to happen, he argued, "it would not only render us a less valuable ally in point of consequence as well as power, but furnish the enemy of both with a new acquisition of naval strength; the sure and natural consequence of possessing the fisher-ies." To retain rights to the fisheries was "of the utmost importance to America," Paine wrote, "and to surrender them is a species of treason for which no punishment is too severe."[196]

Paine supplemented his original essay on the fisheries, which was pub-lished by the *Pennsylvania Gazette,* with two additional letters on the sub-ject for the same publication. In his own replies, Americanus averred that any mention of American access to the fisheries was absent from the 1763 Treaty of Paris, and not widely acknowledged at the time of the Declara-tion of Independence. Therefore, he figured, American usage of the fish-eries was a mere convenience rather than an enforceable right. To this, Paine built upon his previous arguments by asserting that the American rights to fish on the banks of Newfoundland was a natural right rather than a civil privilege. This deduction was consistent with the Lockean proverb that mixing one's labor with the world's resources led to the acquisition of property. Utilization of the fishers could therefore "not be derived from subjection," he explained, "and as we never can but by our own voluntary consent be put out of the possession" of it.[197]

Notwithstanding Paine's vision for peace terms, the war was far from over. In late 1778, Britain began a deliberate shift in its overall war effort by pursuing the "southern strategy"—a calculated attempt to shift many of its resources from northern positions to attack pockets of patriot resistance in the South. The general basis for this decision was the widespread supposition that the South contained large concentrations of loyalists that would aid in the overall British mission to vanquish state militias and the Continental Army. The campaign began with enormous success for the British, as the significant coastal city of Savannah, Georgia, was captured in December. As the commander of the southern department of the Continental Army, General Benjamin Lincoln was tasked with reorganizing a highly disjointed group of patriot soldiers the next year.

After working to rebuild his army, and with the addition of French Navy under the command of Charles-Hector, comte d'Estaing, Lincoln and his force of about 5,000 Continental forces laid siege to Savannah in the fall of 1779. Determined to take the city back, the joint Franco-American force made a tragic strategic miscalculation by deciding to attempt a daring assault upon the Spring Hill Redoubt on October 9. The allies failed to maintain the element of surprise against a defense force of well-trained British regulars, who, with the help of loyalist volunteers, repelled the attempt to retake Savannah, inflicting about 1,000 casualties on the attackers. d'Estaing himself was wounded in the assault before ordering the French fleet to sail away.[198] To make matters worse, Polish military genius Casimir Pulaski, who had been tapped to train the new American cavalry, was mortally wounded by grapeshot.

As patriot hopes were floundering in Savannah, so too were Paine's financial prospects. Now without funds to continue writing, or even eating, he resorted to touching his well-connected friends for money. In a letter to Henry Laurens, for instance, he revealed that he had recently "taken so little exercise, and lived so very sparingly, that unless I alter my way of life it will alter me." He described his plans to publish a two-volume collection of his previous writings and to begin a subscription-based series on the history of the American War of Independence. "I would rather wish to borrow something of a friend or two in the interim," he admitted, until he could establish his new subscription. While maintaining a humble disposition, Paine was pleading with Laurens to support him. In the meantime, he petitioned the Pennsylvania government for compensation he was still due.[199]

By late 1779, Paine had come full circle from his experience with poverty in England. After having climbed to the highest heights of public celebrity, he had now fallen to the lowest lows of personal destitution. As history soon proved, though, Paine still had much to offer the world, and the next year would rank among the busiest in his life. Even though his expositions on the Deane Affair had lost him friends and prestige in the Continental Congress, the radicals in the Pennsylvania General Assembly remained stalwart, appointing him clerk of that body on November 2, 1779.

As Paine was stepping into his new role, the Pennsylvania General Assembly was setting out to fulfill one of his most novel political goals. George Bryan, a friend of Paine and vice president of the Supreme Executive Council of the Commonwealth, took the lead in drafting An Act for the Gradual Abolition of Slavery, which was first introduced in 1779 and further refined into a plan that was presented in February of 1780.

Virtually unprecedented for its time, the bill enacted a system of emancipation whereby every "negro or mulatto child" born after the passage of the bill would be liberated from slavery at age 28. In addition, the bill also freed the slaves of all owners who failed to enter information into a state registry prior to November 1 of the same year. Furthermore, the bill also imposed an absolute prohibition on the import of slaves. Though this step had already been taken by Virginia two years prior, the addition of a ban prevented slaves from pouring into Philadelphia, at that time the most significant American harbor and a lucrative center for the American slave trade.

Bryan's act also imposed other limitations upon slavery and did much to liberalize the treatment of freed blacks in Pennsylvania. Out-of-state residents were then restricted from keeping slaves in the state for more than six months, and a multitude of laws allowing for discrimination against blacks was nullified entirely. Before the law's passage, for instance, blacks were forced to endure trials in special courts that often all but assured convictions with harsher relative sentences. In addition, the law disposed of a ban on interracial marriage that included blacks, as well as restrictions on blacks' freedom to assemble.[200] All of these changes, now universally embraced, were trailblazing measures in an age where slavery was prevalent in virtually all corners of the world.

The act's preamble began with a stirring declaration that those seeking freedom from tyranny had an obligation to extend liberty to slaves. "When we contemplate our abhorrence of that condition, to which the arms of tyranny and Great Britain were exerted to reduce us," the foreword read, "we rejoice that it is in our power, to extend a portion of that freedom to others…to which we ourselves were tyrannically doomed, and from which we now have every prospect of being delivered." As to why men were born of different colors, it was "not for us to enquire," the message read, but "it is sufficient to know that all are the work of the almighty hand." Accordingly, providence had granted the new Pennsylvania republic the rare opportunity of "removing, as much as possible, the sorrows of those who have lived in undeserved bondage, and from which, by the assumed authority of the kings of Great Britain, no effectual relief could be obtained."

Though the introduction of the emancipation law has sometimes been attributed to Bryan, the words used and themes invoked have led some to conclude that Paine himself was the true author. Eminent biographer and abolitionist Moncure Conway, for example, contended that Paine's authorship "can hardly be doubted."[201] Regardless of whose pen was responsible for the prose, the essence of the content was undoubtedly the embodiment of Paine's ideas.

The gradual emancipation law—envisioned in germ by Paine's earliest American publication—was passed by the Pennsylvania General Assembly on March 1, 1780. Though the Vermont Republic adopted a written constitution that abolished slavery in 1777, Pennsylvania's emancipation act was widely viewed as an extraordinary anti-slavery policy that rattled the cultural status quo. It reversed established legal precedent, and led to

a shift in Western civilization in general. Though it stopped short of absolute abolition, the act was substantial enough to affect the lives of thousands, and it emboldened anti-slavery forces throughout the colonies. In
many ways, it was vindication of the state constitution's axiom that "all
men are born equally free and independent, and have certain natural, inherent, and inalienable rights."

Following Pennsylvania's innovative emancipation act, a series of
cases in Massachusetts led the state's highest court to conclude in 1783
that slavery was an inhumane practice that violated the Massachusetts constitution. The same year, New Hampshire adopted a state bill of rights that
was similarly interpreted to have ended slavery. In 1784, Connecticut and
Rhode Island adopted gradual emancipation acts, both of which contained
provisions similar to their antecedents in Pennsylvania. As the dominos
fell, an entire region in North America set slavery upon a path to extinction. At the time, no similar measures existed in Britain, France, Prussia,
India, Russia, or China, making the American states the first true pioneers
of manumission in world history.

Perhaps invigorated by the act, the arrival of French military forces to
North America, or by his new clerkship, Paine made a timely return to *The
Crisis* in the same month. For the eighth essay in the series, which had
been his first offering in almost a year and a half, Paine boasted of American successes when there were actually few. "Five years have nearly
elapsed since the commencement of hostilities," he wrote, "and every
campaign, by a gradual decay, has lessened your ability to conquer."[202]
Placing the command of British forces into the hands of Clinton and shifting strategy to invade the South, he argued, had been indicative of desperation.

In reality, British successes in the South had been tragic for the patriots,
and the element hindering the crown the most was the entry of France.
"The triumphant appearance of the combined fleets in the channel and at
your harbor's mouth," Paine warned, placed Britain "in the condition of
an endangered country," and was destined to bring forth "a truer picture
of promiscuous distress." Now hardened by a domestic war for years, the
penman portrayed Americans as decidedly resolute:

The people of America, by anticipating distress, had fortified their minds against every species you could inflict. They had resolved to abandon their homes, to resign them to destruction, and to seek new settlements rather than submit. Thus familiarized to misfortune, before it arrived, they bore their portion with the less regret: the justness of their cause was a continual source of consolation, and the hope of final victory, which never left them, served to lighten the load and sweeten the cup allotted them to drink.

Because their cause was just, surmised Paine, the fortitude of the American people had masterfully adapted to the adversity of the crisis. In contrast, he condemned the British government for compounding the miseries of a land far off. "Everything you suffer you have sought," he declared. The crown had abandoned any sympathy for the grievances of Americans, now fully focused on its ceaseless desire to conquer the continent. "The world awakens with no pity at your complaints. You felt none for others; you deserve none for yourselves."[203]

Paine's prognosis on the war, and the condition of those resisting the British, could not have been more improperly timed. In mere weeks, Charleston would be lost to the ambitious Cornwallis, who successfully initiated a siege upon the crucial southern port. Undermanned and without a coherent strategy, General Benjamin Lincoln surrendered his 2,500-man Continental Army force in what was the most devastating patriot capitulation of the war. Though the siege resulted in fewer than 300 patriot casualties, the British managed to capture about 6,000 muskets, more than 300 artillery pieces, almost 400 barrels of gunpowder, and about 30,000 rounds of ammunition. Charleston was a great political and military loss—but the catastrophic loss of supplies at a time when they were desperately needed stung even more. Nevertheless, Paine spun the setback as the catalyst for a new rallying call, urging his compatriots to remain firm in their resolve against Britain. "The reported fate of Charleston," he wrote, "has at last called forth a spirit, and kindled up a flame, which perhaps no other event could have produced."[204]

While the anguishes of war compounded for the Continental Army, a political battle was brewing over ratification of the Articles of Confederation, a proposed constitutional framework for the American states. The chief handiwork of John Dickinson, who at first had been reluctant to favor the independence of the states, the instrument was designed to bind the several states into a loose confederation for shared purposes of mutual convenience. Among the powers to be granted to the new government were those of war, treaties, foreign diplomacy, and the issue of currency.

The Articles featured a Congress in which—like the Continental Congress—each state had one vote, regardless of the number of delegates it sent to the body. In stark contrast to the state constitutions, the charter featured no executive, no central judiciary, and no law enforcement apparatus. Rather than issue laws, Congress was designed to pass resolutions that required enforcement by the individual states and their respective governors. The document embraced the principle of enumerated powers, which was designed to be interpreted such that only powers explicitly mentioned in the document could be exercised. This meant that all other government functions were intended to be reserved by the states and the people. As Article II read, each state "retains its sovereignty, freedom, and independence, and every power, jurisdiction, and right, which is not by this Confederation expressly delegated to the United States, in Congress assembled."

Under the Articles, the resolutions concerning most issues of substance required the endorsement of nine states. Delegates to Congress were appointed annually by their respective state legislatures, a process that mostly maintained the status quo under the Continental Congress. The government would be funded by the requisition system—an arrangement by which each state was obliged to pay a sum of money to the central treasury in proportion to the total value of all land within the state. The Articles did not prohibit the states from issuing their own currency—via coinage or paper—or from levying tariffs on goods from other states and countries within the Confederation.

Although it was drafted in 1777, the Articles had yet to be ratified by 1780. While the document by this time had found favor with virtually all other states, Maryland remained the lone holdout against ratification. This was because the Old Line State refused to enter into any confederation that held no regulatory control over the western territories. As the war raged, prominent politicians and speculators had been making land claims that stretched westward all the way to the Mississippi River. This development prompted a bitter dispute between those who deemed any collectivization of the western lands an egregious violation of property rights and those who perceived such territories as joint possessions of the United States.

Entering the fray of another continent-spanning political debate, Paine set pen to paper once again. In what became the most thorough defense of the Maryland position, he composed a new pamphlet, *Public Good*, which rebuked the lofty western claims of Virginia. Placing the western lands into the possession of the states as a whole, he wrote, "is a principal means of preserving harmony and perpetuating friendship." This was because "the hand of providence has cast us into one common lot, by the unanimous consent of the several parts," Paine explained.[205]

Public Good contained several predominant arguments as to why Virginia's grandiose land claims should be opposed in favor of congressional control. First, Paine opined that Virginia's original colonial charter, secured by Sir Walter Raleigh in 1584, prevented an exclusive claim to the territory. This was because the charter granted land to Raleigh and his named successors through a monarchical system of inheritance through royal titles. This arrangement, he argued, was abolished by the state's transition to republicanism in 1776. Additionally, the charter could be interpreted so broadly as to include "all the inhabitants of America, from New England to Florida."[206]

Later charters for the colony, upon which "some of the present Virginians ground their pretension to boundless territory," compounded the uncertainty of the intended limits to the territory. According to Paine, this was because language that related to geography was unclear and subject to varying interpretations. Virginia's 1609 charter contained no boundary restrictions that were "clear, fixed and defined," he declared, for "words which describe nothing can give nothing." Furthermore, Paine claimed that charters were now null and void because the parties to the agreement were deceased. "The charter was a contract between the crown of England and those adventurers for their own emolument, and not between the crown and the people of Virginia," he reasoned.[207]

Central to Paine's argument was the notion that Virginia's westward expansion was representative of a lust for power. The "land scheme" had only counteracted the valiant pursuit of independence and virtue that Virginia had pursued from the earliest days of the Imperial Crisis, Paine lamented. There was no "greater fund of true wisdom, fortitude, and disinterestedness" than that of the colony Virginia, he wrote. Though the colony once exemplified republican principles, Paine contended that the quest of territorial expansion had caused the commonwealth to become absorbed with power, as if "a torpor has overshaded them."[208]

Paine also favored granting Congress the power to dispose of the western lands for logistical reasons. "Those lands are too distant to be within the government of any of the present states," he claimed, and the lives of their inhabitants were destined to be "hazardous and distressing," with "their habitations unsafe and their title precarious."[209] Because only Congress had the power to incorporate new states under the Articles of Confederation, Paine believe those living in the West would feel unavoidably disconnected from their state governments. The remedy for this, he thought, was augmenting the power of the body such that new states could be carved out of the territory in the future.

Borrowing a theme from the eminent political philosopher Charles de Montesquieu, Paine also doubted that a republic spanning such a large continent could long survive:

> It seldom happens that the romantic schemes of extensive dominion are of any service to a government, and never to a people. They assuredly end at last in loss, trouble, division, and disappointment. And was even the title of Virginia good, and the claim admissible, she would derive more lasting and real benefit by participating in it, than by attempting the management of an object so infinitely beyond her reach.

The inevitable disconnect between the westward and eastward peoples of Virginia, he supposed, would lead, ironically, to the same tumultuous conditions that unraveled the bonds between the American colonies and Britain. A distant government, detached from the needs of its people, was certain to fall into the same tendencies of tyrannical rule. Western settlers would appear to Virginia "as revolters," he warned, "and she to them as oppressors," such that "in a little time a total disagreement will take place, to the disadvantage of both."[210] It was a worst-case scenario for all parties, Paine believed.

To bolster his argument, Paine reminded readers that in *Common Sense* he had portrayed the vacant western lands as a common benefit to all the inhabitants of North America. By "resuming the subject where I then left off," he intended *Public Good* to make clear his views had remained consistent and had not been shifted to suit advantageous political winds.[211] In so doing, it appears Paine realized once again how controversial his words would be. He had begun friendships with several prominent Virginians, many of whom had even promoted his work on the dawn of independence. By depicting his position as an unswerving one, then, he hoped to allay some of the impending commotion that was sure to follow the pamphlet's publication.

Under the direction of Congress, Paine proposed that a new state should be carved out of the western territories, where approximately 20 million acres of land should be sold. By his analysis, the land sold for this purpose would generate £4 million—approximately £723 million, or $905 million, in 2019 currency—enough to fund the war for three additional years. Virginians should favor such a plan, he argued, for three general reasons. First, the revenue from the land sales would spare the commonwealth from paying a greater share of taxes to support the costly war effort. Additionally, the new western state would insulate Virginia from Indian incursions, which were a realistic threat in the 18th century. Lastly, the state stood to benefit from an increase in trade proceeds, as the new state's imports would naturally come through Chesapeake Bay, where Virginia collected impost duties.[212]

By taking such a rigid stance against Virginia's claim to the West, Paine placed himself at odds with virtually all of the state's renowned political class. His philosophical ally Thomas Jefferson answered that he could not comprehend the basis upon which Virginia's "right to the western country could be denied which would not at the same time subvert the rights of all the states to the whole of their territory." The attempt to wrangle the West from his state was "unacceptable to us in form only & not in substance," the author of the Declaration of Independence complained. Severance from the western territories, Jefferson clarified, was only defensible whenever the inhabitants of the region "shall think themselves able to stand alone" by their own volition. In similar fashion, James Madison portrayed the scheme to negate the state's title to the lands as a front for rival land speculators, including the Indiana and Vandalia Company. He consequently attacked Paine's sentiments as an "aggression on her rights," and as "sources of calumny and influence."[213]

The commonwealth even went so far as to appoint a committee of stunning repute—George Mason, Thomas Jefferson, Thomas Walker, and Arthur Lee—to create a written repudiation of *Public Good*. Ironically, it was Lee, who Paine fervently defended during the Deane Affair, who fulfilled this aim through the publication of a thorough refutation to the pamphlet called *A Concise View of the Title of Virginia to the Western Lands*. The work contended, in addition to the colonial charters, that cessions of Indian land through the 1744 Treaty of Lancaster and the 1752 Treaty of Logstown supported Virginia's claim. Richard Henry Lee, brother of Arthur Lee and Paine's most trusted friend in the Continental Congress, seemed to break with his fellow Virginians and give Paine's case secret credence. In a private letter, the elder Lee admitted his hope that Congress would see that the "the ceded lands be sold fairly" such that the funds could be "applied to the extinguishing the continental debt." In turn, Virginia would "be reimbursed the expense she has actually incurred in wresting that country from the British possession by her arms alone."[214]

Great embarrassment followed for Paine when it was revealed, confirming allegations in the press, that the penman had actually been a shareholder in the same Indiana Company that hinged its commercial successes upon the negation of Virginia's title to the West. In the middle of yet another controversy, he took to his own defense in written form. Paine explained that he had written *Public Good* prior to receiving any benefit, but shortly thereafter was granted a voter's share of stock from the company. Having forgotten the gift, Paine claimed he was only reminded of it two years later, in 1782, at which point he directed the company to disclose it to the public. The same year, he admitted that the ideas within his work did in fact bolster the aims of the enterprise. "That the pamphlet was of service to the company is certain," he wrote, while arguing that this was a "natural consequence" rather than a calculated exertion of dishonesty. Still, Paine adamantly insisted that his position on the western lands was his alone and had not been corrupted by financial benefit. "The interest of the heart alone has carried me through a thousand things which others would have failed in or staggered at," he declared.[215]

Ultimately, Virginia abandoned its position on the western lands. Following precedent laid out by New York in 1780, Virginia granted a monumental cession of its western lands to Congress in 1781. However, the commonwealth qualified this decision by making it conditional upon the ratification of the Articles of Confederation by all American states. The state's position was shrewd and explicit—Maryland had to accept the framework, or the cession offer would be rescinded. In response, Maryland quickly assented to these terms and adopted the Articles of Confederation the same year. The document therefore took effect on March 1 of the same year.

Paine's agenda for the western territory also had great implications for constitutional government in the United States. By asserting regulatory power over the lands, his plan called for granting Congress power it did not have under the Articles of Confederation. To the contrary, Article IX of the same framework unambiguously guaranteed "that no state shall be deprived of territory for the benefit of the United States." Nevertheless, he thought it necessary to augment the power of Congress to deal with the western territories and other issues. As a mere agent, Paine perceived the body too feeble to handle issues that mutually affected the fledgling states.

Revisiting a theme from *Common Sense*, he again stressed the necessity of establishing a "continental convention" among the states, "with the purpose of forming a continental constitution, defining and describing the powers and authority of congress." Complaining that "the internal control and dictatorial powers of congress are not sufficiently defined," Paine urged his countrymen to "have them marked out legally" to "give additional energy to the whole, and a new confidence to the several parts." By expressing dissatisfaction with the confederation and proposing a course of action that would strengthen the central government Paine foreshadowed several tropes that were ultimately adopted by American nationalists in the run-up to the Philadelphia Convention of 1787.

Though Paine endured considerable scorn from those responding negatively to his musings in *Public Good*, his next project—dedicated to the subject of America's financial disorder—inspired yet another layer of controversy. As the Continental Army languished through the bitterness of 1780, a currency crisis reached its heights in the American states. As the

War of Independence unfolded, numerous states had enacted policies designed to assist debtors, especially the passage of stay laws—which suspended repayment requirements—and emissions of paper-based currency. In parallel, beginning in 1775 the Continental Congress issued the Continental currency—paper emissions that depreciated in value so much that they were essentially worthless by 1781. The substitution of paper for bullion-backed currencies, intended to encourage the settlement of debts, actually amplified the monetary crisis by debasing the existing currency and prompting hyperinflation. The currency lost so much value that it went out of circulation entirely, remembered only by the saying "not worth a Continental," which Americans use to this day when describing something without value.[216]

Concerned about the country's financial state, Paine composed a new pamphlet, *The Crisis Extraordinary*. Published in 1780 at his own expense, the work was a radical indictment upon paper money. Hoping to "place the difficulty to the right cause," Paine pontificated that, rather than the degree of taxation in the states, the country's economic predicament was largely the result of "the scarcity of the medium in which it is paid." It was therefore the "quantity of money that can be spared out of trade" that exacerbated the conundrum, he cautioned.

It was only when Congress at last stifled the dissemination of the Continentals, Paine asserted, that the drastic fluctuation of prices ended:

> When the emissions stopped, the continent was left in possession of two hundred millions of dollars, perhaps as equally dispersed as it was possible for trade to do it. And as no more was to be issued, the rise or fall of prices could neither increase nor diminish the quantity. It therefore remained the same through all the fluctuations of trade and exchange.

The devaluation of America's paper money never manifested "by any advantage obtained by the enemy," he professed, but through Congress itself. Military losses such as Philadelphia and Charleston, he explained, did not affect the value of money so much as the propensity of Congress, "careless of its value," to continue its issuance of paper Continentals. In the words of distinguished Paine biographer Moncure Conway, Paine's new tract was "a forcible reminder of the depreciation of the Continental currency."[217]

The Crisis Extraordinary also made a case to grant Congress a central taxing power, which Paine promoted as a mechanism to raise revenue to support the disheveled Continental Army. "That the people generally do not understand the insufficiency of the taxes to carry on the war," he lamented, "is evident." Because the British system of taxation had provided lucrative support for the country's campaigns in North America, he argued that the lack of an equivalent countervailing measure would cripple the patriots in their quest to end the war.

Paine envisioned an impost tax—whereupon the domestic acquisition of foreign goods would be taxed—as the most preferable method for Congress to generate revenue. This was primarily because it could be applied uniformly and only to products consumed, and therefore could be avoided and paid whenever it suited its buyer. "The power of choosing is an agreeable thing to the mind," he noted. Under his plan, the tax could also be "ascertained and regulated by Congress," sent to the treasuries of each state, granted to Congress by proxy, and paid in gold and silver only. Unlike Parliament's infamous Stamp Tax of 1765, Paine's calculated impost tax would be more palatable to the masses and subject to notable limitations.

To make it easier for consumers to pay his hypothetical tax, Paine called for a policy of free trade with the rest of the world. "The case must show the vast advantage of an open trade," he reasoned. While the trade of the colonies was once "loaded with restrictions" under Britain, their abandonment by way of the separation demonstrated the aptitude for prosperity "when the whole shall return open with all the world." In this opinion he may have been influenced, besides his own observations, by Adam Smith's 1776 economic treatise *An Inquiry into the Nature and Causes of the Wealth of Nations*, which he was known to have read.[218]

Again, Paine's call for a taxing power had sweeping constitutional ramifications and faced a very obvious political hurdle. Short of an amendment, the Articles of Confederation prohibited Congress from levying any taxes in the manner Paine laid out. Because Article XIII of the document required amendments to be "agreed to in a Congress of the United States, and afterwards confirmed by the legislatures of every State," the next years proved that the framework's alteration process itself would be called into question. The unanimous endorsement of each state, on any subject, was soon acknowledged as an uphill battle indeed.

Any reform of the constitutional system, of course, was predicated upon a military triumph over the British forces still in the field—surely no small hurdle after the crushing losses of 1780. Adding to them was the defection of Benedict Arnold, the ambitious Continental general who had played a principal role in both the capture of Fort Ticonderoga and the crucial victory at Saratoga. Convinced he had been unfairly passed over for promotions in the army, the general faced a court martial in 1779 for engaging in financial impropriety. Even though he was cleared of all but two minor charges, Arnold clung to bitterness under the belief that his accomplishments had gone entirely overlooked. After initiating a secret line of correspondence with enemy commander-in-chief Henry Clinton, to whom he provided military intelligence, he was offered £20,000 to surrender West Point to the British.[219] Arnold obliged, but his plot to give up the post was exposed before it came to fruition. Nevertheless, Arnold was given a commission in the British army and his campaigns hindered the patriots for the remainder of the war.

As Arnold was planning his treachery, General Horatio Gates, the celebrated victor of Saratoga, suffered a catastrophic loss at the hands of Cornwallis at the Battle of Camden in South Carolina. Gates sent his numerically superior force on a nighttime raid, even though his men were physically exhausted, malnourished, and ill-supplied. By coincidence, Cornwallis launched his own assault on the very same night. The well-trained British regulars, augmented by cavalry, met and cut through the inexperienced militiamen, who fled in terror. The Continental Army incurred about 650 casualties, and many troops and supplies were captured by Cornwallis.[220] Gates fled northward to Hillsborough, North Carolina, where he offered his resignation to Washington.

Great alarm followed the British capture of Charleston, the treachery of Arnold, and the disaster at Camden—but more calamity was yet to come. In January of 1781, Virginia's capital of Richmond was put to the torch by an army of loyalists led by Benedict Arnold, forcing the commonwealth's republican government to flee. Without forces to commit or time to spare, neither Washington nor the French commander-in-chief, Comte de Rochambeau, could intervene. Thomas Jefferson, who was then governor of Virginia, escaped capture by minutes, and the British invasion of America's most illustrious state seriously injured patriot morale.

After accepting Gates' resignation, Washington appointed Paine's former superior in the Continental Army, General Nathanael Greene, to command the Southern Department of the Continental Army. Soon after he arrived in North Carolina in December of 1780, he ordered the brilliant Virginian general Daniel Morgan and his group of about 600 men to gather supplies, harass loyalist forces, and forage for food and other supplies in the South Carolina backcountry. Greene consciously defied military convention by dividing his broken army, but believed his decision would buy him enough time to rebuild his army and transform it into a respectable fighting force.

When the notorious British general Banastre Tarleton caught wind of Greene's plans, he quickly pursued a major engagement under the direction of Cornwallis. Tarleton had developed extreme disrepute in American ranks for his deeds at the Battle of Waxhaws earlier in the year, where it was alleged that he had deliberately ordered the massacre of surrendered patriot troops. As a widely publicized incident, the massacre became the source of a new rallying cry to resist, and patriots shouted the phrase "Tarleton's quarter!" to profess that they would provide no quarter at all in return for the general's malevolence at Waxhaws.

Now with 1,100 men, Morgan decided to make his stand against the forthcoming British assault on the south side the Broad River. As Tarleton's force of similar numbers approached Morgan's carefully chosen position, he employed a dazzling maneuver whereby the first line of his militia fired shots into the British force, then quickly retreated to join the second line as Morgan had arranged. Subsequently, Morgan's second line of militia followed its own volley, and also withdrew to the rear according to plan. This series of events appeared to Tarleton a full-scale retreat rather than a premeditated tactic, and the general responded by sending his entire line forward against Morgan's strategic position. Americans holding the rear ground executed a daring bayonet charge as planned, and the patriots employed a stunning double envelopment that encircled Tarleton's army.

The British brigade found itself surrounded in an indefensible position, and utter shock consumed Tarleton's detachment, which collapsed in disarray. Morgan's army captured about 700 prisoners, but Tarleton and a few of his men managed to escape. By any measure, Morgan's triumph was a stunning success for the patriots, especially after the string of devastating losses in the region. A grave setback for Cornwallis and the British ministry, Morgan's victory at the Battle of Cowpens greatly discouraged loyalists in the South and jeopardized Britain's entire southern strategy. According to historian Murray Rothbard, "Tarleton's force had been decisively smashed and the flower of the British forces in America had been destroyed."[221]

At the end of 1780, Paine beseeched the Pennsylvania General Assembly to send him to London as a clandestine agent. His goal would be to use his rhetorical skill to sway public debate in Britain through the publication of pro-Whig, pro-patriot propaganda. There was no better way to defeat the British, he reasoned, than through the "channel of the press," which he "ever considered the tongue of the world, and which governs the sentiments of mankind more than anything else that ever did or can exist." He suggested that the undercover mission could be financed, without additional cost, by convincing the Pennsylvania government to send one fewer delegate to Congress in the next term. Pennsylvania refused, so Paine made plans to travel to Europe on his own accord. Before he could do so, however, Greene visited his former subordinate and successfully persuaded him to abandon the effort as a risky and dangerous delusion.[222]

Without impetus to visit London, Paine, still obsessed with providing financial aid to the American cause, held to the precepts he espoused in *The Crisis Extraordinary*. Discouraged by the lack of a mechanism to raise taxes in the United States, Paine drafted a letter to the French foreign minister, Charles Gravier, comte de Vergennes, asking for a substantial subsidy or loan. As Paine lacked civil standing, the letter was never sent, and was instead shown to members of Congress, several of whom aspired to similar aims regardless of the penman's fall from favor as secretary. Congress soon appointed the young New Yorker Alexander Hamilton, Washington's aide-de-camp, to travel to France in pursuit of financial aid. However, Hamilton declined, and the responsibility was passed to Colonel John Laurens, a good friend of Paine and fellow critic of slavery. The South

Carolinian, also an aide to Washington, agreed to the task so long as Paine could accompany him.

Soon after arriving in Paris, Paine was surprised to discover the great extent to which his writings had swept through and influenced France. "I find myself no stranger in France," he wrote to a friend, "people know me almost as generally here as in America." Paine noted in the same letter that the commandant of Lorient, the seaport he arrived at, complimented him on the "great success and spirit of my publications."[223] The warm treatment only foreshadowed the immense praise he would receive upon his return to the country a decade later.

Accompanied by Laurens, Paine was reunited with Benjamin Franklin, who years earlier had helped facilitate his arrival in Philadelphia. With their reunion, Paine had come full circle. The last time the two were in Europe, Paine was relatively unskilled, impoverished, afflicted with numerous setbacks to his personal life, and lacking in social standing. Now, he was an accomplished writer, well acquainted with the most renowned figures of his time and widely recognized as the penman who ignited the flame of independence. The elder statesman's original note of recommendation requested that his son, William Franklin, then the royal governor of New Jersey, assist Paine in obtaining an understanding of America. At this point, he had defined it.

By this time, Franklin had lost favor in Congress. His political rivals believed that in his old age he had become too passive in his efforts to procure additional war funding from France. South Carolinian Ralph Izard, for example, claimed that "the political salvation of America depends upon the recalling of Dr. Franklin."[224] Under the realization that Laurens had been tasked with assuming some of his responsibilities, Franklin took issue with Congress but did not impede the transition. The elder statesman helped groom the 26-year-old Laurens as his successor, and trained him to effectively fulfill his country's request for additional funding from France.

Laurens eventually grew impatient, and broke from Franklin's advice entirely. After making repeated demands of Foreign Minister Vergennes, the spry South Carolinian threatened to flout all diplomatic convention and hand a petition for funding to the king himself—a highly unprecedented gesture that could be construed as an insult. When Laurens actually followed through on his threat, the royal court was livid, but Laurens got his way when France elected to give the United States six million livres—a fortune capable of sustaining the American war effort.

Perhaps to maintain the devotion of his court, and defend his own integrity, King Louis XVI denied Laurens recognition for the gift. Rather than make it known that the young diplomat had secured the deal, the French minister to America recorded that "the king loaded Paine with favors"—meaning that the aid so desperately sought by the Americans was granted in name to the illustrious penman instead. Though records are sparse, it is also possible that Paine himself made his own unofficial attempt at negotiation, perhaps by parlaying the reputation he had gained as a writer into palpable diplomatic success. Paine boarded the *Resolve*, a French frigate, with 2.5 million of the livres granted and a plethora of war supplies. [225]

Notable of Paine's deeds in France was his commitment to the pursuit of American independence, even after many of his peers had worked so diligently to discredit him, remove him from public influence, and obscure his contributions. While Laurens was extolled in the United States for his bold maneuver to acquire the loan, it was Paine who deserved much of the credit. Even so, without calling attention to himself and his role in the matter, Paine seems to have perceived the feat as one to be celebrated by all who shared his aims. Where it may have been much easier to walk away from the national political stage entirely, Paine never discarded his affection for and commitment to the American cause.

Weeks before Paine journeyed across the world and exchanged formalities with America's indispensable European ally, Washington witnessed another horror—this one internal in nature. A mutiny among the Continental Army's Pennsylvania Line materialized upon widespread complaints in regard to pay. At the crux of the unit's qualms was the contention that the bounty system, which granted lucrative cash enlistment bonuses to new recruits, had disproportionately favored novices who had not seen battle over soldiers that had been in the field for years. The men were also fed up with paltry supplies and horrific housing conditions—realities that Washington acknowledged.

Intending to present their financial demands to Congress, the Pennsylvania Line marched from its encampment in New Jersey to Paine's home of Philadelphia, which had been abandoned by the British in 1778. Making matters worse was Clinton, as the British general aspired to meet the financial demands of the men in return for their promise to switch sides in the war. A considerable force of more than 2,000 men, the Pennsylvania Line posed a serious threat to the continuance of republican government, as it likely could have sacked both the state government and Congress.

In desperation, Washington wrote to the governments of the states to plead for greater funding so that the demands could be met without bloodshed. At the same time, he urged delegates in Congress to remain in Philadelphia to hear the protests rather than flee. The latter course, he warned, would only convey distrust and ill-intent. Anticipating the Pennsylvania Line's arrival in January of 1781, Pennsylvania sent Joseph Reed, the president of the state's executive council, to negotiate with the resentful soldiers. By this time, Congress was also working on a plan of its own in response to the crisis.

Ultimately, a settlement was reached that allowed the men to be discharged, at which point they could either retire outright or reenlist to receive the newly-offered bounty payment. Content with this outcome, about half the men retired, a large portion were granted furlough, and others reenlisted. Following the upheaval, the Pennsylvania Line was reorganized. When 200 soldiers from New Jersey decided to follow a similar course to extract additional pay from the state government in Trenton, Washington acted quickly to quell their protest by ordering 600 Continental Army soldiers from West Point to stop them.[226]

While the potential for a coup had been successfully averted without violence, Washington complained that Pennsylvania's attempt to address the issue "had been productive of ill consequences" and compromised the resolution. In a letter to Robert Livingston, the head of New York's highest court, he lamented that there "can be no radical cure" for such dire situations "till Congress is vested, by the several states, will full and ample powers to enact laws for general purposes."[227] The line mutiny seems to have greatly supported Washington's belief that Congress needed to be strengthened to settle disputes between states and the central authority—an opinion Paine came to share.

After Paine's successes in France, the Franco-American high command began to lay plans for a decisive engagement against the British. However, the vital question of where to strike remained. General Clinton had amassed his forces in New York City, a target Washington had long set his eyes upon. Liberation of the metropolis was now within reach, the Virginian figured, because allied forces greatly outnumbered Clinton's. In addition, the combined force of 7,000 men would expend considerably less energy and resources in pursuit of such a goal, because the armies merged in White Plains, just north of New York City.

However, Clinton's subordinate Cornwallis had already pushed into Virginia, where he conducted strategic raids throughout the summer of 1781. He was soon sent to Yorktown with orders to set up a defensive position for a future British offensive on the region surrounding the Chesapeake Bay. Washington's French counterpart Rochambeau hesitated on the proposal to take back New York, and French naval admiral François Joseph Paul, comte de Grasse, after setting sail from the West Indies, insisted on landing his own reinforcements in Virginia. Unable to rebut both Rochambeau and de Grasse, Washington reluctantly agreed to a grand push into Virginia rather than New York City.

Every aspect of the Franco-American plan in Virginia was calculated to preserve the element of surprise. To confound Clinton, Washington authored various communications that continued to signal his intention of taking New York City, and even moved soldiers into position such that it looked like this was truly the allied aspiration. In late August, the hasty march southward began. De Grasse initiated a blockade of Yorktown, and the allied forces converged thereupon. With numerous delays, Clinton remained behind in New York, ensuring that his eventual attempt to provide support to Cornwallis would come too late.

After a siege that lasted several weeks and included a series of Franco-American assaults upon strategic fortifications, the greatly outnumbered British army suffered several tactical losses and the loss of key positions. In the middle of October, Cornwallis attempted to evacuate Virginia and regroup at nearby Gloucester Point, but was hampered by a coincidental storm. After conferring with his officers, Cornwallis eventually agreed to capitulate. The British surrendered more than 7,000 soldiers, who publicly laid down their arms in a giant pile. In defeat, Cornwallis remained too proud to meet Washington per traditional custom, and instead dispatched a subordinate to deliver his sword.[228]

Though some battles were fought over the next two years, Yorktown represented the final nail in the British coffin. From that point onward, the trajectory of overall success for the American patriots would never be reversed. News of the battle's result sent a ripple throughout the world, and its colossal ramifications were felt on both sides of the Atlantic Ocean. If Paine's audacious declaration that Americans had within their grasp an opportunity "to begin the world over again," the result at Yorktown proved to be the true starting point of such a goal. Freed officially from British subjugation, such a prospect—once portrayed as outlandish in the extreme—was now an undeniable political reality.

After news of the surrender reached Philadelphia, the city celebrated for days. Masses of people crowded into the streets, blasting fireworks and drinking toasts to the victors of the war and inheritors of a new future. It was to this ardor that Paine returned, lacking in wealth but filled with pride. The persistence of America had proven "superior to every effort to enslave her," wrote Paine, and Britain was now forced to endure the "mournful story" that was its failures at Yorktown.[229] At the pinnacle of his army's morale, Washington brought his force back to New York, where it remained for the rest of the war.

When British prime minister Lord North heard of the Yorktown surrender, he was aghast. Responding as if he had "taken a ball in his breast," the head of government paced up back and forth "under emotions of the deepest consternation and distress," repeatedly bellowing "Oh God! It is all over!" King George III voiced his "deepest concern" toward the "unfortunate result of the operations in Virginia," while concealing his own distress from the British public.[230] North soon resigned, and the king was forced to rewrite his Speech from the Throne that originally presumed victory. The king briefly considered abdication, but decided against it.

Horror swept through both Parliament and the royal cabinet. After having come to believe that the American military collapse was imminent, fervent Tory and former colonial administrator Lord George Germain was genuinely shocked. In like fashion, Henry Dundas and Richard Rigby resigned from North's cabinet. In stark contrast to the war hardliners, however, the Whigs who had long opposed the war in America—such as Edmund Burke, Horace Walpole, and Charles James Fox—were ecstatic. At

long last, the failures of Clinton and Cornwallis provided the political capital necessary to bring the war to a close. Parliament adopted a resolution
placing a halt on the war effort in February of 1782, and in May passed a
corollary that declared anyone advocating the continuation of war in North
America was to be treated as an enemy of the crown.[231]

Under the terms of the 1778 Franco-American Treaty of Alliance, both
countries were expressly prohibited from signing a peace with Britain
without the consent of the other. However, the alliance proved fragile on
this point, with American diplomats continually at odds with Vergennes,
the French foreign minister. The American negotiators made it their crusade to make all other terms dependent on the immediate British recognition of the independence of the states and their divisive claims to western
lands, but Vergennes believed France should reap the benefits of victory
in the form of some territory to the east of the Mississippi.

To complication matters, Spain, which had entered the war through the
Treaty of Aranjuez in 1779, agreed to a secret arrangement with France
that permitted continued war with Britain until Spain recovered the territory of Gibraltar, the fiercely contested mouth of the Mediterranean Sea.
However, this agreement seemed to breach terms of France's treaty with
the United States, namely on the dictum that the absolute independence of
the American states was instead the clear prerequisite to any peace with
Britain. Consequently, all three powers maintained divergent ambitions,
and even differed on the true aims of the war.

With a keen understanding of these dynamics, American diplomat John
Jay cunningly brokered a unilateral peace with the British, effectively un-
dercutting both France and Spain. Shrewdly acting on the impulse that a
unilateral treaty would yield greater benefits for United States, Jay's maneuver effectively barred Spain from extending its colonial foothold in
North America, prevented the European allies from monopolizing navigation of the Mississippi River, and ended any prospect of France gaining
territory to the east of the waterway. What came to be known as the Treaty
of Paris was finalized in November of 1782. Pushed out of the negotiations, France and Spain were left to conclude their own terms of peace
with Britain the next year.[232]

Britain's treaty with the United States contained several important provisions. The terms of the arrangement were highly generous to the United

States, both from the success of Jay's scheme to deal with the British directly, and as the product of British prime minister Shelburne's Whig inclination toward free trade. By laying the groundwork for good relations with the American states from the outset, Shelburne believed mutual trade relations would result, providing economic benefit to all parties and tempering the potential for future animosities.

The independence of the American states was unambiguously regarded as of the foremost importance. Rather than acknowledging peace with a singular American union, the Treaty of Paris made clear that each state—enumerated individually—was to be considered a sovereign country with independent political authority. To these newly "free sovereign and Independent States" the crown relinquished all claims to its former colonial territory.

In addition, all wartime hostilities between Britain and the United States were to cease, and British forces, including those in occupied forts, were to be recalled with "all convenient speed." As another term, all land north of the Ohio River and south of Canada was to be ceded to the United States. Rights to the fisheries off Newfoundland, which Paine had so ardently defended, were guaranteed to all Americans. To encourage good faith relations, debts between the inhabitants of each country were to be honored and repaid. Prisoners of war on both sides were to be released, and the rights and property of Tories in the United States were to be protected by law. Furthermore, any future attempts to confiscate Tory property in America were explicitly prohibited.

For his failures in the run-up to Yorktown, General Clinton was replaced with Guy Carleton, who organized the British withdrawal from New York in late 1783. In New York City, a lone British flag was replaced by the stars and stripes of the United States and Washington led a procession through the town square. On the same streets, he would be sworn in as president of the United States a half-decade later. Jubilant crowds greeted him to celebrate the occasion. It was the culmination of the enormous hardships, personal sacrifices, immense financial losses, stunning betrayals, and military setbacks of the last eight years.

With Britain ejected from the continent, many of Paine's loftiest ambitions had come true. The American triumph vindicated his devotion to political independence and trademark optimism during the darkest days of the conflict, leaving many of his naysayers to observe in silence. Despite the palpable military and philosophical victory, though, he was far from victorious in his personal affairs. He was not without friends, but he was certainly without money. Made into a pariah of the political class, Paine lived in squalor, having made little from his writings though they had sold many thousands of copies. In embarrassment, he continued to beg friends for financial support while he contemplated his uncertain future. Just as the states had been made independent, Paine had become dependent.

The American War of Independence failed to revolutionize much of anything. As a conflict long predicated on the preservation of English liberties, traditions, and institutions, the conflict failed to produce a fundamental alteration of the American political system. Though Parliament and the king could no longer lay claim to the former colonies, the internal governmental affairs of the states mostly reverted to customs and processes that existed prior to Parliament's campaign to tax the colonies. Despite the conspicuous transition from colonialism to republicanism, the states retained their representative assemblies, commercial affairs, civil institutions, and cultural characteristics. For this reason, many historians have been apt to portray the American Revolution as a conservative—rather than radical—phenomenon.[233]

Understanding these outcomes, Paine's quest to make America ripe for a radical reawakening was to him a job half-finished. Though the chains of the monarchy he so decried had been cast aside, he saw good reason to remain ambivalent about the future of the United States. An emerging economic crisis—to follow the military strife he wrote so much about—soon raised his trepidations. Compounding his uncertainty was his consistent belief that numerous defects in the Articles of Confederation would ultimately undermine the bonds among the states and threaten the gains of the moment.

Chapter 4

Crossroads of the Republic

Principle, like truth, needs no contrivance. It will ever tell its own tale, and tell it the same way. But where this is not the case, every page must be watched, recollected, and compared like an invented story.

- Letter to the Abbé Raynal

The dawn of independence led Paine to an identity crisis. The "Penman of the Revolution," as he has been called, had fallen on tough times just as the victory of self-determination had been actualized in the fledgling country. The newfound autonomy of the American states brought forth new political prospects and economic frontiers for many, but appeared not to yield the same gains for one of the most prominent champions of the patriot cause. Though he had secured the crucial loan from France that ensured victory over the British, Paine received no public credit or reward and struggled even to gather the funds necessary to make his way back to Philadelphia.[234] With the states freed from Britain, Paine no longer had a real foe to fight. Even in the country he helped create, the former alien to America, in many ways, was an alien yet again.

Soon after his return from France, Paine revealed his discontent to select friends. On November 30, 1781—the seventh anniversary of his arrival in America—he wrote to Washington on the subject. While his time in the country had been the "the most honorary time" of his life, he wrote, his recent days had been "most inconvenient and even distressing," and had made him question the moral standing of America itself:

> From an anxiety to support, as far as laid in my power, the reputation of the Cause of America, as well as the Cause itself, I declined the customary profits which authors are entitled to, and I have always continued to do so; yet I never thought, (if I thought at all on the matter) but that as I dealt generously and honorably by America, she would deal the same by me. But I have experienced the contrary—And it gives me much concern, not only on account of the inconvenience it has occasioned to me, but because it unpleasantly lessens my opinion of the Character of a Country which once appeared so fair, and it hurts my mind to see her so cold and inattentive to matters which affects her reputation.

Presuming the trust of the most popular figure in the United States, Paine informed Washington that he intended to leave America permanently. "It is my design to get to Europe," he explained, where his "literary fame" would ensure that he would not "experience worse fortune" than he had in the states.[235]

By early 1781, the paper money crisis had reached its height. Congress refused to accept its own paper money in repayment of debts, and the Continental bills were now so worthless they had ceased to circulate. At the same point, states disseminated their own paper money currencies in their own attempts to assist debtors. Rather than provide relief, however, the debasement of paper bills worsened economic hardships while the value of hard currencies—such as Spanish coins—remained remarkably stable. The paper money calamity spawned a new breed of hard money warriors who vehemently opposed any attempt to resurrect paper money schemes. For example, one enthusiastic supporter of bullion money, Pelatiah Webster, wrote in 1780 that the "compulsory methods to force value into paper money" sparked "irritations and disappointments that so destroyed the courage and confidence" of the American people.[236]

Some still maintained that the reintroduction of paper money was necessary in exceptional times of crisis, but much of the political class was now dead set against it. Having already broached the subject in *Public*

Good, Paine found himself in alignment with the latter bloc. With a stream of new evidence demonstrating that paper money policies had crippled the American economy, he would return to the subject in future writings. Moreover, the topic would also play a prominent role in his next political venture.

Despite his economic misfortunes, the years following the Deane Affair had largely vindicated Paine's inflexible stance against the now-discredited merchant. Deane spent the last years of the war as a Tory apologist, and his writings had become the focal point of attacks by American Whigs. Desperate to salvage his reputation, he authored a pamphlet in 1784 to defend his divisive wartime commercial pursuits, but it fell on deaf American ears. The "warmest of his advocates," wrote Paine, "now very candidly acknowledge their deception." Even some of Paine's most ardent political enemies—such as Robert Morris—reversed position on the subject. Having "been totally deceived in Deane," for instance, Morris "now looked upon him to be a bad man" with a "reputation totally ruined."[237]

Morris had amassed considerable political influence in 1781. Elected superintendent of finance, the Pennsylvanian assumed control over the government's expenditures, a position he accepted only on the condition that he could both unilaterally hire officials into his own department, and dismiss civil officers in any other Congressional branch—including the foreign affairs and war departments. He used his authority to help elevate his friends to high positions in the other departments, including New Yorker Robert Livingston as the head of foreign affairs. By this point, Morris was widely considered the most powerful figure in the government.

In May of 1781, Morris presented a bold plan to Congress—a framework for a centralized commercial bank, the first of its kind on the continent. His model was inspired by the Bank of England, an ostensibly private entity with public duties that had been established in London at the end of the tumultuous 17th century. The Bank of North America, as it would eventually be called, was to possess a monopoly on the issuance of currency. In return, it would lend its inflated notes to the government. Additionally, the imposition of a bank freeze would prevent other banks from operating in the country for a time. Under the program, the bank's wealthy investors would become the holders of public debt, and profit immensely from the issuance of new notes.[238]

While Congress debated the bank, Morris began a friendship with Paine, whom he came to view as a potential ally in the quest realize another political objective despite the fact that the two stood diametrically opposed on virtually all matters of philosophical substance. While Paine was a radical Whig, Morris was a model conservative in the classic conception. Paine was living in poverty, but Morris was a wealthy aristocrat. Paine's talents rested in his capacity to rile the masses through the written word, while Morris' successes were defined by his commercial achievements and backroom political connections. Despite their perceived incompatibility, however, the two men fervently agreed in the necessity of political reform to augment the power of Congress to provide for raising revenue through taxation.

Morris arranged, with approval from Washington and Secretary of Foreign Affairs Robert Livingston, for Paine to be hired by Congress as a writer with a comfortable annual salary of $800. By commissioning Paine to publish in favor of congressional policies, the men—all eventually American nationalists—believed the penman would aid their quest to empower Congress to tax and enforce other resolutions of importance. It was through *Common Sense*, after all, that Paine was able to change the parameters of political debate entirely, successfully using the written word to appeal directly to the American commoner. Morris shrewdly recognized this, and was more than happy to employ a radical former political enemy with whom he now happened to share an objective. The impecunious Paine was no doubt grateful for an unexpected opportunity to pay the rent using his talents for a cause he favored.

The crusade to grant Congress more power was hardly the aim of a small cabal. Washington's young aide-de-camp Alexander Hamilton had already written in favor of the same ends. In one letter that was published in two prominent New York newspapers, Hamilton anguished over the impotency of Congress:

With respect to the Federal Government; if it is too weak at first, it will continually grow weaker. The ambition and local interests of the respective members, will be constantly undermining the usurping upon its prerogatives, till it comes to a dissolution; if a partial combination of some of the more powerful ones does not bring it to a more speedy and violent end.

These flaws made the Confederation government "unable to command the means to pay, clothe, or feed their troops," he professed. The young and ambitious New Yorker offered a simple remedy: "TO ENLARGE THE POWERS OF CONGRESS." Any political response that stopped short of this remedy, he claimed, would be purely "illusory."[239] These sentiments, in germ, were the cornerstones of political nationalism, a political creed embraced by much of the founding generation in the 1780s.

In the end, Morris' cherished plan for a central bank was chartered by Congress in December of 1781. Only one state, Massachusetts, voted against the bank after assembling an anti-nationalist coalition. Even though the Articles of Confederation did not permit the charter of such a corporation, most delegates looked the other way in hopes that the bank would help curtail the catastrophe of the Continental and other fiat currencies that circulated in the states.[240] It was a colossal victory for Morris and his fellow American mercantilists, but the campaign to establish a central taxing power was still left undone.

The idea of writing on behalf of the government—rather than against it—must have vexed Paine. His past works had been created with the intention of benefiting the public by revealing abuses of government, but his recent change in circumstances subjected him to a possible conflict of interest. Everything Paine wrote during this period, however, was wholly consistent with themes he previously espoused. Furthermore, those who saw fit to harness his skills once again—namely Morris and Livingston—maintained their own grievances with the Confederation system. Rather than promote its merits on face value, these men looked to the illustrious author to once again shed light on impediments that, once displaced, would yield a more prosperous country. Instead of painting a rosy portrait of the Confederation government, Paine was quick to point out the defects he saw within it—in full respect of his own philosophical sensibilities and his trademark propensity to criticize government.

In February of 1782, a transcription of King George III's speech at the opening of Parliament found its way to American shores. In his oratory, the monarch admitted that "the events of the war have been very unfortunate for my arms in Virginia, having ended in loss of my forces in that province." War with the American states had been "prolonged by that restless ambition which first excited our enemies to commence it," he grieved. Still, the king expressed his commitment to "restore the blessings of a safe and honorable peace" in the culmination of the struggle. At this point committed to political damage control, he discounted the losses of the war by pointing to commercial successes in the East Indies and elsewhere. "The favorable appearance of affairs," he said, "must have given you satisfaction."[241]

In truth, few were more satisfied than the relentless patriots who persevered through the many hardships of their cause and time. Those who made financial sacrifices and had overcome military tribulations were justly elated, even with America's political and economic future uncertain. Nevertheless, the king mocked the same breed as "deluded subjects" who had left behind "prosperous condition which they formerly derived from a due obedience to the laws" by embracing "that spirit of rebellion." Bitter in the realization that the war was over, the king apologized for the financial burden his subjects were forced to endure, which stood "among the many ill consequences" of his conquest in America.[242]

With no time to waste, Paine committed himself to a scorching response to the speech for his next installment in *The Crisis*. The lofty claim that the Americans—rather than the crown—were to be blamed for instigating the war was to Paine an utterance of grave insincerity. "The very man who began the war," who "invoked every aid of hell in his behalf" was instead guilty of the same crime, he replied. To "turn the tables from himself, and charge another for the wickedness that is his own," wrote Paine, "can only be equaled by the baseness of the heart that spoke it." Furthermore, to the king's assertion that the British war effort had been a noble endeavor, the penman condemned the same exertion as a pursuit of "unequalled barbarity."[243]

Paine depicted the speech as a feeble attempt to obscure the empire's great sins by appeal to the emotional sensibilities of British subjects:

That the man whose ignorance and obstinacy first involved and still continues the nation in the most hopeless and expensive of all wars, should now meanly flatter them with the name of a free people, and make a merit of his crime, under the disguise of their essential rights and permanent interests, is something which disgraces even the character of perverseness.

The king's compliments to his subjects "for their constant, zealous, and affectionate attachment" to the kingdom throughout the toils of war, therefore, were "words which impress nothing but the ear, and are calculated only for the sound."[244]

The king's comments on favorable circumstances in the East Indies came in light of Britain's recent acquisition of trade privileges in the region, after having first having taken Dutch possessions hostage. By coming to such an arrangement peacefully, the country had unmistakably averted added military conflict and opened new avenues for foreign trade. However, Paine wrote that the king's allusions to this episode were made only to shift public attention to matters unrelated to the momentous blunder that was his attempt to subjugate the American colonies. Simply because one event produced more favorable results for the British, he argued, was no reason to buy into a diversion and ignore existing oppression. "One broken leg is better than two, but still it is not a source of joy," he scoffed.[245]

The king's idle words were filled with "sniveling hypocrisy," quipped Paine, though they still reminded the world of the incredible costs involved in securing independence and safeguarding individual rights. As he saw it, the speech should serve as a timely reminder of the debts that had accrued and the financial doldrums of the Confederation government. "But let not America wrap herself up in delusive hope and suppose the business done," he wrote, as the "least remissness in preparation" and "the least relaxation in execution" would "only serve to prolong the war, and increase expenses." Paine reminded his peers that the war against Britain would not be concluded "without trouble and expense," and promised to follow his essay with his case for "vigorously providing for them."[246]

Though ultimately victorious in their campaign to implement a central bank, Morris and his political allies hoped to take another step forward in pursuit of their cherished economic program in 1781. That year, American nationalists proposed a constitutional amendment to sanction a universal five-percent tariff on all imported goods, and arm Congress with the ability to collect the tax. The amendment, described by its sympathetic sponsor as "indispensably necessary to the support of public credit and the prosecution of the war," was designed to generate revenue for the troubled and continually underfunded government.[247] After securing the approval of Congress, the proposal sparked heated debates within the states, the unanimous approbation of which was required, per the Articles of Confederation, to ratify any amendment.

At the same time Paine drafted his latest essay in *The Crisis* series, he maintained a routine correspondence with Morris. In March of 1782, the penman alerted his new friend of his intent to distribute the article to Philadelphia newspapers. In addition, he promised to follow the piece up with another to address "the whole business of revenue" the next week.[248] It was during this juncture that Paine—having already expressed his opinions on the subject in his previous writings—fully absorbed himself in the cause of the impost.

Realizing the hurdles of persuading every state to conform to his opinion in favor of the taxing power, the eager writer professed that he had never predicated his principles upon their perceived popularity:

> When any necessity or occasion has pointed out the convenience of addressing the public, I have never made it a consideration whether the subject was popular or unpopular, but whether it was right or wrong; for that which is right will become popular, and that which is wrong, though by mistake it may obtain the cry or fashion of the day, will soon lose the power of delusion, and sink into disesteem.

To reinforce his claim, Paine reminded his readers that he had maintained the same approach during the Deane Affair. While his condemnation of Deane had caused "every man, almost without exception," to view him in a negative light, the "poison of his hypocrisy" was worth putting a stop to even if it cost Paine his own reputation—a price he paid in many regards. In the same way, he was now writing in support of a new taxing power while knowing full well that Americans were utterly repulsed by taxation. While most viewed the practice of paying taxes to one's local assembly as a duty and necessity, a central tax in the United States in the manner called for was without precedent. The new impost proposal brought forth comparisons to the tyrannical schemes of taxation employed by the British in the buildup to the war. Even so, "where sufficient revenues are not provided," Paine wrote, the country would "be overrun, ravaged, and ruined."[249]

Paine sincerely believed Americans could bear the burden of a new tax. "There are not three millions of people in any part of the universe, who live so well, or have such a fund of ability, as in America," he claimed. As he figured, his countrymen had overcome substantial economic hardships for two general reasons. First, the industriousness of Americans was so apparent and consequential that it allowed citizens to transcend the many impediments they faced. Whether hindered by trade embargoes, the loss of property, or the debasement of currency, Americans found ways to make a living in wartime. Second, he argued that in their infancy, American governments had lived up to the republican ideal of the Lockean conception. In other words, taxes paid to the state governments funded only measures to protect life, liberty, and property. Congress would similarly manage the new revenue on a general level, he wrote, by working to solve problems affecting all states.[250]

At this point calling the "union of America" the "foundation-stone of her independence," and "the rock on which it is built," Paine maintained that the potential for financial corruption would be circumvented so long as the purposes for which Americans were taxed were carefully managed. Making clear delineations between the objectives of the states and those of Congress, he added, was the key to securing the public faith in regard to taxation. Taxes "should be levied, paid and collected, separately, and kept separate in every instance," he wrote, and civil officers of state governments and Congress should never meddle with the powers and affairs of their counterparts. To pay taxes to separate entities, he added, would also carry the advantage of making citizens more aware of what they are paying for. "While the monies of both were blended," Paine observed that Americans remained confused as to the destination of their money, despite having "the same right to know, that they have to pay."[251]

The gains of independence would be lost, argued the Paine in another essay, unless "a revenue sufficient for the protection and good of the country is obtained." To withhold one's portion while American soldiers languished in battle, despite "all hazards and events," was "the highest dishonor man can undergo." Though some states had underpaid or failed to pay their quotas of funds to Congress under the oft-disregarded requisition system, those who devoted their own earnings to the patriot cause did "more for his country's good," according to Paine, "than the loudest talker in America."[252]

To avert the "crisis of destruction by the insufficiency of our public revenues," and a public treasury "furnished with inability," neutral parties must support taxation by way of their own representatives. Only then, Paine insisted, would Americans "be freed from the murmurs of the suffering soldier" and "ignoble and impolitical covetousness." Paine promoted the measure as a temporary prerogative that would expire at the termination of the conflict. "When the war shall cease with us, our taxes for that purposes will cease with it." While acknowledging taxes would naturally "be attended with some inconvenience," he denied the inevitable permanence of such a power. Without the power to tax, Paine concluded, America was merely "a country sunk in corruption and extravagance," but with such an endowment, she would be "one whose object is founded in just principles," characterized by "good management."[253] Public funding was necessary to safeguard the young United States, and fund their mutual interests, he reasoned.

Morris and his associates tirelessly lobbied representatives in the state legislatures to clear the way for a congressional taxing power. They portrayed the power as vital to the war effort, extolled the merits of public debt, and even concealed news of foreign loans from the public so their objective would not be threatened. Their arguments won out in nearly every state, and by late 1782, Rhode Island remained the only holdout. The deeply independent state—first to declare its independence from Britain—postponed its consideration of tariff power beyond its originally planned September date.[254]

In the early 1780s, Rhode Island had flourished under a system of free trade that defined its economy. When the war had ravaged Newport, commerce shifted to Providence, which became a boisterous commercial hub. There, merchants thrived without the burden of taxes on foreign trade, and several conservative-leaning politicians in the state government had been replaced by radicals. Congress responded to the state's recalcitrant posture by sending committees to lobby state lawmakers.[255]

At the same point, Paine converted his philosophical support for the tariff into local activism. From his home in Philadelphia, he wrote a new series of six letters to be disseminated in Rhode Island. Published in the *Providence Gazette*, the essays diverted from his typical brand by making a practical case for the tariff. In addition, he also responded to some of the common arguments made by opponents of the tariff. One of them, "A Citizen of Rhode-Island," claimed the new taxing authority would harmfully permit Congress to transform itself into a supreme oligarchy with the power to exploit the treasury: "Is it expedient, says he, in any government, that the supreme executive power should hold the revenue independent of the people?" Such a proposition, he warned, would have tragic ramifications for America's constitutional system. The authority to raise revenue was therefore more justly lodged in the states, where it applied "more closely upon every individual who is capable of forming a judgment upon the effects." Conversely, the power to tax would raise "a radical question" not sanctioned by the constitutional apparatus.[256]

To this claim, Paine answered unequivocally that no government or council should have the power to command the public treasury without being accountable to the people. It was "the very being, principle, and constitution of the republic," he professed, "that the people have nothing in their government independent of themselves." Such a question "may belong to Turkey or Persia," both of which had autocratic systems "totally independent of the people," but the orientation of the American government was that of a republic, where executive power was "wholly in our hands," and the ability to "unmake, change and alter, as we please" was inherently understood. Members of Congress were elected as delegates by their respective constituencies, and were themselves taxpayers subject to the laws they passed. By presuming representatives were distinct from the inhabitants of the states, Paine asserted that the Rhode Islander's argument undermined itself through faulty premises. "There is no such thing in America as power of any kind, independent of the people," he insisted.[257]

Paine also defended the method of taxation under the proposed plan. Because "commerce is not the local property of any state," but rather the effect of "the produce and consumption" of peoples of various states and regions, he reasoned that "its regulation and protection can only be under the confederated patronage of all the States." By "not coming into the measure with the rest of the states," Paine argued that Rhode Island opponents had overblown the extent to which the indirect form of taxation—applied only to foreign trade—was morally egregious.[258] Unlike direct taxation within a state, or the requisition system that applied tax burden by property ownership, the tariff would be applied equally to all regardless of region. Moreover, it would not disproportionately penalize those who possessed large wealth holdings.

Another strike against the taxing power, according to its ardent enemies in Rhode Island, was that it would grant Congress the "power to keep a standing army, and support a number of pensioners."[259] In that time, even the mere suspicion of prolonged military presence was met with universal alarm. In English constitutional history, there were few circumstances that so riled the anger of the populace than that of a standing military force, and the British occupations of Boston, New York, and Philadelphia, and other areas only magnified this perception. Any political tool that appeared to challenge the republican axiom that the civil authority was to remain superior to its military counterpart, then, was highly suspect.

The idea that the taxing power would pave the way for a standing army, wrote Paine, was a ridiculous fantasy of "illiberal and unbelieved pretenses." Because the power to tax did not confer the power to raise a perpetual force, Paine considered the argument so implausible that he denied that Rhode Islanders "ever could be so duped as to suffer it."[260] Nearly all governments throughout history had the means to generate revenue through taxes, he reasoned, but that did not make standing armies inevitable. Even though the state governments in America enacted similar taxes upon trade, for instance, the same assemblies had not taken such leaps toward tyranny.

Rather than cling to their own financial self-interest, Paine beseeched the merchants who opposed the tax to understand that the consequences of their opposition would "throw the burthen on the shoulders of your neighbors, both in town and country, already more taxed in proportion" than their merchant detractors. For the sake "suffering creditors," a "suffering army," and "for the purpose of equalizing the public expenses," Paine advised his naysayers to drop their fringe resistance to the revenue venture.

Congress had already proven its merits to the commercial class, he argued, by funding the Continental Army in its defeat of the British occupiers. "Had the enemy succeeded in conquering America," he wrote, "the taxes upon commerce would have been an amazing deal more than five per cent." Paine went so far as to cite several examples of this, noting that the British duties on coffee, tea, cocoa, single-brandy, rum, and salt were all more burdensome than that which Congress proposed.[261]

Even prior to the campaign to convince Rhode Islanders of the efficacy of the congressional tariff, Paine portrayed the United States as a singular entity. Rather than a plural league of societies confederated for defined purposes, the United States was, to Paine at this point, "one extended family, one imperial commonwealth, the greatest and most equal in its rights and government of any ever known in the world."[262] However, this conception of a homogenous, aggregated nation was not a predominant one. At the time, states acted almost wholly autonomously, and public policy was carried out at a local level. The states cooperated with each other for mutual purposes through the Confederation system, but even those purposes largely had to be carried out by local authorities. Paine's grand appeal to national unity, aimed at skeptical Rhode Islanders, therefore represented an idealistic desire rather than a political reality.

As the battle over the tariff played out in the press, Paine kept Morris alerted to his undertakings. He expressed that he would not sign his letters by his moniker "Common Sense," as he normally did, so as not to "bring them into more notice than there is occasion for." In an assessment Morris was sure to share, he wrote that the continued antipathy within Rhode Island was the result of unfounded, isolated paranoia among those who disagreed with the necessity of the impost:

> All of these embarrassments are ascribable to the loose and almost disjointed of the Union. The States severally not knowing what each will do are unwilling to do anything themselves. But the point to be considered no is, whether we cannot make the inconvenience a foundation for reform, by applying the inconvenience as a reason for it.

Vexed by the cold reality that Congress lacked true legislative authority, Paine did what came naturally to him by this point, and prescribed a solution that transcended the issue of revenue. He suggested the formation of a continental legislature, comprised of three to five delegates per state, that would meet yearly to "enact law for and in behalf of the whole." If a stronger union was not to be formed, he wrote, we hang so loosely together that we are in danger of hanging one another." His implication that Congress should "stand in a much better and more exalted situation than a present" uncannily foreshadowed the general government that would come to pass in 1789, but it was not to be in the moment.[263]

As Congress launched its effort to lobby Rhode Island, the state sent its own new delegation of Whigs to defend its position of opposition in Philadelphia. After a series of public debates and written propaganda, the final verdict on the tariff was decided by an unexpected party. The amendment was defeated, not by Rhode Island, but by Virginia—which rescinded its endorsement of the impost in December when the British invasion no longer threatened the state. With this about-face by the Old Dominion, Morris' highly publicized quest for the tariff ended in failure. "The impost plan was dead," wrote historian Murray Rothbard, and the pro-tariff "juggernaut had been stopped, almost at the last minute."[264]

Beyond the political brawl over the powers of Congress, Paine's attention was drawn into another project in 1782. As an avid reader of European political tracts that were reprinted in American newspapers, he took notice of a particular work by the Abbé Raynal, one of France's most prominent Enlightenment thinkers and writers. A friend of Diderot and Voltaire, Raynal was the famed author of the *Philosophical History of the Two Indies*, the most influential treatise of economic and political radicalism the country had ever seen. His controversial works were countered by a state-imposed campaign of censorship, and he was eventually forced into exile. In 1781, he released *The Revolution of America*, his own analysis of the imperial struggle between Britain and the United States.

At the heart of Raynal's work was the claim that, while the people in Massachusetts had suffered immensely through the imposition of the Intolerable Acts, the other colonies had not been so adversely affected by British treachery:

The disturbances by which the provinces of Massachusetts was agitated, were repeated in the other provinces. The scenes, indeed, were not bloody, because there were no British troops? But the Americans seize every where on the forts, the arms, and the military stores: they every where expel their governors, and other agents of England; and every where harass such of the inhabitants as appeared favourable to its cause.

Rather than reaching a settlement upon peaceable terms, he wrote, Congress assembled and appointed George Washington to command its army. "Instantly the new general flies to the province of Massachusetts, drives the royal troops from post to post, and obliges them to shut themselves up in Boston." In the process, the Americans dealt with the conflict in such a way that they disregarded the principles they had always espoused by applying force too profusely. "The principles which justified" their rally for independence, he asserted, "were dispersed on all sides."[265]

Raynal also disputed the American gospel—spelled out explicitly in the Declaration of Independence—that all men were naturally endowed at birth with the same inalienable rights as all others. "It has been said that we were all born equal," he wrote, "but that is not so." On the contrary, the Frenchman explained, "there is an inequality of talents, or of strength." Denying "that nature offered to us all the same dwelling," the "same resources," the "same means of defense," or the "same qualities of mind and body," he contended instead that nature made some strong and others weak. "There is amongst men an original inequality which nothing can remedy," he professed. "It must last forever; and all that can be obtained by the best legislation, is, not to destroy it, but to prevent the abuse of it."[266]

In perhaps his most significant departure from the American Whigs, Raynal opined that the 1766 repeal of the Stamp Act had removed most of the animosity that had existed between British Tories and American Whigs. "Revoked after two years of convulsive agitation," he wrote, the formal annulment of the combative law should have averted an armed uprising of the colonies. "But the triumph of the colonies is of short duration," he contended, as the Townshend Acts—which imposed taxes on trade rather than implementing schemes of internal taxation—were simi-

larly opposed in concerted efforts of colonial resistance. Opposing the latter acts was duplicitous, thought Raynal, because several patriot writers
assured Parliament that they held no constitutional objections to taxes
upon trade, and reminded readers that Americans had always paid them
under the British Navigation Acts. By refusing to pay the Townshend duties, the patriots had only created the illusion that the policy was as despotic as the Stamp Act. It was a "subterfuge" designed to conjure the impression of tyranny where there was none, reasoned Raynal.[267]

On the surface, it ironically seemed as if Raynal had shared many of
Paine's political sensibilities. Despite his agreements with some of their
methods, for instance, the Frenchman boldly defended the right of colonies
to declare independence and institute new republican societies. Americans
"are called rebels," he wrote, only "because you will not be taxed but by
your representatives." The patriots across the sea "confined themselves to
a resistance, authorized even by the English laws," he insisted, with the
sole aim of "maintaining the very limited rights which they had hitherto
enjoyed." Because the colonies were "formed of plain, brave, upright men,
proprietors and cultivators of their land in one," they would soon overcome the years of adversity. "The authority of Great Britain over America
must sooner or latest be extinct," he declared.[268]

In alignment with Paine, Raynal also depicted the embrace of paper
money as an acute disaster. "You are overwhelmed with paper," he wrote,
so much so that foreign creditors "know not by what incredible illusion
this fictious money is kept up." The "dreadful consequences" of the paper
money experiment, he concluded, "are beyond our imagination." Likewise, he portrayed the condition of Americans to that of a subjugated people, who justifiably revoked their consent to the monarchical system of
Britain. "Conquest binds no more than theft," he wrote, and "the consent
of ancestors cannot be obligatory upon descendants." In this realm too, he
and Paine agreed wholeheartedly.[269]

Robert Bell, the Philadelphian printer who quarreled with Paine over
royalties after publishing *Common Sense* in its original form, illegally
promulgated a copy of Raynal's *The Revolution of America*. The work
soon made its way to the notorious pamphleteer, who took immediate issue
with Raynal's interpretations of the American struggle for independence.
Throughout the summer of 1782, he carefully worked on a new pamphlet

that would prove his most lengthy yet. Printed by Bell's competitor Melchior Steiner, *Letter to the Abbé Raynal, on the Affairs of North America* was published in September of the same year.

At the crux of Paine's umbrage was the work's assertion that the American Crisis—as he called it—came down to the question of whether the mother country had the right to impose taxes upon the colonies. In this, Raynal had "misconceived and mis-stated the causes which produced the rupture between England and her then colonies." To Paine's indignation, the Frenchman perceived the American Revolution as a historically unique event that had "none of the energetic causes, which have produced so many revolutions upon the globe." In fact, he denied that the British government had done much to meddle in American affairs at all:

> Manners, customs, habits, no object dear to nations had there been the sport of ridicule. Arbitrary power had not there torn any inhabitant from the arms of his family and his friends, to drag him to a dreary dungeon. Public order had not been there inverted. The principles of administration had not been changed there; and the maxims of government had there always remained the same.

While sympathizing to an extent with Americans who resisted British taxes, Raynal denied that the laws were as egregious as radical agitators in the colonies portrayed them. The livelihoods of Americans, he thought, were not disturbed to a degree that necessitated bloodshed in North America. Parliament's laws were thus mischaracterized by firebrands from the colonies, who exploited the situation for political gain.[270]

Paine could not have disagreed more vehemently. According to his philosophical creed, Parliament had oppressed the colonials severely by discarding the governmental apparatus they had operated under for more than a century. While Raynal depicted the repeal of the Stamp Act as an earnest attempt to alleviate American enmity, Paine viewed the same event as an immaterial gesture that only preserved the legal mantra that Parliament could "bind America in all cases whatsoever." The negation of the stamp tax only paved the way for the "infinitely more mischievous" Declaratory Act, which reiterated the same treacherous doctrine that inspired Americans to resistance in the first place:

If then the stamp act was an usurpation of the Americans' most precious and sacred rights, the declaratory act left them no rights at all; and contained the full grown seeds of the most despotic government ever exercised in the world. It placed America not only in the lowest, but in the basest state of vassalage; because it demanded an unconditional submission in every thing, or as the act expresses it, in all cases whatsoever: and what renders this act the more offensive, is, that it appears to have been passed as an act of mercy; truly then may it be said, that the tender mercies of the wicked are cruel.

To Paine, the rate of the tax—or even the power to tax—was inconsequential in comparison to the far more important and overarching doctrine that Parliament had no business in American affairs. Any policy—tax or otherwise—was to Paine an invitation for objection and resistance. "The principle of the act," he contended, "made all tyranny legal." To concede the legitimacy of British taxes required acknowledging the merits of "the universal supremacy of parliament," he explained.[271]

By assuming the power to legislate on behalf of the colonies, Paine argued, Parliament—in collusion with the king—had disregarded the reasons for which colonists elected representatives to their local assemblies. Far from an unauthoritative expansion of colonial power, he wrote, this practice was legitimized under the long-standing colonial charters:

All the original charters from the crown of England, under the faith of which the adventurers from the old world settled in the new, were by this act displaced from their foundations; because, contrary to the nature of them, which was that of a compact, they were now made subject to repeal or alteration at the mere will of one party only. The whole condition of America was thus put into the hands of the parliament or ministry, without leaving to her the least right in any case whatsoever.

Far from unenforceable legal contracts, Paine held that the charters remained the constitutional foundation of the colonial system. In this regard, they could not simply be ignored or supplanted by the whims of Parliament. Britain's attempts to do so represented "a total overthrow" of the

British constitution, and "an annihilation of the foundation of liberty" with "absolute domination established in its stead." In opposition to Raynal's assertion that the catalyst for American resistance was "a slight tax upon the colonies," Paine argued that the tax "was neither more or less than an experiment to establish the practice of declaratory law" under the condemnable claim to "the universal supremacy of parliament"—the true crux of the conflict with Britain.[272]

Another matter of dispute between the two eminent writers was Raynal's allegation that the Franco-American alliance impeded the possibility of a peaceful settlement with Britain in April of 1778. At that time, the British government had sent a group of negotiators to discuss terms of a peace with the Americans. The Carlisle Commission, as it came to be called, offered colonial representation in English Parliament, but did not recognize the independence of the American states. Raynal reasoned that the failure to reach a settlement was due to France's entry into the war, which greatly boosted the confidence of the American patriots. To this, Paine responded that Congress had in fact rejected the English overtures for a settlement on April 22, eleven days before hearing news of the alliance with France. In addition, the prospect of foregoing American independence was never seriously considered by Congress, and the American envoy lacked substantive authority to negotiate.[273]

Paine also took exception to Raynal's allegation that the Franco-American alliance was an unsustainable nuptial that was destined to end badly for both parties. To the contrary, the penman thought the alliance was a natural friendship that would yield fruit for both countries. The union was to him "an alliance not formed for the mere purpose of a day, but on just and generous grounds, and with equal and mutual advantages." Due to France's assistance, "we are now really another people, and cannot go back to ignorance and prejudice," Paine wrote. Consequently, "the mind once enlightened cannot again become dark."[274]

To Paine, the fact that one party to the alliance was a republic and another a monarchy was immaterial. "Forms of government have nothing to do with treaties," he contended, because fulfillment of a treaty's obligations did not depend on political structure. "So long as each performs its part, we have no more right or business to know how the one or the other conducts its domestic affairs, than we have to inquire into the private concerns of a family," he wrote. Paine added that all alliances were premised upon the idea that participating members "are relatively republics with each other," which he deemed "the first and true principle of alliance."[275]

Also within the tract was an unambiguous accusation that Raynal had lifted significant portions of *Common Sense* for his own publications, without citing their source. According to Paine, the French writer "has borrowed freely from the said pamphlet without acknowledging it," so much so that "the idea in *Common Sense* is so closely copied and pursued, that the difference is only in words, and in the arrangement of thoughts, and not in the thoughts themselves." To prove this assertion, Paine went so far as to include side-by-side comparisons between Raynal's writings on the distinction between society and government and that which he included in *Common Sense*. Indeed, the similarities between the two passages were remarkable.[276]

Much of the remainder of Paine's barrage focused upon his own objections to Raynal's accounts of the war. For example, while Raynal portrayed Washington's victories in Trenton and Princeton as accidental achievements, Paine insisted that they were calculated strikes that were well-planned and enthusiastically executed by a well led and highly dedicated Continental Army. "It was undoubtedly a bold adventure," he wrote, "and carried with it the appearance of defiance."[277]

Even as he continued to vindicate the patriot cause against its detractors, Paine's financial struggles continued. In 1784, he was finally rewarded in earnest for his services in the struggle against Britain, when New York's republican government granted him 277 acres of farmland in New Rochelle, which had been confiscated from a Tory named Frederick Davoue who had been taken prisoner during the war before eventually fleeing with his family to Nova Scotia, where he resided until his death.[278]

New York's grant to Paine was read aloud to the state legislature, where the writer was commended for writing works that "inspired the citizens of this state with unanimity, confirmed their confidence in the rectitude of their cause, and have ultimately contributed to the freedom, sovereignty and independence of the United States." By his own account, Paine was grateful for the bestowment, but, having grown accustomed to urban living in Philadelphia, had no interest, initially, in living in the country at least a day's travel away from New York City.[279] Paine rented the property to a tenant farmer, but would eventually return from his sojourn in Europe to live on the New Rochelle homestead in his final years.

The following year in 1785, Paine received another gift from a grateful state government, this time £500 from his home state of Pennsylvania. For a time, it seemed as though Paine would also be awarded financially by the Virginia General Assembly, spurred by the efforts of the renowned Thomas Jefferson and James Madison. The latter proposed granting Paine a swath of land worth about £4,000, but the maneuver was defeated by a campaign headed by Arthur Lee, former friend of Paine who bore a grudge against the writer for his 1780 assault upon Virginia's lofty Western land claims articulated in *Public Good*.[280]

A few of Paine's friends, including George Washington, lobbied Congress to grant the writer a recompense as well. When the process to mull the subject slowed to a crawl, though, Paine grew noticeably impatient. After first allowing Washington and Elbridge Gerry to plead his case, he eventually submitted a claim of $6,000 for services rendered during the struggle for independence. In a note to the Committee of Foreign Affairs, he also expressed personal aggrievement for being forced to wait so long:

> I must declare to the Committee that it hurts me exceedingly to find, that after a service of so many years, and through such a perilous scene, I am now treated and higgled with as if I had no feelings to suffer or honour to preserve.

In the end, Gerry's attempt to secure the amount Paine had requested was defeated by a two-thirds majority of Congress. Ultimately, though, a negotiated settlement of $3,000 was granted to Paine.[281] This financial stopgap ended Paine's long crusade for public remuneration.

Also in 1785, Paine was elected to the American Philosophical Society in Philadelphia. Founded by Benjamin Franklin in 1743, the institution was widely known as the most prestigious academic body of its time in America. Joined in this distinction by many of his era's most noteworthy figures, such as George Washington, John Dickinson, Thomas Jefferson, John Adams, and others, Paine stood out in that he lacked aristocratic background or familial pedigree. No doubt many of the society's members were aware of this, as Paine's membership had been hotly contested—and even denied—in previous years.[282]

By the mid-1780s, those who favored augmenting the power of the central government had plenty of gripes about the Articles of Confederation. Most of these complaints came down to a few overarching claims, all of which were routinely espoused by nationalist politicians. Firstly, many contended that the Confederation government had no real power of taxation, being forced to rely on requisitions—formal requests for money—from the state authorities. Another common gripe held that without centralized control of militia forces, state governments would be continually threatened by rebellions and hostilities. Moreover, many were upset that several states had levied protective tariffs and paper money laws that restricted trade with other states. A constitutional arrangement prohibiting these practices, then, would establish a North American free trade zone that would serve the general benefit of all states.

In 1780, Alexander Hamilton declared that "the Confederation itself is defective," and the framework was "neither fit for war nor peace." According to Thomas Tredwell of New York, "the federal government is not adequate to the purpose of the union." Even Samuel Bryan, future opponent of the Constitution, admitted it had become "the universal wish of America to grant further powers" to Congress, "so as to make the federal government adequate to the ends of its institution."[283]

In the midst of these calls to expand the power of the central government, George Washington himself arranged for a conference to discuss issues of continental importance at his residence of Mount Vernon, which sat upon the Potomac River in Fairfax County, Virginia. While the resultant Mount Vernon Compact of 1785 settled disputes between states regarding navigation, joint waterways were to be shared equally by all citizens of all states, where each had access to all harbors. Navigation expenditures would be apportioned equally, and commissioners pledged to recommend uniform currency, imposts, and even a joint Chesapeake navy.[284] Even with this newfound spirit of cooperation between states, however, nationalist complaints about the Confederation model persisted.

In a candid attempt to bring delegates from all of the states together to discuss practical constitutional reforms, Alexander Hamilton played a key role in organizing a new convention in 1786, to meet at Maryland's capital of Annapolis. James Madison, who also played a pivotal role in the convention, hoped the gathering would help address what he called the "defects of the Confederation." Throughout the same year, Madison immersed himself in an exhaustive study of ancient confederacies and republics. In this pursuit, his goal was to prescribe remedies for the Confederation system under the Articles of Confederation. Ultimately, Madison came to the conclusion that classic confederations often suffered from governmental weakness in the center and squabbles over the division of powers. As a pamphleteer later wrote, by this time the nationalists had abandoned "a mere revision and amendment of our first Confederation" in favor of "a complete system for the future government of the United States."[285]

On September 11, 1786, 12 delegates from five states—New York, New Jersey, Pennsylvania, Delaware, and Virginia—arrived at George Mann's Tavern in Annapolis. Their ostensible aim was to convince the various states to reverse the protectionist trade barriers they had erected against each other, but nationalists such as Hamilton, Madison, George Read of Delaware, and Abraham Clark of New Jersey hoped the proceedings could be used as a springboard for broader political action to centralize greater power in Congress. The Meeting of Commissioners to Remedy Defects of the Federal Government, more commonly known as the Annapolis Convention of 1786, lasted four days.

The meeting ended with the its participants having resolved that a future meeting of state delegates from all the states was necessary to confront the challenges of the Confederation framework, lest the array of issues grow to be "greater and more numerous." Philadelphia was proposed as the location for the future meeting, set for the second Monday in May in 1787. The commissioners also agreed on the need to urge the states to grant delegates to the upcoming meeting "enlarged powers" to discuss all topics, not just trade.

Unfortunately for Hamilton and Madison, the Annapolis Convention proved to be, for several reasons, a relative failure in terms of actualizing the true goals of the nationalists. The immensely popular George Washington, professing that he had retired to Mount Vernon and would no longer take part in politics, was not present at the proceedings, despite his opinion that the Confederation was a "half-starved, limping government, that appears to be always moving upon crutches, & tottering at every step."[286]

Also hindering the potential for successes at the Annapolis Convention was inaction—and even obstruction—from some states. North Carolina, New Hampshire, Massachusetts, and Rhode Island all appointed delegates, but none of them attended the Annapolis convention. In addition, South Carolina, Maryland, Georgia, and Connecticut refused to elect delegates or take any action to support the aims of the convention at all. With only five states represented, the convention carried little weight or influence.

Furthermore, most of the delegates in attendance were only authorized to discuss issues related to trade among the states. Because the delegates were bound to these instructions from their home governments, the potential for actual reform was highly limited from the outset. These dynamics, more than anything, influenced the future Philadelphia Convention to adopt rules requiring oaths of secrecy in order to guarantee that the earnest views of the delegates would be heard.

While political tensions consumed much of the country's aristocracy, such matters were hardly the most pressing concern for the average American. For several years, financial calamity had endangered the young states and their inhabitants. The lack of circulating coins backed by cold or silver made the repayment of debts nearly impossible for most Americans, and tensions between creditors and debtors continued. The emergence of the Bank of North America, and its later counterparts in two states—New York and Massachusetts—only exacerbated the economic debate. Furthermore, protective tariffs that the states instituted against each other remained in place.

Paine took note of these political and economic developments, and foreshadowed them to a great extent through a new pamphlet in 1786, *Dissertations on Government, The Affairs of the Bank, and Paper Money.* Consistent with his writings from previous years, Paine continued to err on the side of those who wished to expand the powers of Congress. Nevertheless, he remained equally committed to hard money and the bank he helped champion. In his introduction, Paine made clear that he was not part of any particular political faction of the day. "As to parties, merely considered as such, I am attached to no particular one," he wrote. Accordingly, he informed readers he wrote on behalf of morality over politics. "There are such things as right and wrong in the world, and so far as these are parties against each other, the signature of Common Sense is properly employed," he wrote.[287]

In typical fashion, Paine began his latest work with a philosophical proposition. All governments on earth, he wrote, contained a sovereign power, "a principle common to all." It follows that, in monarchies, this authority is lodged in a single individual, where "his will is law; which he declares, alters or revokes as he pleases, without being accountable to any power for so doing." In contrast, then, the sovereign power in republican-styled government "remains where natured placed it—in the people; for the people in America are the fountain of power." While the sovereign in a monarchy "is restrained by no fixed rule of right and wrong," a republic is "directed by certain fundamental principles of right and justice." The administration of despotic government was carried out unilaterally by the sovereign himself, whereas republican administrators derive their authority only from their electorate—people who serve as their sovereign superiors.[288]

Paine's purpose in laying out these precepts was to remind the people that republicanism was premised upon the extension of the "public good," or the idea that government should serve the individuals it represents. In his eyes, it naturally followed that people in every republic have the means, and perhaps the duty, to exact recourse when governmental defects are exposed. This process, he thought, exemplified the sovereign will of the people and their eternal prerogative to organize and rearrange the powers of their government in such a way to better suit their happiness—an unmistakable theme in the Declaration of Independence.

Among the shortcomings Paine saw in the American constitutional system was its continuous sanction of paper money, which he condemned as a medium that "has the least intrinsic value of anything that can be put in the place of gold and silver." He reminded readers of the monetary pitfalls the American states experienced in the last decade:

> But the evils of paper money have no end. Its uncertain and fluctuating value is continually awakening or creating new schemes of deceit.

Every principle of justice is put to the rack, and the bond of society dissolved: the suppression, therefore, of paper money might very properly have been put into the act for preventing vice and immorality.

Paper money acted to "turn the whole country into stock jobbers," he claimed, where those who championed the currency and those who denounced it would inevitably work to the detriment of each other. Paper money sent the economy into a vicious tailspin, he claimed, by empowering men to make purchases on credit without the intention to repay, then lobby the government for more paper money emissions afterward. This would allow these ill-designing deviants to "get a deal of it for a little price, and cheat their creditors," repeating the "concise history of paper money schemes" that Americans—and the world in general—had often borne witness to.[289]

The remedy to the evils of paper money, Paine wrote, was a constitutional stipulation that would prohibit it entirely. As a true hard money advocate, he called for an immediate end to both paper money emissions and legal tender laws—which required all merchants to accept a state-endorsed currency as payment. "All tender laws are tyrannical and unjust," he argued, "and calculated to support fraud and oppression." To deliver justice and financial stability, he said, the recent effort of a coalition to repeal the charter of the Bank of North America should be defeated. "The bank is an institution capable of being made exceedingly beneficial to the state," he continued, "as a means of increasing the quantity of hard money in the state. The bank's hedge against inflation by way of bullion deposits and notes that were exchangeable for gold and silver on demand would "combine the security of the government and the bank into one."[290]

In contravention of Paine's outlook, opponents of the bank made several arguments to support its repeal. The most commonplace allegation against the establishment was that its inflationary tendencies raised prices and drove specie out of the country. Other radicals lambasted the bank for receiving anti-competitive privileges from the state, which violated the traditional precept of equality under the law by allowing one class of men to exploit the other financially. A coalition of the bank's adversaries succeeded in revoking the bank's Pennsylvania charter in 1785, but the bank continued to operate under its existing congressional charter, and the Pennsylvania General Assembly renewed the state-level charter in 1786 after conservatives within the state scored an important electoral victory.[291]

Within the pamphlet, Paine also noted his newfound disdain for Pennsylvania's unicameral legislature, an idea he had once advocated. As one of the state's most distinct features, the unicameral legislature was championed by Pennsylvania radicals as a body that would better reflect public sentiment and remain less susceptible to the aristocratic checks and balances that characterized bicameral systems. The author wrote that his support for a single legislature was based on the idea "that whatever personal parties there might be in a state, they would all unite and agree in the general principles of good government." Recent developments had forced him to conclude instead that the emergence of political parties in Pennsylvania deferred this role to whatever party triumphed over the other. "When party operates to produce party laws," he wrote, "a single house is a single person, and subject to the haste, rashness, and passion of individual sovereignty." This flaw made it no different from an aristocratic system, he now alleged.[292] After conservatives took power over in the state legislature a few years later, Pennsylvania's unicameral legislature was replaced by a bicameral system under the 1790 state constitution that supplanted its 1776 forerunner.

Truthfully, *Dissertations on Government* was for Paine a distraction from a true passion he developed at roughly the same time—iron engineering. It is possible he was drawn into such a pursuit by the campaign to rebuild various structures in the states following the destruction of infrastructure during the recent war, which inspired various artisans to utilize modern innovations to solve practical problems. Paine's fascination with the same subject prompted his foray into bridgebuilding.

Up to that time, bridges in the Western world were exclusively built with stone or wood. In the latter case, tall trees were processed, turned into beams, and used as supports to prop up platforms that connected land masses. Wooden arches provided an invaluable asset for humanity, but suffered from the disadvantage of being vulnerable to damage and required regular repairs. Their stone counterparts mostly avoided these limitations, but required much more labor to build and often constricted water flow. In 1785, the mere idea of replacing either substance with iron was a novel idea that challenged engineering norms.

What exactly spurred Paine's design for an iron bridge is subject to debate among scholars. According to his own account, he first developed such an idea upon observing the structure of a spider web and considering its application to the human world. On the other hand, biographer John Keane wrote that Paine was drawn to the topic of bridges due to his fascination with the blend of architectural beauty and practicality.[293] It may also have stemmed from his experience as a staymaker in his youth, during which time he would have noticed that stays performed a function remarkably similar to that of a bridge. Whatever the source of his affinity for the endeavor, the idea for an iron bridge soon dominated his time and attention. He used his newly-granted funds to hire an assistant, John Hall, who had also immigrated to America from England. With an engineering background, Hall's enthusiasm for Paine's aims became quickly apparent, and the two developed a personal friendship as well as a working relationship. The two worked in Bordentown, New Jersey, where Paine was living at the time.

Paine was certainly not the first person in the world to conceive of the utility of iron bridges. In the years prior to his new project, an arch bridge entirely made of iron was built over the River Severn in Shropshire, England by architect Thomas Pritchard and a local ironmaster, John Wilkinson. Their plans were subsidized by Parliament, and put into motion in the late 1770s. Completed in 1779, it was a marvel of engineering, though virtually no one in North America had knowledge of its existence or utility. Though it has been restored several times, it still stands today.

From late 1785, Paine and Hall set to work at designing bridges, with the ultimate aim of attracting financial sponsorship for what would be, if completed, the first iron bridge in America. By mid-1786, Paine and Hall developed both wooden and iron variants of the same bridge design, which they made into cast-iron models. Originally, Paine envisioned his wooden design could be employed to span the Harlem River on a tract of land recently inherited by Gouverneur Morris, the famed Pennsylvania conservative. Paine had befriended Morris, who was not related to the more well-known Robert Morris, in recent years and hoped the Pennsylvanian would back his project.[294]

Unfortunately for the ambitions of the writer-turned-engineer, Morris was not impressed with the idea. Not to be discouraged, Paine then shifted his attention to the Schuylkill River, which ran through much of eastern Pennsylvania, splitting Philadelphia before joining the Delaware River. There, Paine sought sponsorship for his iron bridge, a move that seemed perfectly timed. No bridges in the area performed such a function, and Philadelphia's stature as one of the most important North American metropolises made the location an appealing prospect. Paine's familiarity with the local culture and political climate also may have fed his desire to pursue the project.

Throughout the last half of 1786 and into early 1787, Paine tirelessly lobbied the Pennsylvanian government to back his enterprise. At the same time, his competitors pitched other bridge proposals, but all of them were based on traditional wooden designs. The most notable came from the Pennsylvania Agricultural Society, which sought to build their bridge at a similar location. Paine's ambition to consummate his own project led him to portray the aims of his rivals as disastrous and financially cataclysmic, apparently to persuade representatives in Pennsylvania of the merits of his alternative instead.[295]

Paine and Hall also created a miniature version of their bridge to be displayed at the home of Benjamin Franklin for inspection by the most prestigious figures in the state. According to Hall's journal, several men provided positive feedback, including David Rittenhouse, the famous scientist and surveyor. At the same time, Paine launched a relentless letter-writing campaign to share the news of his design with numerous state representatives, including George Clymer and Thomas Fitzsimmons.[296]

As Paine waged the political crusade for his iron bridge, Massachusetts found itself in an intense financial predicament. The rampant debasement of American money created economic hardships, and Americans often struggled to get by. Because merchants demanded repayment in gold and silver for debts incurred with hard money instead of the inflationary currency, borrowers found it virtually impossible to get out of debt. Though some states issued stay laws to give debtors extra time to repay, or permit the repayment of debts in paper rather than hard money, these strides often alienated the merchant class and other debt holders. The political situation

in Massachusetts, wherein governments struggled to strike a balance between policies that favored debtors and those that aided creditors, was not
uncommon throughout the early American republic.

James Bowdoin was elected Massachusetts governor to replace the
wildly popular John Hancock, who had resigned in 1785 for health reasons. Bowdoin firmly resisted introducing paper money, believing that doing so would just fan the flames of the state's economic crisis. In addition
to the alarming number of debtors, many soldiers who had served in the
recent war were paid in bonds that had greatly depreciated in value by the
war's conclusion. Among them was Daniel Shays, a former Continental
Army soldier who was wounded in action and retired only to find himself
in court for the nonpayment of debts. Shays first took part in local meetings to send petitions of grievances to the government, which went unanswered.

Shays soon began to attract followers who found themselves in a similar predicament, and cultivated a widespread tax revolt. Peaceful protests
gradually became more hostile, and on August 29, 1786, many dissidents
in Northampton clogged a county court, preventing it from sitting.
Bowdoin denounced the action and the Massachusetts government indicted 11 protestors for disorderly and riotous sedition. Shays and Luke
Day, another former military officer, successfully shut down additional
courts in Worcester, Barrington, Concord, and Taunton. The group even
succeeded in breaking imprisoned debtors out of jail in Springfield and
burned the barns of some civil officials. According to the eminent James
Warren, Massachusetts was "now in a state of anarchy and confusion bor-
dering on civil war."[297]

Several famous Massachusetts patriots who had fiercely resisted British tyranny, including Paine's political ally Samuel Adams, did not sympathize with the dissenters whatsoever. Adams based his position on the
notion that individuals could only be legally taxed by the local representatives of the people, and a republican government had now been established with representatives from all regions of the state. Far from acknowledging parallels to the conflict with England, he even helped draft the 1786
Riot Act, which suspended habeas corpus and permitted the government
to detain rebels indefinitely. "Rebellion against a king may be pardoned,

or lightly punished," Adams said, "but the man who dares to rebel against the laws of a republic ought to suffer death."[298]

To Shays and his followers, the last straw came with the attempt to arrest the rebellious leaders. Although warrants were issued for his arrest, Shays recruited about 4,000 followers in the western part of the state, all of whom refused to pay taxes to the Massachusetts government until their grievances were addressed. In contrast to Samuel Adams, the legendary statesman Thomas Jefferson, then serving as a diplomat in France, seemed to sympathize with Shays and his acolytes. "A little rebellion now and then is a good thing, and as necessary in the political world as storms in the physical," he wrote. In another letter, Jefferson defended the "spirit of resistance" that characterized the movement, declaring that "the tree of liberty must be refreshed from time to time with the blood of patriots & tyrants. It is its natural manure."[299]

In the end, General Benjamin Lincoln, the Continental Army veteran who lost Charleston to the British in 1780, solicited voluntary funding for a privately raised 4,000-man army whose sole task was to stop Shays and his followers. After Lincoln launched his march westward, the two forces clashed at Springfield, where Shays aimed to gain control over armament stores. However, Shays' men were stopped by William Shepard, a militia general and subordinate of Lincoln who successfully defended the armory. After the Massachusetts legislature passed a bill authorizing martial law, and expanded the powers of Governor Bowdoin, Shays' Rebellion collapsed at Sheffield and dozens of insurgents were captured.

Many of the remaining dissidents fled to New York, New Hampshire, and Vermont, including Shays himself. In some areas, those who had been branded traitors were even provided shelter and financial support by sympathizers. Shays and some of his top followers were convicted of treason and sentenced to death by Massachusetts, but were later pardoned. In addition, the following legislative election in Massachusetts led to a series of measures that sought to alleviate the woes of the farmers and other debtors.

The conclusion to Shays' Rebellion had long-lasting political implications. Even though the uprising was short-lived and settled internally, nationalist politicians cited the event as reason to vest Congress with greater power to suppress rebellions and insurrections. Perhaps even more significant was George Washington's decision to terminate his retirement and lend his own influence to the growing campaign for constitutional reform. While Paine's energies were dominated by iron engineering at the time, the overarching campaign to augment the power of the central government was certainly a cause he had recently championed.

Unfortunately for Paine, the Commonwealth of Pennsylvania had other priorities than infrastructure in 1787. The government began to lay plans for electing delegates to the forthcoming convention to take place in Philadelphia, and the state hoped to play a major role in the incorporation of the Northwest Territory. As time went on, official consideration of Paine's project stalled, and doubts lingered as to its financially tenability. According to one account, the enterprise never came to fruition due to "the imperfect state of iron manufacture in America."[300] Though his dreams in America were crushed, Paine had not yet given up bridgebuilding for good.

Even by the time *Dissertations on Government* was published, Paine's heart had grown tired of America. His campaign for the Bank of North America and support for strengthening the powers of Congress alienated him from former radical friends while failing to win him any favor with many conservative gatekeepers who had long opposed him. His lack of fortune for many years impoverished him to a degree similar to that which had affected him in England, and he earnestly wondered whether the beneficiaries of American independence could uphold the same streak of civil virtue that helped propel the patriot cause to independence. His failure to secure funding for his ambitious iron bridge was the final nail in the coffin. At the age of 50, he was at last ready to return to England.

He had for several years entertained the idea of returning to live in Europe, but several factors prevented the feasibility of such an option until 1786. Viewing his quest for the iron bridge as a job left unfinished, he hoped to gain support in Europe, where he was known by many simply for authoring his noteworthy pamphlets. To aid him, he successfully sought the assistance of Benjamin Franklin once again, this time for a letter of introduction to French hosts. Still wildly popular in his old age, Franklin contended that Paine's work was published "with great effect on the minds of the people at the beginning of the revolution," and called the penman "an ingenious, honest man." Moreover, Pennsylvania's most well-known polymath praised the iron bridge design.

After Paine left Bordentown, he and Hall shared one last friendly discussion in Trenton, after which he set off for New York to depart for
France. As he set sail, the American states were moving ahead with plans
for constitutional reforms. As biographer Moncure Conway put it, "he who
first raised the standard of independence" was "far out at sea on his way
to rejoin his comrades in the old world, whose hearts and burdens he had
represented in the new."[301]

As the national political discussion in America centered upon constitutional reform, the question of how to organize the Northwest Territory
emerged. The landmass, which was largely the result of major land cessa-
tions by multiple states, left many questions unanswered. Should new
states be carved out of the area immediately? Would slavery be tolerated
in any portion of it? Who would have navigation rights in the territory?
These questions and more demanded answers, and the matters Paine had
tackled in *Public Good*—which proposed mutual American ownership of
the western lands—became relevant yet again.

Three years earlier, Thomas Jefferson had drawn up plans to partition
the territory into ten rectangular polities—Cherronesus, Sylvania, Asseni-
sipia, Illinoia, Metropotamia, Polypotamia, Pelisipia, Washington, Mich-
igania, and Saratoga. Upon acquiring a population of 20,000, each of these
entities would draft and ratify a constitution, become new states, and enter
into the confederation on an equal footing with the remainder. Most notably, his design included an absolute ban on slavery. "After the year 1800
of the Christian era, there shall neither be slavery nor involuntary servitude
in any of the said states," his resolution read.

The specifics of Jefferson's plans were hotly debated, but carried the
support of many in Congress. In the end, though, the Virginian's hopes
were dashed when his 1784 Land Ordinance failed by a single vote to secure passage. Jefferson agonized in response, lamenting especially the prospect of continued slavery in the area:

The voice of a single individual … would have prevented this abominable crime from spreading itself over the new country. Thus we see
the fate of millions unborn hanging on the tongue of one man, and
Heaven was silent in that awful moment![302]

An alternative, the Land Ordinance of 1785, established a survey system for the land, but did not create ten independent regions and did not prohibit slavery within the territory.

By 1787, the dynamics had changed. With the clear intention to carve out new states out of the territories rather than to allow existing states to expand their own territories westward, Congress passed the Northwest Ordinance. The act contained two of Jefferson's key proposals, a provision that would allow regions within the area to create a constitution and petition for statehood upon the acquisition of 60,000 inhabitants and a ban on slavery throughout the territories. While Paine himself played no direct role in the Northwest Ordinance of 1787, its legal character combined two ideas that the penman had long championed: the abolition of slavery and Congressional management over the western lands. *Public Good*, which had been viewed as a radical plan and won Paine many enemies, predated the territorial settlement by seven years.

In May of 1787, the first delegates to planned convention arrived at the Pennsylvania State House in Philadelphia. Among the first orders of business was the imposition of an oath of secrecy to conceal the details of the proceedings from the public—a gesture intended to allow for earnest debate free from outside influences. George Washington was quickly elected president, a nod to the importance of his presence, which provided an aura of legitimacy to the convention. Over the next four months, nearly every subject imaginable was debated. While the convention's stated purpose was to recommend amendments to the Articles of Confederation, various proposals for entirely new constitutional frameworks were discussed almost immediately.

One of the primary subjects of contention centered was legislative apportionment. Under the Confederation system, all member states had equal suffrage in Congress, carrying one vote each on all matters of importance. Preserving this system was of the utmost importance to delegates from states of smaller populations, such as Connecticut and New Jersey. Hailing from the latter state, William Paterson proposed a framework known as the "New Jersey Plan" that featured a unicameral legislature with equal representation from each state.

Conversely, the 1780s convinced American nationalists—including Charles Pinckney, Alexander Hamilton, and James Madison—that such a system of equal state suffrage had overinflated the power of states that lacked the stature of New York, Pennsylvania, and Virginia. As a key facet of Madison and Edmund Randolph's set of resolutions known as the "Virginia Plan," the legislature would have two houses, both of which would feature apportionment by state population. A loathsome prospect to some, this innovation would hand much more power to the larger and more dominant states.

These two incompatible doctrines on representative apportionment caused a notable impasse, which was broken only by a compromise spearheaded by the Connecticut delegation. Under the "Connecticut Compromise," two houses were to be created, one of which would preserve equal state suffrage, while the other would be apportioned by state population. While pleasing almost no one entirely, this agreement blended the aims of multiple factions together into a system that was palatable to nearly everyone.

Also germane to the matter of representation was the question of whether slaves would count toward apportionment. In general, northerners argued against the proposition, realizing this would only augment the power of southern states like Virginia. On the contrary, southerners generally favored having slaves be counted entirely such that they would receive more relative representation. Ultimately, another settlement was made, whereby three-fifths of each state's slave population would be counted for this purpose.

While the Virginia Plan advanced general legislative authority—where Congress would be granted limitless power to legislate on matters of importance—the convention ultimately embraced enumerated powers instead. Under this doctrine, only powers that were expressly delegated to the central government in the document's text could be legislated upon. This decision—though part of the American status quo under the Articles—was a radical departure from the norms that existed in the rest of the Western world, most notably in England, which had been operating under a system of parliamentary sovereignty—plenary legislative authority over the kingdom—since 1689.

Among the explicit powers was the authority to regulate trade with foreign countries, among the several states, and with the Indian tribes. Intending to obviate the combative trade war among American states and create a uniform policy of foreign commerce, this scheme supplanted the decentralized system under the Articles. In addition, the general government was also delegated taxing authority, allowing Congress to impose indirect taxes, which included imposts and excises. In addition, direct taxes that required payments for specific types of property or per person could be levied as well, but only if such taxes were apportioned by state population.

Perhaps most consequentially, the new government was to have three distinct branches. While the Confederation system featured a Congress without an executive or a standing judiciary, the new Constitution created an executive office headed by a president, who would be elected to serve four-year terms through a federally-oriented Electoral College. The executive held the power to enforce the laws of the union, the authority to make treaties with foreign powers upon the advice and consent of the Senate, and the ability to recommend measures of expedience to Congress.

The new federal court system featured a standing Supreme Court—to be filled with judges nominated by the president and approved by the Senate—with the power to adjudicate certain types of disputes, primarily those involving the states. While the new system permitted the existence of inferior courts, their power was greatly under the supervision of Congress, which had the power to call them into being and dissolve them at will. This federal court system was intended to serve mostly as a court of appeals, with a limited array of cases under the purview of the Supreme Court.

Though the Articles of Confederation required every member state to agree to the addition of amendments, the Constitution required but three-fourths of the states to do the same. The existing order largely permitted the states to enact war policy on their own terms; the new one allowed Congress to declare, and the president to execute, war. In addition, Congress could now call forth the militia of the states to suppress insurrections and repel invasions, a primary objective of those who feared military counterrevolutions would disrupt or erase the gains of republicanism. Rather than sanctioning paper money on both a state and central level, the new Constitution prohibited fiat money entirely. As an indictment against the inflationary tendency of the 1770s and 1780s, this measure sought to return the states to a hard money regimen.

While this plan was seen by many as a massive political victory for American nationalists, the same group did not view the new Constitution as such. Madison and Randolph, for example, desired a national legislature with broad authority to make law on all subjects, a supreme judiciary with the power to adjudicate virtually all types of cases, a two-house legislature with both houses being apportioned by state population, and—most importantly to Madison—an explicit veto power by the general government over state law. While securing some of the powers they had hoped for—such as a taxing authority and a mechanism to regulate trade—the new Constitution fell short of the nationalist ideal.

In a letter to Thomas Jefferson, Madison admitted his belief that the Constitution "will neither effectually answer its national object nor prevent the local mischiefs which everywhere excite disgusts against the state governments." Having recommended a quasi-monarchical system wherein the executive would serve for life and the states would be effectively consolidated into a singular political unit, Alexander Hamilton grieved that the Constitution was "very remote" from his own vision.[303] Despite their misgivings, both men later lobbied for the document's adoption in their own states and began writing *The Federalist* series of essays to push public opinion toward ratification.

Even as the Constitution was signed in Philadelphia in September of 1787, the new document served only as recommendation and lacked any standing whatsoever. This was because the framework's ratification process, spelled out in Article VII, required nine member states to assent to before it had any legal standing. To get to that point, each state was given absolute authority to call delegates to conventions that would decide the matter independently of the other states.

The popularity of the proposal differed greatly by region. Some states, such as Delaware and Georgia, ratified almost immediately and with little contention. However, the political aristocracy in more populous states—especially Virginia and New York—were of varying opinions on the subject, resulting in lengthy and quarrelsome debates. The opponents of the document generally complained about the lack of a bill of rights, believed the new judiciary and executive would be too powerful, decried the potential of a standing army, and argued that the government would not be representative enough in relative terms. Champions of the framework, on the other hand, stressed that the instrument would be one of enumerated powers only, where separation of powers and far-reaching checks and balances would curtail any possibility that any one branch of the new government would dominate the other two. To accompany the official state conventions, a grand political debate—both for and against the model—materialized in earnest.

Ratification of the Constitution was secured in the most contentious states through explicit assertions that the general government could not assume undelegated powers. In Virginia, Edmund Randolph claimed that the general government would violate the constitution whenever it exercised any power "not expressly delegated therein." Maintaining the same position, Charles Cotesworth Pinckney of South Carolina opined that Congress had no right to "exercise powers not expressly delegated to it." Lending his hand to the cause of ratification in New York, Madison insisted in *The Federalist* No. 45 that the powers delegated to the general government were "few and defined." At the Hillsborough convention in North Carolina, James Iredell declared that the "powers of the government are particularly enumerated and defined: they can claim no others but such as are so enumerated."[304] These testimonials played an enormous role in reassuring skeptics in some of the most polarized states.

By the summer of 1788, the requisite number of states had approved the new Constitution, guaranteeing its legal standing and effectively terminating the existing Confederation system. Nevertheless, Rhode Island and North Carolina refused to ratify for a time, both remaining as independent republics into the forthcoming Washington administration. The latter state even formed a diplomatic delegation, headed by Hugh Williamson, to travel to the capital in New York to lobby the new government to adopt amendments favorable to the sensibilities of North Carolinians.

At first glance, the new Constitution appeared to actualize many of the political goals that Paine had long desired. Because he repeatedly insisted that the ideal political arrangement for America was a unified front rather than a loosely-confederated group of autonomous states, the new system seemed to embody many of the characteristics of the "Continental Charter" he had promoted in *Common Sense*. Years later, Paine remarked that while he would have voted for the instrument, he viewed several aspects as defects. "I declare myself opposed to several matters in the Constitution," he wrote, "particularly to the manner in which what is called the executive is formed, and to the long duration of the Senate."[305]

Paine took credit for the idea of "consolidating the states into a federal government," which he said he suggested in 1782 to Chancellor Robert Livingston, then the American minister for foreign affairs, a subject eventually pondered by a broader audience that included Robert Morris and Gouverneur Morris. Paine thought such a central legislature necessary to carry the five percent impost amendment that failed to garner the approval of all states. Even so, he came to the conclusion that the new constitutional framework brought about corruption from the beginnings of the Washington administration:

> The lands obtained by the revolution were lavished upon partisans; the interest of the disbanded soldier was sold to the speculator; injustice was acted under the pretense of faith; and the chief of the army became the patron of the fraud. From such a beginning what else could be expected than what has happened? A mean and servile submission to the insults of one nation; treachery and ingratitude to another.

While Paine appreciated the conglomeration of states into a more unified system, he remarked that the drive to do so was spearheaded by ill-designing characters like John Adams and John Jay, "who never contemplated the origin of government, or comprehended anything of first principles." Paine saw immense value in bringing together republican states for specific purposes of continental importance, but not under the rigid, semi-monarchical system he felt some of the most prominent Federalists envisioned.[306]

Paine's journey across the ocean lasted only a month, and he arrived in Paris in June of 1787. Once there, Paine shared his bridge design with a team of accomplished French engineers, and his idea was quickly met with greater praise than it received in Pennsylvania. After providing initial feedback, the commissioners began drafting a report that would inform the crown of its feasibility. Even before the report was released, Paine had a great confidence in his potential for success in Paris. "That the model is strong, and that a bridge construed on the same principles will also be strong," he wrote, was reason enough for celebration.[307]

While in France's capital, Paine happily shared schematics of his iron bridge with Thomas Jefferson, who was serving as an American ambassador to the country. After paying candid attention to the design, the illustrious Virginian was exceedingly impressed. "The execution of the arch of experiment far exceeds your expectations," he wrote. Owing to his reputation as a polymath, Jefferson even provided his own lengthy list of suggestions for how the bridge could be improved.[308] Such a response was not out of character for Jefferson, who dabbled in architecture, music, linguistics, meteorology, and anthropology beyond his obvious political pursuits.

Though Paine faced competitors in Paris who also championed iron-based bridges, his plan was lauded by the commissioners. Their report portrayed the design as "ingeniously conceived; that its construction is simple, sound, and fit to provide the strength necessary to withstand effects arising from loading; and that it is worthy of a trial."[309] His project faced one final hurdle before it received financial support: endorsement from the Ponts et Chaussées, an assembly of inspectors that approved infrastructure within the kingdom.

Notwithstanding the report of the private commissioners, this body opposed Paine's project, though not for engineering deficiencies. The president of the agency, Jean Perronet, opposed iron bridges from the outset, citing the plentiful supply of stone in France. Moreover, Perronet was also a direct competitor to Paine, as the Parisian received financial backing from the crown to build non-iron bridges over the Seine River. For a period, Paine tried to convince other entrepreneurs to adopt his plans for their own projects, but in this too he failed. It appeared that Paine's plans for an iron bridge were as radical to the engineering realm as his ideology was to the political order. Despite his early cause for optimism in Paris, his vision for a bridge was again dashed.

Despite his absorption in the bridge project, Paine decided to write a brief pamphlet, *Prospects on the Rubicon*, which was published in August of 1787. In a mere six paragraphs, he urged Parliament not to get caught up in a fervor for warfare with France, despite tensions between the two countries flaring up once again. "He that goeth to war should first sit down and count the cost," he declared. Paine warned that the "young and ambitious minister," William Pitt, endeavored to involve Prussia and Holland in an alliance against their classic enemy.[310] Continued economic relations between England and France, he argued, were in the best interest of the two countries.

When Europe caught wind of the proposal for a new Constitution in the United States, Paine joined Jefferson and the Marquis de Lafayette to discuss its merits. While no official records of their conversations survive, Paine's later writings reflect his overall endorsement of the document, combined with a few misgivings. While Jefferson decried the lack of a bill of rights and the lack of term limits for the executive, he too commended the document and viewed it as an improvement. Among its merits, he thought, was the strict line of delineation between branches, the compromise on apportionment, and the president's veto power.[311] Given the kinship and philosophical bond between he and Paine, it is likely that the latter shared many of the same sensibilities.

After much contemplation, Paine decided to return to England. Still clinging to hope that his iron bridge design would be accepted in his homeland, he travelled there with the same model in September 1787. That month, he returned to Thetford, where his father had died the previous year. His mother, whom he had not seen in 13 years, greeted him in what was likely a heartfelt moment. According to one account, Paine's mother fasted on July 4 of each year since 1776 in order to honor her son's contributions to American independence.[312]

In his hometown, Paine met up with several friends, who must have seemed to reside in a different world than he had for many years. Among them was Thomas "Clio" Rickman, who had befriended Paine in Lewes. He recorded that Paine's "manners were easy and gracious," that his "knowledge was universal and boundless," and that "his conversation had every fascination that anecdote, novelty, and truth could give it." Few records exist from this time, but that which does tells us that the man felt out of place, likely the product of being swept up in American culture and every tumultuous circumstance that enveloped it. While there, he lambasted the English government as "the oppressor of freedom in all other countries," as he contemplated the rising prospects of war between England and France. A few months later, he admitted to George Clymer that he may never secure funding for his bridge.[313]

As Paine endured entrepreneurial misfortunes in 1788, he made company with some of the country's most influential Whigs, including party leader Charles James Fox, Richard Brinsley Sheridan, Mary Wollstone-craft, and William Godwin.[314] He also befriended Edmund Burke, the legendary Irish statesman and member of Parliament who had zealously opposed the war in North America and defended the rights of the American colonists. At that point, Burke was one of the most tenured and renowned figures in his country. In terms of political philosophy, the two men had much in common. Both emphasized the traditional rights of Englishmen as a sacred construct and viewed property as the cornerstone of Western civilization. Furthermore, each of the two were well known for their skillful writing, and as intellectuals with mastery in multiple fields. It became a true irony, then, when the two would become ideological foes in just a few short years.

In 1788, Paine was also introduced to Peter Whiteside, a wealthy Pennsylvanian merchant in London. The two became friends, and Whiteside agreed to provide Paine financial backing for his bridge so long as he obtained a patent from the government. At this point, Paine pledged that he "had closed [his] political career with the establishment of the independence of America, and had no other business in France than to execute the orders of Pennsylvania with the Academy of Sciences respecting the model of the bridge." By his own account, Paine's passion for politics had faded. "I had rather erect the largest arch in the world," he wrote, "than be the greatest emperor in it."[315]

Jumping through all the necessary bureaucratic hoops, Paine acquired a patent—ironically requested from "His most Excellent Majesty King George the Third," the nemesis he routinely excoriated—on August 26, 1788. In the petition, he described his idea at length:

A method of constructing of arches, vaulted roofs, and ceilings, either in iron or wood, on principles new and different to anything hitherto practiced, by means of which construction arches, vaulted roofs, and ceilings may be erected to the extent of several hundred feet beyond what can be performed in the present practice of architecture.

Paine reiterated that he drew his ideas for the project from a spider web, and "from a conviction that when nature empowered this insect to make a web she also instructed her the strongest mechanical method of construct-ing it." After Jefferson learned that the patent had been granted, he boasted Paine's design would be "cheaper by a great deal than stone," and "admit a much greater arch."[316]

The Englishman spent the next two months leveraging Whiteside's support to gain addition funding for a prototype from local iron kingpins. He eventually attracted the support of Thomas Walker of Rotherham, Yorkshire, and his team of workers began working on the model, which was to be built over the Don River. The project was eventually abandoned for financial reasons, and Paine's dream suffered yet another setback. Meanwhile, a political firestorm had begun to consume France, drawing attention from all corners of the world. The former writer, now a bridge-building visionary, was about to be drawn into yet another revolutionary affair.

Chapter 5

The Rights of Man

Every age and generation must be as free to act for itself in all cases as the age and generations which preceded it. The vanity and presumption of governing beyond the grave is the most ridiculous and insolent of all tyrannies. Man has no property in man; neither has any generation a property in the generations which are to follow.

- The Rights of Man

Even before Paine arrived in Europe, France was plagued by an acute economic crisis. By 1786, the kingdom had contracted immense debts through the expenditures of Bourbon monarchs, especially as the result of several costly wars. In addition, both King Louis XIV and his great-grandson, King Louis XV, devoted massive funding to extraordinary architectural projects, the debt for which King Louis XVI was forced to inherit. France's tax structure was regressive, exempting many from the burden of taxation through noble privilege, inviting added strife. Most significantly, the country had also worsened its debt crisis by financially backing the newly-born American states in their struggle for independence from Britain.

Years prior, Louis VXI had been urged by his director general of finance, Jacques Necker, to initiate rigid tax reforms that included the elimination of royal pensions, the abolishment of various monopolistic fee systems, and an adjusted tax structure. The king refused to assent to Necker's plan, replacing him with Charles Alexandre de Calonne in 1783. Calonne proposed a new tax code that featured taxes on land, the abolition of internal tariffs, and the conversion of statute labor into a money tax. In addition, under Calonne's framework, taxes would be imposed upon clergy and nobles for the first time ever.

With the advice of his council, Louis attempted to solve the kingdom's financial woes through the unprecedented step of convening the Assembly of Notables—France's aristocratic functionaries—for the first time in 161 years. As an extraordinary circumstance, the assembly was to consider Calonne's plan of action for financial reform to reverse the kingdom's ruinous financial trajectory. The notables arrived in Paris in February of 1787, and immediately began mulling the plan. Among them was the Marquis de Lafayette, Paine's friend and America's favorite Frenchman.

After a series of debates, the Assembly of Notables refused to endorse Calonne's financial proposal. This was primarily because the body of 144 was dominated by nobles, princes, archbishops, and others from the classical French aristocracy, whose members stood to bear the load of the newly proposed taxes. Nevertheless, some of the notables were open to new forms of taxation, but differed upon the approach.[317] The body insisted instead that any reform package be placed before the Estates General, France's traditional representational assembly that was called and dismissed by the king on rare occasions. Louis elected to dismiss Calonne and summon the Estates General for the first time such a step had been taken in over a century. In addition, the king sanctioned the collection of cahiers de doléances, official lists of grievances from every corner of the kingdom. These gestures, which aspired to resolve the country's financial straits, ultimately provided the catalyst for a series of events that led directly to the French Revolution and the end of the country's Ancien Régime.

Despite his own claim that he had discarded politics for good, Paine could not help but to stay informed of the country's circumstances, especially through his correspondence with Jefferson. "I feel exceedingly interested in the happiness of that nation," he admitted to the Virginian. With

the reforms on the horizon, Paine saw reason for optimism for the kingdom. "They are now got or getting into the right way," he wrote, "and the
present reign will be more immortalized in France than any that ever preceded it."[318] Paine was ultimately correct, though for reasons he could not
have then imagined.

Consistent with tradition, the Estates General was comprised of three
separate class-oriented groups. The First Estate belonged to members of
the clergy, the Second Estate to the royal nobility, and the Third Estate to
the commoners. Each member received his position within his respective
estate through regional, estate-based elections. "So orderly was the election conducted," Paine wrote, "that it did not give rise even to the rumor
of tumult."[319] The 1200-delegate assembly convened in May of 1789, and
proceedings quickly devolved into controversies over representation and
voting procedures.

When it became clear that more than half of the total delegates belonged to the Third Estate, which vastly outnumbered the other two, the
clergy and nobility launched a shrewd campaign to stifle the influence of
the commoners. Their strategy was to adopt traditional parliamentary rules
that preserved vote by order—a system in which the leanings of each estate
weighed equally. In contrast, the Third Estate favored vote by head, where
each member held a single vote—which would allow the commoners to
dominate every aspect of the proceedings. Moreover, a drive materialized
to enforce rules that allowed only landowners to serve as deputies for the
Second Estate, excluding many—including the distinguished Honoré-Ga-
briel Riqueti, comte de Mirabeau—who sympathized with the plight of the
commoners. The Third Estate balked at the push to diminish their relative
power, and passions were enflamed on all sides.

The controversy over voting rules boiled over on June 20, 1789, when
members of the Third Estate found themselves unable to enter the chamber
doors, which were locked and guarded by French soldiers. As it turned out,
the king himself had ordered the doors closed to ensure a convention that
would be more favorable to him. Not to be disturbed from their quest to
enact their own brand of reforms, the delegates of the Third Estate rushed
to a nearby tennis court. From there, the delegates declared themselves the
new National Assembly of France. Its members proceeded to take the

"Tennis Court Oath," a promise that committed each delegate to meet continuously until a new constitution for France was adopted. The gesture represented an uncharacteristic and overt act of opposition against the king and his desire to steer the assembly in the direction of his own aims.

Louis at first dug his heels in against the Third Estate, condemning its declaration as an illegitimate act. Despite the royal discontent, the National Assembly passed a decree pronouncing all existing taxes illegal. As a radical measure, the deed unbound the commoners from the kingdom's regressive system of taxation, further stirring unrest among the nobility. For a time, the king considered using military force to stop the sitting of the new National Assembly, but he was eventually persuaded against doing so by his advisors, who realized the extent to which the institution enjoyed popular support.

On July 11, the king dismissed Necker, who had been restored to power as France's finance minister. Necker sympathized greatly with the Third Estate both in terms of desired constitutional and financial reforms, and had even done much to grow its base of influence. When news of Necker's dismissal reached Paris, partisans assumed immediately that his ousting was part of a royalist countermeasure that aspired to reverse the establishment of the National Assembly and its intention to impose constitutional reforms. Commoners took the streets, resulting in mass demonstrations and looting.

With rumors of revolution stirring, huge groups of supporters of the Third Estate began gathering arms from royal storehouses. In response, the king's advisors took precautions to move massive quantities of gunpowder so that it could not be seized by the mobs of commoners. Among the new storage locations was the Bastille, an ancient prison within Paris, where 250 barrels of gunpowder were stored. The location housed only seven convicts, but had become a symbol of Bourbon extravagance because it provided a limited function and required costly maintenance. The location was garrisoned by royal soldiers, who were quickly surrounded by a crowd of about 1,000 on July 14.

Initially, the mob of commoners demanded the release of the gunpowder. For a time, it seemed the negotiations would be concluded peacefully through the intervention of municipal authorities, but all such hope was dashed when discussions dragged on into the midday. At that point, members of the crowd rushed forward into the fortress despite the commands of the soldiers to fall back. Gunfire broke out between both soldiers and commoners, but nothing could halt the commoners from swarming into the Bastille. The commander of the fortress, the Marquis de Launay, attempted to allay tensions by ordering a ceasefire, but his petition for safe passage from the Bastille included a vow to ignite the gunpowder within the stronghold, a message that was interpreted by commoners as a thinly-veiled threat.

Believing he had no choice, Launay surrendered in the evening and opened all gates within the fortress. He was then dragged to the Hôtel de Ville—a location that would figure prominently in the years to come—where he was beaten and stabbed repeatedly before bleeding to death. Jacques de Flesselles, a noble official accused of royal sympathies, was also killed. The heads of both Launay and Flesselles were raised upon pikes, and the event was met with the cheers of commoners, the terror of the nobility, and the shock of impartial observers.

News of the Bastille's capture rippled throughout the world. Rarely had such an overt act been consummated against a European monarchy without prompting a swift campaign of retribution, which some royalists soon demanded. Though the structure itself had little significance, the Bastille became metaphorical for the perceived transgressions of the Bourbon regime in particular, and for the excesses of hereditary monarchy in general. As Paine would later write, "the downfall of it included the idea of the downfall of despotism." The fortress "was attacked with an enthusiasm of heroism, such only as the highest animation of liberty could inspire," he wrote.[320] The Marquis de Lafayette, the Frenchman who had played a major role in the struggle for American independence, was appointed to the newly-created Parisian national guard.

After discussions with his advisors, and facing widespread unrest, the king ordered the French military to stand down. Furthermore, he announced he would personally return to Paris to entertain the grievances of his people and to reinstitute Necker as Chief Minister. This apparent change of course caused even some critics to believe the king was now serious about instituting financial and constitutional reforms. Indeed, his grand return to Paris three days later was greeted by jubilant masses of Parisians who praised him as he walked by.

Paine interpreted the recent events in Paris as the beckoning of a new wave of independence. The actualization of political autonomy in America, he thought, had set a powerful precedent that had spread to Europe. He came to believe that the establishment of the National Assembly and the Storming of the Bastille proved that French subjects would no longer tolerate vanity and inaction from their government, an encouraging sign to any republican. From London, he shared his enthusiasm with George Washington, with whom he still maintained a correspondence. "A share in two revolutions is living to some purpose," Paine wrote.[321]

Nevertheless, Paine maintained a disposition toward the French monarchy that was fundamentally divergent from the one he had for its British counterpart. For several reasons, he came to view Louis as a uniquely enlightened monarch in an age of kingly despots, a view no doubt influenced by his willingness to provide financial and military assistance to America in its more dire days. Though sympathizing with the events that challenged his rule, Paine was encouraged by the king's willingness to welcome political reforms that would elevate commoners to a stature they had never yet experienced. Even though he knew the path to that destination would be a rocky one, he was adamant that it was for the best. "With respect to the French Revolution," he wrote to Benjamin Rush, "be assured that everything is going on right—little inconveniences, the necessary consequence of pulling down and building up, may arise, but even these are much less than ought to have been expected."[322] Monarchy itself was still an abject evil, he believed, but Louis was at the very least a good steward of its impositions.

Throughout the summer of the 1789, France's new National Assembly got to work on its most important project yet—the adoption of a declaration of the people's rights. At the forefront of this project was Lafayette, the skilled military commander and an honorary American citizen. As a member of the National Assembly, he drafted—with the help of the renowned Thomas Jefferson—an enunciation of the rights of the French people. The document's themes and verbiage were heavily inspired by the Declaration of Independence, which itself was a project Paine had championed in *Common Sense*. It was a manifesto that defended individual rights on the basis of natural law, recognizing free speech, due process, private property, and freedom of assembly for the first time in the history of the country.

The Declaration of the Rights of Man and of the Citizen was presented to the National Assembly. After some edits by the Comte de Mirabeau, the document was adopted by the same body on August 26, after which it was sent to the king for his endorsement at Versailles, where he had returned after being in Paris. Instead of embracing the document, Louis stalled for several weeks, and unrest grew as the document's legal status hung in the balance. As a result, radicals in the National Assembly feared the worst. As grain riots emerged in Paris, Lafayette attempted to maintain order. On September 19, tensions exploded when the king's response to the Declaration was read. While agreeing to the general spirit of the document, he refused to sign it unless major amendments were made in regard to hereditary offices, taxes, and other matters.[323]

To protest against food shortages and political discontent, a mass demonstration of women working in the Parisian marketplaces formed outside of the Hôtel de Ville on October 5. The mob grew to between 6,000 and 7,000, and the angry women burst into the building. Many of Lafayette's forces sympathized with the crowd, and the general himself was late to the scene. Once there, he was stunned to discover that a large number of his men, rather than oppose the lawless demonstration, instead joined it in its new objective—a grand march to Versailles to confront the king and queen. Although he commanded his troops otherwise, they began to mutiny, and his own life was threatened. Rather than face death, Lafayette agreed to lead the march, hoping to exert some influence on their behavior.

When they all arrived at Versailles, the female-dominated mob was turned away the palace door. The royal guards were soon overwhelmed, however, and participants streamed into the palace doors by the hundreds. For a time, they harassed delegates of the National Assembly, who were congregating inside. The angry mob frightened the king's family and threatened to kill Queen Marie Antoinette, who was seen by the revolutionaries as the personification of corruption and opulence. After some time, Louis grew fearful for his life. After contemplating how to proceed, he went to the palace balcony and made a grand declaration that he would be returning to Paris to heed their demands. The crowd then chanted "Vive le roi!"—or "long live the king!" The monarch was then peacefully escorted to the Tuileries Palace in Paris. At this point, many thought the chaos of the French Revolution would come to an end.

As Paris was consumed by tumult, Paine remained committed to his architectural pursuits. After the death of his bridge project over the Don River, Paine began a campaign to build a test bridge near London. His intention was to display his work more prominently in a public location, so it could be more easily viewed by prospective financiers. To do so, he recruited assistance from a new group of investors headed by Thomas Walker, a leading figure in the iron fabrication industry. To secure the group's monetary commitment, Paine put up for collateral his property in New Rochelle, his house in Bordentown, and $1,000 in stock in the Bank of Philadelphia. In addition, he borrowed money from several friends, including Thomas Jefferson.[324] The ribs to be used in the prototype were shipped from Yorkshire to London by ship, but its assembly did not begin until the summer of 1790.

Paine's sizable model bridge was placed near Lisson Green in the Marylebone district of London, where it sat on the bowling green behind the Yorkshire Stingo, a prominent tavern. The prototype had a span of 110 feet, and was five feet high from its chord. It was completed in September of 1791, and was immediately opened to the public. Despite a large number of visitors and Paine's efforts to promote the model, however, it failed to receive positive attention from the press. The iron structure, which was also largely ignored by academic circles and potential financiers, was taken down after a year of failed attempts to attract funding. By that time, Paine had given up his attempt to market the venture. "The bridge has been put up," he told his partner John Hall, "but being on wood butments they yielded, and it is now taken down." By that time, he had shifted his attention to "a political bridge."[325]

In London, Edmund Burke at first echoed Paine's sensibilities in regard to recent events in France. "Our thoughts of everything at home are suspended," he wrote, "by our astonishment at the wonderful spectacle which is exhibited in a neighboring and rival country—what spectators, and what actors!" The famous Whig was impressed by the Parisian outburst for liberty, but he remained skeptical that they could handle such a swift transition to a free society. "The spirit it is impossible not to admire, but the old Parisian ferocity has broken out in a shocking manner," he wrote. As the weeks passed, however, he adopted a more measured approach to the situation, and soon argued that French subjects were unprepared for revolutionary democracy. While admitting "the people, along with their political servitude, have thrown off the yoke of laws and morals," Burke questioned "whether they are in a condition to exercise any function of decided authority." There existed "a mob of their constituents ready to hang them if they should deviate into moderation, or in the least depart from the spirit of those they represent," he cautioned.[326]

In late 1789, the renowned Welsh republican Richard Price delivered a stirring speech in support of the French Revolution to British radicals. The oratory was later converted to a pamphlet, which was read by Burke. After being prompted by several friends, Burke set out to publish his own response to the letter in early 1790. He worked on the manuscript for several months, revising it many times. As Paine attempted to concentrate on bridgebuilding, he could not help but to follow its path to publication. He eventually presumed that Burke's work would chastise the French Revolution, and told his well-connected friends in the political world that he was preparing a written answer to it. The *General Evening Post*, a Tory-oriented publication in London, quoted him in boasting that "he would answer it in four days."[327] Meanwhile, many of Burke's peers remained confident that his upcoming work would heap praises upon France's transition to republicanism.

Throughout 1790, Paine remained enthusiastic about the recent events in France. The Marquis de Lafayette even presented to him a key to the Bastille, which soon became symbolic of the revolutionary fervor. Paine sent the same "handsomely framed" key to his great friend George Washington, who was inaugurated as president of the United States the year prior. "I feel myself happy in being the person thro' whom the Marquis has conveyed his early trophy of the spoils of despotism, and the first ripe fruits of American principles transplanted into Europe to his master and patron," Paine wrote.[328]

In November of 1790, *Burke's Reflections on the Revolution in France* was finally published. In its original format, it was a lengthy response to

Charles-Jean François Depont, member of the new French National Assembly and acquaintance of Burke, who had asked the statesman about his opinions on the recent events in the country. However, the context of the work spoke more broadly that than of a personal conversation, and was directed toward European thinkers as a whole. As Paine predicted, the pamphlet was a torrent of criticism against the French Revolution and its supporters. Burke called the French Revolution "the most astonishing that has hitherto happened in the world," an episode that produced a "strange chaos of levity and ferocity, and of all sorts of crimes jumbled together with all sorts of follies."[329]

Early in the work, Burke made reference to a bombastic sermon delivered by Price, a radical Unitarian Whig, fellow sympathizer with the American revolutionaries, and head of London's Revolution Society. According to Price, precedents left in the wake of England's Glorious Revolution of 1688 made clear that all free people had the right political self-determination, and, more specifically, the right to "choose our own governors, cashier them for misconduct, and to frame a government for ourselves." In sum, the conception was hardly dissimilar from the principles embraced by those who drafted and adopted the Declaration of Independence in the young United States. In late 1790, the Revolution Society also passed resolutions praising those responsible for saving France "by its deliverance from popery and arbitrary power."[330]

In anticipation of the many counterarguments his pamphlet was destined to attract, Burke carefully drew distinctions between England's tumultuous constitutional history and the circumstances in Paris. In contrast to Price and his Whig acolytes, Burke insisted that the Glorious Revolution upheld traditional English hereditary succession through law, and the subsequent 1689 Bill of Rights only clarified the specifics of that process. Far from establishing "a right by the revolution to elect our kings," he wrote, "the English nation did at that time most solemnly renounce and abdicate it, for themselves and for all their posterity forever." Following the circumstances, Burke admitted that "the nation was at that time, in some sense, free to take what course it pleased for filling the throne," but deliberately retained traditional conceptions of the English monarchy, its constitution, and its civil institutions nevertheless. [331]

Rather than fundamentally transform the English political system, Burke argued the Glorious Revolution inspired a reiteration of the country's customary succession process, but with slight modifications under the law:

> On this principle the succession of the crown has always been what it now is, an hereditary succession by law; in the old line it was a succession by the common law; in the new, by the statute law operating on the principles of the common law, not changing the substance, but regulating the mode and describing the persons.

According to the writer, James II's abdication of the throne terminated only his own connection to the office, not the office itself. "Though a king may abdicate for his own person, he cannot abdicate for the monarchy," Burke professed, and likewise, "by a stronger reason, the House of Commons cannot renounce its share of authority." Rather than "dissolve the whole fabric" of English monarchy, or bring about a manner through which Englishmen could choose their governors, Burke portrayed the Glorious Revolution as a conservative venture. By maintaining "hereditary descent in the same blood," he stressed that England's magistrates conceived of hereditary monarchy as an "inviolable" maxim.[332]

As an Old Whig, Burke had long dedicated himself to traditional liberties and opposed an absolute monarchy. As such, he consistently opposed kingly overreach despite his hardline position against revolutionary passion. Even still, he considered the Glorious Revolution an ideal uprising because it successfully reversed the crown's transgressions without casting aside the traditional customs and institutions that served as the foundations of British society. Indeed, when James was ejected from the throne and William and Mary assumed joint stewardship over the monarchy, the country's political system remained largely unchanged. Moreover, the two new monarchs agreed to be subject to the English Bill of Rights, which placed explicit limitations upon their power without the need for bloody upheaval. Burke portrayed this gesture as a compact between English subjects and their monarch to ensure governmental stability throughout the generations.

From almost every angle, Burke rejected the Lockean mantra that all free people had the right to alter or abolish their government when it ceased to protect the life, liberty, and property of its inhabitants—the same theory Paine championed. Rather than a compact among the living, the statesman described government as a contract "not only between those who are living, but between those who are living, those who are dead, and those who are to be born."[333] This view contrasted greatly with the one held by radical Whigs, who believed every aspect of government was subject to alteration through the will of the present generation.

While he sympathized with the American revolutionaries, Burke was utterly unimpressed with France's new representative assembly. "Of any practical experience in the state, not one man was to be found," he claimed. The Third Estate was overrepresented, and populated with "inferior, unlearned, mechanical, merely instrumental members of the profession." To Burke, the very composition of the National Assembly made the body incapable of judicious governance, and only exacerbated the country's ailments. It was through the body's ignorance, he explained, that the body abolished France's traditional regions in favor of 83 administrative districts, eliminated hereditary privileges for the clergy and nobility, and subdued the political influence of the country's civil institutions. When the French legislature "framed democratic governments," he wrote, "they had virtually dismembered their country." The revolutionary uproar, in his eyes, merely placed into power "men who never had seen the state so much as in a picture," and "men who knew nothing of the world beyond the bounds of an obscure village." In Burke's opinion, this inexperience would inevitably bring about the country's ruin.[334]

At the heart of Burke's argument against the French Revolution was his allegation that the event would necessarily uproot and obliterate political order, the characteristic he felt most responsible for preserving Western civilization. He alleged that the French revolutionaries had "no respect for the wisdom of others," and aspired to "destroy an old scheme of things," inclinations that threatened all historical advances made on behalf of individual rights and stable governance. Erasing all characteristics of the past in attempt to rid the world of evil, he thought, was a pompous approach. "Duration is no object to those who think little or nothing has been done before their time, and who place all their hopes in discovery," he declared.[335]

France's new republican government was doomed, Burke predicted, because the National Assembly had usurped the power of the French monarchy. In turn, it would soon exercise the same powers in an arbitrary and destructive fashion and unleash a wave of tyranny upon its people. "Civil and military anarchy" had become "the constitution of the kingdom," he wrote, and the new authority had already unleashed a wave of oppression:

> They have made no sacrifices to their projects of greater consequence than their shoe-buckles, whilst they were imprisoning their king, murdering their fellow-citizens, and bathing in tears, and plunging in poverty and distress, thousands of worthy men and worthy families. Their cruelty has not even been the base result of fear. It has been the effect of their sense of perfect safety, in authorizing treasons, robberies, rapes, assassinations, slaughters, and burnings, throughout their harassed land.

As the king himself was transformed into a mere figurehead, so too would any semblance of traditional constitutional constraints and other impediments against despotic rule.[336]

Burke also speculated that the gradual degradation of French society would result in an authoritarian, military leader to rule with an iron hand:

> In the weakness of one kind of authority, and in the fluctuation of all, the officers of an army will remain for some time mutinous and full of faction, until some popular general, who understands the art of conciliating the soldiery, and who possesses the true spirit of command, shall draw the eyes of all men upon himself. Armies will obey him on his personal account.

Under the auspices of democracy, France's deluge of revolutionary fervor would eventually yield a concerted lack of confidence in among army military ranks. "The army will not long look to an assembly acting through the organ of false show," he warned, and various army factions would be galvanized against such a body. This trajectory, he thought, was destined to rupture republicanism and bring about military rule.[337] About a decade later, these words were proven prophetic.

Beyond France's political metamorphosis, Burke also lambasted the National Assembly's assault on the country's Catholic religious establishment. In his mind, religion was inseparable from morality. As he put it, "religion is the basis of civil society, and the source of all good and of all comfort." Though a practicing Anglican, the Irishman believed the Catholic Church provided a virtuous foundation for France. The campaign to abolish clerical privileges and confiscate Church property was thus but "a drunken delirium from the hot spirit drawn out of the alembic of hell, which in France is now so furiously boiling." If Christianity was subverted in France, Burke predicted "that some uncouth, pernicious, and degrading superstition might take place of it."[338]

Ultimately, Burke believed the greatest shortcoming of the French Revolution was that its concerted embrace of abstract ideas—no matter how commendable—ignored existing social realities and human nature itself. The statesman denied that man could forge his own political society or constitution, and considered views to the contrary as a reckless proclivity that ignored human nature. In trying to do so, he believed the French revolutionaries had presumed for themselves that which only an omnipotent god could presume.[339]

Reflections on the Revolution in France was met with a divided reception. Many of Burke's political allies disagreed with his narrative, and its publication caused the English Whigs to split into two factions shortly thereafter. After reading the work, some even went so far as to question Burke's mental stability in old age. Among them was Thomas Jefferson, who claimed the pamphlet confirmed "evidence of the rottenness of his mind," a sad deviation in a life that otherwise "wore the mask of virtue and patriotism."[340] At any rate, the pamphlet became an immediate hit. In its first month, 12,000 copies were sold, many of which quickly found their way into the hands of Europe's intellectual class.[341] Among its first readers was Paine.

Even though he anticipated a critical account, Paine was dumbfounded by Burke's unambiguous tirade against the French Revolution. Viewing liberty as the inseparable gift from the creator to humanity, he could not understand how the same blessing should not be applied universally. In his eyes, opposition to monarchy was not a uniquely American penchant, and French subjects held the same rights as those asserted by patriots in their struggle with Britain, namely self-determination and the power to alter or abolish one's government. Furthermore, he was utterly confounded that Burke, a man of immense wisdom and similar philosophical leanings, could feel so differently about the French Revolution. Though Paine swore he had left his former trade by the wayside, he could not remain silent as Burke's work was released to the world. If he had ever been truly vomited forth from the mouth of politics, *Reflections on the Revolution in France* pushed him right back into its jaws.

Paine was not alone in his opposition to Burke's tract among his peers. Mary Wollstonecraft, a friend to both Paine and Burke, soon responded with her own pamphlet, *A Vindication of the Rights of Men, in a Letter to the Right Honourable Edmund Burke*. Wollstonecraft blasted Burke's dissertation as "a mortal antipathy to reason," full of "ingenious arguments in a very specious garb." If government was merely an inflexible compact that bound the current generation and all future generations to the dictates of those who originally created it, she claimed Burke's argument "settles slavery on an everlasting foundation."[342] Wollstonecraft condemned the same deep-seated hereditary distinctions that Burke defended as precedent, and excoriated the statesman for his inconsistency in support of American—but not French—political independence.

Paine took up residence at the Angel Inn in London's Islington district, where he hurriedly put pen to ink on what was destined to become his most painstaking work yet. With his unparalleled eloquence, widespread popularity among the Whigs of Europe, and zeal to defend republicanism and absolute political self-determination, he sat writing by candlelight in his small room. In less than three months' time, he completed the first part of that which was to become his magnum opus.

Paine dedicated *The Rights of Man* to his good friend George Washington, and stressed his intention to defend "those principles of freedom which" the president "so eminently contributed to establish." The author expressed his sincere desire that the pamphlet "may become as universal as your benevolence can wish," and that the Virginian "may enjoy the happiness of seeing the new world regenerate the old."[343] From that point, it was only three years until Paine's friendship with the most respected man in America would deteriorate completely.

In the first pages of his new work, Paine castigated Burke for launching an "unprovoked attack" upon the French people and the country's new republican government. He depicted the statesman's recent pamphlet as a "copious fury of near four hundred pages" that was filled with "flagrant misrepresentations." Even so, Paine sincerely lamented the recent musings of a man he once considered a great champion of liberty and "a friend to mankind."[344] Undoubtedly, his reluctant disappointment with Burke spilled all over the work's remaining 40,000 words.

In response to Burke's contention that the ascension of William and Mary bound English subjects into a condition of perpetual submission to England's hereditary monarchy, Paine offered several counterpoints. First, while England's Parliament of 1688 did indeed possess the right to undermine a tyrannical monarch, he contended that the body "set up another right by assumption, that of binding and controlling posterity to the end of time." Paine portrayed that deed as an act of usurpation against the laws of nature:

> There never did, there never will, and there never can, exist a Parliament, or any description of man, or any generation of men, in any country, possessed of the right or the power of binding and controlling posterity to the "end of time," or of commanding for ever how the world shall be governed, or who shall govern it; and therefore all such clauses, acts or declarations by which the makers of them attempt to do what they have neither the right nor the power to do, nor the power to execute, are in themselves null and void.

The penman insisted that "every age and generation must be as free to act for itself in all cases as the age and generations which preceded it." Any view to the contrary, thought he, was akin to slavery. "The vanity and presumption of governing beyond the grave is the most ridiculous and insolent of all tyrannies," he declared. The natural corollary to this, according to Paine, was that the living possessed the absolute moral and political right to determine their own course of governance. "As government is for the living, and not for the dead, it is the living only that has any right in it."[345]

Secondly, Paine derided Burke's position that Parliament could issue a permanent and unalterable law, while still assuming that the body retained parliamentary sovereignty—the right to legislate on any matter. If it had such power, the writer argued, its supreme authority could certainly reverse the deed. Nevertheless, in contrast to Burke, Paine denied such a power ever existed at all, "for that power must certainly be more than human which no human power to the end of time can alter." He added that Burke's position to the contrary was arguably more despotic than the misdeeds of James II, because that king had, in his deposition, abandoned any aspirations of binding future generations to his will.[346]

Instead of rooting his perspective in "musty records and moldy parchments to prove that the rights of the living are lost," as he accused Burke of doing, Paine promoted prose within the Declaration of the Rights of Man and the Citizen, including its open acknowledgement that rights were "engraved on the heart of every citizen" through natural order. Among them, he continued, was a right to sever all existing connections to one's existing government. "A nation has at all times an inherent indefeasible right to abolish any form of government it finds inconvenient," Paine wrote, "and to establish such as accords with its interest, disposition and happiness."[347] This outlook was completely antithetical to Burke's claim that Englishmen lacked the right to frame a new government of their own choosing.

In comparing France's political upheaval with its English counterpart, Burke's pamphlet paid great attention to the year 1688. While the Glorious Revolution and its aftermath was universally acknowledged a watershed to all Englishman, Burke wrote of the era as if it should be perceived as a new beginning of sorts for English rule. However, Paine contended the origins of the England's political system should not be traced to the year 1688, but instead to the year 1066. Expanding upon a motif from *Common Sense*, Paine cast doubt upon the legitimacy of William the Conqueror, the Norman Conquest he launched, and the hereditary line he produced. As the penman noted, William successfully deposed the Anglo-Saxon king Harold Godwinson, himself part of the centuries-spanning royal line within the country. Far from a sovereign expression of English subjects to choose their own rule, their mode of government had been chosen for them by an invading army.

According to Paine, Burke was hypocritical to base his assertions on the legal impermissibility of Englishman to frame a new government on precedents established by a foreign warlord that did the same by way of military force. Far from monarchy rooted in moral foundations, the kingdom the Normans established was an oppressive tyranny instituted by "bands of robbers" obsessed with internal wars and legal plunder. While English aristocracy ignored these truths for fear that they would ruffle too many feathers, Paine wrote plainly of them in his usual manner. "Though not a courtier will talk of the curfew-bell," he wrote, "not a village in England has forgotten it."[348] By paying such great attention to 1688, Paine wrote, Burke ignored the despotic history of the same royal system he considered unalterable.

If there were any generation of man that had the authority "of dictating the mode by which the world should be governed" for all time, Paine suggested it would be the first generation that existed rather than an arbitrary cohort of Englishmen in 1688. This was because all men had their origin in the same creator, and each generation was therefore beholden to the creator rather than to other generations of men. Only usurpations of God's will, then, could allow one generation to divest another generation of their right to rule themselves by whatever system suited them. "Every generation is equal in rights to generations which preceded it, by the same rule that every individual is born equal in rights with his contemporary," he professed.[349]

In accordance with this creed, Paine applied the same principles to subjects of the Bourbon monarchy in Paris who sought to remake their government. They had suffered long enough under the excesses and subjugations of monarchy, so why should they be exempted from the same gospel preached by the English Whigs? Furthermore, why should British subjects be prohibited from actualizing their own inherent right to alter or abolish their government? While Burke provided an explanation as to why Englishmen lacked such authority over many pages, Paine emphatically maintained that the same power was applicable to all of humanity, whatever their country or government.

Like John Locke and Algernon Sidney before him, Paine professed that all people had the right to invoke such a right whenever it suited them. To him, this was justified on the basis of an ultimate extension of the tenets of natural law, which had long been perceived axiomatic by British Whigs. According to this gospel, men were generally cooperative in a state of nature, but by mankind's failings, life, liberty, and property would become endangered. To protect them, man created a social compact with each other to perform that sole function. Whensoever the agent created by the compact overstepped these clearly defined prerogatives, it ceased to require compliance and was susceptible to alteration by the people.

While Burke sourced traditional English rights to precedents that emerged in history, Paine contended the same were bestowed upon mankind from the time of the creation. This was because God created man in his own image, "and consequently that all men are born equal, and with equal natural right ... every child born into the world must be considered as deriving its existence from God." According to Paine, natural rights had been violated through history "because there have been upstart governments, thrusting themselves between, and presumptuously working to unmake man."[350] Rather than embracing an arbitrary political system, and thereby contravening the rights of man, Paine believed governments should be established with the chief purpose of affirming and protecting those rights.

Countering Burke's claim that France's revolutionaries had rebelled "against a mild and lawful monarch, with more fury, outrage, and insult, than any people has been known to rise against the most illegal usurper, or most sanguinary tyrant," Paine asserted that his peer had completely overlooked the true source of French enmity. The writer contended that the revolution was carried out not against the sitting monarch, King Louis XVI, but instead against the overarching monarchical establishment of France. "The monarch and the monarchy were distinct and separate things," Paine alleged, "and it was against the established despotism of the latter, and not against the persons or principles of the former, that the revolt commenced, and the revolution has been carried."[351]

Incidentally, Paine shared Burke's view that the reigning king of France was a uniquely fair and just magistrate. The penman had long respected the king for being such a friend to the young American states throughout their most trying days, and had established cordial relations with him in his quest to secure financial aid about a decade earlier. "Perhaps no man bred up in the style of an absolute king, ever possessed a heart so little disposed to the exercise of that species of power as the present King of France," Paine admitted. The person of the king and the French hereditary establishment were separate entities that should not be conflated, he argued. "Burke does not attend to the distinction between men and principles," he wrote, and therefore "does not see that a revolt may take place against the despotism of the latter, while there lies not charge of despotism against the former." Paine went even so far as to sympathize with the king for being made to reign over such a despotic system. In his eyes, it was the monarchy that was corrupt, not Louis.[352]

According to Paine, the Bastille was stormed because it was a symbol of despotism, a structure spawned from ages of monarchical tyranny. "The originally hereditary despotism ... divides and sub-divides itself into a thousand shapes and forms, till at last the whole of it is acted by deputation," he observed. Rather than a quest to eradicate the monarch, the French Revolution was to Paine a movement to reverse "a thousand despotisms" that existed in the country. The reasons for the revolt were infinitely more justifiable morally in that they did not stem from personal resentment toward a single man, but instead from a sincere desire to safeguard individual rights. "In the instance of France we see a revolution generated in the rational contemplation of the rights of man," he declared.[353]

In no uncertain terms, Burke's anti-revolutionary diatribe blasted the agitators in France for the bloodshed that resulted from the Storming of the Bastille. "That the Bastille was attacked with an enthusiasm of heroism, such only as the highest animation of liberty could inspired" was not to be denied, but it was not the work of the National Assembly. Instead, it was the work of commoners, who, according to Paine, had learned such behavior "from the governments they live under; and retaliate the punishments that they have been accustomed to behold."[354]

Though the grisly executions of the governor of the prison and the mayor of Paris upon pikes was to Paine a horrifying incident, he alleged it was not extraordinary for Europe. Heads on spikes in England "differed nothing in the horror of the scene from those carried upon spikes at Paris," and all such abominable behaviors were "sanguinary punishments which corrupt mankind." Furthermore, Paine pointed out that in England the punishment of hanging, drawing, and quartering remained in place for certain crimes, a process infinitely ghastlier than that which was seen at the Bastille.[355] Having grown up within view of public execution site near Thetford, he knew this all too well.

The brand of extreme brutality that had transpired in both France and England was to Paine a product of the oppressive regimes that had instituted such punishments long before any group of commoners. The bloodshed arose "as an unavoidable consequence, out of the ill construction of all old governments in Europe, England included with the rest," he explained. The violence in Paris was "not the effect of the principles of the revolution, but of the degraded mind that existed before the revolution, and which the revolution is calculated to reform."[356] Paine lived by these words, and strictly opposed the death penalty under all circumstances even when it became most unpopular to do so.

As to Burke's grievances against the National Assembly on the basis that it acted arbitrarily and foolhardily, Paine could not have disagreed more. Rather than act irrationally or foster conflict, Paine contended the National Assembly acted only in self-preservation in the days leading up to the Storming of the Bastille. This was because the king's brother, the Comte d'Artois—the future Charles X—devised and began to execute a plot to dissolve the body by force and arrest its members. As part of the scheme, the crown summoned thousands of troops and stationed them throughout Paris, placing the legislative body in "the most perilous and critical situation a body of men can be supposed to act in." Far from disturbing innocents and committing atrocities, Paine noted that the National Assembly merely responded in self-defense by organizing its own militia forces against a counterrevolutionary coup. He also commended the body for refusing to launch its own reprisal against Bourbon officials, the crown's forces, or their sympathizers in the aftermath of the event.[357]

According to Paine, the constitutional model Burke endorsed—a series of statues, precedents, and traditions—was a defective construct. Its unwritten nature made it subject to the arbitrary whims of the state, and especially to the king's impulses. It was imperative that "the government is in like manner governed by the constitution," he wrote, so that its power could not extend boundlessly. If any government had the power to remake its constitution simply to fulfill its ambitions, as he believed the English crown had over the centuries, it was in his mind no constitution at all.[358]

As an adherent of the brand of social compact theory espoused by John Locke, Paine believed "a constitution is a thing antecedent to a government, and a government is only the creature of a constitution." Mankind's only reason to create a government out of a state of nature, then, was to protect the liberty of society's inhabitants from infringements upon their life, liberty, and property. It was written document rather than an abstract ideal, and unambiguously laid the foundations and restrictions for a government:

> It is the body of elements, to which you can refer, and quote article by article; and which contains the principles on which the government shall be established, the manner in which it shall be organised, the powers it shall have, the mode of elections, the duration of Parliaments, or by what other name such bodies may be called; the powers which the executive part of the government shall have; and in fine, everything that relates to the complete organisation of a civil government, and the principles on which it shall act, and by which it shall be bound.

Because Burke could not point to such an English constitution in physical form, Paine alleged that the device had no merit whatsoever. "Though it has been so much talked about, no such thing as a constitution exists, or ever did exist" in England, "and consequently that the people have yet a constitution to form," he wrote.[359]

In contrast to England's precedent-oriented series of statutes, traditions, and procedural customs, the constitutional model Paine promoted was that of a written constitution. As an ideal, the France's constitution was a "personal social compact" among delegates elected to frame it, and the authority of future assemblies created by its ratification would be limited to legislating "according to the principles and forms prescribed in that constitution." Unlike England's counterpart, France's constitution constrained the government within fixed boundaries, unambiguously affirmed the rights of its subjects, and, most importantly, and prevented the government from changing its political system arbitrarily.[360]

The Rights of Man defended the merits of nearly every aspect of the French Constitution of 1791, contrasting it with the unwritten constitution of England that Burke championed. Paine first pointed to the addition of new electoral safeguards to protect the people's interests. He celebrated the extent to which suffrage was extended under the new French system. In republican France, every man who paid a poll tax of sixty sous—a nominal fee—was entitled to vote. In contrast, less than one percent of England's populace were granted the same civil right. In addition, he extolled the representation arrangement because it tied representatives to taxable inhabitants within a region, ensuring that more populous regions did not suffer disproportionately. Each region in England, on the other hand, sent two representatives to the House of Commons regardless of population, which led to skewed representational outcomes. As Paine wrote, this resulted in an "unsystematical display of paradoxical rhapsodies." Finally, he praised the National Assembly's two-year terms, which established a frequent legislative rotation.[361]

Next, the penman endorsed the new constitution's reform of French game laws. Prior to the document's ratification, game laws prevented property owners from hunting on their own land. France's new framework prohibited such laws entirely, such that "the farmer on whose land wild game shall be found ... shall have a right to what he can take." In England, however, disputes over hunting rights had been a longstanding topic of contention due to the grant of royal monopolies and expansion of public lands. "Every chartered town is an aristocratical monopoly in itself," an assault on property rights, Paine protested. Consequently, the French system respected a purer form of property rights that could not be found across the English Channel. Paine went so far as to recommend that Burke read Adam Smith's famous 1776 economic treatise, *The Wealth of Nations*, which illustrated the destructive nature of state monopolies.[362]

Paine expressed deep respect for separation of powers, a doctrine borrowed from the works of Charles de Montesquieu, in his tribute to the French constitution for barring National Assembly members from being civil officers in France. Because it untied legislators from the executive authority, this provision would encourage public virtue and act as a safeguard against corruption. It was almost certainly influenced by the recently ratified United States Constitution, which prevented any member of the

Senate or House of Representatives from being appointed as a civil officer of America's central government. Barring those in public office from intermingling and manipulating other power centers would do much to ward against duplicity, he claimed.[363]

The creation of legal barriers between representatives tasked with raising taxes and those in civil office also discouraged the propensity to raise taxes, Paine reasoned. The English system had failed to enact such a precaution, and this defect allowed Parliament to exploit the kingdom's subjects to the ends of its own ambitions. "Everything in the English government appears to me the reverse of what it ought to be," he wrote, because Parliament "is like a man being both mortgagor and mortgagee," analogous to a "criminal sitting in judgment upon himself." In England "the national purse is the common hack which each mounts upon," Paine pontificated.[364]

Another hazard the new French constitution protected the people against was the excesses of war. "War is the common harvest of all those who participate in the division and expenditure of public money, in all countries," he warned, and was "the art of conquering at home." It was little more than a devious scheme to "keep up deceitful expectations which prevent people from looking into the defects and abuses of government," and a tactic to prolong their subjugation. Moreover, the power to wage war was inextricably linked to the tendency to abuse the taxing authority. Paine wrote that "the history of the English government" had revealed that "taxes were not raised to carry on wars, but that wars were raised to carry on taxes." Of all disasters for which government was the catalyst, he believed war to the most catastrophic. "I had seen enough of the miseries of war," Paine lamented, "to wish it might never more have existence in the world, and that some other mode might be found out to settle the differences that should occasionally arise in the neighborhood of nations."[365]

The commencement of war could only be fueled by taxation, he observed, so the French instrument wisely disposed of the king's unilateral war-making power by lodging the power to declare war in the National Assembly instead. In this way, France's new government emulated that which had been done in the United States by way of the Constitution. To Paine, this was not an insignificant shift in political particulars, it was a maneuver that deliberately raised elected representatives over the English monarchy. In contrast, English kings claimed and asserted "this power of war and peace in himself" ever since the days of William the Conqueror.[366] It was a tradition founded in military conquest rather than self-determination.

Paine also advocated for the French constitution on the basis that it undermined the country's ancient system of royal titles and hereditary classes, customs he had long considered outdated and repressive. Furthermore, titles of nobility denigrated the social, political, and commercial contributions of individuals:

> Titles are but nicknames, and every nickname is a title. The thing is perfectly harmless in itself, but it marks a sort of foppery in the human character, which degrades it. It reduces man into the diminutive of man in things which are great, and the counterfeit of women in things which are little. It talks about its fine blue ribbon like a girl, and shows its new garter like a child. A certain writer, of some antiquity, says: "When I was a child, I thought as a child; but when I became a man, I put away childish things." It is, properly, from the elevated mind of France that the folly of titles has fallen.

The new document promoted meritocracy over aristocracy, which Paine believed was of great benefit to mankind. Securing social and political status on the basis of familial happenstance was a characteristic of monarchism he considered especially egregious, for it rewarded the undeserving and punished the blameless.[367]

According to Paine, it was also wise of the French republicans to abolish primogeniture—the legal requirement for the oldest son to inherit his family's estate in its entirety. The concept was "the law against every other law of nature, and Nature herself calls for its destruction," he declared. This was because the custom served as an affront to property rights by prohibiting individuals from disbursing their wealth as they wished. Additionally, it was also a disproportionate setback to large noble families. "Aristocracy has never more than one child," he claimed, as "the rest are begotten to be devoured." In his passionate support for the elimination of primogeniture in France, he likely drew inspiration from Thomas Jefferson, who spearheaded a successful effort in 1785 to put an end to the practice in republican Virginia.[368]

Finally, Paine commended France's new constitution for recognizing freedom of conscience and for barring the state from intervening in the church. This reversal was wise, the penman wrote, because "engendering the church with the state" had created "a sort of mule-animal, capable only of destroying." Established churches, he wrote, had only divided peoples against each other and encouraged civil conflict. The American states, however, had begun to rectify this classical error:

> Persecution is not an original feature in any religion; but it is alway the strongly-marked feature of all law-religions, or religions established by law. Take away the law-establishment, and every religion re-assumes its original benignity. In America, a catholic priest is a good citizen, a good character, and a good neighbour; an episcopalian minister is of the same description: and this proceeds independently of the men, from there being no law-establishment in America.

To Paine, there was a wide gulf that separated the United States from Europe in regard to such matters. Whereas "the union of church and state has impoverished Spain," Paine observed, the disestablishment of official churches and removal of religious oath requirements in several of the American states, such as Virginia and South Carolina, proved more conducive to human liberty and domestic tranquility. "It was by observing the ill effects of it in England, that America has been warned against it," he wrote.[369] Consequently, France should borrow from their brethren in the United States that were reaping the benefits of a system that terminated state-bestowed religious subsidies.

At its core, *The Rights of Man* was an overt denunciation of hereditary monarchy. Paine claimed such system lacked any moral foundation, and disposed of natural order as the creator intended it. Expanding upon groundwork he had already laid in *Common Sense*, Paine lambasted all systems of monarchy as varying degrees of slavery. While Burke insisted that stability necessitated hereditary monarchy, Paine countered that "it was by the government being hereditary, that the liberties of the people were endangered." Furthermore, he categorically denied Burke's assertion that an inherent "hereditary wisdom" ensured political fortitude.[370]

With the exception of the fledgling the United States, most of the world fell prey to corrupt kingdoms that were established by conquest or usurpation, bound together by coercion and military force, and subject to the impositions of those who claimed political power for themselves. In most of these cases, including the esteemed English kingdom, the doctrine of hereditary succession presumed that all subsequent generations were unnaturally and immorally bound to the dictates of the original hereditary family. On the contrary, Paine believed "if the present generation, or any other, are disposed to be slaves, it does not lessen the right of the succeeding generation to be free."[371]

In Paine's perspective, there were only two overarching governmental systems that prevailed in the world, "government by election and representation" and "government by hereditary succession." The latter system was incompatible with morality, for it required "a belief from man to which his reason cannot subscribe, and which can only be established upon his ignorance." In time, he believed, its precepts would be rejected by all. "Mr. Burke talks about what he calls a hereditary crown, as if it were some production of nature…or as if it were a thing or a subject universally consented to," scoffed Paine. "It has none of those properties," he wrote, "but is the reverse of them all." The entire construct was therefore "a thing in imagination, the property of which is more than doubted, and the legality of which in a few years will be denied."[372] To Paine, monarchy was more than a mere misguided idea—it was an outright abomination that defied natural law and plagued mankind from the earliest civilizations on earth forward.

Rather than limiting his pamphlet to a righteous attack against monarchy, Paine also took strides to promote its preferable alternative, republicanism. The world had now borne witness to the precedent of the United States, a league of independent republics that chose to cast monarchy aside completely. "I see in America," wrote Paine, "the generality of people living in a style of plenty unknown in monarchical countries; and I see the principle of its government, which is that of the equal rights of man, is making rapid progress in the world."[373]

To the contrary of Burke's allegation that such an arrangement was quasi-utopian and would inevitably lead to instability, Paine portrayed France's new course as a stroll across a bridge that had already been tested. He knew there would be growing pains, but he perceived in France the same advantages that were inherent to America—a learned, industrious people with zeal for liberty and a newfound thirst to uproot and reverse the oppressions of the past. By issuing a declaration of rights, constituting a new government, and drafting a new constitution, the National Assembly had already taken the hardest steps. In Paine's mind, the country was bound for a bright future by embracing republicanism and entering into a fraternal brotherhood of liberty that all mankind was entitled to.

Paine finished his manuscript on January 29, 1791, his 54th birthday. Liberated from his lengthy streak of writing, he took to celebration in the lounge of the Angel Inn with his good friend Clio Rickman, whom he had known since his days in Lewes. The following day, he brought the completed manuscript to Joseph Johnson, a well-known London bookseller and publisher, who agreed to print its initial run to coincide with both George Washington's birthday and the opening of Parliament on February 22.[374]

While a mass audience of readers anticipated the release of Paine's pamphlet, so too did agents of the crown. If *Common Sense* stood as any precedent, his forthcoming work was guaranteed to disprove the precepts of hereditary monarchy, repudiate England's civil religion, and cause commotion among British subjects. In the days following Paine's delivery of the manuscript to the publisher, Johnson was visited on several occasions by government officers, who likely threatened to charge him with crimes if he published the tract. At that point, only a small number of hardbound copies were ever printed and bound. Apprehending criminal prosecution and possible bankruptcy, Johnson ultimately agreed to terminate the print run on the very day it was completed.

Blindsided by the hurdle, Paine scrambled to find alternative publication avenues. After securing a loan from a friend, the penman was able to convince J.S. Jordan, a rival of Johnson's whose press was located on London's Fleet Street, to take on the project despite the legal risk. With a borrowed horse and cart, Paine hauled the unbound sheets of the Johnson printing to Jordan, who worked tirelessly to complete its publication.

Though the precise reasons are unknown, Paine then made hasty preparations to catalogue his work and leave London. It is known he wished to
arrange a French translation of the work as soon as possible, though it is
possible he also feared harassment by agents of the crown. He entrusted
the few copies of the hardbound Johnson version that existed to three
friends, each of whom agreed to protect them in the case of another publication blunder.

Regardless of the writer's precautions, Jordan came through, and the
90,000-word pamphlet materialized in England on March 13, barely two
weeks after his agreement with Paine. Soon after printing, London publications reported that some of the original prose had been altered, but in
truth it had been copied exactly. The work was originally sold for three
shillings, approximately $15 in 2021 currency.[375] The relatively high price,
which amounted to about a single day's wages for a tradesman, was widely
considered a severe impediment to its potential audience.

Upon its release, *The Rights of Man* resounded like a cannon volley
throughout the public debate in England and the continent. By far, the
work was the most anticipated and exhaustive anti-monarchical treatise
that had ever been written and published in English. Read by Tories and
Whigs alike, it was snapped up by the political class, but it also sold well
among tradesmen, political dissidents, and indisposed commoners, many
of whom had little reason to read the work but for Paine's unique gift at
connecting with them. While hundreds of pamphlets had set out to refute
Burke, it was Paine's that proved best able to do so. Its original printing
was soon followed by versions that made their way to France, Holland,
and Prussia. In spite of its steep price, demand for the tract was so great
that an underground network of printers churned out pirated versions of it,
and many strides were taken to read it aloud to the illiterate.[376]

Paine's radical ally Charles James Fox, the leader of the New Whigs in
British Parliament, declared soundly that *The Rights of Man* "seems as
clear and simple as the first rules of arithmetic." Virginian aristocrat Richard Henry Lee loved the work so much, he commended the author for remaining "so thoroughly in republican in sentiment and fearless in the expression of his opinions." Likewise, the esteemed Scottish poet Thomas
Campbell remarked that the penman "strongly answered at the bar of public opinion all the arguments of Burke," and professed admiration for "the

shrewdness and courage of Thomas Paine." While in France, future president James Monroe professed a commitment to "the equal and inalienable rights of man," and declared that the country would emerge "in the enjoyment of peace, liberty and independence" just as the United States had. His Virginian peer James Madison also praised the work as "a written defense of the principles on which that [our] government is based." French revolutionary heroine Madame Roland wrote that Paine's work made him "one of those celebrated foreigners whom the nation ought with eagerness to adopt."[377]

Paine's like-minded friend Thomas Jefferson, who had returned to the United States to become Washington's secretary of state, ordered several copies of the tract. As he began to upbraid American nationalists for their proclivity to discard republicanism in favor of a more British-oriented monarchy in the United States, he praised *The Rights of Man* for countering the dominant Tory narrative. He was "extremely pleased ... that something is at length to be publicly said against the political heresies which have sprung up among us." He informed Paine that Americans "love what you write and read it with delight." Jefferson helped circulate its original publication in the United States, and expressed "no doubt our citizens will rally a second time round the standard of Common Sense."[378]

Of course, Paine's diatribe did not receive universal acclaim. London's *Monthly Review* blasted the pamphlet as "desultory, uncouth, and inelegant," a work containing "nothing new or ingenious" that was stylistically "awkward, ungrammatical, and often debased by vulgar phraseology." British linguist Brooke Boothby, well known to London's political establishment, alleged it was "written with the logic of shoemakers and the metaphysics of barbers," and filled with "quackery and ignorance." The renowned British lawyer Samuel Romilly assaulted it as "inaccurate in point of grammar, flat where he attempts wit, and often ridiculous when he indulges himself in metaphors."[379]

As word spread of the pamphlet, the presses could not keep up with demand, even at the high price; by May 50,000 copies had been sold, an extraordinary reception that outsold Burke's counterpart by several times.[380] Furthermore, the work spoke to commoners in a way that enabled them to begin to develop basic political consciousness. For the first time in England, one did not require a formal education in constitutional law, legal history, or even current affairs to be persuaded to adopt a position on the most pressing matter of the day. It took only Paine, with *The Rights of Man* as his instrument, to awaken a new class to Whig philosophy and persuade them to support individual rights, defend republican government, and challenge the cornerstones of hereditary monarchy.

In the aftermath of its release, several other pamphlets defending the French Revolution and the radical political ideas it represented continued to appear. Nevertheless, none of them earned as much praise and readership and thus none surpassed *The Rights of Man* as the predominant counterattack to Burke's work. The pamphlet had become an overnight, international sensation, and its popularity was matched by the controversy it created. Paine's overt assault on English political convention, and especially the kingdom's monarchical arrangement, attracted perpetual indignation. As Tories expended great effort to attack Paine's work from every imaginable philosophical angle, British authorities considered charging Paine with sedition.

However, various London publications reported that, after several organized rallies in support of the pamphlet, the law enforcement apparatus of Britain ultimately decided against prosecution. According to one account, even the kingdom's Tory prime minister, William Pitt, who was at the same time organizing a mass propaganda campaign to promote the empire's orderly society and denigrate the unhinged French lunatics, admitted the merits of the work. "Tom Paine is quite in the right, but what am I to do? As things are, if I were to encourage his opinions we would have a bloody revolution," he lamented.[381] It is possible that the British government was worried that any legal retaliation against Paine would merely catapult the popularity of his work to newfound heights. As it turned out, its success required no governmental assistance.

While Paine had labored carefully to avoid outright sedition under England's common law, *The Rights of Man* was unmistakably irreverent in style and certainly ventured into realms rarely visited by polemicists. Indeed, biographer John Keane recognized that Paine succeeded in outflanking Burke "by replacing the accepted courtly standards of literary excellence with the vulgar and quotable language of common speech."[382] He astutely crafted a narrative with vernacular familiar to the common man rather than the landed class, and translated the style of *Common Sense* to fit European sensibilities. More than just a work that condemned the sitting government, the pamphlet challenged both the necessity and legitimacy of the institutions considered most integral to the underpinnings of British society in general. By all accounts, Paine's pamphlet made him a true firebrand in Europe.

Freed from legal turmoil, Paine began an ambitious marketing campaign for his pamphlet to make it accessible to wider audiences, particularly those who could not afford the work at its three-shilling price. Paine worked tirelessly to ensure broader distribution in English-speaking areas outside of Britain and France, even when it meant foregoing royalties. Because "the high price precluded the generality of people from purchasing" the work, Paine also worked to make the pamphlet more accessible "by printing small editions in the country, of only a few thousands each." By "giving the public a cheap edition," he wrote, every man could "read and judge for himself, not only of the merits and demerits of the work, but of the matters therein contained, which relate to his own interest and happiness."[383]

After establishing the new method to make his tract more affordable in England, Paine sought to do the same in France, the new republic where his enthusiasm was now clearly focused. He returned there in April, and took up lodging with a friend. In Paris, he frequently met with Gouverneur Morris, with whom he shared a tepid friendship from their time campaigning for the congressional impost tax. However, that which remained of their relationship likely soured after Morris drifted toward the pro-British outlook the Federalists hoped to adopt, and confessed to Paine that he had supported his removal as secretary for the Committee of Foreign Affairs. While Morris admitted the presence of "good things" in *The Rights of Man*, he found as much value in Burke's *Reflections on the Revolution in France*.[384]

As a result of his new connections with France's political class, Paine was made a guest of the state, and took up residence in Versailles Palace in May. There, he conversed regularly with key figures in the National Assembly, and with his good friend the Marquis de Lafayette, who remained in charge of the country's national guard. While in France, Paine conceived plans to write a follow-up to *The Rights of Man* that would tackle the political situation in Britain and carry the tentative title of "King-ship." Fully captivated by the budding French republic, and viewing its revolutionary genesis as an outgrowth of its American precursor, Paine could not understand how eminent figures of Europe could continue to favor the model of hereditary monarchy over republicanism. Pitt's govern-ment in Britain stood at the precipice of disaster, he believed, while the advent of constitutional monarchy in France would mark the beginning of a bright, new golden epoch in the West.

Regardless of Paine's intention to expand *The Rights of Man*, his deci-sion to dedicate the work to George Washington seemed to have irritated the sitting president. By linking his work to Washington's good name, he was accused of engaging in a political scheme to undermine the potential of a closer relationship between the United States and Britain, an objective that Federalists in the United States were wholly committed to. Washing-ton failed to reply to Paine's gift of 50 copies of the work for nearly a year, and his response was tepid at best. Attributing the delay to the obligations of his public office, he expressed a vague commitment to "the happiness of mankind" such that the "enlightened policy of the present age" would "lay the foundation of happiness for future generations." Even still, he gave no thanks to Paine for his dedication and wrote nothing of the ideas contained within his immensely popular work. As Paine biographer David Freeman Hawke wrote, the letter was "cautious and evasive, coming from one who nine years earlier had joyfully helped Paine set afire air stirred up from the bottom of a river."[385] The letter marked the beginning of a schism between the two friends that would be never be mended.

Without warning, Paine awoke in the heart of Paris one June night to the panicked calls of Lafayette. As he left his bedside, he realized the com-motion extended beyond the civil officers and to commoners who stood in large groups around the government center. As he soon discovered, King Louis and his wife had fled their residence at the Tuileries in the dead of night. In attempt to quell the tensions, a proclamation of the National As-sembly was read to the crowd to assure them that the drafting of a consti-tution would commence regardless of the king's presence. On the street, Paine ran into the Scottish radical Thomas Christie, with whom he conversed for some time. "You see the absurdity of monarchical govern-ments," Paine told Christie, in "a whole nation disturbed by the folly of one man."[386]

That night, Paine received his first taste of true French revolutionary fervor. As the mob formed in the streets, he was mistaken for a royal ab-solutist because he had left his hat decorated by the French tricolor—garb possessed by all supporters of the National Assembly to distinguish them from aristocrats—in his room. In an age where the appearance of interna-tional celebrities was not known to all, the agitators began calling for his execution, and some began preparations to hang him from the nearest lamppost. Paine's life was saved only by the deeds of the bilingual Chris-tie, who recognized him and spoke in his favor.[387] Narrowly avoiding death had shaken Paine, giving him a rude awakening on the realities of the country's political transition.

Though Paine had scoffed at Burke's suggestion the political upheaval in France brought forth "bands of cruel ruffians and assassins" that un-leashed "all the unutterable abominations of the furies of hell," the writer had had now witnessed the same firsthand.[388] The random street violence, which Paine had portrayed in *The Rights of Man* as isolated and unremark-able for its time and place, foreshadowed the massacres to come two years later in the Reign of Terror.

When the uproar settled, it was learned that Louis, his wife Marie An-toinette, and their immediate family had left Paris entirely. Constrained by his close proximity to the most radical revolutionary fervor, the king was continually under the thumb of the radical reformers who sought to chip away at the French absolutism. His situation had led him to make several concessions—such as the acceptance of the Declaration of the Rights of Man and of the Citizen—that he clearly reviled. By absconding from Paris, the king aimed first to escape his immediate living circumstances, and sec-ond to band together with royalist forces in the countryside. His ultimate objective was to reassert his authority as king by igniting a large-scale counter-revolution against the National Assembly and its sympathizers. The king was encouraged to take this route by his wife, who hatched a plan with the help of her staff to relocate to the eastern frontier.

At the Tuileries Palace, the king left behind a document that explicitly rejected reforms that emerged in the wake of the Storming of the Bastille and March of Versailles. Instead, the screed expressed a desire to entertain those instigated by the Third Estate in its original inception. The royal family's private correspondence made clear, however, that they sought a full restoration of the old Bourbon monarchy without any intention of capitulation to radical reforms.[389] After the king's words were published in Paris, passions erupted, with a swell of street violence and roaming mobs desecrating signs bearing the name of the king. As commander of the French national guard, Lafayette was harangued, and radicals even accused him of aiding and abetting the king's departure.[390]

In their haste, Louis and his family made it all the way to Varennes, a small village along the Aire River near the border of the Austrian Netherlands. They aspired to reach the royalist stronghold of Montmédy, but had stopped in the town to change horses and to make contact with their planned escort. As rumors that the Austrians had already invaded the country on behalf of the king spread through Paris, Louis exchanged words with local peasants himself while incognito. After hearing of the incident, the area's local postmaster recognized the king from a portrait in his possession. After gaining confirmation from a local judge, the king and his family were arrested and brought back to Paris in a closely-guarded carriage procession.

As the royal carriage reached Paris, crowds of Parisians stood in silence. The masses continued to wear their pro-National Assembly hats as the procession passed, and the traditional cheers and praises that often accompanied such a spectacle were nowhere to be heard. Popular perceptions of the king had completely shifted, and both royalists and radicals struggled over the question of how to best respond to the situation. The staunchest constitutional monarchists began a propaganda campaign purporting that Louis had merely been kidnapped, but struggled to maintain the narrative because the king had left a detailed letter that was widely printed. The few radical republicans—a small group that included Paine—lacked the political capital to realistically set the monarchy on a course of destruction. Despite the public uproar against the king, monarchists of all stripes immediately engaged in damage control to justify the Flight to Varennes, as it came to be called. Even the most radical members of the same body promoted a constitutional republic that featured a hereditary monarch as its executive.[391]

Never one to be surpassed by others when it came to adopting the most radical position imaginable, Paine hastily professed that the king's recent act of departure from Paris had left the nation with a republic by default. "He has abdicated the throne having fled from his post," he wrote, making him "equally unworthy of the important functions that had been delegated to him." As a result, he continued, French subjects were released from any type of fealty to the monarch:

> In every sense in which this question can be considered, the reciprocal obligation which subsisted between us is dissolved. He no longer holds any authority. We owe him no longer obedience. We see in him no more than an indifferent person; we can regard him only as Louis Capet.

Though he had previously exhibited a soft spot for Louis relative to monarchs he considered more despotic, the recent circumstances were to Paine indefensible. The Flight to Varennes was only the most recent passage in the chronicle of monarchical oppression. "The history of France presents little else than a long series of public calamity," Paine wrote, "which takes its source from the vices of kings; we have been the wretched victims that have never ceased to suffer either for them or by them."[392] He would never again thank the king for supporting the American states in their struggle for independence, or extol him for his kindness and moderation.

As it turned out, Paine's manifesto was the forerunner to a grand shift in France away from constitutional monarchy and toward unadulterated republicanism. With the help of a recently-formed Society of Republicans—which Paine founded alongside four of France's most ardent partisans—he launched a grassroots campaign to win the hearts and minds of Parisians to his cause. The "Republican Proclamation" he authored was spread throughout all corners of Paris in spoken and written form, and was now met with receptive eyes for the first time. According to the writer's translator and confidant, the newly-converted republican and self-described "impulsive nobleman" Achille François du Châtelet, the two set out "to change the governmental system in France" even without the assistance of the most anti-monarchical leaders in the National Assembly. "The idea of a republic had previously presented itself to no one," his friend wrote, "but some of the seed sown by the audacious hand of Paine were now budding in leading minds."[393]

Paine and Châtelet's well-distributed poster caused a public stir, and inspired some debate in the National Assembly, where few members were willing to embrace such a radical position of eliminating the king from France's political system entirely. The principal spokesman in the legislature for constitutional monarchy, Emmanuel-Joseph Sieyès, even took to the presses to deride Paine's argument in the city's leading newspaper, *Le Moniteur Universel*. Pure republicanism was incompatible with the country's circumstances, he alleged, and the liberty of citizens was better protected by a monarchy than a republic. Paine responded by challenging Sieyès to a pamphlet battle on the subject of constitutional monarchy versus republicanism, but the statesman declined and the contest between the two never came to fruition.[394] Sieyès' sentiments found favor in the National Assembly, but ran against the general outlook of commoners. The nation was now in crisis, wholly divided on the king's place in France's political future.

In the end, the Flight to Varennes backfired against the king enormously. Rather than free him from the bonds of inner-Paris scrutiny, it only created a schism between him and the indisposed. Those who sat on the fence between French republicanism and royalism were now openly suspicious of the king, if not opposed to his agenda outright. Gradually, Parisians were persuaded of Paine's assertion that "an office which is the reward of birth," was "in the very nature of things, an absurdity." Despite his newfound animosity for the king, he insisted that France would not stoop to "a spirit of revenge against a wretch who has dishonored himself," and would assure the personal safety of Louis and his family.[395]

To the detriment of royalists, the queen's familial connection to Austria also incited rumors that the Flight to Varennes was actually the work of an Austro-Bourbon conspiracy to safeguard continental monarchy in Europe. For the first time, the prospect of a Europe-spanning royal alliance against the National Assembly now seemed a distinct possibility. Those who still supported the king cited the danger as reason to restore the king to his rightful authority, while those who opposed him invoked the same as reason to restrain his authority. In either case, the king's base of support dwindled from what it once was, both among commoners and politicians. The king's indiscretion in the summer of 1791 was, by all accounts, a critical juncture of the French Revolution—a point of no return for the Bourbon dynasty.

As the chaos played out in France, Paine returned to England, where he intended to finish the second portion of *The Rights of Man*. Republican fervor was spreading throughout Europe, partially due to his own deeds, and he desired to keep fanning its flames in Britain. The first volume of *The Rights of Man* was selling a higher rate than any other political book before it, and its author's return was met with the interest of both friends and enemies. The newfound enthusiasm for republicanism in the country, largely stimulated by Paine himself, was reminiscent of the final days of King Charles I and the rise of the Commonwealth of England in the middle of the 17th century. At the same point, the British government under William Pitt enacted a massive campaign against republicanism. Backlash culminated in riots on Bastille Day, where the homes of many royal dissenters—including Paine's friend Joseph Priestley—were invaded, ransacked, and burned to the ground.

Paine took up residence again in London with Clio Rickman, where he did his best to keep a low profile despite his celebrity status. Paine's arrival was soon met with the publication of an antagonistic biography commissioned by the crown and written by George Chalmers, a Scottish Tory under the pseudonym "Francis Oldys." Beyond revealing Paine's low-born background as a lowly staymaker, the work portrayed the man as a corrupt excise officer, pitiful husband, and wicked atheist. Moreover, it blasted Paine's writing style and berated his usage of grammar in *The Rights of Man*.[396] Regardless, Chalmers' work failed to extinguish the fire that was the pamphlet's incredible popularity in Britain, and Paine, perhaps uncharacteristically, decided not to respond to the assault upon his reputation and writings.

As the penman was coming to grips with his new status as a public figure in Britain, France stood at a political crossroads of the highest stakes. Just as before Louis' dramatic escape from Paris, a committee within the National Assembly began drafting France's first republican constitution. Pitted against each other, rival factions differed greatly in regard to powers of the king, continuance of noble privileges, organization of French districts, citizenship requirements, legislative structure, and

other matters. Though many maintained their own preferences for the document, the king's theatrics clearly emboldened the radicals to institute
sweeping, pro-republican changes. Despite the efforts of Paine and his
friends, however, it remained apparent that the body was unwilling to discard its king.

Before the drafting process concluded, the National Assembly issued a
declaration that Louis would retain the throne under a constitutional monarchy. To ardent republicans, the announcement was taken as an absolute
betrayal, unleashing a renewed season of protest and street violence. Republicans began an arduous mission to persuade the National Assembly to
remove the king, and Lafayette's national guard was placed on high alert.
On July 17, a crowd of about 50,000 gathered to sign the petition at the
Champ de Mars, a large public gathering space in the center of Paris. Using
the presence of isolated trespassers as justification, the mayor of Paris instituted martial law, and soldiers dispersed the group of protesters.

For a time, it seemed as if the clamor had been suffocated entirely. That
was, of course, until a much bigger mob, much more organized and infur-
iated than the first, began to approach the Champ de Mars again the same
afternoon. The gigantic crowd of 20,000 was now led by the daunting
Georges Danton, leader of the populist Cordeliers Club. They brought with
them a new petition that explicitly declared Louis a traitor and fugitive,
and rejected his standing as monarch in the new French system. Lafayette
again attempted to disperse the new mob, firing warning shots into the air
after stones were thrown at guardsmen. No order to fire into the crowd was
given, but shots rang out nonetheless, perhaps because of a breakdown in
communication. When the dust settled, 50 random Parisians lay dead on
the street, and public outcry exploded yet again. The radical presses denounced the guardsmen for what was portrayed as a public execution, and
Lafayette was soon made into the common villain of the people for his role
in the incident.

The event was followed by a reactionary campaign of prosecution
against the protesters. Two hundred radicals were arrested for their involvement, with Danton hastily escaping to London for a time until the
commotion blew over. Without a doubt, the circumstances forced those on
the fence—both in and out of the National Assembly—to choose between
two sides of an ever-widening political division. Those who blamed the

crown for the bloodshed sided with Paine and the radicals, while those who blamed the mob for the same disaster cast their lot with the moderates promoting constitutional monarchy. For the time, though, the latter group won out in the halls of the National Assembly—which was putting the final touches on the country's first constitution.

Ultimately, the French Constitution of 1791 instituted a unicameral legislature that favored democracy over intra-legislative checks. The document abolished "irrevocably the institutions which were injurious to liberty and equality of rights," and eradicated all noble privileges. Each citizen was afforded the ability "to speak, write, print, and publish his opinions without having his writings subject to any censorship or inspection before their publication." Religious oath requirements were eliminated completely, and the free exercise of religion was guaranteed to all. The king's policymaking prerogative was curtailed significantly by the imposition of a suspensive—rather than absolute—veto power that allowed the will of the assembly to override his opposition after two legislative sessions. The boundaries apportioning French districts for centuries were erased, replaced with a new scheme that served the administrative convenience of the central government. In nearly every way, the framework completely uprooted France's Ancien Régime and replaced it with a constitutional monarchy that limited the overall power of the king.

Soon after the constitution's adoption, the National Assembly imposed a self-denying ordinance devised by Maximilien Robespierre, an eloquent lawyer and rising star of the Jacobin Club. Under the provision, all members of the National Assembly were strictly disqualified from election to the first sitting of the legislature under the new constitution. Supporters of Robespierre promoted the effort as a method to check the ambitions of power-seekers, while his enemies portrayed it as a crafty scheme to perpetuate the revolutionary crusade beyond the confines of the government apparatus. In either case, the measure guaranteed that those who had the most vested interest in seeing the constitution succeed—the architects of the document—would be completely unable to defend it from perversion. Moreover, it triggered the rise of powerful political clubs in Paris, which all but assured a more radical turn for the revolution.

Unfortunately for Paine and his ideological brethren, the new constitution meant the opportunity to rid France of monarchy had come and gone.

However, this fact hardly softened his resolve. "I am the declared, open, and intrepid enemy of that which is called monarchy," along with "the evils with which monarchy has scattered over the earth," he professed. In the days he spent working on the sequel to *The Rights of Man*, he sometimes displayed the same intensity at clubs of Englishmen that supported the French Revolution, including the Friends of Universal Peace and Liberty in London. While far more gifted with his hand than he was with his voice, he belted out a speech that was quintessential, unhinged Paine. "We congratulate the French nation for having laid the axe to the root of tyranny," he boasted, "and for erecting government on the sacred hereditary rights of man." Without stopping there, he reminded the cheering crowd of the cornerstone of his radical gospel, the "indefeasible right to constitute and establish such government for itself as best accords with its disposition, interest, and happiness." After all, British subjects were "oppressed with a heavy national debt, a burthen of taxes, and expensive administration of government," all plagues that were sustained by "invented wants of courtly extravagance, ambition, and intrigue."[397] As the crown saw it, his words bordered upon incitement of insurrection against the kingdom, and even some of Paine's closest political allies feared for his safety.

In the summer of 1791, Edmund Burke released a brief response to *The Rights of Man*, which also served as a rejoinder to those who had recently expelled him from the Whig Party. The short pamphlet aimed to vindicate his position on the French Revolution, but dismissed Paine's arguments without confronting them directly. "I will not attempt in the smallest degree to refute them," he wrote. Nevertheless, Burke took the opportunity to imply support for the British crown to counteract Paine's doctrine through criminalization. True opposition "will probably be done (if such writings shall be thought to deserve any other than the refutation of criminal justice) by others, who may think with Mr. Burke," he warned. However, the statesman did assert that Paine's belief that all free people had the right to alter or abolish their government was shared by the most traitorous insurrectionists in British history—namely Jack Cade, Robert Kett, and Jack Straw. In addition, he ridiculed the French Constitution of 1791 for not living up to Paine's standards, and suggested the document was unalterable and therefore bound French posterity forever to its dictums. In reality, Title VII of the same document clarified the amendment process.[398]

As Paine won prestige within Britain's revolutionary circles, he no longer feared prosecution by British authorities for his diatribes against monarchy. This was because the crown had already blundered by giving the subject consideration, thus giving notoriety to Paine's writings. The king's agents had "already tried all the under-plots of abuse and scurrility without effect," he wrote, and bungled their operation against him in such a way as to "make the work and the author the more famous." Surely, the government would not make the same mistake and propel his sales even more. In a letter to William Short, then serving as the United States Ambassador to France, Paine committed to making the second part of *The Rights of Man* even more objectionable to the Tories. "I have but one way to be secure in my next work which is, to go further than in my first," he professed.[399]

Around the same time, insurrection of African slaves broke out in the French colony of Saint-Dominique. Within days, the masses had killed their masters, seized substantial French property, and taken over the Northern Province, the colony's commercial hub. The slaves of Saint-Dominique passed a decree that demanded liberation from slavery, but stopped short of declaring independence from France. Even Paine's intense affection for French republicanism could not stop him from siding with the revolutionaries. The ordeal was "the natural consequence of slavery and must be expected everywhere," he claimed.[400] In several ways, the violent outburst foreshadowed the arbitrary carnage that would come to define the French Revolution's next years. Rebels engaged in street assaults, desecrated huge swaths of property, and even placed the heads of French children upon pikes to be carried by insurgents.

As he labored to finish his manuscript for *The Rights of Man, Part Second*, Paine boasted to friends that he hoped to maximize its political effects by releasing it to coincide with the upcoming sitting of Parliament. His plan was to reissue 100,000 copies of the first part alongside the same number of the new offering. He also hoped to price the works at the incredibly cheap rate of six pence each in order to reach a mass audience and thus infuriate the British authorities.[401] Though Paine was fearless in his plans for publication, publishers themselves were far more hesitant. Joseph Johnson warned friends in the business not to take on the task, and Paine's former publisher J.S. Jordan refused to allow his name to be printed on the title page for fear of prosecution, forcing the writer to look elsewhere.[402]

After a series of discussions, an admirer of Paine's writings, Thomas Chapman, agreed to publish the work. The penman provided a portion of the manuscript that was completed so that Chapman could begin work while he finished drafting the remainder. As the days passed, two major factors plagued the business arrangement between the two. In particular, Paine and Chapman began to quarrel after the latter requested to purchase the copyright of the work, gradually offering Paine successively greater sums of money to do so. The writer refused, realizing that such a sale would allow the publisher to alter the work's contents and treat his cherished project as if it were merely fodder for profit rather than a virtuous instrument to spread the precepts of liberty throughout Europe. After reading the manuscript, Chapman also grew apprehensive under the impression that British agents would treat the writings as seditious libel, drawing their disdain for Paine to himself as well.[403]

Unwilling to risk his business and livelihood, Chapman decided to break the news to Paine that he was no longer willing to publish the work. He did so during dinner with Paine, who had been drinking alcohol, and the revelation led to a fierce argument between the two. The two men insulted each other, with Paine departing Chapman's home in a livid state. Though he likely lacked soundness of mind at the time, the episode must have appeared to Paine as a stroke of déjà vu, given that Joseph Johnson's last-second decision not to print the first volume manifested in such a similar manner. Paine tried to reconcile with Chapman the next morning, profusely apologetic for his outburst. Even so, Chapman refused to reconstitute their agreement, leading the author to conclude that royal agents had already persuaded him not to publish the work.[404]

The printing feud made it impossible for Paine to finish the work on schedule for the opening of Parliament, and the writer took earnest strides to protect his work from confiscation, just as he had the year prior. After bargaining over royalties, he eventually enlisted the assistance of Jordan once more to print the second volume. Key to their contract was Paine's promise to assume all legal liability for the contentious manuscript's publication. He was, after all, completely unwilling to alter his treasured prose simply to strike a more moderate tone. "It is against the whole hell of monarchy that I have declared war," he announced.[405] Whatever the costs, he would willingly endure them in order to broadcast his ideas to the world. Jordan and his crew worked tirelessly to crank out copies, and the pamphlet was officially released to the world on February 17, 1792. With its publication, the sharpest and most brilliant blade yet was thrust into the heart of British monarchy.

Paine dedicated *The Rights of Man, Part Second* to his friend Lafayette, whose reputation had suffered greatly by the Champ de Mars Massacre. "I feel a pleasure in presenting you this small treatise," he wrote, "in gratitude for your services to my beloved America, and as a testimony of my esteem for the virtues, public and private, which I know you possess." A constant theme that ran through Paine's writings, indeed, was that the causes of American and French independence were inextricably linked. He expressed that the culmination of American independence led him to "sit serenely down and enjoy the calm," but recent events in France convinced him to carry the banner for the same principles once again. "But when principle, and not place, is the energetic cause of action, a man, I find, is everywhere the same."[406]

In the preface, Paine asserted his original intention to extend the first volume of his work to account for the subject matter of the second, but chose to conclude it as he had so as not to "make the work too bulky, or contract my plan too much." Because of recent happenings in both Britain and France, he had gained a desire to expound upon the concepts he previously explored. "A great field was opening to my view of mankind by means of the French Revolution," he wrote. Paine noted his desire to hold the second volume until Burke fulfilled his promise to elaborate upon the philosophical differences between the French and English constitutions, a commitment he explicitly disdained his last pamphlet. Mockingly, Paine claimed the matter was a subject Burke "certainly would not have omitted, had the comparison been in his favor." As the firebrand proclaimed, "I am enough acquainted with Mr. Burke to know that he would he would if he could." Though Burke claimed to have "done his part," Paine countered that he had not done so. Instead, he wrote, "he started the controversy, he gave the challenge, and has fled from it."[407]

Paine responded to Burke's implication that his work should be banned by the state rather than answered with a counterargument by claiming such an outlook was inconsistent with liberty generally, and freedom of expression specifically:

> It would be an act of despotism, or what in England is called arbitrary power, to make a law to prohibit investigating the principles, good or bad, on which such a law, or any other is founded ... The defects of every government and constitution, both as to principle and form, must, on a parity of reasoning, be as open to discussion as the defects of a law, and it is a duty which every man owes to society to point them out.

Burke's abandonment of reasoned debate caused Paine to view his former friend as an appendage of the worst aspects of British monarchy—its potential to engage in arbitrary behavior and infringe upon individual rights. "The right of forming and reforming, generating or regenerating constitutions and governments" could not be made, "without invading the general rights of that country" into "subjects for prosecution."[408]

Paine's protest against monarchy's tendency to suppress political dissent, far from an impulsive retort within the context of a personal feud, was to him a cause of colossal importance. Both the French Revolution and the separation from monarchy in United States had demonstrated, at least as he saw it, that societies flourished more where individuals were the free to express their ideas openly. "Mankind are not now to be told they shall not think, or they shall not read," and any attempt to punish authors for controversial material was "not worth the trouble of prosecution," because such a decree "cannot amount to a prohibition of reading." Certainly, Paine believed the creator had placed within man the tendency for curiosity, and any law intending to reverse that quality could never contravene the laws of nature. Even a twelve-man jury, he wrote, could not make such a judgment in good conscience.[409]

To begin his outright assault on monarchy, Paine appealed to the plight of English subjects who had suffered under the institution for centuries. They had been oppressed "by men assuming to be leaders," exploiting them for their liberty and property at every opportunity. It was therefore time to reject the crown's inclination "of stretching taxation to excess," and to "dismiss all those songs and toasts which are calculated to enslave, and operate to suffocate reflection." To do so would require significant political changes, which could be accomplished "without convulsion or rage," Paine wrote. However, he danced verbally around the subject of whether such revolutionary action should be taken in England. "It is not worth making changes or revolutions, unless it be for some great national benefit," and doing so would attract strong and natural opposition.[410]

To Paine, the greatest example of political optimism was to be found in America's transition from a colonial branch of the English crown to an independent republic. Indeed, a common refrain of Paine's worldview was his belief that liberation from monarchy was a cause that belonged to all peoples on earth. By actualizing its independence, then, America "made a stand, not for herself only, but for the world, and looked beyond the advantages herself could receive." For the first time in recent history, the United States had contradicted the commonly held notion that monarchy was necessary for a society to flourish. Even while much of the country was occupied, Paine noted that "order and harmony were preserved as inviolate as in any country in Europe." The common belief that "the abolition of any formal government is the dissolution of society" was a blatant falsehood, on the contrary, a revolution against oppression "brings the latter closer together."[411]

The United States were to Paine a place where "concord, according to common calculation, would be least expected." This was because its inhabitants originated from other nations, spoke different languages, and practiced different religions. Nevertheless, Americans built a republican society where harmony thrived. "By the simple operation of constructing government on the principles of society and the rights of men, every difficulty retires." Paine noted that in the United States, "the poor are not oppressed, the rich are not privileged," commerce "is not mortified by the splendid experience of a court rioting at its expense," and "taxes are few, because government is just."[412] This rosy picture stood in stark contrast to the English monarchy, which he construed as a parasite feasting upon an ethical society.

Instead of being founded on laudable principles, the kingdoms of Europe were formed through the "total violation of every principle sacred and moral." According to Paine, conquest and usurpation had marked the origin of almost all modern governments, and the same governments devoted enormous energy to burying their brutish roots. The embarrassment that was the ruthless Norman Conquest—the true starting point of the present English monarchy—was the reason Tories placed so much emphasis on 1688 rather than 1066 as the country's genesis. In his mind, the fundamental difference between monarchy and republicanism became readily apparent. "The former supports itself by keeping up a system of war; the latter promotes a system of peace, as the true means of enriching the nation." While "the old is hereditary, either in whole or in part ... the new is entirely representative."[413] England would benefit greatly by emulating their American and French counterparts, and by casting aside their cruel schemes of subjugation, he argued.

One technique by which European monarchies relentlessly oppressed their subjects, Paine reasoned, was through gratuitous taxation; the more ambitious and absolute a monarchy was, the more destructive their schemes of taxation had proven. In such systems, "we still find the greedy hand of government thrusting itself into every corner and crevice of industry, and grasping the spoil of the multitude," he mourned. "Invention is continually exercised to furnish new pretenses for revenue and taxation," he wrote. Wealth-hungry monarchies view "prosperity as its prey, and permits none to escape without a tribute." Exacerbating the miseries of their subjects, Paine thought, was the propensity for monarchies to use punitive taxes to fuel wars of conquest:

> All the monarchical governments are military. War is their trade, plunder and revenue their objects. While such governments continue, peace has not the absolute security of a day ... This certainly is not the condition that heaven intended for man; and if *this be monarchy*, well might monarchy be reckoned among the sins of the Jews.

By taxing for the sake of empire, then, monarchies perpetuated a cruel cycle of tyranny that even threatened the very governments that viewed the taxes as their lifeline. "Excess and inequality of taxation, however disguised in the means," had the consequence of throwing the masses into "poverty and discontent," bringing them to "the brink of commotion."[414]

Certainly, a significant cause of both the English Civil Wars and the American War of Independence was the widespread indignance of those languishing under the burden they presented.

Paine reminded his readers that internal wars were encouraged by the hereditary nature of monarchy. "The civil wars which have originated from contested hereditary claims," he wrote, "are more numerous, and have been more dreadful, and of longer continuance, than those which have been occasioned by election." To validate this claim, he cited the long string of civil wars in France, the War of the Spanish Succession, disputes over hereditary officers of the Dutch Republic, and repeated clashes in England, such as those between the York and Lancaster families in the Wars of Roses. The abolishment of hereditary monarchy would naturally terminate the fiery passions of those ravaging their countries by wars over their favored successors, thought Paine.[415]

The Rights of Man, Part Second reiterated Paine's belief that "all hereditary government is in its nature tyranny," and that inheriting a government "is to inheriting people, as if they were flocks and herds." No government had the moral right to condemn successive generations to it, and all free people had the right to dispose of it. Allowing it to take hold over society was to roll the dice of nature, hoping for a good result in a world filled with both the benevolent and the cruel:

It indiscriminately admits every species of character to the same authority. Vice and virtue, ignorance and wisdom, in short, every quality good or bad, is put on the same level. Kings succeed each other, not as rationals, but as animals. It signifies not what their mental or moral characters are. Can we then be surprised at the abject state of the human mind in monarchical countries, when the government itself is formed on such an abject levelling system? It has no fixed character. Today it is one thing; to-morrow it is something else. It changes with the temper of every succeeding individual, and is subject to all the varieties of each. It is government through the medium of passions and accidents. It appears under all the various characters of childhood, decrepitude, dotage, a thing at nurse, in leading-strings, or in crutches. It reverses the wholesome order of nature. It occasionally puts children over men, and the conceits of nonage over wisdom and experience. In short, we

cannot conceive a more ridiculous figure of government, than hereditary succession, in all its cases, presents.

Indeed, the foothold of monarchy was a randomization mechanism by
which subjects could only hope for a palatable ruler rather than to take
control of their own authority to construct government on their own terms.
In an allusion that could easily apply to England, the "mental character"
of kings had proven to be "below the average of human understanding;
that one is a tyrant, another an idiot, a third insane, and some all three
together, it is impossible to attach confidence to it, when reason in man
has power to act." The throne was widely portrayed as an office of divine
importance, but yet one in which "any child or idiot may fill" without pre-
condition. "It requires some talents to be a common mechanic," Paine
wrote, "but to be a king requires only the animal figure of a man—a sort
of breathing automaton."[416] Such prose was the epitome of blasphemy to
Tories, who viewed hereditary line of succession as the most sacred and
indisputable of all the country's political foundations.

The "absurdity of hereditary government" could also be observed in the
descendants of famous men in any line of work. Among one's common
ancestors, "Is there scarcely an instance in which there is not a total reverse
of the character?" Paine asked. Even those with the same pedigree varied
greatly in their aptitude for certain talents, he claimed, which exposed the
folly of hereditary distinction in general. "How irrational then is the hereditary system," Paine heckled, "which establishes channels of power, in
company with which wisdom refuses to flow!" Man is "perpetually in contradiction with himself," he wrote, if he "accepts, for a king, or a chief
magistrate, or a legislator, a person whom he would not elect for a constable."[417]

A primary reason "the ancient governments present to us a miserable
picture of the condition of man," Paine thought, was because the concept
of representation had not developed until many years after the great ancient civilizations. Early democratic forms of government, such as those
of ancient Athens, where "people met and enacted laws … in the first person," degenerated not because they lacked hereditary monarchy, but because their governments became "unwieldy and impracticable" as they ex-

panded in territory and increased in population. Had frameworks of representation been invented and utilized in those times, he argued, there was no reason to believe that the development of monarchical or aristocratical governments "would ever have taken place." It only became possible for hereditary monarchies to take root, then, by exploiting the unsustainability of democracy in society that had grown too large for it to work efficiently. Paine contended that republican representation provided a panacea to the defects of democracy by "embracing and confederating all the various interests and every extent of territory and population" within a state.[418]

When it came to assessing the merits and shortcomings of various governments, nothing was more important to Paine than the source and distribution of power. All power exercised "must have some beginning," he wrote, and "must either be delegated or assumed." In their original inception, then, governments were compacts between sovereign individuals, where certain powers were delegated to a general agent for specific purposes. The act of delegating these powers did not represent a permanent abandonment of the same, and did not deprive the individual of all authority retained and undelegated. The adoption of an original compact among individuals, "each in his own personal and sovereign right," remarked Paine, was "the only mode in which governments have a right to arise, and the only principle on which they have a right to exist."[419] Consequently, government could only be a product of the original compact, and never be a sovereign party to it.

Of all countries, Paine believed the United States best exemplified his conception of social compact theory. This was because each of the original American states was formed through compacts among their inhabitants. Even though "each state acted independently of the rest, in forming its governments," all representatives were vested with the power to supplant their colonial authorities with new republican systems. After formation, each state sent delegates to Congress, which first served as a meeting place of delegates rather than a central government founded in usurpation. As Paine observed, Congress "was nothing more than a deputation from the legislatures of the several provinces, afterwards states; and had no other authority than what arose from common consent, and the necessity of its acting as a public body."[420]

By adopting the Articles of Confederation in 1781, the states produced a new compact, in which each state—rather than the newly formed government—acted as a separate party to the arrangement. This deed "was not an act of Congress," Paine insisted, "because it is repugnant to the principles of representative government that a body should give power to itself." Instead, the states were first provided a proposal that had no legal binding whatsoever, and no obligation of acceptance. It was only through the deliberate endorsement of each, he concluded, that "the states severally agreed with each other, and concentrated in Congress those powers." The writer reiterated this by pointing out that the states followed a similar pattern years later through the ratification of the Constitution, a process that played out in the halls of independently-elected ratification conventions in each state.[421]

In all three cases—the formation of the states, the adoption of the Articles of the Confederation, and the ratification of the Constitution—government never served as or pretended to be a party to the compacts. None were conceived in conquest or usurpation, but were instead created through the voluntary acceptance of individuals through their representatives. America walked a virtuous and unprecedented path, then, by denying government the ability "to make itself a party in any debate respecting the principles or modes of forming, or of changing, constitutions."[422]

In great contrast to the American experience, of course, was the constitution of England, which Paine viewed as a mere fable. This was because England's political system was founded in the Norman Conquest of 1066, an invasion and occupation driven by military force. In its genesis, the Norman system perpetuated hereditary aristocracy, featured no representation schemes by which subjects were represented in government, and accepted no limitations on its own authority. Rather than governing by representation, the Normans governed by coercion. The legacy of Norman rule was to the writer "a perpetual system of war and expense, that drains the country, and defeats the general felicity of which civilization is capable." Even measures cited by apologists to promote the country's constitutional order—such as the Magna Carta, various limitations upon the Stuart kings, and the English Bill of Rights—were mere "restrictions upon assumed power" rather than manifestations of the sovereign will of English subjects, Paine wrote.[423]

Paine went beyond merely defending his conceptions of liberty and acting as an apologist for the French revolutionaries and French republican system. In the conclusion of *The Rights of Man*, he prescribed a radical series of political reforms for England. The primary solution to rectify the woes presented by monarchy, he alleged, was the adoption of a national character, or constitution, which he depicted as an essential ingredient for a prosperous republican system. Rather than a series of traditions, statutes, and legal precedents, Paine's ideal constitution would be written in form. However, Paine made clear that such an instrument was not a fount of rights. "It is a perversion of terms to say that a charter gives rights," he wrote, because "rights are inherently in all inhabitants." Constitutional charters merely placed powers that were first exercised by man in a state of nature "in the hands of a few" for the purposes of protecting life, liberty, and property.[424]

According to Paine, the adoption of a written constitution in the country would "restrain and regulate the wild impulse of power," threaten the "irrational and tyrannical" nature of its law, and make the country's law enforcement apparatus less "vague and problematical." Such a framework would also prevent the gradual growth of government through legal precedent, a phenomenon that always created "a deeper policy than at first sight appears." Paine described how the invocation of precedents in England had led to a tragic cycle of oppression:

> Government by precedent, without any regard to the principle of the precedent, is one of the vilest systems that can be set up. In numerous instances, the precedent ought to operate as a warning, and not as an example, and requires to be shunned instead of imitated; but instead of this, precedents are taken in the lump, and put at once for constitution and for law.

As governments cited bad precedents to justify the continuance of bad policies, the same policies became that much tougher to restrict or abolish, he observed. "Either the doctrine of precedents is policy to keep a man in a state of ignorance," he wrote, "or is a practical confession that wisdom degenerates in governments as governments increase in age."[425] This phenomenon certainly flew in the face of Paine's conviction that all free people had the absolute moral authority to substitute a government of their choice for their archaic and repressive counterpart.

In addition to implementing an American-style written constitution, Britain should follow France's example and eliminate all aristocratic titles and privileges, Paine argued. "The evils of the aristocratical system are so great and numerous," and "so inconsistent with everything that is just, wise, natural, and beneficent," he declared, that all of virtuous character "wish to see such a system abolished." He also reiterated his desire to abolish primogeniture, a cause he first visited in the first volume of the *Rights of Man*. The system "occasions a waste of natural property," he wrote, by forcing the public to pay for the maintenance of lands not yet inherited by the oldest male child. Primogeniture also corrupted elections, he claimed, by the "overbearing influence" that resulted from the accumulation of aristocratic wealth in a small number of individuals.[426]

The major area in which Paine diverged from his shining American example was in his preference for a single-house national assembly rather than a bicameral system. He campaigned for the former as an institution that better reflected the voice of a country's citizens by preventing systematic resistance to the democratic impulse. A two-house system, on the other hand, featured checks and balances that improperly presumed one of the two houses was "wiser or better than the other," and therefore yielded outcomes where "the minority governs the majority." To avoid hasty policy-making, he suggested creating legislative partitions within a single house whereby laws could be debated in each part successively before a final debate and vote is taken.[427]

In the concluding section of his work, Paine asserted that England should enact a series of political reforms to improve the living conditions of the kingdom's impoverished class, a goal no doubt influenced by his own meager upbringing and personal struggles with poverty. Groundbreaking for their time, his plans had monumental policy implications and were at least as novel as his call to abolish hereditary monarchy. Before addressing the specifics of his aims, though, he made clear that his relief agenda should not be considered as mere charity, but instead as the natural inheritance of free people. As he explained, this was because all wealth that existed in the world was the original product of man's interaction with resources placed in the commons. Because God arranged the world in such a way—rather than grant wealth through individual acts of bestowment—a portion of wealth generated since the origins of man was the collective property of mankind generally.[428]

Rather than treat his readers to platitudes alone, Paine offered a rigorous analysis of England's demographics, complete with statistical references alongside each of his assessments. Paine's plain desire was to eliminate England's taxes for the poor entirely, absolving about two million of the kingdom's seven million inhabitants of all tax liability. In addition, 252,000 poor families would be paid from the public treasury an annual sum of money equal to double their current rate of taxation, a total of four million shillings. To fund this proposal, Paine recommended that Parliament slash military spending rather than impose additional taxes. In addition to raising the less fortunate to their proper dignity, Paine also claimed the relief would keep the poor out of jails and reduce the frequency of foreign wars.[429]

Another branch of Paine's aid program for the poor involved the creation of system for education funding. A just government "should permit none to remain uninstructed," he professed. His solution called for publicly-funded education for one million poor children. Specifically, each child under the age of 14 would receive four shillings per year, with a total projected cost of about 2.5 million shillings under Paine's assumption that it would apply to about 630,000 children per year. The penman invoked both humanitarian and economic justifications in defense of the proposal. As he saw it, the plan ensured that poor workers "with good natural genius" would not be hindered from the lack of "common education" when young. In turn, England as a whole would reap the benefits of the greater number of skilled workers. However, Paine admitted "public schools do not answer the general purpose of the poor," and intended to restrict the funding to "on the spot" programs that "enable the parents to pay the expenses themselves."[430]

To accompany his plans to provide financial relief the poor, Paine devised another program to grant financial support to the elderly. Paine divided the aged class into two groups—an "approach of age" group that included persons aged 50-59 and an "old age" group of individuals aged 60 and above. Those in the first category were to receive six shillings per year from the public treasury, while those in the second were to receive ten. Based on the author's estimates in regard to the number of persons in both groups, he predicted the total cost to be amount to about 1.1 million shillings annually. Anticipating the natural opposition to this plan, Paine insisted that public support of the elderly was "not of the nature of a charity but of a right." As he explained, this was because the taxes paid over the course of their lives—more than two pounds annually—should be returned to them in a way less egregious than the manner in which the crown typically returned public funding—through war and oppression. The "right" Paine called for, then, was a form of restitution for those languishing under England's oppressive system of taxation.[431]

Paine's public relief agenda also included ambitious plans for a workfare system, or "asylum," where poor individuals committing to at least three months of work would be provided lodging, meals, and a stipend for their labor. The work asylum system would require the construction of "two or more buildings" within a metropolis such as London, and would be designed to house 6,000 individuals at a time. The poorhouses and the associated hospitality would be funded by England's coal tax, which had been "so iniquitously and wantonly applied to the support of the Duke of Richmond" in the form of an aristocratic subsidy. With an asylum system to guide troubled poor toward a better future, "the crisis of a life of ruin" may be averted, and the commonplace "thefts and pilferings that lead to greater" offenses "may be prevented."[432]

In order to "relieve a great deal of instant distress," Paine's public aid package also called for one-time payments of 20 shillings to the parents of each newborn child and 20 shillings for each newly-married couple. Though it remains a bit unclear how he arrived at such figures, the author believed payments for only one-fourth of the country's 200,000 annual births would be claimed. Paine also saw need to commit £20,000 of public money to the funds of those who had died "at a distance from their friends." In his day, local churches typically covered such costs, so the stipulation was a device to free them from exorbitant costs and devote their funds to other essential purposes. "By relieving parishes from this charge, the sick stranger will be better treated," he wrote.[433]

To enable the funding of his welfare system, Paine pitched a drastic reformation of England's system of taxation. The kingdom's existing tax edifice, which extracted wealth from subjects through apportionment—taxes on land—and through impost—taxes on foreign goods. According to the writer, this apparatus should be abolished, and replaced by a progressive income tax that would tax total individual estates rather than land holding alone, a method designed to "restore justice among families by distribution of property." In addition, taxes on windows and houses should be eliminated entirely, as the tax fell "heavy on the middle class of people." In sum, the tax was calculated "to extirpate the overgrown influence arising from the unnatural law of primogeniture."[434]

In totality, Paine's public relief agenda was a prototype for Western civilization's first welfare state. An untested and radical set of proposals, no other political treatise had so thoroughly laid out such a plan before. He felt both morally and philosophically justified in his objective to create a more ideal world, and boasted of its potential:

> When it shall be said in any country in the world, my poor are happy; neither ignorance nor distress is to be found among them; my jails are empty of prisoners, my streets of beggars; the aged are not in want, the taxes are not oppressive; the rational world is my friend, because I am the friend of its happiness: when these things can be said, then may that country boast its constitution and its government.

Such widespread plans for a wealth redistribution system to aid the poor had never been formulated, even by Paine's most radical Whig friends or their philosophical forerunners. The pamphleteer insisted his motivations were "dictated by no passion but that of humanity," and denied receiving any financial bribes in return for proposing them. "Independence is my happiness," he wrote, "and I view things as they are, without regard to place or person; my country is the world, and my religion is to do good." Paine's carefully-developed aspirations to alleviate poverty were bold, radical, and without parallel world history.

As a whole, Paine's treatise championed three overarching notions—that monarchy was unfit to exist, that Britain deserved a true republican form of government with a written constitution, and that mankind's dignity and a society's morality was dependent upon a social welfare system to assist the poor. His narrative was filled with his trademark irreverence, in a form sure to catch fire once again with a class of commoners he so successfully reached in *Common Sense*. Soon enough, he was both a national pariah and hero of unrivaled character.

Just as *The Rights of Man, Part Second* was sent to booksellers, the newly appointed American Minister to France, Gouverneur Morris, recorded his growing contempt for Paine and his work. In so doing, he revealed much about the penman's outlook in contrast to his own:

> I read Paine's publication today, and tell him that I am really afraid he will be punished. He seems to laugh at this, and relies on the force he has in the nation. He seems to become every hour more drunk with self-conceit. It seems, however, that his work excites but little emotion, and rather raises indignation.[435]

Though many critics like Morris perceived Paine or his writings in such a way, thousands of readers eagerly anticipated the work in an unprecedented manner. The further he ventured into anti-monarchical thought, the more he galvanized fellow radicals and boosted his own notoriety. In a matter of time, the growing rift between Morris and Paine became a gaping chasm.

Paine's decision to forego royalties resulted in an extraordinary circulation of *The Rights of Man, Part Second*. Whig organizations supporting the French Revolution bought all copies they could find, and booksellers in London could not keep them stocked in their shelves. Even England's taverns, inns, and coffee houses purchased copies to read aloud to visitors. As in France, the pamphlet even inspired the activities of London's political clubs. The London Corresponding Society organized in support of his work, while the perhaps inaptly-named Friends of the People campaigned against it. Paine was even the focal point of a rift in the Society for Constitutional Information, which splintered into two competing factions over the work. A supporter of the group and prominent Whig reformer, Christopher Wyvill, even denounced Paine for stirring animosity "among the lower classes of the people, by holding out to them the prospect of plundering the rich."[436]

Paine's influence extended into France, Ireland, and the United States, where his recent and most fiery work attracted a cult following of supporters. "Throughout the British Isles," biographer John Keane wrote, "Paine's name became identical with the agitation, at a depth and with an intensity unheard of since the failed revolution of the 1640s" that had preceded the English Civil Wars.[437] The crown, of course, took notice. Almost immediately after its release, the government assigned Charles Ross to monitor Paine's movements in and around the house of Clio Rickman, where Paine was still staying. Now the lightning rod of England, it appeared as if those warning Paine of governmental retribution may soon be proven true.

At the time of its release, *The Rights of Man, Part Second* was by far the most widely read political work ever published. Its initial record-setting sales only grew exponentially as word of its publication spread throughout every corner of the British Empire, and multitudes of commoners and political militants went to great lengths to secure copies. Though sales figures are difficult to calculate, one account attests that 200,000 copies were sold in England, Wales, and Scotland within the first year of its release. The pamphlet also caught fire in Ireland, where its sentiments only exacerbated the growing animosity toward England, especially among poor Catholic dissenters. In the United States, it was well received by the Jeffersonian Republicans, who were deeply embroiled in a philosophical squabble with the Hamiltonian Federalists over the true legacy of the American Revolution and its implications for the fledgling republic. The work had even inspired John Quincy Adams, writing under the pseudonym "Publicola," to attack it in the presses. In England alone, the pamphlet sold 1.5 million copies by the time of Paine's death in 1809, an unprecedented reception for a work of its kind.[438]

In the spring of 1792, the revolutionary tides of Europe were shifting. As masses of Englishmen were swept into a fervor over *The Rights of Man,* Paine's political allies brought him out of London and into the village of Bromley to protect him from possible prosecution by the government. Meanwhile, France entered into a new phase of its revolution. Soon after the new Legislative Assembly was seated, tensions between the government and its European neighbors exploded. The Hapsburg monarch and Emperor of the Holy Roman Empire Leopold II, along with Prussian King

Frederick William II, assumed an aggressive posture toward the new republic. To the delight of French noble émigrés who fled the country, the two issued the Declaration of Pillnitz, which denounced France's internal antagonism toward King Louis XVI and swore to protect his safety. Soon afterward, Leopold summoned troops to the Franco-Austrian border. In combination with the Flight to Varennes, the deed sounded alarms within France that a royalist invasion was about to transpire.

French leadership perceived Austria as a regime in decline, whereas the Austrian leadership regarded France as a republic in disarray. Though Louis himself opposed an aggressive foreign policy, France's new minister of war, Louis Amalric, comte de Narbonne-Lara, believed it was necessary to restore the king's executive authority. The king responded to their disagreements by dismissing Narbonne-Lara and filling his department with Girondins, members of a political faction who had split from the Jacobins. At that point, the Girondins had risen to prominence under the guidance of Georges Danton and Jacques Pierre Brissot, both of whom worked tirelessly to exploit the optics of the Champ de Mars Massacre. In contrast to the other clubs, the loosely-connected faction of revolutionary reformers rallied around the cause of spreading the French Revolution beyond France itself. The merits of the revolution should be extended outward, they argued, for humanity to flourish under a new system of cooperation and harmony. According to Girondist dogma, these objectives should be secured at all costs, even it meant war against rival monarchies.

With these dynamics at play, the Girondin Ministry hyped the fissure between France and Austria. The king himself asked the new Legislative Assembly to declare war against Leopold's successor, Frances II, and the body complied overwhelmingly. Over the next months, disaster would plague the disorganized French military, and the botched war led indirectly to the downfall of Louis and the collapse of the French monarchy in general. Dissenters circulated rumors that the king, with the assistance of an aristocratic cabal, intended to lose the war in order to aid the Austrian plot to reassert his power as an absolute monarch. After initial setbacks against Austria, thousands of national guard forces were summoned to defend Paris, while a multitude of regulars were sent to the front lines.

Back in London, the government of William Pitt the Younger grew concerned that the waves of the French Revolution, aided by the penman's blockbuster pamphlet, would soon flood England. Sounding the alarm, Pitt issued a declaration that demanded an end to "wicked and seditious writings," a thinly-veiled reference to Paine's latest offering. It was the crown's intention to "carry the laws vigorously against such offenders." In a meticulous effort, the kingdom's law enforcement agents were dispatched throughout the country to gather information on the work's printing and distribution network. Paine's friend Charles James Fox blasted the operation in Parliament, decrying it as a treacherous exertion of royal overreach.[439] Indeed, Pitt had fired the first shots in what was to be an unrestrained information war.

The next days featured a relentless crusade of censorship against the penman and his words. Businesses that held public readings of *The Rights of Man* were forcibly closed, the activities of sympathetic political clubs were disrupted, and those selling and distributing the pamphlet were arrested and imprisoned. The publisher of the *Leicester Herald*, Richard Phillips, was charged, convicted, and sentenced to a year and a half in prison for selling the work. Government officers even conducted house-to-house "loyalty canvasses" where subjects were obliged to swear fealty to the king and against Paine's woeful brand of radicalism. In addition, the Pitt turned to the presses in attempt to combat the pamphlet's momentous influence, and public monies were illegally funneled to authors willing to condemn Paine's work.[440] Those courageous enough to defy the scheme blasted the government for its excesses, drawing comparisons to the despotism of England's most nefarious kings, such as John and Charles I.

When its intimidation campaign failed to yield immediate results, Pitt's government even went so far as to ramp up their efforts to put pressure on Paine's private life. In attempt to force him into voluntary exile, agents shadowed him wherever he went, and even attempted to pressure local taverns to deny him patronage. Beyond their attacks on his writings, the Tory presses excoriated him personally, and went to such lengths as to satirize his corset-making background and to portray him as a malformed hunchback in ragged attire. Another poster depicted him as part of a three-headed monster, united with "Sin" and "The Devil," with a list of "intercepted" instructions "from Satan to Citizen Paine." Tories held public ceremonies hanging him in effigy, with the mock corpse dangling for all to see. In one demonstration in Littletown, a man chopped to bits a wooden likeness of Paine so fiercely it made his hands bleed. In another display, a straw figurine of the man was stood against a lamppost, where it was "shot amidst tremendous hootings" of "church and king!" and "down with Tom Paine!"[441]

In May, the government indicted J.S. Jordan for having released the pamphlet, prompting Paine to beg the publisher to fight the charges in what was to be a highly visible trial. He went to such lengths to secure this outcome that he offered to pay all of Jordan's legal fees, and provide him the services of his own Whig lawyer and attorney general to the Prince of Wales, Thomas Erskine. To Paine's dismay, though, Jordan lacked the passion to contest the charges and stand tall in defense of his own provocative beliefs. Ultimately, rather than suffer the loss of his trade and personal well-being, he decided to plead guilty and pay a fine. Though he was disappointed, the penman did not hold Jordan's decision against him. "I make no objection against him for it," Paine wrote, taking the printer's guilty plea only as an admission he had published the work, not as a concession his musings were seditious.[442]

Days after learning Jordan had been targeted by the crown, the Pitt ministry issued a notice to Paine that he too would be tried for seditious libel for the contents of *The Rights of Man*. Regardless, Paine did not alter his behavior whatsoever, and sent correspondence to the Jacobin Club in Paris that boasted of the rise of radical political clubs in England. Amazingly, he also sent a written response to Pitt's adviser and Home Secretary Henry Dundas, which was widely published. Within, he warmly received the action against him. In his aspiration to "break the chains of political superstition," Pitt's prosecution campaign would "serve to hasten that dissolution," he professed. After defending his onslaught against "all the vices and defects" of hereditary monarchy, Paine heaped praises upon American's republican counterpart:

This is a government that has nothing to fear. It needs no proclamations to deter people from writing and reading. It needs no political superstition to support it. It was by encouraging discussion, and rendering the press free upon all subjects of government, that the principles of government became understood in America, and the people are now enjoying the present blessings under it. You hear of no riots, tumults, and disorders in that country; because their exists no cause to produce them. Those things are never the effect of freedom, but of restraint, oppression, and excessive taxation.

Pitt's expertise was "confined to the means of extorting revenue," he taunted, and Dundas was little more than an aristocratic parasite "rolling in luxury at the expense of the nation." Most humorously, he signed his name in a manner that defied polite convention. "I am, Mr. Dundas, not your obedient humble servant," Paine wrote, "but the contrary, THOMAS PAINE."[443] In every way, Paine's utterly fearless letter was bound to generate more antipathy toward himself.

Paine's direct tirade against his accusers did not stop with his message to Dundas. Within days, the penman also sent another letter addressed to the crown, this time to Sir Archibald Macdonald, England's attorney general. Remaining defiant against the prosecution against him, he accused the government of planning to "enter into a negotiation" with Jordan to secure information to be used in "a future trial" against himself. He urged Macdonald to "cease the prosecution against the publisher" if Dundas had been truthful in his claim that Jordan was indicted only because Paine could not be found. Directing "the whole process against me," Paine wrote, would "do the cause full justice, as well as for the sake of the nation, as for my own reputation." Moreover, he believed that jurisdictional limitations would hinder the prosecutor from securing his desired outcome. "Because a jury in London cannot decide upon the fact of publishing beyond the limits of the jurisdiction of London," he argued, thousands of printings would simply be "republished over and over again in every county in the nation." The strategy would therefore fail to uproot "the right of public discussion and investigation of principles and systems of government" brought up in *The Rights of Man*.[444]

Most interestingly, Paine's letter also accused Edmund Burke of collecting a secret pension from the king in return for encouraging the prosecution against him:

I believe that Mr. Burke, finding himself defeated, and not being able to make any answer to the Rights of Man, has been one of the promoters

of this prosecution; and I shall return the compliment to him by shewing, in a future publication, that he has been a masked pensioner at
£1500 per annum for about ten years.

The claim was the continuation of Paine's statement that the Whig patriarch was "a stickler for monarchy, not altogether as a pensioner, if he is
one, which I believe, but as a political man." According to the penman,
Burke's duplicity meant that "the public money is wasted, and the dread
of public investigation is produced." While Burke certainly implied Paine
should be punished in *An Appeal from the New to the Old Whigs*, the allegation that he was receiving payment from the public coffers was never
substantiated by the polemicist, despite the rumor's prevalence among radicals. The tale apparently had its origin in the account of William Godwin,
the proto-anarchist philosopher and future husband of Mary Wollstonecraft.[445]

With a court date set for June 8, Paine stood firm, fully intending to
answer the charges of his accusers with the support of Erskine. As the
summer days passed, his likeness continued to be hanged in effigy at town
meetings, and the government persevered in its mission to suppress the
distribution of Paine's writings. Meanwhile, Paine continued to converse
with friends, made some public appearances, and persisted in correspondence with Britain's most radical political leaders. On July 4, he celebrated
the anniversary of the Declaration of Independence's adoption in Lewes,
where his radical sensibilities first materialized. At the home of Clio Rickman, he even sat for a portrait by George Romney, the most renowned
portrait artist of his era. For the first time in his life, Paine was not at a
financial impasse. His latest work was an unparalleled smash hit, and its
author was collecting substantial earnings in royalties for the first time in
his life. Regardless, his newfound financial success did nothing to sully
his virtue. After being made aware he was owed £1,000 in royalties, he
acted as he did even in poorer times, and donated the sum to the Society
for Constitutional Information.[446]

Two days after his letter to Dundas, Paine arrived at the King's Court
only to discover that his trial had been postponed to December, a decision
that had been politically motivated. Prolonging the process, thought the

Pitt ministry, may provide enough time to the subdue radical agitators supporting Paine, hinder any manifestation of an actual revolution against the government, and leave the writer psychologically defeated. Ironically, the decision only seemed to energize the man. Not to be disturbed from his work, he boasted days later of his great "honor and happiness to be the author" of *The Rights of Man*. The legal assault on his standing, he wrote, was "purposely calculated to give an impression to the jury before whom that matter is to come." The boastful message was addressed to Lord Onslow, a local magistrate who publicly applauded the proclamation against his "seditious and wicked" musings. Onslow was guilty of "aiding and abetting" the "illegal purpose" that was the crown's war against Paine's character, which the writer characterized as an overt violation of his due process rights.[447]

By all accounts, the summer of 1792 was in many ways a season of political firestorms on both sides of the English Channel. France's war against Austria had been an utter failure, and the mismanaged affair brought forth the march of soldiers toward Paris. Rumors of coups, counterrevolutions, and imminent enemy occupations were pervasive. Many blamed the military shortcomings on the king himself, and the radical masses continued to clamor for an end to French monarchy entirely. Leaving his post in command of a French unit, Lafayette appeared before the Legislative Assembly on June 28, where he proposed a crackdown upon the Jacobin Club and the Cordelier Club. Though his reputation had already been tarnished, his suggestion was met with outright hostility. After being dismissed by the body, he attempted to appeal to Louis, who gave him an even colder reception. At this point, the king believed Lafayette a traitor for standing down to the mob that coerced the royal family to abandon Versailles for Paris. The recipient of Paine's dedication in *The Rights of Man, Part Second* decided to return the front, but was now viewed as a universal villain by all sides.

On July 11, the French Legislative Assembly passed a desperate measure that permitted the enactment of emergency powers and a suspension of the Constitution of 1791. Sold as a wartime measure, the deed elevated radical political ideologies to the forefront of policymaking. As failures in the field captured the attention of French citizens, the boisterous Danton prepared to mobilize against the French monarchy. Rallying masses of commoners to open militancy, Danton's desire to overthrow the monarchy was aided by the Brunswick Manifesto, an Austro-Prussian decree that threatened punishment against French citizens if the royal family were harmed. In utter distrust of the National Assembly, Danton and his compatriots declared themselves an "insurrectionary commune," and on August 10, the Girondin leader united his confederation of commoners, radicals, and allies within the national guard.

Tipped off to the events, Louis and his family slipped into a room in the Legislative Assembly, which they perceived as a safe haven. After a brief skirmish, Danton's ragtag masses murdered the remaining royal guards, flooded into Tuileries Palace, and converged upon the king's location. The royal family was then taken captive, the king's authority was suspended, and under the pressure of coercion, Danton was appointed Minister of Justice by the beleaguered National Assembly. It was the beginning of the end of the Constitution of 1791, the Legislative Assembly, and the French monarchy. By fortune alone, Paine the Englishman would soon have a word in the French king's fate.

Back in London, Paine's personal friends and political allies grew more concerned about his future than the scribe himself. According to one account, this group even included the young poet William Blake, who urged Paine to flee. While Blake's friendship with Paine and reverence for his work is certain, the story of warning is likely mythical.[448] Even though Paine responded pompously to the legal volley against him, he decided on the evening of September 13 to flee England and preserve his personal safety. In every way, it was a bittersweet departure. Though made an outcast by the Tories, Paine clearly wished to fight the charges against him, if only to further expose the malignant nature of hereditary monarchy and its existential assault upon individual liberty. Nevertheless, he relented under the guidance of trusted company.

Along with his friend John Frost, Paine united with Frenchman Achille Audibert, municipal officer of Calais. Astoundingly, Audibert carried news that the Englishman—defying all convention—had not only been granted honorary French citizenship for his writings, but was also elected to the newly-created French National Convention as representative of Calais. "Come, friend of the people," the letter read, "to swell the number of patriots in an assembly which will decide the destiny of a great people, perhaps of the human race."[449] The stunning offer was the result of several factors, including the popularity of the French translation of *The Rights of Man*, political trends toward radical republicanism within the country, Paine's personal fame, and perhaps a stroke of luck. Undoubtedly, the news brought forth an incredible contrast of receptions. On one side of the waterway, he was treated as a traitorous outcast, while the other welcomed him with the greatest admiration.

En route to France, the group travelled southeast to Dover, where they checked into the York Hotel. Inside, they encountered and unexpected hurdle when a government agent stopped the three and demanded access to their luggage under the authority granted by the recent proclamation against seditious material. The agent claimed to possess "information" against the group, but refused to substantiate it openly. Paine protested the invasive act and attempted to impede the search and seizure, but his belongings were eventually searched, along with those travelling with him. Among his possessions were letters from George Washington, Gouverneur Morris, and Charles Pinckney. After leaving their room for a time, though, the British officer admitted to finding the proclamation against him "ill-founded," and returned the group's belongings.[450]

With the way cleared for Paine to set sail for France, the group awoke the next morning to masses of locals who had been tipped off to the writer's presence. As they headed for the Port of Dover, he was verbally assailed by spectators, a reception he had grown accustomed to from his recent days in London. Nevertheless, a journalist from the *London Chronicle* reported that "he trembled every joint," likely the result of exhaustion from the all-night ordeal with the officer rather than a personal response to the hecklers. The mob "loaded him with abuse" as he and his two companions boarded the *Quay*, a ship bound for Calais in the Port of Dover. The mob continued to harangue him. "Every mark of disapprobation and contempt" was hurled against him, along with promises of "a cheap coat of tar and feather," as he entered the ship's lower deck.[451] His view to the shore was the last he would ever see of his native soil.

As the ship approached Calais, a mixture of emotions must have engulfed Paine. His departure allowed the Pitt ministry to declare victory, albeit a pyrrhic one, against him and his supporters, and moderated the spread of radical agitation that filled the year. Still, his writings had captivated the radicals of France, who were more energized, empowered, and receptive to his ideas than at any other point in the French Revolution. The notoriety he gained from Pitt's unyielding campaign against him, then, had only propelled his celebrity in France. Even while England prepared to convict him in absentia, a French region granted him actual power in government for the first time in his life, an unprecedented honor for a man who could not even speak the French language. Just as his star dimmed in Britain, it was burning bright across the English Channel.

Chapter 6

The Age of Reason

Royalty, its fanatical éclat, its superstitious idolatry, the delusive assumption of its necessity, all these fictions have been invented only to obtain from men excessive taxes and voluntary servitude.

- Anti-monarchal Essay

Just as Paine was run out of his native land by the British authorities, he enjoyed a hero's reception in France. As the *Quay* docked in Calais, jubilant masses of Frenchman packed the area. By all accounts, the crowd cheering his arrival was the antithesis of the horde that berated him in Dover. Soldiers fired shots to salute his entry, and officers approached to welcome him. A beautiful woman pinned a cockade to his hat, and townsfolk belted out repeated chants of "long live Thomas Paine!" At the local Constitutional Society, he was met with a special ceremony, and given an ornate box specially crafted "For the author of *The Rights of Man*." In the words of one biographer, "the prosecution of Paine in England had its counterpart in a shrine across the channel." His reception was one that "hitherto had been accorded only to princes."[452]

While still in Calais, Paine met with locals and hurriedly did what he could to prepare for the obligations demanded by his new office. In a matter of days, he arrived in Paris just in time to witness the realization of one of his sincerest aspirations. On September 21, the National Convention voted to abolish the French monarchy and adopted a full republican system. Furthermore, it replaced the country's existing calendar system with one that began anew along with the newly inaugurated political order. Under the new revolutionary calendar, 1792 had become the Year I. Furthermore, the body decided to create a new purely republican constitution to coincide with the monarchy's demise. The deed was the final nail in the coffin of the Constitution of 1791, which had already been put on life support by the Legislative Assembly. It was the final rung on the ladder of Danton's rise to power, and his ultimate aspiration. In just one year, the idea of substituting republicanism for constitutional monarchy had gone from a theoretical fantasy to a tangible political fact. The transition must have seemed an incredible triumph to Paine, the man who had done the most to spread anti-monarchical, pro-republican ideas throughout Europe. What to do about the former king, however, remained an open question. All that was known at the time was that he would now be "Citizen Louis" rather than Louis XVI.

Within hours of arriving in the France, Paine's new legislative duties required that he hit the ground running despite little knowledge of parliamentary procedure. On September 22, he first raised his voice in a discussion regarding the dissolution of the final remnants of Bourbon rule—administrative, municipal, and judicial subordinates of the king. Danton proposed a hasty termination to their offices, but Paine advised additional discussion and reorganization over outright annulment. Royal positions should be eliminated, he argued, but removing those with extensive knowledge of the law jeopardized judicial reforms and consistency in law enforcement. Granting the National Convention all power over both subjects, he believed, would put too much power in too few hands—a creed derived from the ideas of French philosopher Charles de Montesquieu. In the end, Paine failed to get his way. It was decided that new administrative positions would be filled by popular election, and all constitutional prerequisites for municipal or judicial positions would be eliminated.[453]

The emergence of the National Convention as the de-facto French legislature also brought forth new factional dynamics. Robespierre organized the Montagnard, or "Mountain," a group of radicals that inherited its name due to their presence in a section of high-rising seats on one side of the convention hall. Opposite the Montagnard sat the Girondins, led by Brissot and Danton, who sat in their own section opposite their rivals. Between the two factions was the Plain, a group of fence-sitting independents who occupied seats on the convention floor and lacked the partisan attachments of their peers. Though each group had different priorities, there was overlap among them. The Girondins emphasized the importance of property rights, free trade, and spreading the ideas of the revolution beyond France. The Montagnards, on the other hand, focused upon egalitarianism and policy through democracy, both ideas derived from their political progenitor, Jean-Jacques Rousseau. While all factions clashed with each other in a series of power struggles over the next years, few entertained the prospect of a restored monarchy of any type.

Finding a break from the pomp and circumstance that was his welcome, and his policymaking responsibilities, Paine drafted a letter of thanks to his constituents on September 25:

> I receive, with affectionate gratitude, the honour which the late National Assembly has conferred upon me, by adopting me a Citizen of France: and the additional honor of being elected by my fellow citizens a Member of the National Convention? Happily impressed, as I am, by those testimonies of respect shown towards me as an individual, I feel my felicity increased by seeing the barrier broken down that divided patriotism by spots.

The new French citizen was in decidedly high spirits, especially in comparison to his previous month in London. With his new focus on the development of the budding government, he reiterated his commitment to ideals he promoted in *The Rights of Man.* "Convinced that the cause of France is the cause of all mankind, and that liberty cannot be purchased by a wish," he wrote, "I gladly share with you the dangers and honors necessary to success." The new French republic, he assured his constituents, "shall blot despotism from the earth, and fix, on the lasting principles of peace and citizenship, the great republic of man." Paine declared that "the same spirit of fortitude that insured success to America" would envelop France as well, and professed that "a new ray of light will be thrown over the world" as the principles of the French Revolution were "universally understood" by humanity.[454]

Paine's inspiring letter of revolutionary unity contrasted greatly with the young republic's looming discord. In the government's earliest days, a feud was sparked over the most pressing issue at hand—the fate of the king. A special commission was quickly formed to consider his malfeasance, and virtually all sides agreed the monarch bore some responsibility for the government's downward spiral and lack of military successes. Whether or not Louis should be put on trial for crimes against the country was a matter of great contention, and the debate was made even more complex by the diverse array of opinions regarding an appropriate punishment. The Montagnards generally favored trial and execution of the king, while the Girondins were divided among those who favored legal immunity, those who supported full clemency, and those who preferred a lesser form of punishment than death. Allowing the king to live would only encourage a royalist insurrection to restore him to power, some argued, while others contended that sparing his life and allowing him to transition into the life of a normal citizen would best demonstrate the benevolent merits of republicanism to the world.

In his first weeks in France, Paine devoted most of his time and energy to the country's new constitutional project. On October 11, the writer-turned-representative was appointed to a nine-member committee to create such a framework for France. Also appointed to the same committee, ironically, was his intellectual rival Emmanuel-Joseph Sieyès, whom Paine had sparred with a year prior in the presses over the necessity of republicanism verses constitutional monarchy. Their new shared task, which conceded that constitutionally monarchy was entirely out of the question, had made Paine the tacit victor of the dispute. The committee was dominated by Girondins, and also included both Brissot and Danton—truly a who's who of France's most legendary revolutionary figures at the time.

By this point, Paine began to gravitate toward the Girondins, which aided him in securing the appointment to the constitutional committee. At first, the association seemed an unnatural one. Paine was opposed to the continuance of offensive war against Austria—a Girondin cause—and held out hope for an armistice to end the fighting. After a string of French military triumphs on the eastern front that fall, the Prussian king had "proposed to negotiate," he reported glowingly, and the penman greeted the end "to any further operations."[455] By all accounts, Paine thought the revolution was best spread through hearts and minds rather than on the battlefield. Even so, he was adamantly opposed to putting the king to death, a position that put him in the good graces of the Girondins. This stance, along with his reputation as a writer and defender of the French cause, won over the trust of Brissot and Danton. The faction may have decided to welcome Paine into their clique simply to prevent the eminent writer from being recruited by the Montagnards.

Beyond the immediate political considerations, Paine's experience in the subject matter made his appointment to the Girondin constitutional committee a logical one. After all, it was he who first proposed a "Continental Charter" in America, outlining its particulars in *Common Sense*. The proposal came to fruition in the form of the Articles of Confederation, and later the Constitution. His influence in America was also apparent among Philadelphia radicals, who grafted many of his ideas into the Pennsylvania Constitution of 1776. Furthermore, *The Rights of Man* openly touted a written constitution for England that eschewed monarchy entirely, and articulated his republican ideals meticulously. Despite having no direct role in the formulation of the American constitutions, he was widely viewed as an expert on constitutional affairs, and the stars aligned to give him great influence within France's new republican order.

In addition to his legislative duties, Paine also took to France's presses to promote the country's transition to republicanism. In *Le Patriote Français,* Brissot's revolutionary publication, he lashed out against the recently terminated Bourbon system. "The perjuries of Louis, the conspiracy of his court, the wildness of his worthy brothers," he wrote, "have filled every Frenchman with horror. The country's hereditary monarchy, he continued, was "dethroned in their hearts before its fall by legal decree." The Bourbon system was merely one dynasty in a long string of endeavors to "subvert a country, place it under tribute, seize its lands," and "enslave its inhabitants." With the "expedition completed," he wrote, "the chieftain of the robbers adopts the title of monarch or king." Hereditary succession thus "breeds monsters as a marsh breeds vipers," and was "the most shameful fantasy that ever degraded mankind."[456]

Paine also aspired to debunk those portraying republicanism as nothing more than a utopian fantasy. Disputing the notion that a king was needed to "preserve a people from the tyranny of powerful men," Paine insisted that a firm Constitution, the elimination of aristocratic privileges, free trade, and freedom of the presses guaranteed good laws, and by extension, an inability for ambitious men to rise as tyrants. To the idea that a king was necessary to stop a legislature from usurping authority, he countered that representatives with clearly defined duties, reelection considerations, and active constituents would thwart the possibility of "any months of tyranny." In response to the claim that a king was needed "to give force to executive power," Paine argued to the contrary, that it was actually "the existence of a hereditary prince" that encouraged "perpetual distrust among the friends of liberty."[457]

As a representative in the National Convention, Paine was an aberration in every way. At the age of 55, he was among the oldest members in the assembly. Though other deputies were accomplished writers, the Englishman's background as a staymaker made him one of the only representatives who came from the artisan class of tradesmen, a demographic that almost never obtained any political authority to speak of in Europe. The body was dominated by lawyers, businessmen, and intellectuals, all of whom Paine was now quite familiar with, but he was still an alien to their pedigree. Most unique to the penman was his status as a foreigner, a characteristic shared only with one other representative. Regardless of his unlikely presence in the National Convention, Paine appealed to unity under the banner of republicanism. "Let us begin the new era by a greatness of friendship, and hail the approach of union and success," he pledged.[458] He could not have known it at the time, but his tenure as a deputy would be short-lived, and there would no French unity whatsoever in a year's time.

Paine's ability to succeed in his duties as a regional deputy was often hindered by his own cultural limitations. Though he had visited France on several occasions, he lacked a command of French cultural norms, a hurdle that made it harder to navigate the channels of French politics despite his great notoriety. Given his inability to speak basic French, he was assigned translators, which made his committee work a tedious affair, and his conversations always ran the risk of being misinterpreted by others. Despite these shortcomings, individual rights were to Paine the shared gift of all humanity, and his clarion call for liberty was a cause that all could rally toward regardless of cultural circumstances. France had raised "the standard of liberty for all nations," he wrote, "and in fighting her own battles, contends for the rights of all mankind."[459]

In late 1792, most of Paine's attention was captivated by his responsibility to contribute to the next French constitution. His primary goal for the project was to ensure the inclusion of a declaration of rights. As he saw it, individual liberty was the essential foundation of a republican framework. A constitution "made conformable to the declaration of rights," he argued, would do much to restrain "contradictions" that "served to divide the opinions of individuals at home, and to obscure the great principles of the revolution in other countries." Echoing his passions on this point was Marie Jean Antoine Nicolas de Caritat, marquis de Condorcet, who would become Paine's closest friend in the convention. The two worked together for long hours at a time, discussing philosophy as they inked their ideas into the new constitutional proposal for France.[460]

Gouverneur Morris, who was still in Paris serving as American minister to France, had by now hardened toward Paine completely. While a conflict in philosophy had already weakened the relationship between the two men, the development of the French Revolution had threatened the potential for warmer American relations with Britain, then a primary objective of Washington and the Federalists. The culmination of absolute French republicanism, despite its obvious corollary to the American experience, had become a lightning rod emboldening Jefferson's Republican faction to reiterate its obligations to support American's instrumental ally in the struggle against Britain. Besides his own country's political considerations, Morris expressed that France's radical turn proved it lacked the "cool reflection which appears needful to consolidate a free government." As the country prepared to try the king, he also warned a friend that "it grows every day more probable that England will declare war."[461]

The debate over the king's fate continued to swell toward the end of 1792, and Paine was caught in the middle. By the time deputies began to debate procedures and penalties, Paine had already made his opinion known in the press. After originally defending Louis as a uniquely enlightened monarch and friend to America, he had soured on the monarch completely by the fall of 1792. "The perjuries of Louis, the conspiracies of his court, the wildness of his worthy brothers, have filled every Frenchman with horror, and this race was dethroned in their hearts before its fall by legal degree." Even so, he contended the king was merely a figurehead— the current embodiment of a broken, despotic system. Consequently, it was much more essential to eradicate monarchy from the earth than it was to execute its current occupant. "It is little to throw down an idol," Paine wrote, "it is the pedestal that above all must be broken down."[462]

While deputies formulated and issued various opinions on Louis and his future, the National Convention created two commissions to explore the subject. The first commission was established to collect the monarch's papers and effects in order to weigh the strength of the evidence against him. The second endeavored to comb through legal history to determine whether the king, who had been protected by the now-extinct Constitution of 1791, could rightfully stand trial. The convention as a whole began discussions on both matters on November 13. Before any penalties were proposed, several deputies claimed it was impermissible to try the monarch, regardless of his deeds. After all, France had never tried a king for treason, and the mere idea of doing so was unprecedented and outlandish. Under the Bourbon system, the king was the sovereign, which, by definition, could only be the target, not the perpetrator, of treason. In addition, the Constitution of 1791 explicitly provided the king with legal immunity from prosecution.[463]

The tides of the discussion seemed to change entirely when the young Jacobin Louise Antoine Léon de Saint-Just rose to speak. Rather than debating the finer points of law, the radical deputy from Aisne launched into a verbal tirade against the king. Louis was a villain who had betrayed his country, he asserted loudly. "I see no middle ground," he shouted, "this man must reign or die!" As he saw things, the king "oppressed a free nation, declared himself its enemy," and "abused the laws." Only his death would "assure the repose of the people," he insisted, "since it was his mind to crush the people to assure his own." Even putting the king on trial, he claimed, would be a concession to the possibility of his innocence—a blatant contradiction to the new republican system. "One cannot reign innocently," he declared.[464] Saint-Just's vociferous oratory was met with thunderous applause, and his chief points were soon adopted by Robespierre and the Jacobins.

As many of his colleagues stood in awe of Saint-Just's arguments, Paine's sensibilities were put off entirely by their implications. With help from his translator, Paine weighed into the matter on November 21. The sincerest adversary of monarchy on the planet was now in the awkward position of pleading for the life of the king. His primary motivation to do so was his conviction that the former monarch was now a citizen, and therefore had little remaining significance in the absence of a hereditary system to empower him. Louis was now "an object beneath the notice of the republic," he insisted, and his death would do nothing to erase his crimes or fortify the young government. To the contrary, Paine claimed that France's standing would only be made weaker by a regicide, because such a drastic action would only enflame all the monarchies of Europe and hinder the cause of continental peace. Moreover, Paine believed the worldwide spotlight on France had afforded a crucial opportunity to demonstrate that every man—including a monarch—would be subject to the law in a republican system. Putting the king to death would eliminate such possibility, he cautioned.[465]

On the same day, Robespierre rose to counter Paine's argument. Borrowing from Saint-Just, the Jacobin trailblazer expressed that any defense of the king's life was by extension an assault against the republic. This was because a judgment had already been imposed Louis on August 10, he alleged, when the Paris Commune put an end to his rule. Robespierre concluded this meant the king must be denied the benefit of a trial, and should instead be put to death immediately after charges against him were relayed. The stance was a remarkable shift for Robespierre, who had built his political career largely upon his fervent opposition to the death penalty. Regardless, the charismatic lawyer was willing to make an exception for a king. In his eyes, the French republic and Louis could not coexist in the same world. "Louis must die that the nation might live," he proclaimed that December.[466] The newly-cemented Jacobin position in favor of execution had the strategic effect of putting the Girondins on the defensive by making regicide the litmus test for commitment to the revolution. Beyond all doubt, it was a harbinger to the bloody wave of violence and terror that would soon engulf France.

The National Convention ultimately concocted a legal justification to try the king in court, a decision that fell short of Robespierre's yearning for immediate execution. To the surprise of all, the legal case against Louis was enhanced considerably by a stunning revelation on November 20, just days before his scheduled trial. That day, a hidden safe was discovered in the king's bedroom in the Tuileries Palace. When opened by its locksmith, the container revealed extensive correspondence between the king and various enemies of the French republic. Among the most damning evidence were his written pleas to the Austrian leaders to invade France to restore him to the throne as an absolute monarch. He also expressed contempt toward the Constitution of 1791, mocked the National Assembly, and instructed his subordinates to lie to cover for his actions and assist émigré opponents of the revolution. By confirming the monarch's traitorous deeds, and giving credence to the Austro-Bourbon conspiracy that so many had warned of, the discovery greatly undermined the king's legal case and sealed his fate in the court of public opinion. In turn, it emboldened the Montagnard crusade for execution.

Louis went on trial in early December. Among the many charges against him were allegations that he dissolved the Estates General, ordered a French army to march against French citizens after the fall of the Bastille, bribed sympathizers to help him maintain absolute power, conspired with Austria against his own country, and spilled the blood of Frenchmen at the Champ de Mars Massacre and August 10 insurrection. The monarch, appearing in court as "Louis Capet," answered that France's constitutional system empowered him to take many of the actions he was accused of. On other matters, he blamed his advisors in an attempt to shift responsibility away from himself. When presented with damning documents written in his own handwriting, he refused to acknowledge their authenticity. Louis and his defense team did their best to deny some of the charges and justify others, but it was of no use. The deputies overwhelmingly found him guilty on January 15.

When the penalty phase came, Robespierre and his Montagnard allies reiterated their demand for the king's head. The Girondins attempted to secure lower forms of punishment, but the new evidence against Louis and his responses in court turned many against him. With a prewritten speech in his hand, Paine rose again to address the convention with the help of his translator. "I voted that Louis be tried," he said, "because it was necessary to afford proofs to the world of the perfidy, corruption, and abomination of the monarchical system." Louis' actions were not "more heinous than those of his predecessors," he argued, but were the product of "the lamentable, degraded state" in which he had been restored to power as monarch by the Legislative Assembly. Paine reminded the body that he and his radical friends in the Society of Republicans had campaigned vigorously against the restoration of the king in order "to erect on its ruins the republican system" with "equal representation." Their proposal to banish Louis to exile would have prevented the king's later evils, he preached, and the Legislative Assembly made a colossal mistake by allowing him to retain such power under the Constitution of 1791. "I am far more ready to condemn the Constituent Assembly than the unfortunate prisoner Louis Capet," Paine declared to the amazement of the king's greatest enemies.[467]

In one last measure of desperation, Paine again beseeched the body to spare the life of the king, who he—and everyone else—recognized as a traitor. As he saw it, the trial had already accomplished all of its necessary objectives. First, the "treacherous defects in the constitution had been brought to light," equipping the deputies with the knowledge necessary to favor pure republicanism over constitutional monarchy. Secondly, the proceedings had suitably ruined the reputation of Louis Capet, and more importantly, France put its grand rejection of monarchy on display for the whole world to see:

> The people have beat down royalty, never, never to rise again; they have brought Louis Capet to the bar, and demonstrated in the face of the whole world, the intrigues, the cabals, the falsehood, corruption, and rooted depravity, the inevitable effects of monarchy government.

Lastly, the trial afforded the deputies with an excellent opportunity to nullify the power of Louis without killing him. Paine claimed that sending Louis to live in the United States as a normal citizen would be the most efficient way to render him politically impotent in Europe, and prevent him from being martyrized by royalists. "Far removed from the miseries and crimes of royalty," the former monarch would learn "the true system of government consists not in kings, but in fair, equal, and honorable representation." By providing Americans "that support which enabled them to shake off the unjust and tyrannical yoke of Britain," Paine believed

Louis performed a great deed despite his copious wrongdoing, and therefore earned a semblance of leniency. An execution would only endanger the virtuous drive to "abolish the punishment of death," he professed, even making reference to Robespierre's "excellent oration" in support of the same position. Implicitly, Paine warned that banishment should be preferred by those who thought the same, lest they appear as hypocrites.[468]

Despite his earnest appeal, Paine's attempt to save the king's life failed in the end. After a failed attempt by Girondins to put the king's punishment to a referendum of the French people, the convention voted on January 18, by a narrow margin, to execute the king. The next day, Paine expressed his deepest regrets, and suggested the momentous decision, portrayed as "an act of justice," would one day "appear an act of vengeance." As he did so, the ardent Jacobin Jean-Paul Marat interrupted his lamentation. Marat complained that the foreigner had only arrived at his perspective on the basis of his Quaker religious beliefs, which he claimed should negate him from having a voice in the dispute. "I submit that Thomas Paine is incompetent to vote on this question," he declared.[469]

As the writer continued his speech, Marat grew so indignant that he accused Paine's interpreter of twisting the Englishman's words to put him in a better light. In response, Paine provided his own copy of speech to prove otherwise, a fact that was confirmed by both his interpreter and a third party. Rather than act in accordance with any religion, Paine maintained he voted against execution "from both moral motives and motives of public policy," an explanation consistent with his writings and speeches on the subject. After his answer, loud commotion swept through the chamber, with tensions flaring on all sides. According to one account, it is likely that Marat's interruption was calculated to diminish the body's great reception to Paine's sentiments.[470]

Contrary to Marat's allegations, by this time Paine had almost certainly abandoned any attachment to institutionalized religion, including that of his own Quaker upbringing. His religious nonconformity was confirmed unambiguously two years later upon the publication of the first volume of *The Age of Reason*, his written defense of deism. Regardless of his true motivations, Paine's open support for the king and alignment with the Girondins made him persona non grata in the eyes of ardent Montagnards, including Robespierre, Marat, and Saint-Just. In time, all three would play a role in the commencement of the Reign of Terror, during which he was arrested, confined, and narrowly escaped death.

By a relatively narrow margin, the National Convention voted on January 15 to execute Louis, and an attempt to grant him reprieve the next day failed. With the king condemned to die, the government made speedy arrangements to carry out the sentence. His situation was now comparable to that of Charles I of England, the Stuart king put to death in 1649 by English republicans. Both were accused of shedding blood, igniting civil conflicts, and conspiring with enemy nations. Similarly, the two monarchs were both defiant in the face of the charges against them, and were tried by republicans in unprecedented, extralegal courts. On the morning of January 21, Louis attended his last Mass, before boarding a carriage led by a procession of drummers. Arriving at the Place de la Révolution, a massive public square, the disgraced former king stepped onto the scaffold, surrounded by more than 100,000 observers. In a brief oratory, he declared himself innocent of the charges against him, pardoned those who sentenced him, and prayed that his death would not tarnish France's future. After his hair was cut, his head was placed into the guillotine, and the blade fell. With the death of Louis, the last remnant of the Ancien Régime was extinguished, and the onlookers roared with jubilance. Still, the devoutly anti-monarchical Paine had no reason to celebrate. The spectacle was to him a hollow victory, if a victory at all.

Paine's status as deputy in France of course had no bearing on his standing in England. Indeed, as the fate of the French king was debated in Paris in December of 1792, the English government began its in absentia prosecution of Paine for seditious libel at the Guildhall in London. Both Pitt's desire to uproot political opposition and Paine's resentful message to Macdonald likely contributed to the decision to push the matter to trial, regardless of the writer's whereabouts. As Paine predicted in vexation, his trial featured a hand-picked jury of subjects who were hostile toward him and his ideas. He was represented by the cunning lawyer Thomas Erskine, with whom he had consulted prior to his departure from England.

As Paine's adversaries packed the King's Court, his commoner and radical sympathizers surrounded the building despite the frigid cold. To begin the proceedings, future Prime Minister and junior counsel Spencer

Perceval presented a summary of the charges. Thomas Paine, who he described as "a wicked, malicious, seditious, and ill-disposed person," had done much to "scandalize, traduce, and vilify" the English constitutional system brought about by the Glorious Revolution of 1688. Consequently, the writer was guilty writing and publishing "a certain false scandalous, malicious, and seditious libel" against "the late happy revolution," England's "hereditary regal government of the said kingdoms and dominions," and the kingdom's "present sovereign lord the king."[471]

After the charges were read, Erskine rose to present an epic four-hour opening address. The well-prepared lawyer skewered the English government in a manner that enraged Tories, who had already attacked the lawyer's character for his decision to represent the country's most notorious firebrand. His primary argument in defense of Paine was his assertion that the crown's grand campaign to convict the author of seditious libel violated a key maxim of Britain's constitutional system—liberty of the press. Favoring Whig principles of natural law over the doctrine of parliamentary sovereignty, Erskine contended that free speech could not be merely governed away by Parliament. Unless Paine "clearly stepped beyond that extended range of communication which the same ancient wisdom and liberal policy of the British constitution has allotted," said his counsel, he should be acquitted of all charges against him. He reinforced this point by stressing that Paine's doings fell short of the standard established by England's Libel Act of 1792, which required the state prosecutors to demonstrate that those charged with libel had been motivated by "an overt act of wickedness" rather than good intent.[472]

Freedom of speech was but "an empty sound," professed Erskine, if it did now allow any man to "enlighten others with what his own reason and conscience, however erroneously, have dictated to him as truth." Any English subject may therefore "analyze the principles of its constitution, point out its errors or defects, examine and publish its corruptions, warn his fellow citizens against their ruinous consequences," and prescribe remedies to injustices. Additionally, Erskine denied the common Tory allegation that absolute freedom of the presses meant opening the door to bloody political revolution. This was because each individual is responsible for their own interpretations of any written work, and their subsequent actions. Paine's "opinions indeed were averse to our system, but I maintain that opinion is free, and that conduct alone is amenable to law," his lawyer declared. After quoting extensively from *The Rights of Man*, Erskine concluded that Paine's own outlook on the English system's defects "can never be seditious" because his leanings "can never change ours concerning it." The English government depended upon the notion "that the government leans on the universal will for its support" rather than that of one man, he maintained.[473]

After Erskine concluded his substantive opening remarks, the prosecution rose to present their reply. Seconds before delivering the response though, the court was stopped by a surprise interruption of the jury foreman, who announced that he and his fellow jurors agreed to save the court's time by rendering an immediate verdict of guilty. Without presenting any case whatsoever, the state thereby obtained the conviction of the most accomplished political writer in British history. The judgment carried with it the sentence of death, should Paine ever return or be extradited to Britain. Erskine was quickly whisked away from the court room, and the untamed masses that crowded around Guildhall flocked to his side, showering him with praises. The radicals unhitched his carriage from his horses, carrying it on their backs in a parade through London, making their way to his lodging at the Serjeant's Inn as the energetic crowd of supporters enthusiastically chanted their homages to him, Paine, and liberty of the presses.[474]

Paine's trial concluded in a way that seemed to confirm all the writer's most allegations regarding the corrupt nature of hereditary monarchy. His jury was engineered to include only those who despised him and were guaranteed to overlook exculpatory evidence and issue a guilty verdict. For Pitt, the trial established a crucial precedent for his greatest ambition—the furtherance of his street war against political dissidents and radical published works. Over the next years, the Tory government expanded these efforts against those inspired by Paine's words, with the Prime Minister going so far as to suspend the writ of habeas corpus while jailing radical Whigs for their activism. His primary targets were those who reprinted *The Rights of Man*, some of whom were defended by Erskine, who lost his position as attorney general to the Prince of Wales for taking to Paine's cause. The crown succeeded in putting an end to Paine's freedom in England forever, but failed to stop the revolution of ideas his mind helped inspire.

The trials of Louis and Paine, in sum, seemed the crescendo to a dramatic winter in Europe. For the moment, it appeared the most contentious period of the French Revolution was coming to a close, and that an era of normality would soon replace the confusion and strife that followed the August 10 insurrection, formation of the National Convention, and termination of the Constitution of 1791. Paine wrote that the French republic "still stands unshaken, unsubdued, unsubduable, and undaunted," even in the midst of external war and internal discord. Nevertheless, he concluded that "France can never fall; but by misapplying her own strength."[475] These words would soon prove eerily prophetic, as the lull in political tumult after the death of Louis was only a prelude to a new wave of chaos that would drench France in blood.

With the execution of the French king, Paine became somewhat jaded with French politics. The widening schism between the Dantonist Girondins and Robespierre's Montagnards was to him a pot beginning to boil over. The violent precedent of violent political retribution, he thought, would almost certainly be expanded to punish those opposed—as he had been—to the deed. The downfall of the king, then, may soon prove to be the downfall of a republic he desperately wished to see flourish. Paine's private dealings around this time captured his gloomy attitude. "If the French kill their king, it will be a signal for my departure, for I will not abide by sanguinary men," Paine told a friend.[476] It was an overt jab at the Jacobins, whom he believed were driven not only by an uncompromising impulse to execute the former monarch, but also by a desire to punish those who voted to save his life.

As Paine and his Girondin allies returned their focus to the new French constitution, the new year brought numerous geopolitical challenges for the inexperienced government. In January of 1793, both Spain and Portugal entered the Austro-Prussian coalition against France, and Britain began preparations to enter war as well. In retaliation to the execution of Louis, the Pitt government expelled the French ambassador to Britain, the Marquis de Grosbois, on February 1. In turn, the National Convention declared war on Britain, a decision that was much less contentious than the runup to war with Austria. Now, the French republic was surrounded by European enemies in every direction. Though naturally averse to foreign wars, Paine had confidence in France's capacity to endure. "The first characters in Europe are in arms," he wrote, and "the tyrants of the earth are leagued against France; but with little effect." [477] His confidence may have been inspired by the newly adopted plan to recruit 300,000 military volunteers and organize them into an army loyal to the new republic. The framework was the prototype for the Grand Armée—or "Great Army"—which would see immeasurable time in battle over the next two decades.

On February 15, the Girondin-dominated constitutional committee presented their plan for a new French constitution, to which Paine was a major contributor. The framework was comprised of three separate parts—a philosophical foundation, a declaration of rights, and the actual constitutional document. The lengthy philosophical exposition—primarily authored by Paine's friend, the Marquis de Condorcet—expressed an intention to provide a constitution "founded solely on the principles of reason and justice," guaranteeing "to citizens the fullest enjoyment of their rights." The manifesto justified the abolition of the French monarchy, promoted the merits of republicanism, explained the reasons for the structure of the government, and asserted that the individual was the true source of all political sovereignty.

Paine's chief contribution to the plan came in the form of a declaration of rights, in his mind essential to any republican constitution. According to its prose, republicanism was predicted upon the notion that the "object of all union of men in society" was "maintenance of their natural rights, civil and political," the very "basis of the social pact." The declaration held that all individuals were vested with "the right to do whatever is not contrary to the rights of others," with each right having "no limits other than those which secure to other members of society enjoyment of the same rights." Evocative of the Declaration of the Rights of Man and the Citizen, and the various declarations of rights adopted by the American states, the document proceeded to enumerate a list of rights intended to be out of the purview of government infringement. Among those specified included the authority to "make known his thoughts and opinions," absolute "freedom of the press, and every other means of publishing one's opinion," the right to exercise one's religion, the guarantee of due process, and the assurance of equality under the law. The transcription concluded with Paine's strong conviction that "a generation has no right to subject a future generation to its laws; and all heredity in offices is absurd and tyrannical."[478]

The Girondin constitution would feature a national, centrally-administered government rather than a decentralized federation, and reinstate a unicameral legislature with one representative for each group of 50,000 citizens. Executive power be vested in a single individual, who would be aided by an executive council populated by a secretary and seven departmental heads. Citizenship would be granted to all men 21 years and older who had lived in France for at least a year, and all those obtaining the age of 25 could run for public office. Citizens would be empowered to serve as the republic's militia, where individuals appointed officers to the French national guard. The model allowed for amendments by an elected convention every 20 years, or whenever convened by citizens by way of a national referendum. France's ancient civil and criminal courts would be merged into a uniform, republican judicial system. Most ironically, the Girondin constitution would also outlaw the death penalty—an instrument of oppression that would soon be carried out with brutal frequency.

Regardless of its virtues, the entire Girondin constitution was dead on arrival. It was soundly defeated in the National Convention by a temporary coalition of Montagnards and their allies, who successfully portrayed the framework, and its supporters, as traitorous to the republic. A new constitutional committee, this time filled with those loyal to Robespierre and Marat, was hastily formed and began work on a new constitutional proposal to supplant the Girondin counterpart. The last remaining opportunity for Paine and his friends to stabilize France's government had been quashed, and the revolution was already sliding into its most arbitrary and violent phase yet. Under political duress, Paine shed his legislative duties in favor of solitude. "I went but little to the Convention, and then only to make my appearance; because I found it impossible to join in their tremendous decrees, and useless and dangerous to oppose them," he wrote. Paine's decision was attributed to his unambiguous opposition to the execution of the king, which made him an obvious target of his political rivals. His trepidations extended beyond his own fortunes, however, and he anticipated the outbreak of disaster in France. "We are now in an extraordinary crisis," the result of "the continual persecution of the Jacobins, who act without either prudence or morality," Paine lamented in a letter to Thomas Jefferson.[479]

Despite his recent political failures, Paine remained a celebrity in Paris. Admirers flocked to White's Hotel, a crucial hub for English-speaking radicals, where he was lodged. He was soon reunited with Clio Rickman, his old friend from Lewes, who had fled London as Pitt's crusade to stop the circulation of *The Rights of Man* centered upon him. His friend and biographer recorded that he became so swarmed with visitors that he reluctantly embraced an appointment system to make time for them. Ultimately, though, he withdrew from the busy city center. "Annoyed and disconcerted with a life so contrary to his wishes and habits," Rickman wrote, he retired to Saint-Denis, a country village about five miles from the heart of Paris. There, he rented an apartment where he was visited by both French and British friends. Among them was Mary Wollstonecraft, his intellectual ally in the pamphlet war with Edmund Burke.[480]

At Saint-Denis, Paine enjoyed several distractions from politics. He typically woke early in the morning, shared breakfast with republican friends—especially William Choppin, a prominent member of London's Constitutional Society, and William Johnson, an English doctor so enthralled by Paine that he followed him from London to Paris. The group reminisced about their past, passed the time playing marbles, cribbage, and chess, and engaged in intellectual discussion outside the entrapment of political life. The isolation of the village allowed Paine to begin putting words to his thoughts on religion, a venture that gradually expanded into a full-fledged narrative. Rickman also records that Paine often walked through the garden adjacent to his quarters in Saint-Denis, where one day he happened to notice a spider web. The writer told his friend that the same style of web served as the inspiration for his old passion project, the iron-ribbed bridge. Those who lodged with him would later look back on their days with Paine in fondness, as the calmness of the location provided everyone with a joyous reprieve from the turmoil nearby.[481]

Beyond the internal conflicts that defined 1793, the fortitude of the French republic was also threatened by the military hurdles that stood against their avowed goal of spreading the revolution throughout Europe. One of them came through the undertakings of Charles François Dumour-

iez, a French general who played a major role in the planning and execution of the war on the eastern front. A revolutionary idealist, Dumouriez
aligned his interests to the Girondins, and shared their general zeal for
spreading revolutionary ideals through military force—a concept despised
by Robespierre and his allies. As Dumouriez launched an invasion of the
Austrian Netherlands in late 1792, he planned to do exactly that. He was
successful in leading his army through a string of overwhelming victories
that winter, but still made himself into the bitter enemy of the Jacobins for
his opposition to the beheading of Louis.

Dumouriez suffered a stunning defeat at the hands of the Austro-Dutch
alliance at the Battle of Neerwinden on March 18. Knowing that he was
likely to be forced out of command by the Jacobins, he concocted a rogue
scheme in attempt to maintain his standing. When the National Convention sent a four-member commission to investigate his conduct, he had the
deputies arrested and turned over to the enemy, who held them captive. In
a desperate maneuver, Dumouriez tried to rally his troops to align with the
coalition enemies, raise troops, and march on Paris, where they would
overthrow the National Convention and restore the constitutional monarchy under the Constitution of 1791. While his own soldiers had little sympathy for the French government, Dumouricz's idea was widely perceived
as a step too far, and the elaborate plan failed miserably. His army muti-
nied, and the general escaped into Austrian territory as a defector with the
Duke of Chartres, the eventual King Louis Phillipe I. The disastrous Dumouriez affair greatly compromised France's military position in Europe,
and armed the Jacobins with even more political firepower against the Girondins, with whom he identified.

Always one to exploit any opportunity to assail his rivals, Marat published a torrent of essays that excoriated both Girondins and foreigners
living in France—a group that included Paine—for their supposed treasonous deeds and associations. His attacks were widely embraced by the
Jacobins, who soon elected him president of the Jacobin Club on April 5.
Marat's editorial campaign against those accused of conspiring against the
revolution was quickly followed by a reading of his signed circular letter,
which called for the immediate purge and arrest of Girondin moderates, in
the National Convention. The proposal was met with immediate jeers, and

the body responded by arresting Marat instead. The same day, it was decided he would stand trial before the country's new Revolutionary Tribunal for endorsing "murder, assassination, and massacre."[482]

Upon learning of Marat's outburst against foreigners, Paine's admirer in Saint-Denis, William Johnson, attempted suicide by cutting himself with a blade. He was ultimately stopped short of carrying out the act, but had drafted a will in which he left everything he had to Paine himself. Paine's disposition was shattered, and with his republican ideals subverted by the Jacobins, he no longer believed France capable of becoming the beacon of liberty he imagined. "Had this revolution been conducted consistently with its principles, there was once a good prospect of extending liberty through the greatest part of Europe," he wrote, "but I now relinquish that hope." Paine planned to await the unveiling of the new Jacobin constitutional model, "and then take my final leave of Europe," he told Jefferson. He planned to return to America, the only place he could find solace at this point.[483]

During Marat's trial, Paine was called to testify to his firsthand account of Johnson's suicide attempt. The dejected writer stated Johnson tried to kill himself after learning of Marat's tirade, which he interpreted as a plot against him. Marat lashed out at this assertion, insisting overtly it was Paine toward whom his attacks were aimed, not Johnson. Johnson's later testimony weakened the case against Marat, as the doctor revealed it was his love for Paine in the midst of attacks against him that led him to suicide, rather than fear for his own life. Marat was then afforded the opportunity to defend himself, and his remarkable oratory overwhelmed a receptive audience. His speech centered upon the crucial role the presses played in a free society, and the absolute right to publish one's political beliefs, no matter how controversial. Ironically, the Jacobin's case echoed many of the same themes from Erskine's defense of Paine in London. Marat was then acquitted of the charges against him, and a jubilant mob of sympathizers carried him through the streets as a hero.[484] Undoubtedly, the outcome confirmed the political tides were shifting in the favor of the Jacobins.

With little recourse left, Paine drafted a letter to Danton relaying his sadness toward the "distractions, jealousies, discontents and uneasiness that reign among us," which he believed would inevitably "bring ruin and disgrace on the republic." The despair of France "arises not from the combined foreign powers," he professed, "but from the tumultuous misconduct with which the internal affairs of the present revolution are conducted." Instead of issuing only complaints, though, he suggested a plan to steer the revolution back to a virtuous course. First, the Girondins should organize a new coalition of friends in the National Convention alleviate the economic miseries of the people. This could be done, he wrote, by rejecting all price ceilings on commodities, which he warned would result in widespread shortages, and by terminating the country's paper money venture, which had already led to the utter debasement of the French currency. His experience in America, he wrote, convinced him of the terrible effects of both polices.[485]

Paine believed the best recourse to stop France's spiral of self-destruction was to resist the urge to condemn the Jacobins as traitors, and to instead lead by example by mending animosities through candid reconciliation:

> There ought to be some regulation with respect to the spirit of denunciation that now prevails. If every individual is to indulge his private malignancy or his private ambition, to denounce at random and without any kind of proof, all confidence will be undermined and all authority be destroyed. Calumny is a species of treachery that ought to be punished as well as any other kind of treachery. It is a private vice productive of public evils; because it is possible to irritate men into disaffection by continual calumny who never intended to be disaffected. It is therefore, equally as necessary to guard against the evils of unfounded or malignant suspicion as against the evils of blind confidence.

Unfortunately for Paine, his prescription found no audience. The Jacobins were more emboldened than ever to uproot counterrevolutionary activity, and the Girondins were as powerless as ever to prevent it. On the same day, the Englishman sent a letter to Marat, his bitter enemy, wherein he may have proposed a similar olive branch. However, its contents are lost to time.[486] In another age Paine might have been able to prevent the coming Reign of Terror—as certainly he seemed to anticipate it with repulsion—

but it was not such an age. Rather than negotiate, both the Jacobins and Girondins were ready to purge.

In March, the National Convention grew to believe France was in immediate peril due to the rampant military losses, the rumor of looming internal revolts, and the traitorous deeds of Dumouriez. With Danton's support, the National Convention created the Committee of Public Safety, a nine-member body vested with extralegal emergency powers to thwart various threats to the republic. Thereby, the power to administrate the war, mange finances, appoint judges, and enforce the laws was taken entirely from the National Convention and placed in the hands of a small oligarchy, suspending any aspirations of a new constitutional order. Rather than apprehend its tyrannical potential, Danton viewed the committee as the essential solution to restore order and reverse the country's internal political strife. Instead, the next year proved it was the greatest miscalculation of his life.

On May 12, Paine was called as a witness in a criminal trial yet again—this one regarding the deeds of Francisco de Miranda, Venezuelan soldier of fortune and high-ranking subordinate of the disgraced Dumouriez. The traitorous general blamed his grand loss at Neerwinden on Miranda's strategic blunders. In April, an investigatory committee cleared him of all wrongdoing in the field, and articulated their findings into a report. As it was read to the National Convention, Montagnard partisans shouted down the committee chairman. Instead of absolving Miranda of misconduct, as was intended, Girondin adversaries forced a vote in the National Convention that resulted in his imprisonment and trial. As a friend who had known Miranda since his aid to the cause of American independence, Paine was called to testify to his character. The accusations against him must be without any merit, professed Paine, as the general was a principled devotee of the republic. To demonstrate this, the writer cited Miranda's desire to foment revolution in Spanish America, a project he had already began planning. The jury unanimously acquitted Miranda of all charges, partially due to Paine's attestation. Still, the Englishman dreaded the repeated accusations of disloyalty and the specter of arbitrary arrest.

With tensions between French political factions at an all-time high, several members of the Paris Commune began clamoring for armed insurrection against the National Convention to remove Danton and his friends from power. In response, Girondin deputy Marguerite-Élie Guadet openly denounced the Paris Commune as a bastion of anarchy, avarice, and political domination on May 18. A vote among the deputies to legally dissolve the institute failed, but a committee packed with 12 Girondins was formed to investigate the body as a possible insurrectionary establishment. The committee adopted Marat's antagonistic tactics and ordered the arrest three members of the Paris Commune, including Jacobin Jacques René Hébert, who published a scathing attack on Girondin leaders.

As a result, all hell broke loose. The Paris Commune demanded freedom for those arrested, and continued to lambast the Girondins. Rather than comply, President of the National Convention Maximin Isnard, an outspoken Girondin, lashed out in a rage, promising additional vengeance. "I declare to you, in the name of all France, that Paris will be blotted out, and it will soon be questioned on the banks of the Seine whether such a city has ever existed," he shouted in a fit of rage.[487] These words allowed a united front of Jacobin propagandists to assert that the Girondins would go so far as to destroy Paris if it meant eliminating their rivals, and commoners bought into the message. To prevent a public relations nightmare, Danton made a failed attempt to strike Isnard's words from the record. With both sides refusing to make amends, the Girondins had already lost their last remaining grip on power.

At the Jacobin Club, Robespierre implored adherents to initiate an armed uprising against the National Convention and arrest Girondin traitors to the revolution. In warm compliance, the enraged members of the Paris Commune raised their own army of volunteers. Combined with furious masses of commoners, its size amounted to 80,000. Both the National Convention and the Committee of Public Safety resisted the urge to raise an army to combat it, believing the gesture would inflame tensions and bring about the doom of the government. Even though Paine had soured on revolutionary politics, he felt obligated to return to Paris and assist those trying to preserve the National Convention, in his mind the most essential element of French republicanism. Making his way through the riled masses in the Tuileries courtyard, he was turned away at the palace gates by newly reorganized national guard, now commanded by the Paris Commune. Danton, who was standing nearby, warned Paine he would risk his life to enter, as doing say may lead to his arrest as an enemy of the

Jacobins. He soon came to realize that the soldiers had arrested many of the Girondin leaders, and forced the resignation of others—a list that included several of his friends. At gunpoint, the deputies were forced to take their seats and authorize the purge.

At the end of a three-day struggle, the Girondins largely ceased to be. Having succeeded in their insurrection, the Jacobins scrubbed the National Convention clean of Girondin influence, removing them from the state bureaucracy and replacing them with ideological allies. Several Girondins managed to evade arrest and go into hiding. Among these was Paine's good friend the Marquis de Condorcet, who likely committed suicide after he was discovered and arrested nine months later. The new state bastion, the Committee of Public Safety, was also scrubbed of Girondin influence. After failing to secure the clemency of his beleaguered friends, Danton was soon ejected from the body and made into a pariah. Days later, he was replaced by the triumphant Robespierre. Soon enough, various zealous Jacobins, including Saint-Just and Georges Couthon, were added to the committee was well. For the Jacobins, the political feat accomplished the dual objective of removing all legislative hurdles, and transforming the ultra-powerful Committee of Public Safety into a weapon of their bidding.

The sum of these circumstances led Paine to fear for his life. Without hope of retaking his seat or making friends of the new powerholders in France, he returned to Saint-Denis, where he fell into a state of depression and avoided political activism. In June, two separate petitions condemned the Jacobin coup as an unambiguous affront to the rights of man, but Paine's name was not listed on either document. Later that month, representatives from Calais arrived in Paris to announce their vote of no confidence in him, a move possibly prompted by his time spent away from his legislative duties. The notice resulted in the loss of his seat, for which he cared little by this time. Now weary of the revolution's brutal trajectory, he occupied himself with anything but politics, and likely took to drink. Gouverneur Morris reported that Paine was "so besotted from morning till night," and was "so completely down he would be punished, if he were not despised"—an account that may have been embellished to humiliate his philosophical rival. The diplomat went so far as to accuse the penman of being consumed by "vain ambition."[488] In reality, Paine lacked any ambition whatsoever by this time, except for his ambition to leave France.

Robespierre and his allies wasted no time when it came to implementing their program. The Montagnard Constitution of 1793 was presented to and approved by the National Convention in June. Almost immediately afterward, though, the framework was suspended due to the state of "national emergency"—and along with it any constraints upon the insurrectionary government. All power now belonged to the Committee of Public Safety, which transformed the National Convention into a subordinate entity. The event represented the end to any illusion the government was operating under the direction of representatives, and was the final nail in the coffin to the universal liberties of the people. Potential conspirators were sought out in all corners, and political indifference was often interpreted as a sign of noncommitment to the revolution. In July, Paine's name was linked to a rumored plot against the new government. The origin of this allegation seems to have been a scandalmonger, who claimed Paine had been persuaded by actors in America to undermine the new French state. Thankfully for Paine, the claims were not taken seriously, and writer remained cordial with the authorities.

In contrast to the rumored anti-governmental plots, one true anti-Jacobin plot did transpire on July 13. As Paine's bitter rival Marat was bathing to treat a debilitating skin disease, a young Girondin sympathizer named Charlotte Corday gained access to the fervent editorialist by claiming she had knowledge regarding the whereabouts of Girondins who had escaped the recent purge. Instead of providing the information promised, she delivered the fatal strike of a knife to the chest of Marat. Having been lionized following his trial, Marat became a martyr to the revolution. The writer's corpse was quickly depicted by the most eminent artist of the era, Jacques-Louis David, who falsified his appearance to make him appear more unblemished than he truly was due to his skin condition. The entire National Convention attended his ceremonial funeral, where he was compared to Jesus Christ in a eulogy. Corday was tried, convicted, and executed just days later by the guillotine, which was soon transformed into an instrument of mass death.

In the midst of the chaos in Europe, Franco-American relations became strained. Despite French Minister Edmond-Charles Genêt's pleadings for American support under the terms of the 1778 Treaty of Alliance, President Washington was persuaded that the agreement was voided by the death of the king, with whom it was negotiated. In addition, the president was concerned that continued alliance with France would jeopardize his hopes of securing better relations with Britain, France's wartime enemy. By that time, Washington had already issued the Neutrality Proclamation, a commitment to stay impartial when it came to the raging wars of Europe. In early 1794, the Montagnard-dominated government issued a warrant for Genêt's arrest while the ambassador was still overseas. Fearing his failure to secure American aid would lead to his beheading in France, Genêt sought and was granted asylum in the United States. The botched diplomacy was the first in a series of incidents that ended in outright hostility between the two countries in a matter of years. Furthermore, the occasion contributed to the growing rift between the Federalist supporters of Alexander Hamilton and the Jeffersonian Republicans.

For reasons that remain obscure, in September Paine crossed paths with Bertrand Barère de Vieuzac, who had recently been elected to the Committee of Public Safety. As a key leader of the Plain, he had little attachment to either end of the country's factional paradigm, and claimed to respect Paine for his writing ability. Barère sought the writer's advice as to whether additional ambassadors should be sent to the United States after the conclusion of the Genêt affair. Through an interpreter, Paine also learned that Barère desired help to procure large quantities of flour from the United States. Thinking the Frenchman's keen interest in both subjects meant the Jacobins planned not to persecute him, the sullen former representative of Calais aimed to please, and replied to Barère in the form of a letter. His package also included a draft of the Girondin constitution he helped draft, which had been requested by Barère, though his reasons for doing so remain unclear—it is quite possible this was a ruse to flatter Paine and gain his assistance.

According to Paine, it was "very necessary at this moment" for the Jacobin administration to send new commissioners to negotiate with Congress. Strategically, it would be better to appeal to the proclivities of Jefferson, "an ardent defender of the interests of France" as secretary of state, rather than Morris, a man "badly disposed" toward the French republic as American minster. While the latter had been sent to represent the Washington administration, Paine insisted that many other Americans, such as Morris's half-brother Lewis, were "excellent patriots" who supported the

French Revolution. To demonstrate this, Paine went so far as to send Barère a letter written to him by Lewis Morris, who possessed pro-French sensibilities and "writes like a good patriot." The downtrodden, yet helpful writer recommended using the fleet of 45 stationary American vessels at Bordeaux to carry the proposed convoy across the sea. Besides extending diplomacy, the fleet could also return to France with the cargoes of flour that Barère had requested. Paine conveyed his intention to return to America in October, noting that his affairs "suffered considerably" in his long absence, most notably an accidental fire that destroyed his property in New Rochelle.[489]

It is almost certain that Paine was so polite and cooperative in his response because he feared for his life. His few remaining political allies had by now either been removed from power, imprisoned, or branded as outlaws in their escape from Paris. At this point, even mere political indifference was interpreted by Jacobin fanatics as evidence of tepid dedication to the revolution—or even worse—evidence of traitorous behavior. Despite his intentions, though, Paine's plan to depart on ship to America never came to fruition. Because his correspondence was sparse, it is difficult to ascertain why, though it was almost certainly due to trepidations he would be captured and identified by the British navy, which would have meant extradition and death as punishment for his conviction for seditious libel. While some accounts suggest he chose not to cross the Atlantic for fear of political reprisal within France, this reasoning is unlikely given his willingness to reveal his plans to both Danton and Barère.[490]

The end of 1793 was, in many ways, also the end of all moderation in France. Marat's assassination served as justification for a new operation against Jacobin political opponents, and Paine was caught in the middle of it all. False rumors purported the writer had openly engaged in anti-Jacobin rabble-rousing, and the National Convention specifically declared him a traitor in early October. After the doors of the chamber were locked, the fierce denunciation was read:

At the same time the Englishman Thomas Paine, called by the faction [Girondin] to the honor of representing the French nation, dishonored himself by supporting the opinion of Brissot, and by promising us in his fable the dissatisfaction of the United States of America, our natural allies, which he did not blush to depict for us as full of veneration and gratitude for the tyrant of France.

Amazingly, Paine's repeated and widely-circulated defense of the French Revolution had fallen on deaf Jacobin ears, and did nothing to absolve him from association with the Washington administration, with which he vehemently disagreed. In the eyes of the government, he was now indistinguishable from Brissot, who had called for a return to constitutional monarchy just prior to the Jacobin coup.[491]

The official admonishment of Paine was also accompanied by a broad, all-encompassing condemnation against all Girondins, a considerable leap from the existing approach to target and eliminate specific Girondin leaders. To his great credit, Danton courageously opposed this scheme, imploring his peers to pardon the remaining Girondins and members of the royal family. It was the beginning of his demise. Rather that heed his advice, the government began a host of show trials in the Revolutionary Tribunal, with subsequent executions. Those tried and convicted included Paine's former friend Brissot, Pierre Vergniaud, and Queen Marie Antoinette. Furthermore, a colossal dechristianization effort was enacted. State authorities confiscated church lands, plundered the treasuries of churches, removed religious iconography from French institutions, altered the French calendar to eliminate religious holidays, and most harshly, subjected priests refusing to swear allegiance to the state—and those who gave them safe haven—to death by the guillotine without due process. The Jacobins made clear that widespread horror was now official state doctrine, with the ultimate aim of achieving political purity through violence. The Reign of Terror had begun.

Now named a traitor to France, Paine fell into a panic, struggling under the pressure of both personal and political threats. He lamented to Jefferson that without reprieve, the internal madness within France and the war in Europe would continue unabated:

There is now no prospect that France can carry revolutions into Europe on the one hand, or that the combined powers can conquer France on the other hand. It is a sort of defensive War on both sides. This being the case, how is the War to close?

Perhaps not realizing the extent to which the Washington administration had dismissed any aspiration to participate in the French Revolutionary Wars, the penman urged the secretary of state to send commissioners to play a lead role in negotiating a peace between enemy powers in Europe. "Perhaps a long truce, were it proposed by the neutral powers," he wrote, "would have all the effects of a peace."[492] Given the political situation in America, his request was a pipedream.

In November, terror struck close to home for Paine. A warrant was issued for the arrest of his fellow housemates and admirers, Choppin and Johnson, who narrowly escaped persecution due to the efforts of Paine. Despite his conflicts with Morris, he used his connections with the American Foreign Ministry to secure the delivery of passports that allowed the two men to escape to Switzerland before they could be arrested. About a month later, state guards returned to the Saint-Denis lodgings to arrest the landlord of the property, leaving Paine as its sole inhabitant. Like any good republican, Paine was reluctant to broadcast his personal hardships, and often kept details of his personal life and religious beliefs to himself. Nevertheless, his focus was captivated by his musings on religion, which had by this point developed into a narrative that would become *The Age of Reason.* In October, Paine arranged the publication of its French language prototype, *Le Siècle de la Raison, ou Le Sens Commun Des Droits De L'Homme*—"The Century of Reason, or The Common Sense of Human Rights." However, the pamphlet was not widely printed within France, and its content differs substantially from its 1794 English counterpart.[493]

Several factors underscored Paine's conspicuous shift from politics to religion. The circumstances in Paris almost certainly led him to believe that his life was in immediate danger as the direct result of the Reign of Terror, an operation that claimed the lives of many of his political allies and personal friends. The episode undoubtedly encouraged him to contemplate salvation, the afterlife, and divine will. On the surface, the subject seemed to give him absolution from the political nightmare that was the collapse of ideal republicanism in France, a cause he fought so vigorously for. However, his musings on theism were directly entangled with politics. This was because many of his ideas served as a refutation of the sweeping Jacobin dechristianization effort, which was fixated on the atheistic notion that there was no creator or afterlife. In addition, Paine hinted several times of his intention to expound upon his religious beliefs, but had yet to deliver. According to his longstanding adversary John Adams, the penman "expressed a contempt of the Old Testament and indeed the Bible at large" in 1776, and told the New Englander he would postpone writing on the subject "to the latter part of life."[494] As such, completing an account on religion may have been for Paine something of a lifelong aspiration.

In late December, Paine put the finishing touches on the English version of *The Age of Reason*, which would not make waves until the next year. To celebrate the occasion, he indulged in a rare dinner in Paris with his few unconfined friends on Christmas Eve at White's Hotel, where he had spent much of his early days in France. After a long discussion, Paine decided to stay overnight at the hotel, as the long walk back to Saint-Denis seemed overbearing at such a late hour. Before dawn, he was awakened abruptly to by knocking upon his door, and soon stood in the presence of several state agents. Acting as an interpreter, the hotel manager informed Paine that the men had arrived to seize him by the decree of the Committee of General Security. Paine was to be "arrested and imprisoned, as a measure of general security; that an examination be made of their papers, and those found suspicious put under seal and brought to the Committee of General Security." The directive also applied to Anacharsis Cloots, a Prussian nobleman who had been the only foreigner—other than Paine—to be elected to the National Convention. Robespierre's obsessive lust for vengeance upon foreigners—whom he believed were naturally opposed to revolutionary aims—had finally focused on Paine.

Paine notified the agents he intended to comply with the arrest after dressing himself. Before taking him away, the officers allowed him to go to the room of Achille Audibert, the English-speaking liaison from Calais who had brought Paine into Paris. His request to see Audibert may have been prompted either by a desire to have a trusted friend serve as a translator, or a desire to gain assistance in removing incriminating documents from his possessions in Saint-Denis. Through Audibert, Paine told the agents that his effects were with Joel Barlow, his American friend and fellow radical Whig. After some delay, the group tracked down Barlow at his residence in the Great Britain Hotel. The businessman produced all he had of Paine's documents—an early version of *The Age of Reason* that amounted only to 31 pages. Sensing deception, the officers rummaged through Barlow's property in attempt to find additional writings, but found none.[495]

The officers brought Paine and Barlow to the author's residence in Saint-Denis, where they uncovered both the final version of Paine's most recent pamphlet and his recent correspondence with Barère. After laying out and reading "all the papers found" in Paine's apartment, the French authorities conducted a "scrupulous examination" of the content, after which they concluded that "none of them has been found suspicious." The agents summarized their findings into a written document, which was signed by all parties, including Paine. The Englishman was then "led to jail; to which he complied without any difficulty."[496] After picking up Cloots, the officers brought the two to the Palais du Luxembourg, a former palace now converted to a prison for purged Girondins and other enemies of the Jacobin-controlled French republic. Before entering, he handed Barlow the completed manuscript of *The Age of Reason* for safe keeping.

Paine was placed in a cold, damp room on the ground floor of the prison, "level with the earth in the garden and floored with brick." His confinement deprived him of both exercise and basic necessities. "The state of my health requires liberty and better air," he wrote, and the jailers provided neither "a knife to cut our victuals with, nor a razor to shave." Compounding his suffering was the ground of his cell, which became "so wet after every rain" that he was constantly ill. As Paine soon found out, the National Convention—the same body that had granted him honorary French citizenship the previous year—had now revoked the same measure. Despite the fallen writer's miseries, the man most equipped to attain his release seemed to relish his recent treatment. "In the best of times," Morris wrote, "he had a larger share of every other sense than of common sense." In another letter, Morris further mocked Paine's situation. "Thomas Paine is in prison, where he amuses himself with publishing a pamphlet against Jesus Christ," he told Jefferson.[497]

Despite the meager provisions, security in Luxembourg was surprisingly lax. Prisoners were allowed to roam through the former palace in the afternoon, where they could converse in a common area or step outside to the gated courtyard. After breakfast, inmates were required to keep their own living spaces clean and attend to other basic prison duties. Paine's room had only a small bed, a chair, and a chest for personal items. Along with food, certain amenities were available for purchase, including newspapers and candles—which he made great use of.[498] Within the prison walls, Paine began work on what was to become the second part of *The Age of Reason*, and kept tabs on European news. He often chose to discuss politics and religion with Cloots, perhaps because he was best acquainted with the Connecticut-born radical. Compared to the overcrowded and horrific prisons of the French Revolution, such as the dreaded Conciergerie, Luxembourg was much less insufferable.

For a time, Paine remained hopeful that his freedom would be restored as the direct result of his American citizenship. While the Jacobins could rescind his honors in France, such an action would have no bearing on his standing in the United States, a country that had remained neutral in the wars engulfing Europe. Also, Paine learned from other prisoners that two fellow inmates had already been released from bondage after proof of their American citizenship was presented to the National Convention. With little recourse, Paine wrote to Morris, hoping to persuade the American Foreign Minister to intervene on his behalf and vouch for his American citizenship. Though Paine was in dire straits, Morris' note to French Foreign Minister François Louis Michel Chemin Deforgues in response to the request was characteristically unsympathetic to his plight and did little other than to inquire upon the reasoning for his detention:

> Sir, Thomas Paine has just applied to me to claim him as a citizen of the United States. Here (I believe) are the facts relating to him. He was born in England. Having afterwards become a citizen of the United States, he acquired great celebrity there by his revolutionary writings. In consequence he was adopted a French citizen and then elected Member of the Convention. His conduct since this epoch is out of my jurisdiction. I am ignorant of the reason for his present detention in the Luxembourg prison, but I beg you, sir (if reasons unknown to me prevent his liberation), be so good as to inform me, that I may communicate them to the government of the United States.

To this, Deforgues responded that Paine's acceptance of French citizenship in 1792 invalidated his standing in America. It was, as he saw it, an act that "renounced the protection which the right of the people and treaties concluded with the United States could have assured him." However, Deforgues promised to confer with the Committee of Public Safety to gain an understanding of "the motives of his detention." Privately, Morris informed Jefferson of his belief that Paine's justification for release was unfounded. "I believe he thinks, that I ought to claim him as an American citizen," but "his birth, his naturalization in this country, and the place he filled" made his case "inexpedient and ineffectual," he wrote.[499] Following his exchange with the French minister, Morris did nothing to testify to Paine's American citizenship, and the correspondence confirms his attempt to secure Paine's release was half-hearted at best.

Deforgues' letter angered Paine immensely. After reading it, he reached out to Morris once more, this time demanding additional action in explicit terms. "You must not leave me in the situation which this letter places me," he insisted. "Though you and I are not on terms of the best harmony," he admitted, "I apply to you as the Minister of America," and "expect you to make Congress acquainted with my situation, and to send them copies of the letters that have passed on the subject." Desperation radiated from the letter, with Paine discarding the pleasantries that accompanied virtually all written correspondence of the age. "A reply to the Minister's letter is absolutely necessary, were it only to continue the reclamation," he wrote, "otherwise your silence will be a sort of consent to his observations."[500]

Paine had written in futility. When they learned of the letter's reception by Morris, the French authorities adopted a hardline approach, putting an immediate end to all communication to and from Luxembourg. For the next six months, Paine had no connection to the outside world, save for visits by local friends. The writer began to suspect that this act may have been a result of collusion between Morris and the French government to punish him. "However discordant the late American Minister Morris and the late French Committee of Public Safety were," Paine wrote," it suited the purpose of both that I should be continued in arrestation." Paine suspected Morris obstructed his release so the writer would "not expose his misconduct," and the French government so he could not "publish to the world the history of its wickedness."[501]

This perspective clashed with his earlier suspicion that Robespierre himself was the architect of his imprisonment. Supporting this theory was a revelation that materialized when the arch-Jacobin's papers were uncovered and presented before the National Convention. Within his effects, Robespierre left a handwritten reminder to himself to "demand that Thomas Paine be decreed of accusation, for the interests of America, as well as of France." Beyond these two explanations, it may be true that Morris was simply trying to walk a delicate line with Paine's situation given the Washington administration's adamant desire not to jeopardize its neutrality by inflaming tensions with either Britain or France. Whatever the case, the widespread corruption and arbitrary arrests of the period make virtually certain that Paine was tormented for reasons beyond his foreign status. Most likely, his staunch opposition to the king's execution, testimony against Marat, and his gravitation to the Girondins in general led him to such a fate. As he wrote some months later, "It was the literary and philosophical reputation I had gained in the world" that led to his cruel incarceration, and Paine was as such "the victim of the principles."[502]

Early in 1794, Joel Barlow organized a group of Paine's closest living friends, who drafted a petition that vouched for his character and pleaded for his release. "Our experience of twenty years has taught America to know and esteem his public virtues and the invaluable services he rendered her," the letter read. The petition heaped praises upon Paine's accomplishments and character. The penman was a "man whose courageous and energetic pen did so much to free the Americans, and whose intentions we have no doubt whatever were to render the same services to the French republic." In stark contrast to Morris, this group did attest to Paine's American citizenship and laudatory deeds, citing both as reasons to liberate the troubled writer:

As a countryman of ours, as a man so dear to the Americans, who like yourselves are earnest friends of Liberty, we ask you, in the name of that goddess cherished of the only two republics of the world, to give back Thomas Paine to his brethren and permit us to take him to his country which is also ours.

The petition was signed by eighteen men in total, including Barlow himself, all of whom offered to serve as Paine's security during "the short stay he may make" following his release.[503]

On January 20, sixteen of Paine's friends huddled around the National Convention, hoping to deliver the petition, and, if possible, to affirm to Paine's character in person. Though they were granted seats as spectators, only one was allowed to speak on behalf of the prisoner. As the petition was read in the chamber, where numerous "members hissed during the reading." After the session concluded, the petition was answered several days later by Marc-Guillaume Vadier, who was now the President of the Committee of General Security. Vadier affirmed the importance of the alliance with America, acknowledging that the states "have broken the chains of despotism," and like the French republic, "have sworn the destruction of kings and vowed an eternal hatred to tyrants and their instruments." Nevertheless, "Thomas Paine is a native of England," he declared, and such a truth was "undoubtedly enough to apply to him the measures of security prescribed by the revolutionary laws." Vadier snidely accused the penman of perceiving the French republic "only in accordance with the illusions with which the false friends of our revolution have invested it," a clear reference to the fallen Girondins. With the petition rejected, the cause for Paine's freedom was now at an impasse, where it would remain for almost a year.[504]

When the response to his appeal reached his cell in Luxembourg, Paine was overcome with hopelessness. The country he had promoted so favorably in *The Rights of Man* had turned on him entirely. He was once to all around him, including his enemies, an emissary of the French republic. Now, he was an outcast to the same government, a simple criminal worthy of no praise or commendation. To some extent, the feeling was mutual, as Paine had cast aside any lingering conception of France as a model republic. His time in confinement overlapped the bloodiest phase of the Reign of Terror, the most calamitous period of the French Revolution. From his cell, he witnessed hundreds of prisoners taken away for execution, including personal friends. In a single night, 169 were taken away—always in the dead of night—for the same reason. "The distress that I have suffered at being obliged to exist in the middle of such horrors" weighed heavily upon him. The circumstances caused him to settle into a deep depression.

"My life is but of little to me in this situation, though I have borne it with a firmness of patience and fortitude," he wrote.[505] Without even the ability to write to outsiders, he had no respite from his agony.

The spring of 1794 brought forth the downfall of many of the French republic's most eminent figures. Jacques René Hébert, who had himself attacked Danton, fell out of the graces of the Jacobins for playing a lead role in the violent dechristianization effort—which Robespierre hoped to temper—and for accusing Marie Antoinette of committing incest with her son. For his deeds, he lost his head in March. Georges Danton, who lambasted the pervasive campaign of religious prosecution and urged immediate peace with European powers, soon brought himself into the crosshairs of the Jacobin war against internal enemies. Robespierre's most enthusiastic acolyte, Louis Antoine Saint-Just, launched an attack against the former Girondin leader for subpar dedication to the revolution.

Danton retained popularity in many circles, and the thought that he vied for power in a post-Jacobin administration greatly worried Robespierre, Saint-Just, and Barère. Robespierre nullified the friendship he had formed with Danton, gave him a show trial at the Revolutionary Tribunal, and put him to death by the guillotine in April. Before the Jacobins had his head, he was placed in Luxembourg, where he recognized Paine, and the two shared a melancholy reunion. "That which you did for the happiness and liberty of your country I tried to do for mine," Danton lamented. "They will send me to the scaffold," he said, promising to "go gaily."[506] Camille Desmoulins, the young writer who did much to promote the revolution following the Storming of the Bastille, was executed the same day. Paine's friend and colleague from the constitutional project, Marquis de Condorcet, was arrested from his place of hiding, confined, and died in prison—likely by suicide—while awaiting the same fate.

To right the wrongs of Hébert, Robespierre played the lead role in enacting religious reforms in the summer of 1794. Though he remained greatly opposed to traditional religion, and especially the Catholic Church, France's most powerful man believed France's atheist-oriented dechristianization campaign had gone too far. Through the Committee of Public Safety, he pronounced the existence of God, human creation, the afterlife, and determined the French republic's official religion would be the Cult of the Supreme Being, a deistic state religion based on reason, moderation, justice, and human virtue in general. To consecrate the occasion, Robespierre organized the Festival of the Supreme Being, an elaborate ceremony to take place upon a stage on the Champ de Mars. Every meticulous detail was choreographed by the joint effort of Jacques-Louis David and Robespierre himself.

Thousands of Frenchmen bore witness to the spectacle that was the Festival of the Supreme Being. The festivities included a grand procession of the National Convention, led by the jubilant Robespierre himself, songs of praises to reason and the French republic, and a speech by the lead Jacobin at the top of a hill symbolizing heaven. In its finale, Robespierre, clad in an intricate costume of feathers, golden trousers, and a blue coat, and holding fruit in his hands, came down from mountain in a manner reminiscent of Moses leading his people to the promised land. To many, Robespierre's prominence in the ceremony was overbearing, and the sounds of cackling and hostility from some clashed with the cheers of others.[507] By this time, several of his colleagues—and former friends—believed he had gone mad.

The Reign of Terror continued without abatement, and even expanded its horrifying reach. On June 10, Georges Couthon succeeded in pushing through a plan, known as the Law of 22 Prairial, which streamlined the trial process by limiting trials to three days, and barring defendants from counsel, calling witnesses to attest to their character, and speaking on their own behalf. Moreover, the law obligated citizens to turn in their fellow man for engaging in conspiracy and treason against the revolution. As the direct result, those branded counterrevolutionaries were tried and executed at a rapid pace. In all, the period claimed the lives of about 40,000, a sum that included both those executed and those who died in prison without trial.[508]

In June and July, Robespierre engaged in a series of activities that alienated many of his most powerful peers in France. For a full month, he left Paris for the countryside, with many believing he had suffered a nervous breakdown. When Robespierre returned from this hiatus, entered into a fit of rage and publicly accused several respected deputies of the National Convention, including Jean-Lambert Tallien and Joseph Fouché, of conspiring against the revolution. Few agreed with his outlandish assertions, leading to his embarrassment. Robespierre's outburst also brought him into struggle with Barère, aimed to raise the Committee of General Security beyond its position of subordination to the Committee of Public Safety. The discord culminated in an abrupt departure from a meeting of his committee, where he slammed the door behind him in anger. When proposals were made to end the Reign of Terror, Robespierre even brought his erraticism to the Jacobin Club, where he denounced his new political foes. Even Saint-Just, Robespierre's closest remaining ally, agreed to enter into discussions with Barère on the standing of his committee.

Also aiding Robespierre's downfall, in parallel with the rivalry between committees, was the conclusion to the Battle of Fleurus. There on June 26, the French army triumphed over Austria, destroying the Dutch Republic and ending the "emergency conditions" used to justify the elevation of the Committee of Public Safety over a republican constitution. Rather than demand an immediate end to the bloody wave of executions, though, Robespierre called instead for a new purge of those trying to undermine him, as well as the complete dissolution of both the Committee of General Security and Committee of Public Safety. When asked to name those who needed to be purged, he cowered in silence. Within the legislature, Pierre-Joseph Cambon declared that "one man paralyzes the assembly, and that man is Robespierre." Committee of Public Safety member Jacques-Nicolas Billaud-Varenne, himself an architect of the Reign of Terror, professed he would rather allow his corpse to be made into "a throne to the tyrant" than to become the "accomplice of his crimes."[509] After Robespierre's tirade, nine members of the two committees convened in secret, ultimately deciding that the Jacobin kingpin had to be eliminated.

Robespierre's closest living ally, Saint-Just, drafted a speech to defend his friend and shift the blame to their mutual enemies. However, when he recited it on July 24, his voice was hastily interrupted by a whirlwind of condemnations against Robespierre. At this point, all factions within the National Convention aligned against him, including the Montagnards, a group he helped nurture; Saint-Just sat in reluctant silence as 35 deputies spoke against his friend. In the chamber, Robespierre himself made a last-ditch appeal to the Plain, a group whose moderation he often disparaged, and was sharply rebuffed.

Robespierre tried to commit suicide by shooting himself through the jaw, but failed to succeed, and was left bleeding. For a single night, he was placed on a bed once occupied by Danton in the horrific Conciergerie prison, and was carried off to the gallows the next morning. Joined by his brother Augustin, his allies Saint-Just and Couthon, and 18 other "Robespierrists," he was executed on July 28. The masses shouted for joy as they witnessed the event at the Place de la Révolution, the exact place where King Louis XVI was executed. The irony could not have escaped them.

Toward the end of June, Paine developed a fever that lasted more than two weeks. While ill, he was brought into a larger cell with three fellow prisoners, all Belgians. The group endeavored to save his life, feeding him by hand, cleaning him, and even changing his clothing that had become wet and soiled because of incontinence. Paine was unable to move, concentrate, or converse at all during these trying days, and his roommates believed he would soon die. Paine later wrote that his condition made him "incapable of knowing anything of what happened in the prison or elsewhere," and his recovery "remained doubtful." The trio gained permission from their jailers to leave the cell door open, such that the cool breezes of the prison corridor could reach his feverish body.[510] This fact, while appearing wholly mundane on the surface, would in fact save Paine's life.

While Paine was sure he would soon lose his head, his life was spared from execution in what amounted to a stroke of complete luck. Within Luxembourg, jailers used chalk marks to indicate the cells of prisoners that were to be taken at night for execution. On July 24, mere days before the fall of Robespierre, an attendant designated Paine for execution. In doing so, however, he erroneously placed the mark on inside of his door rather than the outside, the result of the door being "open and thrown back against the wall of the corridor" at the time. The group of Belgians shrewdly shut the door, concealing the marked side from the view of the guards. Later that night, the execution commissioner, not seeing the mark, passed by Paine's cell. In Paine's words, "the destroying angel passed by it." As a result, the penman survived the crucial days leading up to Robespierre's highly-publicized collapse.[511] As he had done as a young and daring privateer, an outlaw in Britain, and a polemicist caught up in revolutionary fervor in Paris, he had narrowly escaped death for a fourth time.

News of Robespierre's demise did little to comfort Paine, who had suffered in Luxembourg for eight months. Earlier in the year, his friend Anacharsis Cloots was executed, and the steady stream of those around him disappearing into the night dampened his already-low spirits. When the prohibition on his correspondence was lifted, Paine wrote to the National Convention for amnesty. His stated reasoning for reaching out to the body now, rather than before, was due to the now-deposed administration. "Robespierre was my inveterate enemy," he wrote, "as he was the enemy of every man of virtue and humanity." The fallen Jacobin had, "by the most consummate hypocrisy and the most hardened cruelties," rendered all attempts "to obtain justice not only useless but dangerous." In a passage that could have been lifted from *The Rights of Man*, he noted that "it is in the nature of tyranny to strike a deeper blow when any attempt has been made to repel a former one."[512]

After submitting "with patience to the hardness of my fate," Paine welcomed the arrival of "better days" that replaced those dominated by Robespierre. In his letter, he reminded the deputies—some of whom had served as his peers—that he had always displayed "the earnest and disinterested desire of rendering every service" on behalf of the French Revolution. "This long sacrifice of private tranquility" amounting to seven years, removed from his personal life and friends, was undeserving of the "long imprisonment" he had "silently suffered." So as to separate the madness of Robespierre from the French republic in totality, Paine made clear that "it is not the nation but a faction that" had done him "this injustice." While professing to be a "citizen of the United States, an ally of France, and not a subject of any country in Europe," he conveyed doubt that his status as a foreigner was the true reason behind his confinement. "But any excuse can be made to serve the purpose of malignity when in power," he digressed. The pained writer wished "fraternity and prosperity to France, and union and happiness to her representatives," and wrote of his hope to be freed by their compassion. "I can have no doubt but your justice will restore me to the liberty of which I have been deprived," he concluded.[513]

Unfortunately for Paine, his letter never reached the legislature, and he continued to languish in prison.[514] The fall season brought good fortune, however, and the political trajectory shifted in his favor, both internally and externally. His friend James Monroe, whom he had known since the American War of Independence, replaced Gouverneur Morris as American minister to France in August of 1794. Additionally, Robespierre's downfall triggered the Thermidorian Reaction, a transition to back to normality in republican France. Anti-religious purges, arbitrary jurisprudence, and all-powerful oligarchical committees were replaced by a drive toward moderation, a stable government, the end to emergency measures, and the establishment of a new constitution.

Upon learning the news of Monroe's appointment, Paine immediately put pen to paper. "A new minister from America is a joy to me and will be so to every American in France," he wrote. He explained that his recent illness "nearly put an end" to his existence, and attached the petition he "sent to the convention after the fall of the monster, Robespierre." Paine also made known his bitterness toward Morris, Monroe's predecessor. "Morris has been my inveterate enemy, and I think he has permitted something of the national character of America to suffer by quietly letting a citizen of that country remain almost eight months in prison without making every official exertion to procure him justice," he grieved. Two days later, he sent the new Virginian ambassador a summary of his history in France, the failure of his friends to secure his release in Paris, and information regarding his arrest and state's claim that his foreign status justified his predicament. "I hope that your authority will release me from this unjust predicament," he ended the letter.[515]

Unlike Morris, Monroe began an immediate effort to press Paine's appeal for release. As he was doing so, in a rare departure from his usual style, Paine revealed the grim nature of his experience as a prisoner of the Reign of Terror:

> While the Robespierrian faction lasted, I had nothing to do but to keep my mind tranquil and expect the fate that was every day inflicted upon my comrades, not individually but by scores. Many a man whom I have passed an hour with in Conversation I have seen marching to his destruction the next hour, or heard of it the next morning—for what rendered the scene the more horrible was that they were generally taken away at midnight, so that every man went to bed with the apprehension of never seeing his friends or the world again.

Despite the profound horrors of those months, when men disappeared into the night never to be seen again, he now had some hope. "There is now a moment of calm," he wrote, while acknowledging that he was "not out of danger till I am out of prison." Viewing Monroe as his sole lifeline, Paine continued writing to the minister throughout September and October. Monroe urged patience, but committed himself to Paine's liberation. In response, Paine maintained a direct, but polite, tone. As to patience I have practiced it long," he replied, while reiterating the conditions of his depravity. Even so, he expressed thanks to Monroe for his diligence that stood in stark contrast to that of Morris. "I am inclined to believe you have attended to my imprisonment more as a friend than a minister, he wrote, and "as a friend I thank you for your affectionate attachment."[516]

Paine's desperation for freedom grew to such heights that in October, he supplied Monroe with a sample letter to be used to argue in his favor, which was to be supplied to the Committee of General Security. The plea reminded the body that Paine was given French citizenship "only as a mark of honorary respect" rather than an abnegation of his American citizenship. The letter would have Monroe insist unambiguously that Paine still held the same status in the United States, and embellish upon his stature therein:

> In consequence of the vote of this Convention declaring him to be a foreigner the former Committees have imprisoned him. It is therefore my official duty to declare to you that the foreigner thus imprisoned in a citizen of the United States of America as fully, as legally, and as constitutionally as myself, and that he is moreover one of the principal founders of the American Republic.

Furthermore, the National Convention's decision to imprison Paine on account of his foreign status was to be regarded as an "infraction" of the two 1778 Franco-American treaties, "which knows no distinction of American citizens on account of the place of their birth." By "a strict adherence to moral justice, to the equality of civil and political rights, to the system of representative government, and an opposition to all hereditary claims to govern," the letter espoused that "no man" had "gone beyond Thomas Paine in promulgating and defending them, and that for almost twenty years past." The immediate deliverance of Paine, "which the injured state of his health absolutely requires," was therefore a moral imperative.[517]

Though Monroe borrowed some themes in regard to Paine's character and patriotism when he appealed to the Committee of General Security, he decided to tread more carefully than the penman suggested. Rather than ascribe nefarious motives to the writer's imprisonment, or imply a governmental desire widen the schism between the United States and France, Monroe's plea instead avoided contention and asked the government to release Paine if he was guilty of no offenses, and to try him in court if he was. Regardless, Monroe reminded the committee that "the citizens of the United States can never look back to the era of their own revolution, without remembering, with those other distinguished patriots, the name of Thomas Paine." The writer's contributions "made an impression of gratitude which will never be erased, whilst they continue to merit the character of a just and generous people," his plea concluded.[518]

The new American minister to France presented his petition on November 2. After two meetings, the Committee of General Security approved Paine's release without delay on November 6. Monroe had the order forwarded immediately to Luxembourg, then took the extraordinary step of personally travelling to the former palace to collect Paine. The grey-bearded, 57-year-old Paine was at long last now freed from the shackles of imprisonment, returning by carriage with Monroe to Paris "in good spirits." Along the way, Monroe graciously invited Paine to live with him in Paris. His offer extended "till his death or departure for America, however remote either the one or the other event may be." Monroe asked only that Paine not write anything about America's diplomatic affairs for public consumption while he stayed, so as not to endanger his mission.[519]

While Paine was in prison, he had devoted much time at first to the second part of *The Age of Reason*. As time went on, however, personal illness and the unavailability of candles in prison made it impossible for him to remain focused on that endeavor.[520] However, as Paine agonized in his cell, Joel Barlow had been working to bring the first part of *The Age of Reason* to the masses. After Paine was arrested, Barlow had escaped to London, where he quickly arranged for the work's publication. The first version was sold for the measly price of three pence. By no surprise, the work was quickly banned by the authorities, but illegally printed versions were widely printed and sold, with many copies making their way overseas to the United States. In tandem with Barlow's efforts, François Xavier

Lanthenas, a former Girondin deputy of the National Convention, translated the work into French which aspirations of having it published locally.

Paine began the first part of *The Age of Reason* with an introduction that stressed his purpose. It had always been his intention, "for several years past," to publish his "thoughts upon religion." In his mind, the monumental dechristianization crusade in France, however, made its publication even more crucial:

> The circumstance that has now taken place in France, of the total abolition of the whole national order of priesthood, and of everything appertaining to compulsive systems of religion, and compulsive articles of faith, has not only precipitated by intention, but rendered a work of this kind exceedingly necessary, lest, in the general wreck of superstition, of false systems of government, and false theology, we lose sight of morality, of humanity, and of the theology that is true.

To expound upon this, Paine declared his basic convictions on religion. "I believe in one God, and no more," he wrote, "and I hope for happiness beyond this life." So too did he believe "that religious duties consist in doing justice, loving mercy, and endeavoring to make our fellow-creatures happy." With that plainly stated, he declared he would, "in the progress of this work, declare the things I do not believe, and my reasons for not believing them."[521]

In a statement that put him at odds with virtually everyone in the Western world at the time, he professed that he did "not believe in the creed professed by the Jewish church, by the Roman church, by the Greek church, by the Turkish church, by the Protestant church, nor by any other church that I know of." All institutionalized churches, of any denomination, were in his mind mandate falsifications of God's will. "My own mind is my own church," he declared, and all church establishments were merely "human inventions set up to terrify and enslave mankind, and monopolize power and profit." While stating his opinion in the most overt manner possible, he acknowledged that he did "not mean by this declaration to condemn those who believe otherwise," as all free people had "the same right to their belief as I have mine."[522] The absolute free exercise of religion and freedom of conscience—whether practitioners aligned with his own inclinations or not—was to Paine an essential element of liberty.

The historical propensity for government to impose upon men an obligation to believe in a certain religion, according to Paine, was a condemnable "moral mischief" that "has so far corrupted and prostituted the chastity of the mind, as to subscribe his professional belief to things he does not believe." In the 18th century, strains caused by the near-immutable bond between church and state were hard to deny. Religious dissenters were punished or hindered in virtually every way—politically, economically, and culturally—in almost every corner of the world. "The adulterous connection of church and state," wrote Paine, had "so effectually prohibited, by pains and penalties, every discussion upon established creeds, and upon first principles of religion." Besides shutting down conversation, strife between religious factions was amplified. In England, Test Acts that prohibited those of minority religious beliefs from obtaining civil office led to lengthy political battles, and the close ties between the state and religious establishments contributed to the outbreak of the English Civil Wars and the Glorious Revolution of 1688. After publishing *Common Sense*, Paine "saw the probability that a revolution in the system of government would be followed by a revolution in the system of religion," a shift he hoped to inspire.[523]

Paine first took aim at divine revelation, in his mind the starting point of every religion. By "pretending some special mission from God, communicated to certain individuals," he argued, men brought the word of the creator to followers, and thereby established churches. Paine wrote that revelation, while held as sacrosanct, had the limitation of applying only to information given by God to a single man. When the original recipient of revelation "tells it to a second person, a second to a third, a third to a fourth, and so on, it ceases to be a revelation to all those persons." According to Paine, divine communication was "revelation to the first person only, and hearsay to every other," leading him to conclude that all other parties "are not obliged to believe it." The children of Israel were not obliged to believe that Moses received the Ten Commandments from God, then, because only he was privy to the revelation that brought them into the world. At the same time, Paine conceded the inherent value of moral lessons contained within the same stone tablets. More controversially, the penman wrote that there was no reason to believe Mary, being a virgin, was able to bear Jesus as her son. "Such a circumstance," like many others of its kind, "required stronger evidence" than the word of men allowed.[524]

Though Paine denied the miracles of Jesus Christ in the New Testament, he admitted the worth of the moral lessons he conveyed to humanity. "He was a virtuous and amiable man," Paine wrote, and "the morality that he preached and practiced was of the most benevolent kind." The gospels were "altogether the work of other people," and subject to the same errors that befall all of humanity, he contended. The miraculous conception of Christ had the advantage of being unable to be disproven easily, "and it was impossible that the person of whom it was told could prove it himself," Paine surmised. Subjecting the Christian savior's resurrection from the dead to reason, also, failed to allay skepticism of its truth. "A thing which everybody is required to believe, requires that proof and evidence of it should be equal to all, and universal," he insisted. Instead, Paine continued, "a small number of persons, not more than eight or nine, are introduced as proxies for the whole world, to say they saw it, and all the rest of the world are called upon to believe it."[525] To make any belief that could not be established through logic such a crucial element of Christianity, he thought, invalidated the nature of such a religion.

For the same reasons Paine denied the divine nature and miraculous aspects of Jesus Christ, he denied Satan's fall from heaven and subsequent temptation of Adam and Eve while assuming the form of a snake. Furthermore, Paine alleged that the historians who invented Satan's story deliberately chose not to "send him back again into the pit," giving him instead "a triumph over the whole creation" such that his presence could be used as a perpetual symbol of evil to be avoided. Religious apologists "could not do without him," Paine wrote, "and after being at the trouble of making him, they bribed him to stay." The writer also contended those who "invented" the biblical account of Satan also implied the evildoer held "power equally as great, if not greater, than they attribute to the almighty." In so doing, he reasoned, Christian fundamentalists must subscribe to the belief that Satan was both "an angel of limited existence," but also capable of "liberating himself from the pit" and expanding his power "to infinity." To believe in both things was to embrace palpable contradictions, the Englishman thought.[526]

Rather than hinging one's belief on divine miracles, Paine believed the natural world was sufficient to prove the existence of God. "It is only by the exercise of reason," he wrote, "that man can discover God." The world and its surroundings stood as direct confirmation, via "internal evidence," that man did not make himself. To justify this, Paine spent a great deal of time expounding the structure of the galaxy, composed, as he wrote, of "many worlds in each solar system." The seemingly boundless size of the universe was an inference that God's power was also comparatively boundless, and as Paine deduced, "the creator made nothing in vain." In his mind, man's size relative to that of the immense oceans and landmasses also served to confirm the same concept. Additionally, Paine opined that a cursory examination of the origins of all humans, animals, and plants, proved that no being could make itself. "Every man is an evidence to himself, that he did not make himself; neither could his father make himself, nor his grandfather, nor any of his race; neither could any tree, plant or animal make itself," he expounded. This truism revealed to him the existence of "a first cause eternally existing, of a nature totally different to any material existence we know of"—that which "man calls God."[527]

Two great objects of Paine's incredulity were miracles and prophecies, both of which he considered incongruent with reason. "Of all the modes of evidence" that existed to prove a point, he wrote, "that of miracle" was "the most inconsistent." Miracles, Paine argued, were natural circumstances that were mistakenly attributed to divine will. For instance, Paine cited "performances by sleight of hand," the fallibility of human senses, and the scientific manifestation of things that man had a limited understanding of, such as electricity. To be certain of biblical miracles, such as those of involving Jonah's safe passage in the belly of a giant fish, the miraculous conception, and Christ being carried to the top of a high mountain by Satan, was to degrade "the almighty into the character of a showman, playing tricks to amuse and make the people stare and wonder."[528] In contrast, Paine's viewed the creator as an entity who imparted knowledge to man through nature, leaving each individual to discover universal truths through deductive reasoning.

Prophecy, by extension, was derided by Paine as mere mysticism that could instead be explained by the nature of ambiguous predictions. The penman elaborated that biblical prophets, even if their forecasts in the Bible were taken as be true, made their assertions in such broad terms that they were bound to be fulfilled in some tangential way. "The supposed prophet," he wrote, "happened, in shooting with a long bow of a thousand years, to strike within a thousand miles of a mark, the ingenuity of posterity could make it point blank." In contrast to fulfillment by elasticity, Paine would only accept fulfillment by specifics. If a future truth from God were truly communicated through a prophet, he reasoned, "it is consistent to believe that the event so communicated would be told in terms that could be understood, not related in such a loose and obscure manner as to be out of the comprehension of those that heard it."[529]

In contrast to traditional, institutionalized religion, Paine championed deism, described synonymously as "true religion." In his age, a deist was one who believed in God as an omnipotent architect who created the world, set it into motion, and granted man ability to reason without intending to intervene in the development of the same world. Moral lessons were to be ascertained not through miracles, prophecy, threats of condemnation, or religious doctrine, but by applying reason to circumstances in nature. As Paine put it, "the true deist has but one deity; and his religion consists in contemplating the power, wisdom, and benignity of the deity in his works, in endeavoring to imitate him in everything moral, scientifical, and mechanical." In contrast to some deists of his time, however, Paine believed in the immorality of the human soul. "I content myself with believing, even to positive conviction" he wrote, "that the power that gave me existence is able to continue it, in any form and manner he pleases, either with or without this body."[530]

To conclude the first part of *The Age of Reason*, Paine reiterated that the natural world was enough to prove the existence of God as a singular entity. "It proclaimed his power, it demonstrates his wisdom, it manifests his goodness and beneficence," he avowed, and "the creation we behold is the real and ever existing word of God, in which we cannot be deceived." The moral duty of man should therefore be to "do the goodness of God to all men," and, conversely, to consider "persecution and revenge between man and man" as "a violation of moral duty." This moral framework remained relevant, he believed, from the outset of the world. "Adam, if ever there was such a man, was created a deist," Paine declared, "but in the meantime, let every man follow, as he has a right to do, the religion and worship he prefers."[531]

Paine's religious treatise featured the same irreverent style of *Common Sense* and *The Rights of Man*, bringing a subject mostly confined to enlightenment scholars to commoners for the first time. While many of the ideas within the pamphlet had been raised by other philosophers—especially David Hume and Voltaire—it was Paine who was most responsible for exposing the masses to religious skepticism. A clue to the latter's influence may reside within his homage to Voltaire in *The Rights of Man*, where he commended the French satirist's "forte in exposing and ridiculing superstitions which priestcraft, united with statecraft, had interwoven with governments." Also contributing to many of the themes may have been the writer's upbringing as a Quaker, a sect of religious dissidents that Paine portrayed as "the nearest of all others to true deism."[532]

Despite his view that the Bible was merely "a book of riddles that requires a revelation to explain it," Paine originally wrote the tract in response to the dechristianization effort in France, which he feared was "running headlong into atheism." However, the atheist-oriented campaign of fierce religious persecution was already scaling back in favor of religious toleration, and as such, the pamphlet's impact was not widely felt there. Though copies spread through the underground after it was banned in Britain, the work was understandably viewed as sacrilege in many corners of the devoutly-religious world. Even so, like in the case of *The Rights of Man*, negative notoriety was notoriety nonetheless, and only helped spread word of the pamphlet's existence. English versions of *The Age of Reason* first appeared in the United States in 1794, where passionate readers even setup local sects based on Paine's religious views. The American embrace of Paine's brand of deism was short-lived and applied only to a niche audience, however, and the work was met ultimately with intense scrutiny.[533] While in Europe, he was shielded from much of the work's negative reception, but in the end its publication in the United States would cost him many friends.

Even after almost a year of imprisonment, Paine could not discard his attachment to world politics. The same month he was released, John Jay, acting as an American diplomat in London, finalized a treaty with Britain.

The Treaty of Amnesty, Commerce, and Navigation, Between His Britannic Majesty and the United States, more colloquially known as the "Jay Treaty," sought to ease lingering tensions between the crown and her former colonies. Before the United States Senate even had a chance to consider its merits, it drew immense controversy. Jeffersonian Republicans, who sided with France over Britain, continued to argue that the treaties signed with France in 1778 should still be honored. The Washington administration's gesture, then, seemed to profess devotion to an adversarial monarchy over a budding republic that was more naturally suited to American friendship. To the Republicans—with whom Paine ultimately sided on this matter—the treaty was an overt act of betrayal the principles for which the recent war had been fought, and a sign that the Federalists aspired to establish a monarchy in the United States. The settlement also raised tensions because the settlement was established by Jay, who was the Chief Justice of the Supreme Court at the time. By sending Jay to represent the executive branch in conjunction with his judicial duties, Washington was accused of abnegating the separation of powers doctrine that underscored the United States Constitution.

Besides the general optics of the Jay Treaty, its particulars also brought about immeasurable scorn. According to leading critics, the pact left many outstanding American issues with Britain sitting on the table. Namely, Jay's negotiation failed to achieve financial compensation for American slaves that were emancipated by the British in 1783, a clear violation of the Treaty of Paris that had remained a source of bitterness for many Americans. President Washington, who expressed his anger toward British General Guy Carleton for his role in the manumission, seemed now to disregard the gripe.[534] The treaty also stopped short of ending the widely-despised practice of British impressment, where captured American sailors were enslaved into the service of the Royal Navy. Both issues were left unresolved, responded Federalist advocates of the agreement, to guarantee the British evacuation of North American forts, establish a northern territorial boundary, and to reopen trade with Britain on a most-favored-nation basis.

Antagonism toward the Washington administration was at an all-time high, and the likeness of Jay was hanged in several corners of the republic.

Nevertheless, the president ultimately sided with Hamilton and the Federalists, giving his own assent to the plan such that it would be placed in
front of the Senate for ratification. By the narrow margin of 20–10, exactly
equal to the minimum threshold of two-thirds, the body endorsed the pact.
By all accounts, the Jay Treaty widened the growing schism between the
Republicans and Federalists. Upon learning of its specifics, Paine lashed
out against its American architect in a letter to his old friend Samuel Adams. Jay's declaration that the "United States has no other resource than
in the justice and magnanimity of his Majesty" was "satire upon the Declaration of Independence," and more becoming of a "character of aristocracy" than "the manly character of a republican," he ranted. Years later,
Paine grieved that the Jay Treaty "had so disgracefully surrendered the
right and freedom of the American flag.[535] Though the penman never made
his association to any faction so rigid, the Jay Treaty did much, in addition
to Washington's inaction during his imprisonment, to place him firmly in
the camp of Jefferson and his devotees.

In late 1794, Paine was astonished to learn that the National Convention had unanimously adopted a motion to reinstate Paine as deputy of
Calais in the same body. At the forefront of the effort was Antoine Claire
Thibaudeau, a moderate Montagnard-aligned member who heaped praises
upon the Englishman. To demonstrate he "could bear an injury without
permitting it to injure" his "principles or disposition," Paine accepted.[536]
With the help of a translator, he expressed his thanks in a letter to Thibaudeau, who assured him that he could take a leave of absence in order to
travel to America in the spring as he planned. After collecting back pay of
1,800 livres, the equivalent of one year's salary as a deputy, Paine took his
seat once again in Paris. In a reception that diverged completely from the
one he received from his Jacobin enemies, he was openly praised by the
revolutionary legislature and even given official honors for his literary
works.

With the Thermidorians now in power, temperament seemed to right
many of the wrongs of the previous two years. The National Convention
resumed its position as the sovereign legislature of France, and the Committee of Public Safety's role was reduced to a subordinate department that
oversaw diplomatic relations and the war effort. The mass persecution

campaign against religious adherents ended, and the Cult of Reason effectively ceased to exist. The Jacobin Club was dissolved, and the militant Paris Commune was disbanded. Painstaking strides were made to erase or subdue almost every remnant of the Reign of Terror, a devastating period that drenched Paris in blood and claimed the lives of more than 40,000 people. While the Thermidorian Reaction involved violent acts against the masterminds of the bloodshed and their followers, and some Jacobin resistance remained, almost all political influence of the previous regime was swept into the dustbin of history.

Chapter 7

Directory to Dictatorship

It is worthy of observation that every case of failure in finances, since the system of paper began, has produced a revolution in governments, either total or partial.

- The Decline and Fall of the English System of Finance

One of the most pressing aims of the new French administration was its desire to establish a new treaty of peace and commerce with the United States. Because the Washington administration held that the previous Franco-American treaties were nullified upon the death of Louis XVI, the National Convention resolved that it was best to act quickly—while acceptance of the Jay Treaty was still up in the air—to restore good will with its republican counterpart. The French authorities planned to send a delegation of commissioners to the United States to discuss terms for a renewed alliance, a task Monroe thought Paine perfectly suited for. In a letter to the Committee of Public Safety, the Virginian made a formal request to appoint Paine to the task, which was to be a confidential expedition. The committee declined Monroe's request, in Paine's mind because adding the restored legislator to the commission would have required application for passport, and thus exposed the clandestine operation. Appointment of the restored deputy may also have been denied for fear that he would bring the treachery of the Reign of Terror to America.[537]

Paine remained in France, committing his energy to the post-Jacobin political settlement, influencing the new republican constitution, and doing his part to restore legitimacy to republicanism in France. Furthermore, he devoted significant energy to several writing projects, including the second part of *The Age of Reason*, as well as two unplanned ventures that became *Dissertations on the First Principles of Government* and *Agrarian Justice*. As the natural result of these projects, his plans to return to America in the spring of 1795 never came to fruition, but for reasons different from those that prevented him from returning in 1793.

In 1795, the Constitution of the Year III, whose primary authors were François Antoine de Boissy d'Anglas and Pierre Daunou, was proposed with the hope it would establish a new conservative order. Specifically, the framework was crafted with the explicit intention of diffusing political authority into multiple centers of power, and obstructing the tyranny of the majority, a tendency inherent in a unicameral legislature. Specifically, this would be accomplished through the creation of a bicameral body composed of a lower house called the Council of Five Hundred and a Council of Ancients, an upper house. All legislation would originate in the former body, while the latter had the ability to negate or endorse laws submitted to it. According to its architect Boissy d'Anglas, the Council of Five Hundred was to serve as "the imagination of the republic," with the Council of Ancients acting as "its reason."[538] Executive power was to be held by a five-member board known as the Directory, whose members would be elected by the Council of Ancients from a list submitted by the Council of Five Hundred.

As an advocate of Montesquieu's separation of powers doctrine, Paine always favored dividing power within government, and this inclination attracted him to France's new constitutional proposal. "A better constitution has never yet been devised by human wisdom," he wrote of the Constitution of the Year III. "Free from the vices and defects to which other governments" suffered, it offered true promise. Among its best features, he explained, was its system of electoral rotation that replaced one-third of the assembly each year, its partition of legislative authority into two separate bodies, and its plural executive model that deliberately cast aside any semblance of a single powerholder. When it came to executive authority, "an individual by election is almost as bad as the hereditary system," he wrote, "except that there is always a better chance of not having an idiot." Substituting an executive plurality, beyond checking the impulses of ambitious office-seekers, would "give opportunity to discuss all the various subjects that in the course of national business may come before it," without bureaucratizing the role to such an extent it would "endanger the necessary secrecy that certain cases, such as those of war, require." Paine was also impressed by the system's checks and balances, which he thought excelled at preventing the "abuse of power that might arise by letting it remain too long in the same hands."[539]

Despite his great praise for the general Thermidorian constitutional plan, but he took issue with the new framework for a very particular reason—namely, that it eliminated universal suffrage. Instead, the Constitution of the Year III granted voting rights only to those who met minimum property ownership thresholds. As the "only defect in the constitution," Paine believed the narrowing of suffrage smacked of noble privilege, landed aristocracy, and every other crooked remnant of hereditary monarchy.[540] He was so passionate in this perspective that he drafted a new manifesto, *Dissertations on the First Principles of Government*, to elaborate upon his grievances regarding suffrage in the summer of 1795.

The work stressed the paramount importance of the representation in a republican system, of which universal suffrage was a critical element. A republic "comprehends all individuals of whatever age, from just born to just dying," according to Paine, and "the rights of minors are as sacred as the rights of age." Differences among persons, he deduced, were differences of classification only, and not of rights. Therefore, depriving the right to vote from some on arbitrary grounds would be "to subjugate him to a system of government to which" he "could neither consent nor object." Taking a jab at the suffrage limitations in the Constitution of the Year III, Paine further declared that "the rich have no more right to exclude the poor from the right of voting, or of electing and being elected, than the poor have to exclude the rich." The right to vote was to Paine "a species of property of the most sacred kind," and belonged to all humanity, just as the right to alter and abolish one's government was.[541] The Thermidorian suffrage plan, by extension, was a dreaded callback to France's aristocratic monarchy, contravening what Paine believed to be the basic tenets of republicanism.

On July 5, with the help of a translator, Paine testified to the same principles in the National Convention. Paine cited passages from the Declaration of the Rights of Man and the Citizen to demonstrate that the constitutional proposal would defile the most fundamental principles of the French Revolution by limiting suffrage rights and citizenship. "Persons excluded by this inequality can neither be said to possess liberty, nor security against oppression," he cautioned, which the enumeration of rights demanded. Granting the state power to determine who would and would not be a citizen based on the payment of direct taxes would "subvert the basis of the revolution," putting in its place "nothing but a cold indifference and self-interest, which will again degenerate into intrigue, cunning, and effeminacy."[542] The Thermidorians were therefore presented with an opportunity to right this wrong by inaugurating an otherwise favorable framework for government. It was a stern but sincere plea, and contained all of Paine's principled abrasiveness.

Unfortunately for Paine, his audience was in no mood to accept the pitch. In the hearts and minds of the sitting deputies—some of whom had also been persecuted by the Jacobins—universal suffrage had been at the heart of the calamities of the previous two years. Many representatives instead came to the belief that revolutionary stability necessitated the revocation of voting rights from ardent French commoners who fanned the flames of the Reign of Terror. Eradication of monarchy, in their minds, did nothing to disturb the perspective that decisions in government should still be left to the most experienced, capable, and landed members of French society. Paine's attempt to amend the suffrage planks failed, with none rising to support his cause. The National Convention endorsed the new constitution in August, and submitted it to a national referendum. It received the popular support of more than a million eligible voters, and was ultimately approved on September 6, 1795. The two new legislative houses, as well as the Directory, would begin operating in two months' time. The duties of the deputies in the National Convention, including Paine, had now come to an end.

In the period between the old and new regimes, Paine suffered lingering health issues as the result of his lengthy confinement. Sporadic chest pains had hindered him since his release, but had not been debilitating. In September, however, he was afflicted with typhus, a disease contracted through bacterial infection. Then known as "gaol fever," the condition was easily spread in overcrowded areas of poor sanitation, as Luxembourg had been. By September, Paine's illness reached critical severity. Monroe reported that the penman had only months to live, and Paine reported to James Madison, then a member of Congress, that his ailment had "taken a malignant turn." To be sure, Paine understood his risk of succumbing to the disease. "It would be agreeable to me to live," he told the Virginian, "but if it is not to be so I can quit life with as much tranquility as any man that ever passed that scene, for I have done an honest part in the world." The *Philadelphia Aurora General Advertiser* even reported the false rumor that Paine had died of the illness.[543]

Even while sick, Paine fought on toward completing his current passion project. *The Age of Reason, Part Second* was finished in October of 1795, and printed the same year. The primary focus of this entry was its rejection of the Bible as the divine, unadulterated word of God. In the first chapter Paine took issue with the Old Testament's records of the killing of women and children, and the cleansing of nations who were enemies of the Jews with acts of violence, which "were done by the express command of God." To accept the clear meaning of the text, he thought, would force one to "unbelieve all our belief in the moral justice of God," and "undo everything that is tender, sympathizing, and benevolent in the heart of man."[544]

According to the deist, Old Testament books ascribed to Moses, Joshua, Samuel, and others failed to withstand the scrutiny of reason in that they "testify of things naturally incredible," raising doubt as to both the authorship of those books and the credit given to the testimony itself. Despite the common propensity of his detractors to argue the Bible was "as well established as that of any other ancient book," Paine insisted instead that ancient works of timeless value, such as those written by Plato, Aristotle, Demosthenes, Cicero, had been given such adoration for their propensity to record natural truths, with a few exceptions. The writer granted that Homer's tale of the Trojan Horse, for example, was believed by no one, and meant to convey meaning through metaphor rather purporting to record a divine truth. Without accepting the miracles of the Old Testament, on the other hand, there was little value in the deeds of the biblical Jews in the eyes of Paine. Homer's literary contributions meant "the merit of the poet will remain, though the story be fabulous," but without his miracles, "there remains nothing of Moses in our estimation, but an imposter," he wrote.[545]

In *The Age of Reason, Part Second,* Paine aspired to prove that Genesis, Exodus, Leviticus, Numbers, and Deuteronomy, rather than divine texts, were "spurious," not authored by Moses, and written hundreds of years after Moses' time. To support this, he pointed to several passages within the five texts that, had they been authored by the leader of the Israelites, must then be interpreted as contradictory. For instance, the mention I Numbers 12:3 that "Moses was very meek, above all the men which were of the face of the earth" could only have been written by a very overbearing man. "If Moses said this of himself," he declared, "instead of being the meekest of men, he was one of the most vain and arrogant coxcombs." In another example, he cites Deuteronomy 34:5–6, which records the death and burial of Moses, and mentions that "no man knoweth of his sepulcher unto this day." The narrative was given in third person with a clear reference to the past, Paine contended, making it clear that Moses was not the writer and the book was instead written at "great length" after the time of his death. Paine's position on Mosaic authorship of the Pentateuch—the first five books of the Old Testament—aligned exactly with the writings of Dutch philosopher Baruch Spinoza, making it likely he drew inspiration from the 17th-century deist.[546]

Paine also took aim at parts of the New Testament he believed defied reason, including its account of the birth of Jesus. Paine wrote with his trademark irreverence that the story of Christ's birth amounted to "an account of a young woman engaged to be married, and while under this engagement, she is, to speak plain language, debauched by a ghost." In addition, the cynical scribe noted differences in the recorded genealogy of Christ in the gospel accounts, both in terms of number of generations removed from David and actual names provided. As for lack of corroboration among the four accounts, Paine believed them all subject to falsification, or at the very least, contradiction. Furthermore, he raised Matthew's account of the happenings after Christ's death—where graves were opened, bodies were resurrected, and the arisen saints ventured into the holy city and appeared to many—to note that such a stunning scene was omitted from all other gospel accounts. To Paine, the spectacle could not have been missed by other observers of the time. "It was not possible," he wrote, for Mark, Luke, and John, "as true historians, even without the aid of inspiration, not to have recorded them."[547]

In contrast to the "true religion" that Paine espoused, "there is none more derogatory to the almighty, more unedifying to man, more repugnant to reason, and more contradictory in itself, than this thing called Christianity," he declared. Its biblical foundation was "too absurd for belief, too impossible to convince, and too inconsistent for practice," he wrote, and Christianity merely served "the purpose of despotism" and "the avarice of priests." Paine's theistic preference, of course, was much more romantic. "The only religion that has not been invented, and that has in it every evidence of divine originality, is pure and simple deism," he wrote. Compared with the Bible of traditional adherents, the Bible of the deist "is inexhaustible in texts," Paine asserted. As he saw it, "every part of science, whether connected with the geometry of the universe, with the systems of animal and vegetable life, or with the properties of inanimate matter is a text as well for devotion as for philosophy." Rather than a miraculous apparition, the God of deism was "the great mechanic of the creation, the first philosopher, and original teacher of all science."[548]

In sum, *The Age of Reason, Part Second* portrayed the Bible as a book filled with fables, falsely attributed writings, and circumstances that could not be corroborated. The few redeemable moral lessons it contained, he thought, were overshadowed by a host of nonsensical parables, impossible situations, perversions of ideal moral lessons, and gratuitous violence, some of which were even purported to be ordered by God. "The most detestable wickedness, the most horrid cruelties, and the greatest miseries, that have afflicted the human race have had their origin in this thing called revelation, or revealed religion," he lamented. Contrary to religious fundamentalists, Paine believed that conviction in the Bible's perfection was "the most dishonorable belief against the character of the divinity, the most destructive to morality, and the peace and happiness of man, that ever was propagated since man began to exist."[549]

The pamphlet's sacrilegious prose and unapologetic impertinence was destined to make it even more controversial than its predecessor. In Britain, the work spawned a new pamphlet war, much like *The Rights of Man* had done several years earlier. Even some of Paine's most devout apologists did not follow him on his bold assault upon traditional religion. Among them was Joseph Priestley, Paine's eminent English friend who had promoted the merits of *The Rights of Man*. In *An Answer to Mr. Paine's Age of Reason*, the English Whig accused the author of mistakenly conflating "the corruptions of Christianity, and even those of a very late date, with Christianity itself." Out of convenience "for his purpose," *The Age of Reason* omitted passages that reveal the contradictions Paine alleged were not contradictions at all, Priestley wrote, but instead wrongful assertions based on false premises. In addition, Paine's attack on the Mosaic creation account, largely for his allegation that it was merely borrowed from Greek and Roman counterparts, was simply mistaken. Rather than a repurposed variant of the Greek and Roman stories, extant biblical texts confirmed the Mosaic account was "at least a thousand years older" than surviving pagan counterparts.[550]

In the years following the publication of *The Age of Reason, Part Second,* several dozen English-language rebuttals appeared in addition to Priestley's work. The radical writer had become became the most notorious pariah of theologians of every denomination, who insisted Paine's deistic treatise—which aimed to expose the Bible's fables—was itself filled with myths and misinterpretations. According to Anglican bishop Richard Watson's well-distributed repudiation, *An Apology for the Bible*, Paine had "attempted to lessen the authority of the Bible by ridicule, more than by reason."[551] As it had several years prior, Pitt's government authorized a wave of prosecutions against those who dared to print either version of the pamphlet, which remained banned in the country for several decades. In 1818, Richard Carlile, the brilliant bookseller and radical agitator, was even tried and convicted in criminal court for selling the pamphlet. As with much of Paine's work, the monumental controversy generated interest in the tract that would not have existed otherwise.

In France, *The Age of Reason, Part Second* had little impact in comparison to its reception in Britain and the United States, as the economic and political subjects captured the attention of most citizens. As a new constitutional era was ushered in, France was afflicted with economic depression as the result of food and materials shortages. This was driven largely by labor losses driven by mass emigration from France, direct and indirect implications of the Reign of Terror, widespread conscription mandates, and the commencement of war in Europe. Compounding the people's miseries was the collapse of the assignat, a French paper currency issued by the National Convention. Ostensibly backed by centrally-held assets, authorities ultimately refused to exchange the notes for bullion during the course of the revolution, and the assignat rapidly depreciated in value to the point of worthlessness. As the assignat collapsed, the cost of producing food and supplies exceeded the price ceilings the Jacobins had imposed on them, forcing farmers out of the market and destroying the supply of food. The Thermidorians repealed the price ceilings at the end of 1794, but the return of labor to the market was sluggish. While the new government mulled the appropriate response, multitudes suffered from malnourishment.

Among those purporting to hold the answer to the economic doldrums was François-Noël Babeuf, a controversial journalist and proto-socialist revolutionary from the city of Saint-Quentin in northern France. During the Reign of Terror, Babeuf, a local officeholder in the city of Roye, was accused of fraud for altering the specifics of a land-transfer deed. Escaping imprisonment, he fled to Paris, where he dubbed himself "Gracchus Babeuf" after the Gracchi brothers of the Roman Republic, who aimed to redistribute aristocratic lands to the plebeians. From the capital, the rabble-rouser wrote editorials calling for the absolute economic extension of Jacobin political maxims. Beyond endorsing egalitarianism in strict terms of political rights, Babeuf insisted that equality of economic outcomes must also be imposed, lest the revolution be an abject failure. Babeuf therefore insisted on the enactment of wealth distribution programs, and lambasted the Thermidorians for their tempered approach to central economic planning. His agitation attracted several thousand "Babouvist" disciples, who joined their mentor in encouraging renewed revolts and a resurrection of the Jacobin Constitution of 1793.

In the midst of the economic crisis, Paine recovered from typhus in the home of Monroe, but continued to suffer chest pains and an abscess in his side. Even so, in the winter of 1795–1796 he was inspired to use his pen yet again to propose a remedy for the French economy. The result of the project was *Agrarian Justice*, a work Paine decided to publish after learning of Bishop Richard Watson's declaration that God had "made both rich and poor." In his preface, Paine professed that "it would be better that priests employed their time to render the general condition of man less miserable than it is," which he set out to do. While he wrote the ideas within the work were not intended "for any particular country alone," it was repurposed into the form of a letter to be sent both to the Directory and the new French legislature.[552] The pamphlet devised a plan of relief that was entirely novel compared to both the Babouvists and reform proposals from the French government.

Much like the second part of *The Rights of Man*, this latest work empathized with the plight of the poor, and recognized public relief as "one of the first objects of reformed legislation." Reflecting upon the natural progress of the world economy, Paine asserted that the concept of landed property came about through agricultural cultivation. There was a clear distinction, he argued, between absolute ownership of land and the value derived from cultivation alone. He concluded that "it is in the value of the improvement only, and not the earth itself, that is individual property." By extension, he declared that land proprietors, far from holding plenary ownership over swaths of land, "owes to the community a ground rent" for "the land which he holds." In a free republic, Paine purported that "every man, as an inhabitant of the earth, is a joint proprietor of it in its natural state," but that "it does not follow that he is a joint proprietor of cultivated earth. While acknowledging the necessity of private property, he did not feel such a right conferred the ability to take from others their natural inheritance. [553]

Paine's views diverged from those of his philosophical forebear John Locke, whose outlook he harnessed and endorsed on almost every other point. Among Whig patriarch's most widely recognized contributions was his labor theory of property, which alleged that God had given all the benefits of the world to humanity as a whole, that the original acquisition of property transpired when man first mixed his labor with that of the world's natural resources, and that the original extraction of property in such a way was a moral endeavor.[554] Paine, like Locke, believed that "the earth, in all its natural uncultivated state, was, and ever would have continued to be, the common property of the human race." Unlike the eminent English philosopher, however, he contended that all men maintained a rightful claim—no matter how minute—to property acquired from the commons.

Paine's remedy to the property inequality and the denial of the natural inheritance of earth the was a "national fund" that would provide relief. It was to be supported by a land tax, applied to land holders once per generation in proportion to the amount of land owned. Whenever citizens reached the age of 21 years older, the fund was to pay £15—approximately $2,500 in 2021 United States dollars—in addition to £10 annually, "as compensation in part, for the loss of his or her natural inheritance." Payments from the fund would "be made to every person, rich or poor." The system would, in Paine's eyes, "immediately relieve and take out of view three classes of wretchedness—the blind, the lame, and the aged poor," and would "furnish the rising generation with means to prevent their being poor."[555]

Paine stressed that his program, far from a charity, was instead the natural right of all free people, a form of restitution that provided a universal answer to economic injustice:

> In advocating the case of the persons thus dispossessed, it is a right, and not a charity, that I am pleading for. But it is that kind of right which, being neglected at first, could not be brought forward afterwards till heaven had opened the way by a revolution in the system of government. Let us then do honour to revolutions by justice, and give currency to their principles by blessings.

Paine insisted that the world's existing wealth disparities were "not in the present possessors," but "in the system" that had "stolen imperceptibly upon the world" from time immemorial. Despite the historic transgressions against humanity in sum, he wrote, "the fault can be made to reform itself by successive generations" without "deranging the property of any of the present possessors." To demonstrate his commitment to the plan, Paine pledged the gigantic sum of £100 to both France and Britain, should the fund be established in either country. By committing even his personal wealth to the notion that a revolution in economics was "the necessary companion of revolutions in the system of government," Paine believed he held the key to generation-spanning economic miseries.[556]

Paine completed *Agrarian Justice* in early 1796, but it remained unpublished until 1797, when he was riled by Watson's sermon. Atypical to his normal publication process was his decision not to supervise the French translation, instead leaving the task to a trusted friend. Paine's characteristic attention to the localization his writings was interrupted by his decision to travel with Monroe and his family to the French port of Le Havre in May of 1796, where he entertained the idea of setting sail for America once again. There, he was persuaded not to attempt the journey for the same reason that had stopped him before—legitimate fear that the British maritime patrols would capture him.[557]

In the spring of 1796, any influence Paine's pamphlet may have made, had it been released at that point, would likely have been overshadowed by the "Conspiracy of Equals," a meticulously organized insurrection against the French republic by Babeuf and his followers. As French citizens continued to suffer through the rapid depreciation of the assignat currency, soon replaced by the similarly inflationary mandate, the socialist agitator's influence expand. Babeuf instituted a de facto resurrection of the Jacobin Club, drafted a revolutionary thesis, the "Manifesto of Equals," and even wrote an ideological anthem that was widely sung by rowdy patrons in cafés and taverns. His greatest base of support came from former Jacobins, poor commoners, and disaffected revolutionary soldiers. The Directory launched a crackdown in early May, and Babeuf and his accomplices were tried by the newly ordained court system. He was eventually convicted, sentenced to death, and executed, his program of revolutionary socialism perishing with him.

Economic disorder was not the only challenge posing a threat to the French state. On October 3, 1795, a royalist uprising threatened the National Convention, which was set to dissolve the following month. The Thermidorian leader Paul Barras, who would soon be elected to the Directory, mobilized to protect the republic. As the commander of France's national guard, Barras appointed a young and talented artillery officer, Napoleon Bonaparte, to lead the defense forces near the Tuileries Palace, the seat of government. Barras had become aware of the young Corsican from his actions at the Siege of Toulon, where he used his budding military acumen to force the withdrawal of an Anglo-Spanish force in late 1793. Now, he was given an even more crucial task—that of protecting the central government itself.

On October 5, Bonaparte and his 6,000 men hastily seized nearby reserve cannons, and the commander personally organized their arrangement in strategic locations along the streets of Paris. The royalist insurrection of 7,000 men was thoroughly routed, and the victory catapulted Bonaparte to great fame. Now a national hero, he was promoted by the new French government to become Commander of the Interior and given control of France's Army of Italy. He was also soon introduced to Joséphine de Beauharnais, the widow of a victim of the Reign of Terror and former mistress of Barras, whom he would marry on March 9, 1796. Bonaparte left for his command the same spring, hoping make territorial inroads against the Austrians. In a few years, he would return to Paris to overthrow the same government he saved.

In April, Paine authored *The Decline and Fall of the English System of Finance*, a work that predicted the collapse of the British pound within 20 years. To justify this prognostication, Paine pointed to the country's enormous foreign debt, accumulated through numerous wars, which had set "the funding system to destruction." The gradually-increasing cost of England's last six wars, he wrote, could not be offset by the Bank of England's reserves. Specie holdings amounted to just £1 million, whereas debt amounted to £400 million. "The sum in the bank is not sufficient to pay one-fourth of only one year's interest of the national debt," he warned. At the heart of most monetary crises, he explained, were disastrous paper money experiments, which had already crippled both America and France:

> In both those cases the whole capital was emitted, and that whole capital, which in America was called continental money, and in France assignats, appeared in circulation; the consequence of which was, that the quantity became so enormous, and so disproportioned to the quantity of the population, and to the quantity of objects upon which it could be employed, that the market, if I may express it, was glutted with it, and the value of it fell.

The English system "approaches the same fate, and will arrive at it with the same certainty," he wrote, because of its propensity to emit bank notes in place of traditional, bullion-backed currency. According to Paine, the "farce of the funding system" was the fact that interest was regularly paid, but in inflationary paper. "As bank notes can always be coined for the purpose, this payment proves nothing," he asserted.[558]

The pamphlet's most provocative musing may have been Paine's prediction that the "case of failure of finances," such as those experienced by both France and the United States, would bring about a monumental political shift. "If, then, we admit of reasoning by comparison of causes and events," he observed, "the failure of the English finances will produce some change in the government of that country." As to the specifics of how this governmental change would manifest, Paine did not elaborate, except to note that Pitt had ironically predicted bankruptcy in France for its inclination to utilize similar schemes. With the claim that the "eyes of all nations" would be fixated upon the "fraudulent system" of English finances, Paine concluded his work.[559]

By many accounts, *The Decline and Fall of the English System of Finance* was the writer's most well-received work in France since *The Rights of Man*. It was translated and sent to both houses of the new French legislature, where it was endorsed heartily by representatives. The Council of Elders even voted to commission a mass printing, quite an honor for the former deputy. The Directory itself responded even more warmly by declaring the work "the most combustible weapon which France could at this moment employ to overthrow and destroy the English government." In tandem, the new administrators worked to distribute the pamphlet to holders of British assets, where economic warfare would result from the liquidation of the same commodities. The Directory even went to extreme lengths to expand the program by translating the work to German and transporting copies across enemy lines by way of secret French agents, where its use could be expanded. This process was repeated for Low German, Swedish, and Italian versions as well.[560]

As it turned out, the Bank of England suspended the conversion of its paper notes to gold in 1797, largely vindicating Paine's opinion that the English pound—at least in its present state—was doomed. In a letter to Jefferson, he boasted that "several people who affected to laugh at my *Decline and Fall of the English System of Finance* now see it in another light." As Paine saw it, the mass distribution of his work proved it was his effort that pushed the British financial system beyond its breaking point:

That little work was translated into French and sent by the French government to all their foreign agents and was also translated into German, Low Dutch—Swedish and Italian. It demolished the credit of the English funds in those countries, and caused a great pulling out ... The Bank of England is now stopped. For my own part I cannot see how it is possible the Bank of England should ever open again. Were it to open tomorrow the run upon it would be so immense, they would be obliged to shut it up immediately ... I much question if England has gained any thing by trade for an hundred years past; that is, ever since the funding system began. She has pushed her manufactures about the world at great risk and often at loss, and the bustle it made gave her the opportunity of pushing forth a vast quantity of paper at home, which the commercial idiots mistook for gain and wealth; but now she comes to wind up her affairs she finds she has not so much money as she had a hundred years ago.

In addition, the writer bragged of France's economic improvement to Jefferson, a fellow supporter of hard, bullion-based money. "In France nothing is seen but money," he wrote, and "paper is entirely gone." He reported that the decision to disregard paper notes made every provision "cheaper, better, and more abundant than before the revolution."[561]

Paine had done much to settle into post-imprisonment life and carve out new endeavors for himself. He had written a bold sequel to *The Age of Reason*, proposed a remedy to the marked divide between rich and poor, and even dabbled in monetary economics. He had gained the respect of both the National Convention and subsequent Directory, both of which considered him instrumental to their cause. Despite his successes, however, he continued to maintain bitterness toward his old friend George Washington, whom he believed complicit in his long imprisonment. Their friendship had been strained by the Virginian's decision to distance himself from *The Rights of Man*, but Paine felt personally insulted by the president's inaction during his greatest time of need. His position seemed to be confirmed by Washington's private correspondence, which revealed his belief that those arrested and confined in France were there under their own volition. "If the citizens of the United States in foreign countries commit acts, which are repugnant to their laws or usages," Washington wrote, "they certainly expose themselves to punishment."[562]

The president was very careful to restrain his administration from even the appearance of intervention into the French Revolutionary Wars, believing any improper exertion could jeopardize his policy of neutrality. In addition, the groundwork for easing tensions with Britain was being laid as Paine languished on the cold floors of Luxembourg, and Washington's subordinate Morris did everything he could to encourage it. In February of 1795, Paine drafted a letter of protest to the president. "As it is always painful to reproach those one would wish to respect, it is not without some difficulty that I have taken the resolution to write you," he admitted. He expressed his great sorrow at Washington's silence during his life-threatening incarceration:

> The dangers to which I have been exposed cannot have been unknown to you, and the guarded silence you have observed upon the circumstance is what I ought to have expected from you, either as a friend or as President of the United States. You know enough of my character to be assured that I could not have deserved imprisonment in France; and, without knowing any more than this, you had sufficient ground to have taken some interest for my safety. Every motive arising from recollection of times past, ought to have suggested to you the propriety of such a measure. But I cannot find that you have so much as directed any enquiry to be made whether I was in prison or at liberty, dead or alive; what the cause of that imprisonment was, or whether there was any service or assistance you could render. Is this what I ought to have expected from America, after the part I had acted towards her, or will it redound to her honor or to yours, that I tell the story?

With his acrimony leaping from the pages, Paine vainly declared that the president had "not served America with more disinterestedness, or greater zeal, or more fidelity, than myself." While he had "ventured into new scenes of difficulties to extend the principles which that revolution had produced," Washington, he wrote, "rested at home to partake of the advantages." By all accounts of the age, it was a lofty charge. Paine's efforts were appreciated in America, where his writings were celebrated nearly universally, but he never approached the eminence of Washington, who was widely praised for personally financing the Continental Army, winning the war, and for refusing to seek political power in the aftermath. Even still, Paine was convinced Washington's feckless response to his plight was deliberate rather than a result of being unaware. "You folded your arms, forgot your friend, and became silent," he professed.[563]

Paine's letter veered from personal enmity to critique the president and his subordinates for abandoning republican principles in France, especially in regard to the Jay Treaty. "If the inconsistent conduct of Morris exposed the interest of America to some hazard in France, the pusillanimous conduct of Mr. Jay in England has rendered the American government contemptible in Europe," he wrote. Paine remained adamant that Washington's decision to mend ties with Britain, a hereditary monarchy, had thrown the cornerstone maxims of republicanism to the wayside and enraged republican France. The Neutrality Proclamation was "an assumption on the part of the executive not warranted by the Constitution," he wrote, and was partial to Britain in consequence. Paine concluded his letter with bewilderment over whether Washington's "ungenerous and dishonorable silence" toward him was the result of such a policy.[564]

In the end, Paine never sent the scathing letter to Washington. He was stopped from doing so by Monroe, who realized its insinuations would give rise to controversy, and would likely destroy the reputation of Paine without damaging Washington's. For a time, Paine's desire to honor Monroe's request not to embroil himself in political controversy while a guest in his house was honored, and the penman stopped short of letting his angers against the president loose. On September 20, 1795, however, he reneged on this decision, electing to let his feelings flow in a second letter that borrowed heavily from the themes of the first. By this time, he was convinced that the president thought his confinement expedient to his political ambitions. "I cannot understand your silence upon this subject upon any other ground, than as connivance at my imprisonment," he wrote.[565]

Paine asked Washington to send him any correspondence, or official papers that would "remove that suspicion," and cast his actions in a more understandable light. He added that Robespierre's memorandum against him was justified by its notation that his arrest would serve "the interests of America as well as of France," interpreting this to mean that America's indifference to his condition provided "connivance and consent." By wavering, Washington "was tacitly giving me up," Paine grumbled. "I shall continue to think you treacherous," he wrote, "till you give me cause to think otherwise." He had taken Washington's lack of attention to his situation as more than just political incompetence, but as a personal betrayal. Whether Washington's indiscretion was intended to "gratify the English government," give the president more justification to "exclaim the louder against the French Revolution," or "meet with less opposition in mounting up the American government," it was "reproach" he would "not easily shake off."[566]

Washington received Paine's contemptuous letter, but declined to respond in any way, either to justify his position or to apologize. To the penman, the lack of response was absolute confirmation that his qualms toward Washington were justified, and that the president cared not to make amends with him. Paine, now eager to expose the moral shortcomings of Washington to the world, set out to put his thoughts to words. As Monroe put it, the writer "thinks Washington winked at his imprisonment," and was preparing an attack upon him of the virulent kind." Monroe "endeavored to divert him" once more, but "without effect."[567] With the publication of his next pamphlet, in the form of a long public letter to Washington, the two who wielded the pen and the sword of the American War of Independence—each so integral to the success of the other—were now at irreconcilable odds.

At some point preceding the summer of 1796, Paine had left Monroe's residence to live for a time at Versailles Palace, where he was set free from his friend's mandate to avoid stimulating Franco-American controversy. The public letter, intended to be published as a pamphlet, was finished in July and sent to Paine's friend Benjamin Franklin Bache, editor of the *Philadelphia Aurora General Advertiser* and fellow Republican firebrand. Its contents were warmly accepted by Bache, the grandson of Benjamin Franklin, whose newspaper had done much to promote antagonism toward the Washington administration.

Paine introduced his open letter with the brutal statement that he would offer Washington "no apology" for writing it. He painted a written portrait as Washington as a disappointing man who double-crossed the underlying axioms of American republicanism:

> There was a time when the fame of America, moral and political, stood high in the world. The luster of her revolution extended itself to every individual; and to be a citizen of America gave a title to respect in Europe. Neither meanness nor ingratitude has been mingled in the composition of her character. Her resistance to the attempted tyranny of England left her unsuspected of the one, and her open acknowledge of the aid she received from France precluded all suspicion of the other. The Washington of politics had not then appeared.

Implying that the transition from virtuous republicanism to quasi-monarchy was aided and abetted by Washington's stewardship, Paine expressed opposition to some aspects of the United States Constitution, namely the structure of the executive office and six-year term of the Senate, which he believed too long. "I also declare myself opposed to almost the whole of your administration," he wrote, "for I know it to have been deceitful, if not perfidious."[568]

Before the ink had time to dry on the on the new Constitution, the Washington began endeavoring to replace America's "rising prosperity" with the "germ of the corruption," he claimed. According to Paine, "monopolies of every kind marked" the presidential administration "almost from the its commencement," and the "chief of the army became the patron of the fraud." To validate this assertion, Paine alleged lands gained through wartime successes "were lavished upon partisans," and that "the interest of the disbanded soldier was sold to the speculator."[569] Paine's accusation was a reference to Continental Army bonds, which had been issued to soldiers in lieu of hard money. Financial speculators bought up the bonds for fractions of their value, many times through fraudulent schemes, and Hamilton's repayment plan made no effort to grant restitution for the scam.

Washington was guilty of "encouraging and swallowing the grossest adulation, the acrimonious author wrote, and "travelled America from one end to the other to put yourself in the way of receiving it." Beyond the Washington himself, Paine blasted the president's closest political allies. He condemned John Adams as a closest monarchist who sought "to set up and establish hereditary government," and accused John Jay of angling for a Senate with life terms.[570] In his tale, the president and his compatriots were a band of swindlers that subverted the revolution's most sacred principles, and let him rot in prison so as not to compromise their efforts to entice monarchist Britain.

Beyond his personal and political gripes with Washington, Paine also went so far as to purport the president's military reputation was undeserved. The renowned Virginian had "not the talent of inspiring ardor in an army," and his tepid responses to British advances—rather than the Continental Army's innumerable disadvantages—had led to the loss of Boston, Long Island, Fort Washington, Fort Lee, and Philadelphia. Washington was greatly outshined by Horatio Gates at Saratoga to the point that his replacement as Commander-in-Chief was widely and seriously entertained, and "nothing was done in the campaigns of 1778, 1779, 1780" by his command except the capture of Stony Point. According to Paine, Washington was guilty of behaving in battle much as he had in regard to his imprisonment—with an obvious streak of "inactivity." He was as "treacherous in private friendship" as he was "a hypocrite in public life," Paine wrote, "and the world will be puzzled to decide" whether the man was "an apostate or an impostor." As he saw it, posterity would look back and wonder whether Washington "had abandoned good principles, or whether" he "had any" in the first place.[571]

To the great surprise of many, Monroe drafted his own critique of Washington, though less personal and incendiary, called *From a Gentleman in Paris to His Friend in the City*. The anonymous letter provided a glowing account of the progress of the French Revolution, but also contained an explicit denunciation of the Jay Treaty. When its authorship was discovered, Washington quickly recalled Monroe from Paris and replaced him with Charles Cotesworth Pinckney, who would serve as the minister to France until 1797. Pinckney went so far as withhold information of the change from Monroe for six weeks, for fear that the Virginian would return to the United States in time to campaign against the president's Federalist successors.[572] Though his sense of professionalism differed from that of Paine's, Monroe's letter made clear that he shared many of the penman's hostilities toward Washington's pro-British policies.

While many had lost their confidence in Washington and the Federalists, Monroe was ultimately correct in his prediction that Paine's disdainful assault on the president's character would ruin the Englishman's reputation among the American public. Even some of the most outspoken opponents of Washington and the Federalists openly admitted that their qualms with the Virginian's administration were political, rather than personal, in nature, and the president's personal integrity was rarely questioned even among his fiercest rivals. Even by this point, Washington was widely viewed as an American Cincinnatus, a man so uniquely principled and averse to ambition that even his harshest critics must admit to his indispensability. Paine's letter thus read to many as a petty outburst by a desperate, bitter man who had misinterpreted the admiration's diplomatic position as a personal affront.

Almost immediately after Paine's condemnation of Washington was published by Bache in early 1797, the president's most loyal partisans returned fire at Paine. According to Boston's *Columbian Centinel*, his attack on Washington was what one "might expect from a traitorous scribbler, saturated with brandy." One prominent pamphlet charged "the enthusiastic, the depraved, the ungrateful Tom Paine" of "sacrificing the last little remnant of imputed patriotism, to a faithless and cowardly attack on his early benefactor and friend." Another tract accused the penman of being "intoxicated with vanity" in his "treacherous and ungrateful" attempt to damage the president's reputation. "If Mr. Washington and La Fayette are not true republicans, you may put up your pen, and call your *Rights of Man* a visionary farce," the anonymous writer ranted.[573]

Washington never wrote or spoke much about Paine's letter after having received it. Even though the matter received great attention in the news, he never provided any public explanation one way or another as to the reasons why Paine's situation was neglected. Furthermore, he never sought to justify his actions, or defended his character against the account. The president's only reference to the tract was in January of 1797, when he depicted it as part of deceitful French propaganda scheme designed to undermine him "particularly and personally." Paine's scandalous letter, "printed in this city, and disseminated with great industry," was merely an attempt to spread "erroneous impressions of the conduct of this govern-

ment towards France." The president concluded his only surviving correspondence on the subject with his endorsement of a recently published assault on Paine by British-born Federalist William Cobbett, who called the
penman "an infamous miscreant" and "the prince of demagogues." The
"one thing on earth nearer to the heartens of all true Americans," he insisted, was "the spotless character of their chief." Paine's letter was a "brutal attempt to blacken this character" without merit, and was a stain on
whatever semblance of integrity the writer still maintained. "You never
before sunk to a level with the damned," Cobbett raged, "but now you are
plunged beneath them."[574] Paine and the eminent American patriarch
never reconciled, even by the time of Washington's death in 1799.

After leaving Monroe's home in Paris, Paine moved in with Nicolas de
Bonneville, a French radical who served as publisher of the *Tribune of the
People* and founder of the Society of the Friends of Truth, a political club
that dissolved after the downfall of the Girondins. The change of residence
was one that lasted for five years, as Paine was still reluctant to return to
the United States. Throughout the next years, the writer resumed his pre-
imprisonment habits. He received visitors at his study at Bonneville's,
strolled through the city streets, corresponded with friends, and maintained
his connections with the political class in Paris. From there, he wrote a
letter to James Madison expressing he had "lost all confidence in the
American government" as the result of the elevation of Timothy Pickering
to secretary of state and the election of John Adams to the presidency. He
could not help but slip in a word of bitterness toward Washington, who he
blamed for his poor health and called the "Chief of Scoundrels."[575]

While the new French constitution and the Directory both aimed to in-
troduce stability, a new threat to the fledgling government began to take
shape. Royalists scored substantial gains in the elections of March and
April of 1797, where one-third of the seats in the assembly were up for
grabs, and monarchist François-Marie, marquess de Barthélemy became a
Director. Soon afterward, public memorials to Louis XVI were held, new
royalist pamphlets emerged, and monarchy-sympathizing émigrés began
returning to France from all parts of Europe. The royalist revival led many
to fear that an anti-republican coup was on the horizon, and a genuine plot
to bring the German-exiled Louis XVIII to the throne materialized.

Though the French government was divided in regard to how to best respond to the threat, the ideas of Paul Barras—who favored a hardline response against the royalists—ultimately prevailed. After winning the support of key members of the government, Barras gained the support of the French army, which was now firmly in the hands of anti-royalist reactionaries. Under the ruse of an Irish invasion, the Directors ordered the military to march through Paris in defiance of the constitution, where they were to arrest the royalist leaders in the French Councils, forcibly annul the recent elections, and shut down royalist newspapers. The coup, which became known as the Coup of 18 Fructidor, was extraordinarily successful. Directors Lazare Carnot and Barthélemy were ousted, with the former escaping into exile and the latter arrested. While in Italy, Napoleon Bonaparte played a role in the scheme by supplying intelligence and sending troops to Paris. The remaining three Directors usurped the authority of the legislature, suppressed dissent, outlawed royalist political expression, and established an operative dictatorship.

Barras' coup was strikingly reminiscent of the Jacobin uprising against the Girondins, but Paine reacted much differently to the event. In a new pamphlet, *Letter to the People of France and the French Armies on the Events of the 18th Fructidor*, the scribe went so far as to justify the anti-royalist crackdown. The uprising endangered the fabric of French republicanism, and stood to reverse all the gains of post-Jacobin rule, he argued, and the situation required a last-ditch reprisal by the government. "Everything was at stake, and all national business at a stand," he insisted. "Shall the republic be destroyed by the darksome maneuvers of faction," Paine asked, "or shall it be preserved by an exceptional act?"[576]

To justify his position—which likely flabbergasted many of his readers—Paine compared the coup to various post-war uprisings during the American War of Independence. As in France, the government of Pennsylvania had also suspended the legislature and imposed martial law in 1780, a move that ultimately protected the government from destruction. As British forces advanced toward Philadelphia in late 1776, the penman also reminded readers that the Continental Congress disbanded, fled to Baltimore, and vested George Washington with dictatorial authority. Specifically, the general was granted "full power to order and direct all things relative to the [military] department, and to the operations of the war," in

Paine's mind a necessary measure of republican self-preservation similar to the recent French purge. Glossing over the dictatorship's clampdown, the penman alleged that "the public has suffered no inconvenience" by the Coup of 18 Fructidor. "It was a great stroke, applied in a great crisis," he wrote, "that crushed in an instant, and without the loss of a life, all the hopes of the enemy, and restored tranquility to the interior."[577]

In another time or place, he would have reproached French or British monarchies for engaging in the same underhanded scheme to uproot political opposition and preserve the continuance of government by force. For the sake of preserving republicanism in France, Paine contended that desperate times called for desperate measures. "These events taken in a series, mark the progress of the republic from disorder to stability," Paine wrote, and the coup was vindicated by "the happiness of its consequences."[578] Unlike the series of radical uprisings that ended in the dissolution of the French monarchy, Paine perceived the royalist insurrection as a dire threat against the popular will of the electorate. He also thought it a swift repudiation against Britain and its perpetual attempts to destabilize the inner-workings of the French republican government, with which the kingdom was still at war.

By all appearances, the Coup of 18 Fructidor was to France what Sulla's March on Rome was to the late Roman Republic—open proof that the foundation of a representative government, no matter how well-designed it was, could not easily withstand the imposition of military force by a popular commander. Just as Sulla's crackdown planted the seeds that facilitated the rise of Julius Caesar and the end of the Roman Republic, Barras and his fellow conspiratorial Directors instigated the creation of a new order in France based on arbitrary authority and military coercion. As in Rome, France would soon witness the emergence of its own Caesar.

Napoleon Bonaparte, now an accomplished, well-connected general, had decisively routed the Austrians in Italy before pushing deeply into Austrian territory in 1797. By the fall of 1797, the Austrians' position was indefensible, and the Hapsburg monarchy reluctantly sued for peace. Its capitulation resulted in the Treaty of Campo Formio, a settlement granting astonishing territorial gains for France. In addition, Bonaparte's army confiscated a significant number of weapons, precious metals, gems, and even valuable artwork from Austria. The ambitious general even founded two newspapers—one to elevate his standing within his own army, and one to build a cult of personality around himself within France. To a great extent, his accomplishments obscured the country's internal tumult, and gave citizens hope for the future. After breaking the back of France's greatest continental adversary, Bonaparte returned to Paris in December as a national hero.

In the last years of the 18th century, Paine wrote little for public consumption, and confined his pen mostly to correspondence with friends. However, he did contribute a short article in defense of the recently-recalled Monroe, whose character he defended in earnest. The allegation that the Virginian "was the cause of rupture between the two republics" of America and France was merely "a perfidious and calumnious" falsehood spread by the Washington administration, which was dead set on "signing a treaty injurious to the French republic." Monroe's work in Paris was instead "characteristic of an excellent citizen," wrote Paine, and the diplomat was only made into "an object of public hatred" by the Federalists because of his sincere attempt to cultivate the Franco-American alliance.[579]

The same transatlantic union that both Paine and Monroe strove for was soon endangered by another event in 1787. The new American president, John Adams, entered into office with plans of reestablishing peaceable relations with France, which had begun seizing American ships in the Caribbean in an attempt to disrupt trade between the United States and Britain. In response, he sent a commission of three noteworthy American aristocrats—Charles Cotesworth Pinckney, John Marshall, and Elbridge Gerry—to Paris to quell hostilities. When they arrived in Paris in October of 1797, the commissioners were approached by informal agents of the Directory rather than the France's foreign affairs department directly. Though they aspired to gain the audience of cunning French Foreign Minister Charles Maurice de Talleyrand-Périgord, better known by his colloquial name Talleyrand, the agents insisted upon two favors as a prerequisite. Only after the Americans provided a sizable loan to the French government, as well as a £50,000 bribe to Talleyrand himself, would they be able to begin negotiations.

The payment arrangement was not out of the norm for the French Foreign Ministry under Talleyrand, but was certainly was to the American commissioners, who considered it a glaring insult. A series of backchannel discussions and bureaucratic runarounds left all parties an impasse. In April of 1798, Pinckney and Marshall departed from France in disgust, while Gerry remained behind in Paris to continue trying to negotiate a Franco-American peace agreement unilaterally. In departure from all diplomatic convention, Talleyrand even threatened to have France declare war against the United States if the New Englander holdout returned as well.

All three commissioners reported their experiences to Adams, who mulled how to respond. When rumors of the XYZ Affair, as it was called, leaked to the outside world, the Jeffersonian Republicans responded in kind. Adams was accused of orchestrating the diplomatic abortion as a means to justify an offensive war against France, with whom the Republicans widely sympathized. In reality, Adams wished to keep the dispatches secret so the American public would not be riled to the point of calling for war against France. After being derided in the presses for several days, Adams ultimately called the bluff of the Republicans by releasing the communications, revealing to all the extent of France's ambassadorial duplicity. Though the gambit effectively silenced his political opponents, Adams' revelation also prompted Federalists to demand a military response. The events led directly to the Quasi-War, a series of naval clashes, primarily in the Caribbean, between the United States and France.

After Bonaparte's incredible triumph against Austria, the renovated French Directory began considering its next move in its war against Britain. Several actors within the French government favored the idea of a naval invasion of England. This pitch was supported by the general belief that France's recent territorial gains meant that the country's chief rival now stood alone in Europe, in a more precarious and isolated position than it ever had before. Ending the war in Europe meant invading Britain, taking strategic targets, threatening the central government in London, and, ultimately, delivering a fatal blow to the administration of William Pitt. Not taking this final step quickly enough, some thought, meant the crown would use its superior position in the Caribbean and warming relations with the United States to rebuild, regroup, and strike back on the European mainland.

At the very end of December, Paine served as one of the chief advocates of an invasion of England. The cause inspired him to opine on the subject in Bonneville's newspaper, *Le Bien Informé*, and to draft a new essay, *Observations on the Construction and Operation of Navies with a Plan for an Invasion of England and the Final Overthrow of the English Government*. Between the two writings, he laid out elaborate plans to accomplish such a task, combining his knowledge of military affairs with his natural talents as an engineer. Strategically, Paine believed the French should use coastal territory on the North Sea, by way of the country's new alliance with the Dutch, which could be used as the invasion's staging point. Rather than France's standard naval fleet, the invasion force should consist of brand new, light-outfitted vessels that could maneuver quickly and quickly evade the Royal Navy. Rather than "a ship of the line," or any other frigate "depending upon the wind for motion," the invasion detachment would be specifically built to "elude and disembark."[580]

Paine's invasion plans called for a grand fleet of a thousand gunboats, each carrying a single 24-pound, front-facing cannon and eight men, would pass through the North Sea and land on the eastern English coast, where the writer felt their defenses would be weakest. Paine thought the contingent should target the River Thames, which ran directly through London, where he believed there would be little "to obstruct the expedition." His assessment relied upon the presumption that the vast majority of the Royal Navy would be lodged in the English Channel, which would be too slow-moving to respond in time to stop the French landing. Tides and weather patterns led Paine to suggest targeting the invasion for May of 1798, giving the country about five months to mobilize. The chief goal of the mission was to "get possession of London as soon as possible, for when this is obtained all the power, means and resources of the government are cut up."[581]

As he had before in several writings, Paine went so far as to suggest a financial arrangement by which his bold project could be funded. According to his calculations, the 1,000 gunboats he envisioned would cost at most 3.6 million livres, which he claimed would be "less than the expense of building and fitting ships of the line for sea." Instead of imposing new taxes, France could employ voluntary requisition similar to that which existed during the American War of Independence, he asserted. To demonstrate support for its feasibility, Paine personally contributed 100 livres to the cause, and with the help of Monroe as a translator, sent his plans to the

Directory in January of 1798. "There will be no lasting peace for France, nor the world," he wrote, "until the tyranny and corruption of the English government be abolished."[582] Like most of his political ideas, Paine's plans for a military invasion scheme defied all established convention. At the time, European navies depended on the performance of large, slow moving ships that could impose blockades and carry greater number of troops. His quick-moving gunboat proposal was untested at best, and unfeasible at worst.

Standing in the way of his proposal was France's new favorite son and victorious general, Bonaparte, who balked at the prospect of launching an amphibious invasion of England. The country's fleet was too insufficient to overcome the might of the Royal Navy, he thought, and the potential for unfavorable weather only amplified the risks. Instead, the popular commander proposed undermining Britain economically rather than militarily. He would do so by obstructing the country's access to lucrative trade in India, a route that ran through Egypt. If Britain and its Ottoman allies could be stopped there, France would be placed in an even more advantageous position to obtain a formal peace agreement.

Years later, Paine told Jefferson that the Directory initially adopted his plan and built 250 of the planned 1,000 ships to launch the invasion, only to abruptly change course. Before proposing the Egyptian expedition, Bonaparte showed great interest in the strategy and held a private meeting with Paine, where he showered the Englishman with praises. "A statue of gold should be erected to you in every city in the universe," he told Paine. Bonaparte even went so far as to tell the man he slept at night with a copy of *The Rights of Man* under his pillow. The general proposed that Paine should serve as one of five leaders of a provisional English republic after the endeavor was successful. "Only let us land," and the plan would commence, Bonaparte told Paine.[583]

Enamored with Paine's invasion plans, Bonaparte called upon Paine to present his scheme to the Military Council of Paris, the government's war ministry. With a burning desire to free England from the bonds of monarchical tyranny, he attended the meeting at the general's request. At the conference, he was greeted by a group of officers that, by one account, were "already all of opinion that the measure was impracticable and dan-

gerous." The pitch was ridiculed especially by General Jean Claude d'Ar-
çon, who openly laughed at the project, and contended France "might as
well attempt to invade the moon as England." Bonaparte's advisors insisted that there was no way for an armada of small, swift-moving boats
to evade the Royal Navy, even in the presence of favorable weather conditions.[584]

When called upon to speak, Paine testified that England could only be
crushed if France were to "annihilate her commerce." Paine told the council that his experiences in the country led him to believe the English people
were "greatly disaffected" and perhaps ripe for an internal uprising, but
one major hurdle stood in France's way. Even if the planned stealth expedition force was able to land in England, Paine warned that the forces deployed would be "cut to pieces" by the British army. Bonaparte's faith in
Paine was shattered when the writer unexpectedly answered that the only
way to subdue England—rather than the invasion plans he presented to the
Directory—was through a Franco-English peace. The sudden shift in the
Englishman's position seemed to defy Bonaparte's expectations for the
meeting, causing the Corsican to distrust Paine forever. He would never
speak to the man directly again, let alone seek his military or political advice.[585]

As Bonaparte consolidated power over the next years, while also obtaining victory after victory against France's continental adversaries,
Paine still clung to the belief that he may still employ a modified version
of the plan. In 1798, though, Bonaparte and The French Directory ultimately aligned that the next military target would be Egypt rather than the
English homeland. According to Paine, this decision was arrived to both
by the council's decision to shoot down his invasion plans, and for the
eagerness of Bonaparte's military rivals to "get rid of him any way they
could" for the time.[586] As they saw it, there was no better, more isolated
placed in the world to contain the popularity of the ambitious general than
Egypt.

Paine's supposition that subjects in England were aching for a republican revolution and needed only the spark of a French invasion to set the
cause in motion was almost certainly a miscalculation. The Reign of Terror and enactment of arbitrary government in Paris soured many within
England to the idea of republicanism, and English Whigs certainly lost

considerable political capital as a result of France's internal strife. Another factor that worked against Paine's lofty vision was the outbreak of a republican revolt in Ireland in May of 1798. Pitt's repressive government successfully transformed its anti-republican censorship campaign into a pro-war propaganda effort, diminishing the influence of Whig dissidents within England. In addition, the British military succeeded in dismembering the core of the rebellion through the acquisition of intelligence on the position and movement of enemy rebels in and around Dublin. While fighting lingered on as loosely organized Irish guerillas clashed with British regulars, the revolution was plagued by setbacks and ultimately failed. By late 1798, most of the remaining pockets of resistance were overcome, and Ireland was subjected to a harsh settlement in the form of the 1800 Acts of Union.

As Paine dreamed of an England set free from centuries of monarchy, Bonaparte launched his military campaign in Egypt. The resolute general secured initial victories at Malta, Alexandria, and Embabeh, where the Pyramids of Giza were visible from a distance. Those opposing him in the fields of battle were the Mamluks, slave-soldiers beholden to the Arabian dynasties with social status above that of Egyptian commoners. Despite his triumphs on land, the French navy suffered greatly from the arrival of the Royal Navy, which began terrorizing the French fleet in the region. In August of 1798, the eminent Horatio Nelson gained a decisive victory at the Battle of the Nile, where the French Mediterranean fleet was completely destroyed. The British were then able to initiate a blockade of Malta, which ruined French supply and communication lines.

Now restricted to land, Bonaparte worked tirelessly to maintain order in Egypt by establishing an occupational government and suppressing anti-French uprisings. In the pursuit of these goals, he turned to propaganda, his greatest tool. His widely-distributed proclamations praised Islam and the local culture, and depicted himself as a great liberator of the commoners from their local rulers. "I shall be able to unite all the wise and educated men of all countries," Bonaparte told a local chief, "and establish a uniform regime based on the principles of the Quran which alone are true and which alone can lead men to happiness."[587] His effort to make himself into a Franco-Muslim was met with mixed results. Bonaparte's forces managed to put down a significant revolt in Cairo, but Egyptian discontent lingered afterward.

As Bonaparte took to war in the sands, The French Directory forcibly shut down *Le Bien Informé*, Bonneville's publication. Its reason was that Bonneville had published an article critical of Emmanuel-Joseph Sieyès, once the target of Paine's wrath for his defense of constitutional monarchy over absolute republicanism and now a Director. After he learned of the moratorium on Bonneville's newspaper, Paine immediately came to his friend's defense. Bonneville was a man of virtue and integrity—as well as a great friend, husband, and father—and his readership was filled with committed patriots, he argued. Paine's good reputation among the French aristocracy may have done his friend a great favor, as the government ultimately reversed its position and allowed Bonneville to reinstitute his newspaper. Nevertheless, because of Paine's rigid defense of Bonneville, and his interactions with an accused British spy, the Paris police distrusted his loyalties.[588]

In the process of exploring the possibility of building a canal that would link the Mediterranean Sea to the Red Sea, French forces under Bonaparte marched southward through the Isthmus of Suez in early 1799. His march through the territory was impeded by the Ottoman Empire, which aspired to use their own army to expel him from the continent. In the spring, the French pushed into Syria, an Ottoman stronghold. Bonaparte was successful at overcoming Ottoman-controlled Jaffa through a siege, but failed to do the same at Acre, where his soldiers suffered a crippling loss. The French army was forced to retreat from Syria, returning to Cairo in a haggard condition. While he was defeated on every imaginable level, Bonaparte orchestrated a grand display of propaganda that depicted him as a victorious hero. Upon his return, bands played, flags were flown, and the general was given lavish gifts.[589]

After regrouping in Cairo, Bonaparte launched several land campaigns in upper Egypt with mixed success. In time, he grew restless under the realization that the destruction of his naval fleet meant he could not be supported or reinforced. Furthermore, his dwindling and ill-supplied forces meant that he could no longer project the mighty image he valued so much. Throughout 1799, he also kept a close eye on news from Paris. French military setbacks in Germany, Switzerland, and Italy had mostly rolled back all of his gains from 1796 and 1797, and Bonaparte suspected corruption in the Directory was at fault.[590] By the summer of 1799, he was convinced the time was ripe to return to France and take advantage of the situation. On August 22, Bonaparte slipped out of Egypt on a frigate, abruptly leaving the doomed French expedition there to a subordinate.

Even though he had actually suffered a series of palpable military blunders, Bonaparte's propaganda in France had created the illusion that his campaign in Egypt and Syria was every bit as successful and glorious as his operations in Italy and Austria had been. When he returned to Paris in October, therefore, the public was still enamored by the Corsican. Sensing an opportunity to take advantage of the circumstances, the crafty Sieyès approached the general with a surprisingly bold idea that would propel both of them to power—a joint coup against the Directory. The basic plan involved spreading news of a false rebellion against the government, isolating the government and surrounding it with troops loyal to the plot, and forcing its top members to resign. Then, the Council of Ancients and Council of Five Hundred would be persuaded to draft a new Constitution that granted extraordinary power to both men. Having already conceived of a plot to overthrow the government on his own, Bonaparte obliged, and the two entered into a treasonous partnership. What Bonaparte didn't reveal to Sieyès, however, was that he was devising a scheme within the scheme with the assistance of his brother Lucien, who was then the President of the Council of Five Hundred, to ensure that he would emerge as the lone powerholder in France.

Almost immediately after his return to Paris, Bonaparte and his brother used the general's deeply-entrenched propaganda machine to spread false information that a Jacobin coup threatened the central government. The Directory fled three miles west of Paris to the Château de Saint-Cloud, where members of the government expected to be safe from the uprising. Under the planned coup—which was disguised by its instigators as a security plan—Bonaparte was tasked with preserving the safety of both councils, giving him command of national troops and ensuring his proximity to the government in refuge. On November 9, 1799, Sieyès, Roger Ducos, and Paul Barras resigned as Directors, preventing an executive quorum and emasculating the French administrative apparatus. The two legislative councils, now under the realization that they faced an actual coup from Bonaparte and his collaborators, assembled in an attempt to thwart the conspiracy.

Bonaparte and his collaborators hoped the effective dissolution of the Directory alone would be enough to terminate the government. However, it failed to do so, and the next day the Council of Ancients scrambled to reorganize. As the body passed a resolution calling for the election of a new Directory, Bonaparte and a small group of armed partisans barged into the chambers, making clear his intention to end the government. Despite the great number of troops surrounding the location, the assembly responded to the Corsican's demands with ridicule, and Bonaparte left the council. He then entered the hall of the even more antagonistic Council of Five Hundred, where representatives greeted his entry with cries of "down with the tyrant!" Deputies in the chamber soon surrounded the coup's mastermind and assaulted him. With the help of his grenadiers and Lucien, Bonaparte narrowly escaped the building, completely shaken by the experience.[591]

For a moment, it seemed the coup had been a disaster, and that the reputation of France's national hero would be tarnished forever. Indeed, the Council of Five Hundred immediately drafted a resolution naming Bonaparte an outlaw and traitor to the republic. Just when it seemed all hope for Bonaparte was lost, his brother Lucien seized an opportunity to salvage the botched coup with one final ruse. In an emotional oratory, he told the soldiers guarding the building that the Council of Five Hundred was in the process of being overrun by a group of dagger-wielding deputies. As proof of this, Lucien pointed to the pale face of his traumatized brother, and promised to drive his sword through him if he were truly a traitorous usurper. "I wanted to speak to the deputies," Napoleon alleged, "and they answered me with daggers."[592] With the encouragement of both Bonaparte brothers, the soldiers then poured into the chambers, causing the representatives to flee in terror. Under the threat of force, those who remained declared Sieyès, Ducos, and Napoleon part of a new three-member oligarchy called The Consulate, and the group was conferred power to ordain a new government. The Directory was over.

Following the Coup of 18 Brumaire, as it came to be called, Bonaparte initiated the second phase of his ploy for power, this part unknown to fellow conspirators Sieyès and Ducos. Rather than allow his two fellow peers to outshine him and impose their own constitutional vision upon France, the general and his allies quickly developed the Constitution of the Year VIII, a governmental framework that vested almost all tangible authority in himself under the invented position of First Consul. The constitution allowed Bonaparte to bypass the legislative process and draft laws unilaterally, created an aristocratic-style election system that gave him great discretion over the composition of the legislature, and made the other two consuls into figurehead advisors rather than concrete powerholders. While preserving the optics of a republic, the document was designed to impose a military dictatorship with Bonaparte at the head.

For Paine, the Coup of 18 Brumaire was cause for great disappointment. The writer had always condemned the centuries of conquests and usurpations that set one aristocrat above another in Europe. Furthermore, he was the world's most tireless advocate for free elections under a republican system where the military would always be subordinate to the civil authority. Bonaparte's ascension to power by force, then, contradicted his most hallowed maxims and caused him to reassess his feelings toward the man who shared his unique desire to free England from the shackles of monarchy. His gloom was compounded by the government's surveillance of him, which likely spurred his decision to leave Paris for a time. In the winter of 1799–1800, he travelled to Bruges, a city in southwest France, where he stayed with his friend and former prison mate, Joseph Van Huele.[593] Certainly, their brief liaison eased Paine's dismay over the end of French republicanism for a time.

When he returned to Paris in early 1800, Paine found himself under increased scrutiny from the government. An order from The Consulate claimed the Englishman had been "behaving irregularly," perhaps due to his flight to Bruges, though the writer was later told by a state agent that some of his writings in Bonneville's newspaper aroused suspicion for their subversive nature.[594] The negative attention likely affected Paine deeply, as he resisted writing or publishing anything in the realm of politics for over a year. Though he continued to correspond with friends through letters and held personal meetings at Bonneville's home, he did his best to stay out of the new regime's crosshairs.

Paine's last months in France must have tested his long-held belief that representative republicanism was the universal gift to mankind. Free elections had been replaced by military coercion, and republicanism had fallen at the hands of an ambitious general. France maintained a respectable footing in the field of battle against its European adversaries, but faced an internal dictatorship that was arguably more dangerous than the Jacobins when it came to preserving Paine's conceptions of ideal government. The public appreciation he had received from the Directory died with Bonaparte's ascension to power, and he was now the focus of a new state censorship apparatus that must have seemed wholly reminiscent of that which he experienced in London before his departure. In early 1800, he shared his miseries with an anonymous recipient. "I have no object in view in this country otherwise than I crave its prosperity," he admitted. "My intention is to return to America as soon as I can cross the sea in safety."[595] Once again, the only thing in his way was Britain's Royal Navy.

During Paine's period of relative silence in the presses, Bonneville drew trouble to himself once again for publishing an article lambasting Bonaparte as a usurper and comparing him to Oliver Cromwell. He was arrested, placed in jail, and his newspaper was dismantled—permanently this time. The circumstances ruined Bonneville financially. When he was freed from prison, he was placed under close police surveillance in the town of Évreux, where he stayed with his father for a time. Paine remained in Bonneville's home, keeping a low profile throughout his friend's predicament and retiring his pen for the moment.

As the months passed, he gradually revealed his repulsion toward Bonaparte and his new military government. His outlook on the aspiring general may have been solidified by a dinner the two attended shortly after Bonaparte's return from Egypt in late 1799, where Bonaparte glared at Paine from across a table of distinguished guests and said, "The English are all alike; in every country they are rascals." After that point, Paine agonized with fellow republicans, including his old friend Joel Barlow, over the tyranny of Bonaparte and his new regime. In 1802, Paine told a visitor, fellow English radical Henry Redhead Yorke, that he detested and despised the general. Bonaparte was "the completest charlatan that ever existed," he declared.[596]

Back in America, the political rift between the Republicans and Feder-alists was at its widest point. The administration of John Adams had riled a substantial coalition of opposition as the result of foreign affairs and the Alien and Sedition Acts of 1798. The most contentious of the new laws, the Sedition Act, went so far as to make criticism toward the president and members of Congress a criminal offense, and partisan Federalists ruth-lessly prosecuted and jailed those who dared to cast Adams and the Fed-eralists in a negative light. A campaign of resistance followed, which in-cluding a clandestine effort by Paine's friends Jefferson and Madison, to craft a set of resolutions—the Kentucky and Virginia Resolutions of 1798—to render the egregious acts "unauthoritative, void, and of no force" within both states. To committed Republicans, the scheme was overt evi-dence that Adams and the Federalists' desire to take the young republic and transform it into a monarchy, and Jefferson himself described the sit-uation to "a reign of witches."[597]

While Americans feuded over domestic affairs, Adams worked to end hostilities between the United States and France, despite accusations from Republicans that he was actually trying to expand the conflict into a full-scale war. His commissioners in Paris succeeded in obtaining an end to the Quasi-War with the Convention of 1800, a treaty that also repealed the Franco-American Treaty of Alliance and Treaty of Commerce. However, tensions between the two countries continued to linger, especially in light of the Jay Treaty, America's commitment to commerce with Britain. The peace settlement was not enough to contain the Republican opposition, however, and the bitter presidential election of 1800 ended with Adams losing to both Jefferson and fellow Republican Aaron Burr, who had in-tended to be vice president. Jefferson and Burr received an equal number of electoral votes, forcing a deadlocked Congress to decide the winner. On the 36th ballot, Jefferson was finally chosen as the next president.

When news of Jefferson's victory reached Paine in France, the writer was filled with a renewed sense of vigor and hope. "There has been no circumstance, with respect to America, since the times of her revolution," Paine wrote to the Virginian, "that has given more general joy." For his part, Jefferson took the "Revolution of 1800," as he called it, as a mandate against the Federalist program and for the principles for which the War of Independence was fought. He promised "Equal and exact justice to all men, of whatever state or persuasion, religious or political; peace, commerce, and honest friendship with all nations, entangling alliances with none." The states, rather than a subordinate unit of the general government, would be restored as "the most competent administrations for our domestic concerns and the surest bulwarks against antirepublican tendencies."[598]

Jefferson's assurances were followed by immediate executive action. Shortly after taking office, the new president pardoned those convicted and still imprisoned under the Sedition Act, eliminated all internal taxes, including the whiskey excise, and reiterated his commitment to free speech and free presses—even for those who opposed him. Furthermore, the Republican Congress repealed the Judiciary Act of 1801, otherwise known as the "Midnight Judges Act," which served as Adams' attempt to extend Federalist power into the federal courts. Jefferson even went so far as to restore the optics of American republicanism, which he believed had suffered greatly under the Washington and Adams administrations. He dressed as a commoner in his official duties, ended presidential dinner parties and balls, and even delivered his state of the union address in written form rather than through a more imposing speech to Congress. The new American administration represented, by all appearances, a concerted return to ideal republicanism as Jefferson and Paine saw it.

With the establishment of Jefferson's presidential administration, Paine began preparing for his return to America. He kept the president apprised on European affairs, especially relative to the French Revolutionary Wars, but also revealed he had been putting his engineering skills to use. In his time away from political writing, he had built two models for carriage wheels that stood apart from traditional models for their reinforcement by concentric circles. Additionally, he had constructed at least two additional model iron bridges, one of which he claimed, "in the opinion of every person who has seen it," was "one of the most beautiful objects the eye can behold." Paine planned to use the models to start his own business in America, and promised to return as soon as he could "pass the seas in safety from the piratical John Bulls."[599]

In 1800, Paine also drafted a series of articles—in sum the "Maritime Compact"—designed to promote the commerce of neutral countries caught within the complicated worldwide war. The essays were combined into a pamphlet in France, where it was translated by Bonneville and widely circulated in continental Europe. Paine also sent the English manuscript to Jefferson, who saw that it was printed in the United States as well. Accompanying the pamphlet was a lengthy letter on European affairs, including France's progress in all theaters of the war.[600] Paine also learned of the appointment of Robert Livingston as secretary of foreign affairs in France. A former Federalist turned Republican from New York, Livingston was a well-respected lawyer and skilled diplomat who played a great role in mending Franco-American acrimony in the years to come.

Circumstances beyond Paine's control seemed to make his return to America feasible in 1802. In March of that year, France and Britain established an indefinite peace through the Treaty of Amiens. Under the agreement, both powers made significant concessions. Britain abandoned some of its wartime conquests, while France withdrew from Egypt and Naples. The settlement allowed Britain to focus on restoring trade with continental Europe, and France to institute a series of domestic reforms including the Napoleonic Code, the country's civil framework. The treaty's long-term feasibility was doubted by all parties, but it held off war between the major European powers for the time being. Most importantly for Paine, the ceasefire also meant naval restraint and the ability to return to America.

Paine paid Bonneville no rent during his stay of multiple years, and it is likely his contributions to the publisher's newspaper fell short of his keep. Even so, by 1802 he had become a very close friend of the Bonneville family. The Frenchman and his wife even named one of their three sons after him, and made Paine his godfather. In light of Bonneville's financial ruin, Paine promised at some point to provide refuge in America for the family, an offer that was taken up by Bonneville's wife Marguerite. She and the three Bonneville sons planned to return with Paine to New Rochelle, New York, while Bonneville would reestablish a living for himself in France. The printer planned to rejoin the family at some point in the future, though his timing was uncertain.

The year prior, Jefferson had already arranged for Paine's return on board the *Maryland*, a public vessel with immunity from capture. "I am in hopes you will find us returned generally to sentiments worthy of former times," the Virginian wrote. Paine responded that he would instead await the public vessel carrying Livingston to France. However, when Jefferson's political enemies in the United States caught wind of the offer, they blasted the president for offering to bring the detested Paine back to America via public monies. After Paine learned of the commotion, and resolved ultimately "not to come by a national ship."[601]

His course decided, Paine made final arrangements to depart from France. His friend and future biographer Clio Rickman even travelled from England to join him in his travel to the port of Le Havre, where he would be sent on his way across the sea. "I shall bid adieu to restless and wretched Europe," he wrote shortly before his departure.[602] He had long accepted that republicanism in France was an unsustainable project, and had for years grown weary in the direction of French Revolution. By nearly every measure, his painstaking efforts to promote and nurture France's young republic had failed. He was successful in authoring the most popular and definitive republican treatise ever printed to that point, but the country had suffered through a decade of anti-republican power struggles, bloody political purges, and continental war. His advocacy for free religious exercise did nothing to stop a coercive dechristianization effort, his hard money sensibilities could not prevent debasement through paper fiat, free elections were subverted by military coercion, and the kings he ridiculed under the Bourbon system were replaced by equally ambitious and tyrannical executives. Rather than the virtuous republic he strove for, France had become a military dictatorship.

Regardless of the French Republic's decline, Paine's return to the United States must still have aroused his trademark optimism. He had played a pivotal role in America's transition from imperial colony to representative republic, and even though he despised the Federalist administrations, the emergence of the Jefferson administration seemed to set things back on course. He still held property stateside, and even though it suffered from damage and neglect, he now had an opportunity to enjoy the fruits of his labors from 20 years in the past. While he still held views on religion that were destined to raise controversy, his sensibilities were more conducive to the American experience than any European alternative. At the age of 65 and in high spirits, he gathered together with Mrs. Bonneville and the three Bonneville children, boarded the *London Pacquet*, and set sail for America from Le Havre on September 1, 1802.

Rickman, who had known Paine for more than 40 years, knew it was the last time he would see his friend. Teary eyed, he channeled the bittersweet occasion into a poem that still remains:

> Thus smooth be thy waves, and thus gentle the breeze,
>   As thou bearest my PAINE far away;
> O! waft him to comfort and regions of ease,
> Each blessing of friendship and freedom to seize,
>   And bright be this setting sun's ray.
>
> May AMERICA hail her preserver and friend,
>   Whose 'COMMON SENSE' taught her aright,
> How liberty thro her domains to extend,
> The means to acquire each desirable end,
>   And fill'd her with reason and light.
>
> One champion of all that is glorious and good
>   Will greet him sincerely I know;
> No supporter of craft, of oppression, and blood,
> The defender of liberty long he has stood;
>   Of tyranny only the foe.
>
> Yes JEFFERSON! well in his principles school'd,
>   Will embrace him with the gladness of heart;
> His value he knows and is not to be fool'd,
> Nor his wisdom and knowledge one moment o'er ruled;
>   By falsehood, corruption, and art.
>
> Tho bitter, dear PAINE, is this parting to me,
>   I rejoice that from EUROPE once more,
> From FRANCE too, unworthy thy talents and thee,
> Thou art hastening to join the happy and free;
> May the breezes blow gently, and smooth be the sea
>   That speed thee to LIBERTY's shore![603]

France had lost its most renowned republican icon, and America had regained him.

Chapter 8

Return to America

"But as laws may be bad as well as good, an empire of laws may be the best of all governments or the worst of all tyrannies."

- To the Citizens of the United States

After a two-month journey, Paine arrived in Baltimore on October 30, 1802. Once landed, he sent notice of his arrival to Jefferson, and made arrangements to travel to Washington, D.C., the new federal city. In those days, the town was a sparsely inhabited, swampy piece of land without any similarity to other national capitals in Europe. Its position was determined a decade earlier by way of a complex political agreement between Hamiltonian Federalists and Jeffersonian Republicans, where the former faction agreed to move the capital south from Philadelphia in exchange for the latter's acceptance of the Assumption Act of 1790, by which the federal government took on all state debts. In time, Jefferson considered the "dinner table bargain" to be a catastrophic mistake. "Of all the errors of my political life," he wrote, "this has occasioned me the deepest regret … Hamilton's system flowed from principles adverse to liberty, and was calculated to undermine and demolish the republic."[604]

Paine notified the president of his safe arrival, and planned to meet him in person as soon as he could. At the time, few extended such good graces to Paine as the American president. *The Age of Reason* had made Paine a pariah in the middle of the Second Great Awakening, a continent-spanning Protestant religious revival in North America. Even though he had played such a crucial role in the actualization of American independence, the news that he had been seen dining with the president at the presidential mansion, and "was seen walking arm in arm with him in the street any fine afternoon," was a minor scandal. Indeed, his presence as a lightning rod was immediately clear. "You can have no idea of the agitation my arrival has occasioned," Paine wrote in a letter to Rickman, "every newspaper was filled with applause or abuse."[605]

While the writer may have exaggerated the applause, he was completely transparent about the abuse. Even before Paine's voyage, a firestorm of negative press surrounded his prospective return. The *Baltimore Republican, or The Anti-Democrat* called the scribe a "loathsome reptile," and Philadelphia's *Port Folio* skewered him as "a drunken atheist, and the scavenger of action." To his greatest foes, he was now a "lilly-livered sinical rogue," a "demi-human archbeast," and "an object of disgust, of abhorrence, of absolute loathing to every decent man except the President of the United States." The *Gazette of the United States, and Daily Advertiser* branded him "the infamous scavenger of all the filth which could be raked from the dirty paths which have been hitherto trodden by all the revilers of Christianity," and another article from the same publication expressed that American agriculture would benefit from Paine's return, should he be turned into manure.[606]

Despite the crass reception from many circles, the *National Intelligencer* adopted a much different tone. "Be his religious sentiments what they may," an article read, "it must be their [the American people's] wish that he may live in the undisturbed possession of our common blessings, and enjoy them the more from his active participation in their attainment." A week later, the same publication reported Paine "received a cordial reception from the Whigs of Seventy-six, and the republicans of 1800, who have the independence to feel and avow a sentiment of gratitude for his eminent revolutionary services."[607] Though he found himself in the favor of the new presidential administration and its natural allies, antagonism toward the former hero of independence was overwhelming, and certainly unexpected to an extent.

None of the venom in the presses manifested toward Paine as he set foot in America. To the contrary, he was he greeted upon shore by a group of admirers, including several Federalists who recognized his merits. From there, he walked with the group to Fulton's Tavern, where he drank brandy and conversed with the locals. He admitted that Jefferson's invitation provided the reason for his American homecoming, and, in good humor, even engaged in self-deprecating humor by poking fun at his distinctive long nose. More eager to discuss engineering than politics at this point, he shared his model iron bridges with several dozen spectators in a room of the tavern, and pledged to showcase them in short visits to Frederick, Philadelphia, and New York.[608]

Paine's warm reception lasted only a moment, and vitriol followed him until the end of his life. After Benjamin Bache, the founder of the *Philadelphia Aurora General Advertiser,* died in 1798, his understudy and editor William Duane warned the new president of the potential adverse ramifications of a close relationship with the widely-despised writer. Appearing to confirm this were the allegations of James Callender, editor of the *Richmond Recorder* and likely his era's most infamous muckraker. According to the Scottish-born scandalmonger, Paine, Jefferson, and Madison all believed the birth of Jesus Christ was "an obscene blasphemous fable, and that all three men should publicly burn their Bibles to demonstrate their sacrilege.[609] In many ways, the attacks echoed of those levied against Jefferson during the 1796 and 1800 presidential campaigns, where the Virginian was portrayed by the Federalist presses as an atheistic Jacobin who would unleash the chaos of the French Revolution on American shores. In this way, the patriarch of the Republican faction should have been the first to realize such an association could jeopardize his administration at the outset.

As the country's most prominent pro-Jeffersonian newspaper, the *Aurora* defended Paine's character but took care to distance itself from his controversial views on religion. Still, the writer was determined to complete a third volume of *The Age of Reason* in America. The next entry would "make a stronger impression than anything I have yet published on the subject," he told a deist friend earlier that year.[610] As always, it was almost as if the increased antipathy toward him inspired him to write even more provocatively than he otherwise might have. After all, Paine was now in Jefferson's America, shielded from political retribution in ways he was not when he lived under the rule of Europe's most erratic regime. As the attacks of the presses continued, so too did his energetic hand.

Despite the advice of some Republicans, Paine frequently enjoyed the company of Jefferson during this period, and the two men often conversed at the presidential mansion. Their lasting friendship may have been maintained by a shared commitment to friendship and personal loyalty over political considerations, which contrasted so sharply with Paine's perception of Washington's behavior a decade prior. Besides agreeing on virtually all national political matters, Paine and Jefferson adhered to similar religious ideas, particularly in regard to their mutual skepticism toward institutionalized churches and miraculous aspects of the Bible. "I am of a sect by myself, as far as I know," Jefferson revealed some years later—an admission strikingly evocative of Paine's famous declaration that his mind was his own church. Furthermore, Jefferson meticulously crafted his own customized Bible with a razor and glue in such a manner as to remove all references to the divinity of Christ, the Trinity, and miracles.[611] Perhaps most importantly of all, the two also bonded over their joint faith in the common man, and his ability to create economic and political prosperity without any need for aristocratic overseers.

Just weeks after Paine landed on American shores, the attention of Americans was captured by the matter of the Louisiana Territory, a vast swath of land west of the Mississippi River that had been controlled by the Spanish from the end of the Seven Years' War until 1800. That year, Spain ceded the immense territory to France in exchange for land in Italy under the Third Treaty of San Ildefonso. The settlement was seen as beneficial to Americans, who had been denied access to New Orleans since 1798 as the result of Spanish policy. The city held immeasurable value as a cultural center, bastion of trade, and gateway to navigation through the Mississippi River. In addition, some argued the arrival of French forces in city meant that Bonaparte planned to instigate a slave uprising in America and invade the southern states. With all of this in mind, Jefferson sent instructions to Livingston in Paris to inquire about purchasing the city.

When Paine caught word of the Jefferson administration's attempt to pry New Orleans from Bonaparte, he quickly composed a letter to the president from Lovell's Hotel in Washington. If the government began its attempt to acquire New Orleans by inquiring about the entire Louisiana territory instead, the strategy would avoid "the appearance of a threat" and potentially pique Bonaparte's interest. To avoid appearing too eager, Paine also recommended that the subject of the territory as a whole could "be stated as a matter of information" rather than an overt request.[612] As in Jefferson's case, it took Paine little time to recognize the colossal value of the vast western land. Besides pushing potential European adversaries off the continent, the transfer would embolden countless American homesteaders to pursue a better life for themselves in the yeoman tradition. The prospective acquisition would, by the estimations of both men, incentivize the most morally redeemable lifestyle imaginable.

To everyone's great surprise, when hearing of the United States' interest in New Orleans, Bonaparte indeed offered the entire Louisiana Territory to the United States for the shockingly low price of $15 million. From the perspective of the first consul, the landmass was utterly indefensible, especially in light of the French failure to retake Saint-Dominique from Haitian revolutionaries. The move would also end conflicts with the United States in the Caribbean, and allow France to deploy nearly all of its resources—including naval forces and supplies—to the European war effort. The American ambassadors had Jefferson's approval to pay up to $10 million for New Orleans, but the greater opportunity to obtain the Louisiana territory at such a cheap rate stunned them. Worried that Bonaparte would renege on the deal at any moment, the commissioners agreed to the deal, certain that it would be accepted by the president and approved by the Senate. The treaty was negotiated and signed by French diplomat François Barbé-Marbois, Livingston, and Monroe, who made a return to Paris to help Livingston to secure the deal. "We have lived long, but this is the noblest work of our whole lives," Livingston declared as he signed the document.[613]

When news of the deal reached America, the ire of the Federalists quickly shifted from Paine to the president. Believing that the territory would diminish the relative power of New England in general and his state of Massachusetts in particular, Senator Timothy Pickering even suggested that his state should secede from the union if Louisiana were to be acquired. "There will be … a separation," he predicted. Senator James Hill-house of Connecticut joined this choir, declaring that "the eastern states must and will dissolve the union and form a separate government of their own, and the sooner they do it the better."[614] In every way, the possibility of adding the gargantuan western territory tore open the same sectional and ideological wounds that festered throughout the 1790s.

On the surface, gaining the Louisiana Territory for such a surprisingly low price seemed as one of the greatest gifts the young country could ever have received. However, there was one problem—Jefferson didn't think it was constitutional. In fact, the president adamantly maintained that the general government lacked the power under the Constitution to acquire foreign territories, despite his own wishes to buy the territory. Still desir-ing the territory, his proposed remedy was the addition of a constitutional amendment that would explicitly permit the acquisition. Jefferson there-fore sent the following proposed amendment to Congress:

> Louisiana, as ceded by France to the U S. is made a part of the US. Its white inhabitants shall be citizens, and stand, as to their rights & obli-gations, on the same footing with other citizens of the U S. in analogous situations. Save only that as to the portion thereof lying North of an East & West line drawn through the mouth of Arkansa river, no new State shall be established, nor any grants of land made, other than to Indians in exchange for equivalent portions of land occupied by them, until authorised by further subsequent amendment to the Constitution shall be made for these purposes.

According to the president, the United States lacked the "power of holding foreign territory," and thus a constitutional amendment "seems necessary" to obtain the region.[615] Those in Jefferson's cabinet, several of whom wrote letters that justified the treaty on constitutional grounds, vehemently disagreed with the president. Under the belief that land acquisition was an inherent extension of the treaty-making power in the Constitution, the Re-publican-dominated Senate also disregarded Jefferson's position. Land purchase treaties were among the universally recognized types of treaties at the time, and even the United States itself had acquired its original territory from Britain under such an arrangement via the 1783 Treaty of Paris. Ultimately, the Senate ratified the treaty by the wide margin of 24 to 7.

As the controversy over the purchase of the Louisiana Territory played out, Paine was occupied with his plans to promote his bridge and finalize *The Age of Reason*. From late 1802 to the middle of 1803, he also devoted his attention to a grand reprisal against the Federalists who despised him and his ideas. "After an absence of fifteen years, I am again returned to the country in whose dangers I bore my share, and to whose greatness I contributed my part," he declared. According to Paine, the early accomplishments of the Jefferson administration were reason for elation. "A spark from the altar of seventy-six," he wrote, "is again lighting up, in every part of the union, the genuine name of rational liberty." Moreover, he made clear that he was not angling for a position in the presidential cabinet. "I have no occasion to ask, and do not intend to accept, any play or office in the government," he asserted. "I must be in everything what I have ever been, a disinterested volunteer," whose "proper sphere of action is on the common floor of citizenship." Paine proclaimed that his life experiences made him impervious to the attacks of his detractors in America. "The government of England honored me with a thousand martyrdoms, by burning me in effigy in every town in that country, and their hirelings in America may do the same," he professed.[616]

In the mind of the writer, the former ruling party in Washington had at first adopted a respectable brand. If a Federalist was "one who was for cementing the union by a general government operating equally over all the states, in all matters that embraced the common interest," Paine claimed "to stand first on the list of Federalists." To validate this, he reminded readers of his support augmenting the Articles of Confederation to include a congressional tariff, and revived his belief that the states of that period operated more autonomously than he preferred. "The several states were united in name but not in fact," he alleged, "and that nominal union had neither center nor circle." In their quest for national authority, though, Paine argued that Federalists betrayed their promise to be good stewards of the new republic in exchange for power and prestige. To the Hamiltonian faction, the label merely "served as a cloak for treason, a mask for tyranny." Under their watch, "federalism was to be destroyed, and the representative system of government, the pride and glory of America, and the palladium of her liberties, was to be overthrown and abolished." The Alien and Sedition Acts safeguarded those in power "within a magic circle of terror," and the Adams administration sought to "overturn the representative system" and keep American citizens "in continual agitation and alarm."[617]

Though to some degree he detested the rise of factions for the same reasons Madison expressed in *The Federalist,* No. 10, Paine could not have made his alignment clearer than he did in a series of letters to the *National Intelligencer*. The publication's editor, Samuel Harrison Smith, was a close friend of Jefferson, and gladly provided Paine a new outlet for his fierce attacks against the president's Federalist adversaries. "Had America been cursed by John Adams' hereditary monarchy, or Alexander Hamilton's Senate for life," he wrote, it would have been subjected to a bloody civil struggle that had been stifled only by the electoral success of Jefferson and the Republicans. The previous Federalist administrations were merely a gang of power-hungry deviants responsible for creating a "Reign of Terror in America," and Jefferson's predecessors were "the same sort of men" as Robespierre. Paine accused Federalists of acting "hostile to the representative system," and terrorized citizens into believing a French invasion was imminent. In sum, the Federalist program exhibited "the treason of apostasy."[618]

In early 1803, Paine's focus was also drawn to the matter of Aaron Burr, who had been elected vice president but became persona non grata in the Jefferson administration. Burr attracted controversy from political friends and foes alike by angling for the presidency after making clear during the 1800 campaign that he was only seeking the vice-presidential role and supporting Jefferson for president. Until the House of Representatives chose Jefferson as the victor of the presidential race, there was a true chance that Burr would be selected by the same body as the result of the tie in the Electoral College. Despite all the rumormongering, Burr was never complicit with any such backroom deals that would have placed him into power, and therefore "escaped the danger to which they exposed him, and the perjury that would have followed," Paine contended. The penman called upon both the Jefferson and the Burr sects of the Republican faction to condemn the deeds of Aaron Ogden, a Federalist senator from New Jersey whom Paine blamed for "tampering to obtain a president on private conditions."[619] Despite the Englishman's pleadings, Burr never regained his political stature. Instead, he was discarded by the political class entirely after killing Hamilton in a duel. Several years later, he aroused even greater suspicion after being accused of plotting the "Burr Conspiracy," a scheme to establish a new independent country in the American Southwest.

In his first two months back in America, Paine was preoccupied by everything but his original stated goals upon his return—to show off his bridge designs and publish the third volume of *The Age of Reason*. Both subjects had been delayed by his inclination to inject himself into American's political scene. By that time, his reflections on religion had become well known, making him a true apostate to many in America. In late 1802, he received an unexpected letter from Samuel Adams, who had kickstarted the opposition effort to the British in Boston on the eve of American independence. On the surface, the two men shared several similarities, especially their mutual fondness for representative government, organized noncompliance in the face of tyranny, and radical political agitation. "Your *Common Sense* and your *Crisis* unquestionably awakened the public mind, and led the people loudly to call for a declaration of our national independence," Adams expressed. As a devout Congregationalist, though, the New Englander could not imagine why Paine had strayed from orthodox Christian doctrine. "When I heard that you had turned your mind to a defense of infidelity," he wrote, "I felt myself much astonished and more grieved that you had attempted a measure so injurious to the feelings and so repugnant to the true interest of so great a part of the citizens of the United States." According to Adams, Paine should abandon plans to continue future writings on religious if he hoped to salvage his legacy. "Do you think that your pen or the pen of any other man can unchristianize the mass of our citizens," he asked, "or have you hopes of converting a few of them to assist you in so bad a cause?"[620]

Paine responded to Adams on New Year's Day, 1803. "I received with great pleasure your friendly and affectionate letter of November 30 and I thank you also for the frankness," he wrote. After giving honest thanks to the Bostonian for recognizing *Common Sense* and *The Crisis*, he promised to be "as frank with you as you are with me" when it came to the matter of religion. To answer the assertion of spreading "infidelity," the writer first stressed that both he and Adams' ancestors had deviated from conventional religious norms from their own time, especially when England was under established Catholicism. By extension, therefore, "all of us are infidels according to our forefathers' belief." He added more brashly that institutionalized churches had corrupted his conception of true religion, which featured the creator speaking through nature alone. "The case, my friend, is that the world has been over run with fable and creeds of human invention," filling the earth "with persecution and deluged it with blood," he claimed. Historically, Paine wrote that competing religions had only created wars "of creed against creed, each boasting of God for its author, and reviling each other with the name of infidel."[621]

After reiterating his belief in a single God, Paine alerted Adams to the fact that he had been called infidel once before, by the Jacobins, ironically for opposing the French faction's adamant predilection toward atheism. Rather than an infidel, Paine portrayed himself as a defender of religion as he saw it—where the presence of God could be perceived in the natural world:

Do we want to contemplate his power? We see it in the immensity of the Creation. Do we want to contemplate his wisdom? We see it in the unchangeable order by which the incomprehensible Whole is governed. Do we want to contemplate his munificence? We see it in the abundance with which he fills the Earth. Do we want to contemplate his mercy? We see it in his not with holding that abundance even from the unthankful.

On matters of theism, both he and Adams would "have to answer to our creator and not each other," he determined. Still, Paine remained adamant that "the key of heaven is not in the keeping of any sect, nor ought the road to it be obstructed by any." Any individual "who is a friend to man and to his rights, let his opinions be what they may, is a good citizen, to whom" he would extend "the right hand of fellowship"—a class that included Adams.[622] The standard-bearer of revolution in New England died just nine months later.

The letter was noticeably more tempered than some of Paine's responses to other critics, possibly due to the immense admiration he had for Adams and his role in the American struggle for independence. In addition, Paine intended to have his response published, so he sent a copy to the *National Intelligencer* for that exact purpose. He may have wanted its broad distribution to make especially clear what his fiercest critics refused to admit—that he believed in a divine creator and was not simply a godless heathen. Even still, he was unmoved from his decision to push forward and finish *The Age of Reason*. Another man may have heeded the warnings of a man as esteemed as Adams, but Paine was a different creature altogether. The volley of hostility toward his religious writings, to the contrary, may have convinced Paine that the third volume was an absolute necessity.

In addition to finalizing his trilogy on religion, Paine planned to spend the year promoting his iron bridge and original carriage wheels—projects he had discarded professionally and treated only as a hobby for the last decade. To do so, he would return to Bordentown, New Jersey, where he would showcase his models from France to possible financiers. Paine had lived in the town from 1778 to 1787, at which time he rented his property in New Rochelle to a tenant. Its close proximity to Philadelphia made it the perfect place for him to socialize with supporters, and possibly leverage his reputation from War of Independence. The success of his writings in Europe had made him wealthy for the first and only time of his life, but his advancing age may have inspired one last effort to put his designs into reality. Paine endeavored to seek Jefferson's opinion on his models, but grew impatient when the president was slow to respond. "But you have not only shewn no disposition towards it," and neglected the subject "by a sort of shyness," he wrote.[623]

Jefferson responded that he meant no offense by the delay, and to the contrary of Paine's supposition, had "openly maintained in conversation the duty of shewing our respect" to Paine since his return. He explained his delinquency by his stringent schedule as president, which consumed his days and left little time to himself. On the subject of the models themselves, "they are all interesting to the public," Jefferson wrote. To Paine's delight, the president expected the designs would attract the attention of

builders, and even expressed interest in procuring several of Paine's carriage wheels for himself. "I imagine somebody at your new establishment
will set up the trade of making them; and when that is the case I will apply
to him for a pair," he assured his friend. The feedback seemed to boost
Paine's spirits, and the writer-turned-inventor spent the next months getting his models into a museum in Philadelphia owned by the renowned
patriot artist Charles Peale.[624]

In his last days in the capital, Paine's reputation as a heretic continued
to haunt him, even amongst allies. His published letter to Adams had been
reprinted throughout the country, as he had hoped, but it also provided his
detractors with additional ammunition to use against his character. At a
dinner party hosted by Secretary of War Henry Dearborn, Paine and a variety of guests were discussing political matters when a guest produced a
letter that he claimed was written by Congressman Manasseh Cutler of
Massachusetts. The letter strongly denounced Paine and his religious beliefs, and the infamous writer responded in great anger. According the
Philadelphia Aurora General Advertiser, he raised his voice "to ridicule
religion, and blaspheme the Nazarene in the most shocking manner." The
occasion caused resentment from Dearborn's wife, who held her door open
and demanded that Paine leave the home immediately. In an awkward silence, he did so as the other guests "sat in amazement."[625]

It was later discovered the guest who had the letter in his possession
was a Federalist, and its content was a total counterfeit. When details of
the incident were reported in the press, Cutler denied ever having written
the letter or having such feelings toward Paine. The ruse was therefore a
cunning scheme to draw out Paine's most controversial opinions on religion and taint his standing among Republicans close to the president. Regardless, specifics of the letter and Paine's reaction to it were widely circulated by newspapers throughout the United States, and the writer was
forced to spend his last three days in Washington as an outcast.[626] By all
accounts, including his own, the same disrepute followed him like a specter for the rest of his life.

In February of 1803, Paine returned to Philadelphia, where he hoped to
display his bridge and catch up with old friends. In the city, Peale brought
him through his museum, which was then filled with various inventions,
animal bones, and his own paintings of famous American figures. The

painter promised to devote an exhibition to Paine's models, which still had
to be shipped via a packet to Philadelphia. Despite his prestige in some
circles, Paine received a cold reception from his old friend Benjamin Rush.
The patriot doctor, who once befriended Paine and encouraged him to
write *Common Sense* at the height of the crisis with Britain, now refused
to see the writer at all. As a result of *The Age of Reason*, Rush now considered the man an apostate unworthy of his own company. A few days
after arriving in the former capital, Paine made his way across the Delaware River and to Bordentown, where he briefly stayed with his friend
Joseph Kirkbride and reunited with Mrs. Bonneville and her three sons.
There, his old ironworking partner John Hall wrote that he "appeared jol-
lier than I had ever known him," and was "full of whims and schemes and
mechanical inventions."[627]

After a few days, Paine decided to travel to New York City to meet
with his old friend James Monroe, who had obtained Paine's release from
prison in France and hosted him in his home for several years afterward.
His journey to the northern hub could not have been more acrimonious.
After eating dinner in Trenton, New Jersey, he was denied entry on two
separate stage coaches to New York, even after Kirkbride helped book the
trip himself. "I'll be damned if he shall go in my stage," one stagecoach
owner bellowed. A second prospective operator responded even more
harshly. "My stage and horses were once struck by lightning, and I don't
want them to suffer again," he quipped. By the time Paine and Kirkbride
finally secured a carriage, news of Paine's presence swept through town,
and an antagonistic mob formed around the two men. The unruly crowd
flung stones at Paine, and the polemicist managed to defuse the situation
by refraining from "fear or anger," and making a calm but stern statement
that such behavior "had no tendency to hurt his feelings or injure his
fame."[628] Ironically, it was in the vicinity of the same city that Paine
drafted *The Crisis* and carried a rifle in the Continental Army. His virtuous
acts so many years ago on behalf of the liberty of those in New Jersey had
done nothing, therefore, to save him from public ostracism.

Paine's arrival in New York that March was greeted warmly by a host
of citizens who wished to meet the famed writer. Notwithstanding the re-
gion-spanning effort to soil his reputation, many could not ignore the author of *Common Sense* and *The Rights of Man* merely for his heretical

religious views. However, affable treatment in the metropolis was hardly universal. During a brief period of several weeks at the City Hotel, Paine met admirers and worked on his writings. On one occasion, he joyfully received a local clerk from the local Scottish Presbyterian Church, Grant Thorburn, who shook the writer's hand while under a spell of considerable nervousness. For daring to meet with the stigmatized Paine, Thornburn was suspended from psalm-singing for three months. This incident, more than possibly any other from the time, illustrated the degree to which Paine had been made into an outsider. In either case, Paine attended social gatherings, including a dinner thrown in his honor on March 18. The dozens of guests—all supporters of the renowned writer—gave him toasts and sung patriotic hymns in his presence. Future biographer James Cheetham wrote that a fit of habitual drunkenness consumed Paine's time in New York.[629] The accusation was the origin of one of the most prevalent themes of ridicule against him for the next two centuries.

Monroe met with his former housemate shortly before he left for France to assist with the acquisition of Louisiana, and Paine happily provided his own strategic advice regarding how to close the deal with Bonaparte. His chief recommendation was to gain the immediate support of Spain's diplomats for the transfer, even if it "cost something as a compliment." According to Paine, this step was crucial in case France at any point reneged on the offer, because Spain would likely intervene in favor of its fulfillment.[630] Monroe did his best to put the suggestion into motion, but it failed to affect the bargain. Bonaparte insisted upon an immediate decision that did not allow for the Spanish involvement in the deal, and never rescinded the offer after it was agreed to by the American delegation.

After his meeting with Monroe, Paine returned to his farm at New Rochelle, where the main house had burned to the ground while he was in Europe. He paid workers to restore a cottage there instead, which still stands and can be visited today. The modest two-story dwelling served as his main residence in the last years of his life. When he returned to his farm, Paine found himself in a precarious financial situation. His tenant of nearly two decades not only refused to pay rent, but demanded payment from Paine for fencing he had built on the property. According to Hall, the squabble resulted in a lawsuit where Paine not only lost his suit, but was required to pay his former tenant's legal fees in addition to his own. Dejected, he sold 60 acres of his 277-acre plot to recoup his losses, and evicted the farmer.[631] In his last years, he lived frugally as he supported the Bonnevilles in America.

Paine's iron bridge models finally reached Philadelphia in the summer of 1803, where they were put under the care of Pearle. In conjunction with this, their creator drafted "The Construction of Iron Bridges," and sent the letter to Congress "to put the country in possession of the means and of the right of making use of the construction freely," and to refuse patent rights for his designs. Within the message, Paine documented the history of the models and his failed attempts to have a full-sized permanent version built in the 1780s. Additionally, he praised the merits of the few iron bridges that had been built in the West, calling their utilization "an object of importance to the world." He proposed that Congress fund an iron bridge project, "of about 400 feet span" to "remain exposed to public view," such that "the method of constructing such arches may be generally known." Paine did not intend to benefit financially in any way from the endeavor, and promised to assist by providing additional design specifications if Congress chose to pursue the plan. The letter was completely ignored by Congress, likely the result of the Republican-dominated body adhering to strict constructionism and the position that the Constitution did not permit the enactment of such a project. Nevertheless, the suggestion served as a forerunner to decade-spanning clashes between those favoring "internal improvements" and those opposing them.[632] After the ordeal, Paine abandoned bridgebuilding, and shifted his attention to other matters.

In August, Paine ventured to Stonington, Connecticut to visit his friend Nathan Haley, a privateer famous for his exploits on the high seas. Soon after arriving, his presence attracted a stream of visitors. In high spirits, he discussed philosophy and politics with those who wished hear his opinions. While there, he drafted a letter to Jefferson about the ongoing Senate debate over Louisiana. Like most Republicans, Paine did not believe a constitutional amendment necessary to consummate the bargain and approve the treaty. "The cession makes no alteration in the Constitution," he wrote, "it only extends the principles of it over a larger territory." Unlike many of his political allies, however, he didn't believe the acquisition was covered under the treaty-making power. "It appears to me to be one of those cases with which the Constitution has nothing to do," he wrote, "and which can be judged only by the circumstances of the times when such a case shall occur."[633]

His lengthy communication tackled several other topics, including his new plans to serialize his most famous writings in America, the war in Europe, and prejudice toward Jefferson for his religious views. As two of the only people in America who dared to eschew institutionalized religion and deny the miraculous aspects of the Bible, Paine and the Virginian president shared a unique bond. With this in mind, Paine confided to Jefferson that "a man that is not of any of the sectaries will hold the balance even between all; but give power to a bigot of any sectary and he will use it to the oppression of the rest." In addition, he blasted the transatlantic slave trade in no uncertain terms. "It is chiefly the people of Liverpool that employ themselves in the slave trade and they bring cargoes of those unfortunate negroes to take back in return the hard money and the produce of the country," he complained. "Had I the command of the elements," he declared, "I would blast Liverpool with fire and brimstone. It is the Sodom and Gomorrah of brutality."[634]

Paine returned to New Rochelle again at the end of 1803, where he learned that Kirkbride had died. "Bordentown has lost its patron, and I my best friend," he lamented. The somber news disrupted his plans to chop wood on his property and sell it to the local market, and put him into a deep depression. His mental anguish was made worse by physical torment that plagued his aging body. "I have been so unwell this winter with a fit of gout," he wrote to a friend the next year. Paine took up temporary residence with Daniel Pelton, a man who owned a general store in town. The change in location helped him recover at first, but his health issues were worsened when he suffered a fall on ice that covered Pelton's garden. The incident debilitated the scribe for a full month, and he ached so bad he could not write. [635] At the age of 66, he could no longer carry himself with the same fierce demeanor that filled his writings, and his plans to republish *Common Sense* and *The Rights of Man* never came to fruition. He could barely move for a time in his frail condition, but his health began to improve a little by the spring of 1804.

During his recovery, Paine kept close tabs on the situation in Europe, clinging to hope that he may live to see the corrupt government of his homeland taken down through the scheme he once shared with Bonaparte. An annulment of the Treaty of Amiens in 1803 meant the renewal of war between Britain and France—and with it the revived possibility for a French invasion of Britain. "The present impolitic war by the English government has now renewed the plan, and with much greater energy than before, and with national unanimity," he alleged. According to Paine, the "plan of a descent upon England by gun-boats" may still "hold the English government in terror, and the whole country in alarm, whenever she pleases, and as long as she pleases, and that without employing a single ship of the line." Since the days of the French Revolution, Pitt's government had only grown more oppressive, priming itself for a new representative order that would come at the hands of the French. "It is a revolution in naval tactics," he declared, "but we live in an age of revolutions."[636]

Paine's longstanding animosity toward Bonaparte for his personal ambitions and political duplicity did not stop him from flattering the general for his military exploits. Bonaparte was "the most enterprising and fortunate man ... the world has known for many ages," he wrote, and "not a man in the British government, or under its authority, has any chance with him." Bonaparte again considered the maneuver, but ultimately decided against it for reason of its incredible risk, the presence of an inflation crisis, and because of France's failure to maintain naval control over the English Channel.[637] He turned his sights away from England in favor of waging continental war instead, and Paine's dream of a French invasion of England was never realized. Later that year, Bonaparte crowned himself Emperor of the French in an elaborate ceremony in Paris, and any semblance of republicanism that lasted beyond his coup was vanquished.

Mere months after the Senate ratified the Franco-American treaty approving the Louisiana Purchase, the French inhabitants of the territory petitioned Congress for immediate statehood on equal footing with the existing states. Their appeal made clear they intended to form a government that allowed both the continuance of both the international slave trade and slavery itself. In addition to expanding sugar cane ventures, the advent of the cotton gin in 1793 only increased the demand for slave labor in the region, and French Louisiana sought to protect its planter and merchant classes. In addition, the grievance criticized the congressional act on

March 26, 1804 that portioned the territory into two separate regions because doing so necessarily prolonged its transition to statehood. In direct contradiction to the wishes of the disgruntled inhabitants, the same law also explicitly barred the importation of slaves into the territory.

In retort to the appeal, Paine lashed out in his typical fashion by excoriating the petitioners for making demands of the United States without laboring to secure the same rights they wished to enjoy. "We obtained our rights by calmly understanding principles, and by the successful event of a long, obstinate and expensive war," Paine wrote, "but it is not incumbent on us to fight the battles of the world for the world's profit." The Frenchmen in the region were therefore "already participating" in "the blessings of freedom acquired by ourselves," despite never enduring "all the dangers and hardships of the revolutionary war." The protest against territorial division was also without merit, he claimed, because the complaint assumed a wrongful attempt "to govern a territory that we have purchased." Contrary to their wishes, precedent from the Northwest Territory established that Louisiana would likely be "divided into twelve states or more," but such a question would be decided by Congress rather than the petitioners.[638]

Paine reserved the brunt of his rage against the supplicants for insisting upon the expansion of negro slavery. In his mind, slavery was a form of bondage that blatantly reject natural law in the same way monarchy did—by forcing men to be bound to "in all cases whatsoever" to an illegitimate ruler. In his eyes, calling for the "right" to slavery was to defy the creator and embrace hypocrisy of the highest rank. It was a "direct injustice," he excoriated the signers, to "petition for power, under the name of rights, to import and enslave Africans!"[639] The statement was telltale Paine, wholly characteristic of his lifelong view that slavery was a moral atrocity that should be expunged from the earth. Ultimately, the Jefferson administration succeeded in securing an outright ban on all slave importation into the United States in 1807, as soon as it was constitutionally permissible.

In 1804, Paine also joined up with his deist convert Elihu Palmer, the most successful promoter of Paine's religious views in New York. A former Presbyterian minister, Palmer gushed at the penman's brilliance, and was smitten by Paine's religious works in particular. According to the theologian, Paine's writings represented "the most striking relation to the immediate improvement and moral felicity of the intelligent world," and the writer himself was "probably the most useful man that ever existed upon the face of the earth."[640] The two worked in tandem to launch a deistic organization known as the Theistic Society. To promote the organization, Palmer inaugurated the *Prospect: or, View of the Moral World*, a monthly magazine in New York. Paine was honored to be so involved in the project, and was happy to contribute to the periodical.

Within, he expanded upon concepts he first invoked in *The Age of Reason*. In his first essay, he returned to the oft-repeated theme that biblical tales could not withstand earnest scrutiny. Christianity "put tradition in place of evidence, and tradition is not proof," Paine claimed, and "the obscene and vulgar stories in the Bible" were repugnant to deistic ideas. The creator of the universe could be proven by nature and reason alone, he argued, and unbelievable fables only tarnished the "perfect purity" of his creed. "It is the reverence of the deists for the attributions of the deity that causes them to reject the Bible," he concluded. Paine argued that biblical parables should be discounted for defying the laws of nature, contradicting themselves, and even for copying other farfetched legends. For instance, the story of Cain and Abel in Genesis appeared to be a mere retelling of the story of Typhon and Osiris, a classic Egyptian tale. According to the self-styled heretic, all miraculous stories should also be disregarded, and acceptance of their truth was unnecessary to celebrate the gifts of a benevolent creator. "The wonderful structure of the universe," Paine wrote, "and everything we behold in the system of creation prove to us, far better than books do, the existence of a God, and at the same time proclaim his attributes."[641]

According to Paine, "the belief of the redemption of Jesus Christ altogether" was an invention of the Catholic Church rather than the "doctrine of the New Testament." Instead, the writer contended that the New Testament authors meant to prove "the resurrection of the same body from the grave" rather than absolution from sin. To justify this, Paine pointed to 1 Corinthians 15, which he said was "full of supposed cases and assertions about the resurrection of the same body, but there is not a word in it about redemption." The notion that Jesus died for the sins of mankind, then, was to the penman "the fable of priestcraft invented since the time the New

Testament was compiled," and caught on among the public only by an "agreeable delusion" that answered "the depravity of immoral livers." Believing the Christian myth of redemption, he wrote, was "dangerous to morals in this world" for its propensity to provide "such a cheap, easy, and lazy way of getting to heaven."[642] This allegation was likely the most controversial observation on traditional dogma that Paine had ever put to ink, a statement that put him at odds with the cornerstone belief of virtually all Christian sects.

Ultimately, Paine and Palmer's joint effort to disseminate deism through the United States proved unsuccessful. Even even amongst its targeted audience of radical religious dissidents, the *Prospect* failed to catch on, and the publication ended in early 1805. Palmer renewed his attempt to spread the word through speaking tours, and died abruptly during one such venture in 1806. His most famous work, *Principles of Nature; or a Development of the Moral Causes of Happiness and Misery among the Human Species*, was published posthumously through the assistance of Richard Carlile, a radical instigator in Britain who was himself imprisoned for seditious libel. Paine's advanced age and focus on other affairs left him unable to continue the venture, and Theistic Society died with his loss of commitment. Nevertheless, the essays he wrote to promote the organization undoubtedly solidified his standing as American's leading religious apostate and emboldened his adversaries.

The 1804 presidential election pitted Paine's friend Jefferson against Federalist Charles Pinckney, a planter from South Carolina who had served with distinction in the Continental Army, represented the Washington administration as minister to France, and played a leading role in writing and ratifying the United States Constitution. In its runup, Paine stated his intention of staying out of the contest. "It is not my intention to publish any pieces or letters on the ensuing presidential election," he wrote to a friend, "because I think there will be no occasion for it." However, he also reserved the right to reconsider this position "if any champion of the Feds whether priest or mousquetaire throws the gauntlet." Paine's general reluctance to involve himself in the campaign was likely the result of his keen awareness that many of his Republican allies feared intertwining the now-wildly unpopular writer of *Common Sense* with Jefferson. Even though the Virginian president admired Paine, he was widely considered a political liability. In the previous year, though, the penman made his support for the president unambiguous. As he saw it, Jefferson's gravitation toward "wise economy and peaceable principles" contrasted so greatly with the "outrage, coxcombical parade, false alarms," and "continual increase of taxes and unceasing clamor for war" of the Federalist administrations.[643]

By the crushing margin of 162 to 14 electoral votes, Jefferson and his vice-presidential running mate George Clinton of New York easily triumphed over Pinckney and Rufus King. The outcome could not have been more different from that of the 1800 election, which was bitterly divisive and remained unsettled for many months. In many ways, it was the beginning of the end for the Federalists on the national stage, and the faction never succeeded in recapturing Congress or the presidency. On the other hand, Jefferson and his administration rightly earned the trust of American citizens, Paine wrote, "by keeping a country well informed upon its affairs, and discarding from its councils every thing of mystery, that harmony is preserved or restored among the people, and confidence reposed in the government." In many ways, the 1804 election preserved "a state of tranquility" never seen in the first two presidential administrations.[644]

Even though Paine's preferred faction had prevailed over the Federalists, he grew concerned in the face of local political overreach. In 1805, well-connected financiers in New York successfully lobbied the state legislature to grant financial monopolies to the Merchant's Bank, an institution created by Alexander Hamilton in 1803. As he saw it, this deed was entirely impermissible because the state's 1777 constitution did not provide for such a power. "There is no article in the constitution of this state, nor any of the states, that invests the government in whole or in part with the power of granting charters or monopolies of any kind," he avowed. According to Paine, disobeying this rule—in his mind the primary maxim of American constitutionalism—was to undermine the cause at the heart of the War of Independence.[645]

The principal reason to elect legislators periodically, he argued, was to provide a check against the proclivities of the body that preceded it, and to right the wrongs of the immediate past. Conversely, the same process also allowed voters to endorse policy by re-electing those responsible for its creation. In either case, representative assemblies could not justifiably

make their impositions binding upon future generations. "The very intention, essence and principle of annual election would be destroyed" if the
legislature "had the power to place any of its acts beyond the reach of succeeding legislatures," he maintained. This meant that free New Yorkers
had the legitimate power to reverse the banking charter after the scheme
was revealed. Any allegation to the contrary reeked to him of the British
constitutional framework, "the most corrupt system in existence," which
held as its chief axiom that Parliament's acts were binding upon all future
generations.[646] Failing to allow a succeeding legislature to repeal the banking charter, or other long-term acts of its kind, would therefore subvert the
state's constitutional system and negate the purpose of periodic elections.

During the same timeframe, Paine also contributed two anonymous essays to New York City's *American Citizen*, in which the writer defended
Jefferson from the merciless attacks of the Federalist presses following his
victory in the 1804 presidential election. Specifically, he took exception
to the allegations of Thomas Turner, an editorialist for Boston's *Repertory*,
which Paine called a "repository of filth." To Turner's charge that Jefferson wrongfully abandoned Richmond as governor of Virginia when the
British forces swarmed the city, the penman responded simply that "he did
what was his duty to do" by evacuating the government from the beleaguered capitol. "It is nonsense to talk about a seat of government when a
country is invaded," he asserted, and attacking his character on such
grounds was foolhardy. It was also "malignant and impotent" to berate the
Virginian for fleeing from his own residence at Monticello as forces under
British Colonel Banastre Tarleton conquered Charlottesville. In his haste
to depart from his property, Jefferson suffered a dislocated shoulder from
falling from his horse, a circumstance that left him physically disabled for
a time and convinced him to resign from the governorship. The circumstances only highlighted Jefferson's "patriotism and integrity," Paine
wrote, and "a mere skunk, such as Turner has proved himself to be," would
have surrendered to the enemy invaders, hid in his home, or defected to
the British.[647]

Turner also attacked Jefferson for funding the notorious Scottish polemicist James Callender, who in his words printed "the blackest effusions
of the blackest calumny that ever escaped the envenomed pen of a villain"
in his attacks against the Adams administration. In Paine's mind, it was

obvious why Callender's work would be disregarded to such an extent by a closet monarchist such as Turner, or "with any conspirator concerned in the treasonable project of bringing over a foreign royal blackguard to be king of America." Far from feeling shame, Jefferson should be proud of supporting Callender's outbursts against Adams and the Federalists, he thought. The continuance of American republicanism depended on opposing the previous presidential administration's pro-Tory policies before they could take root and become precedent. Jefferson's decision to fund Callender at the time, far from a treacherous deed, was in his eyes "a praise worthy act." Callender eventually turned against Jefferson because the president denied him a position as postmaster in Richmond, so he raised funds to smear the Virginian president in the *Richmond Recorder*. A disagreement with the newspaper's owner led to the publication's failure, however, and Callender fell into the James River in a drunken haze and drowned in 1803. Though Callender had "turned into a scoundrel and expiated his crime by drowning himself," Paine wrote, this did not negate his earlier work that exposed the misconduct of the Adams administration.[648]

In August, Paine also composed a lengthy essay calling for a new convention in Pennsylvania to revise the state's 1790 constitution. He considered the document "clogged with inconsistence of a hazardous tendency," and far inferior to the framework's 1776 predecessor he had helped inspire. One major defect of the existing constitution, he claimed, was the presence of an absolute veto, a facet "copied from the English government, without ever perceiving the inconsistent and absurdity of it, when applied to the representative system." The power was historically "derived from conquest, and not from any constitutional right by compact," designed to prevent any law "that might abridge, invade, or in any way affect or diminish" hereditary monarchy. Paine declared the veto power in Pennsylvania should therefore be modified to allow for a veto override, such that "a wise man would not choose to be embarrassed with it, and a man fond of using it will be overthrown by it."[649]

Paine also blasted the state senate, with its lengthy four-year terms and extensive powers, as "an imitation of what is called the House of Lords in England." This issue could be fixed, he wrote, by allowing the two houses to conduct debate and vote on legislation independently, but eliminating

one house's annulment power over the other. Though Paine had long admitted the shortcomings of unicameral system, his ideal would move
Pennsylvania closer to the democratic orientation of the 1776 constitution
by counting the votes of both houses together for "the final decision."[650]

Additionally, rather than restricting voting rights to freemen over the
age of 21 who had been taxpaying residents of the state for two years,
Paine thought wealth, "having no stability, cannot and ought not be made
a criterion of right." As in France, he advocated universal suffrage in Pennsylvania, which did not make "artificial distinctions among men." Furthermore, the state judiciary—which had been populated by political appoin-
tees that served for life during "good behavior"—should be replaced by an
electoral system. In contrast to the current system, "judges ought to be held
to their duty by continual responsibility," he wrote, as the impeachment
mechanism was insufficient to combat inadequate "conduct and character." To avoid bringing "dishonor to the national sovereignty," the propensity to use foreign legal precedents to justify American legal opinions
should also cease. American jurisprudence should entirely supplant its
British counterpart, which he viewed as a corrupt arrangement from which
the United States deliberately escaped. "The case of every man ought to
be tried by the laws of his own country," he insisted.[651]

Paine concluded his essay on constitutional reform in Pennsylvania by
reminding his readers of the central element that set the representative system of the American states apart from every other political system devised:

America has the high honor and happiness of being the first nation that
gave to the world the example of forming written constitutions by conventions elected expressly for the purpose, and of improving them by
the same procedure, as time and experience shall show necessary. Government in other nations, vainly calling themselves civilized, has been
established by bloodshed. Not a drop of blood has been shed in the
United States in consequence of establishing constitutions and governments by her own peaceful system. The silent vote, or the simple yea
or nay, is more powerful than the bayonet, and decides the strength of
numbers without a blow.[652]

Despite Paine's intention for the article to serve as the catalyst for an actual constitutional convention in Pennsylvania, it never came to be. However, the work was printed in pamphlet form by the *Philadelphia Aurora General Advertiser*, which was still under the direction of editor William Duane. In addition, many of the ideas within the tract were at the heart of the state's 1805 gubernatorial race, and likely played a role in securing victory for Thomas McKean over his opponent, the Republican-aligned Simon Snyder.

Paine's writings that summer radiated with the same fiery style that made his earlier works famous, and for a time it seemed the old firebrand had rediscovered his way. Even in old age, it seemed as though the old writer may possibly settle into his solitary lifestyle in New Rochelle, where he could continue to read and write at leisure. At such a pace, he may even have regained some of the respect lost in his denunciation of George Washington and promotion of deism. However, his brief return to form did not last long. *Constitutional Reform* was to be his last political pamphlet, and his attention was soon dominated by personal turmoil.

In America, Paine tried his best to provide for the Bonnevilles as he assumed the role of a "family man" for the first time in his life. In private, however, he expressed bitterness toward the situation. Though he felt personally indebted to the Bonnevilles and intended to honor his financial commitment to them, he grew inwardly frustrated with Marguerite's inability to adapt to her new circumstances. The family matriarch complained of boredom in Bordentown, and insisted on staying in New York City instead, where Paine was at the time. Despite the writer's displeasure at bearing the cost of her stay, she brought all three of her children to live with her at a boardinghouse owned by James Wilburn. During her residence, she accumulated unpaid debts in New York to the point of being brought to civil court in late 1804. Paine managed to win the case, but still agreed to pay the disputed sum of $35 to appeal to the good will of the public and free him from additional controversy.[653]

Despite the legal resolution, Mrs. Bonneville still struggled to take to domestic affairs as Paine expected over the next months. She had become "an encumbrance upon me," Paine complained to a friend, and "would not do anything, not even make an apple-dumpling for her own children." Unable to converse or write well in English, she often required cultural and linguistic guidance that the aging man struggled to provide. On top of that, her tastes were expensive, and she showed no sign of being willing to live thriftily as he did. "I am master of an empty house or nearly so," Paine remarked to a friend, with only "six chairs and a table, a straw-bed, a feather-bed," and various kitchenware.[654] The matriarch's behavior compromised his mission to provide an inheritance to the Bonneville children, and Paine grew worried about his financial situation.

Faced with economic uncertainty, Paine desperately appealed to Jefferson, one of his last remaining friends. In a manner similar to his pleadings during the 1780s, he beseeched the president to encourage Congress to grant him a new estate. The bestowment of his farm and home in New Rochelle, a product of New York's thanks to Paine "for voluntary services during the revolution," was suddenly insufficient recompense for his contributions to America's struggle for independence. The elderly essayist now asked Jefferson to ensure "the matter to be brought over again." Free of Mrs. Bonneville's distractions, he believed he could end his life concentrating on that which had given him purpose—connecting with the public through the written word. If Congress were to "take up the subject … and grant me a tract of land that I can make something of," he wrote, he could navigate "the economy and extreme frugality" through which he was living. "I have been a volunteer to the world for thirty years without taking profits from anything I have published in America or in Europe," he noted in his pitch to the president.[655]

When Jefferson failed to respond within a month and half's time, Paine renewed his pleas in subsequent correspondence. The writer desired "to be informed if he received a letter from him" in regard to "making an acknowledgement to Thomas Paine for his services during the revolution."[656] Still, his plea went unanswered by the Virginian president. Despite his open friendship with Paine, Jefferson's lack of response was likely due to his unwillingness to generate new controversies over his relationship with the outcast penman. Moreover, his rigid position against enacting legislation beyond those powers expressly enumerated in the constitution may have prevented him from broaching the subject even if he thought nothing would come of it in the antagonistic presses.

Soon after the conclusion of Paine's legal battle with his deceitful former tenant, he took up a new one in Christopher Derrick, who became the new steward of his farm. Under their arrangement, Derrick would care for the property and perform basic maintenance to preserve its condition in the absence of Paine and the Bonnevilles. During a period of several months, the two bickered over financial matters and the specifics of the lease. The matter grew agonizing for Paine, who finally asked Derrick to vacate the property at the end of the year. Believing the matter resolved, Paine returned to his property in New Rochelle during the Christmas holiday, where he was joined by the son of a neighbor. On Christmas Eve, 1805, Paine was sitting in the rear room of the lower floor when Derrick approached the home in a drunken stupor.[657] After making his way through the snow, he positioned himself by the window, where he could make out the likeness of Paine through a window. He took aim at the unsuspecting writer with his musket, then fired directly at him.

The event rattled Paine, who immediately ran out of the house with the neighbor's boy. "I directly suspected who it was," he wrote to a friend, "and hallowed to him by name," such that "the party who fired might know I was on the watch." Paine determined the gun must have been placed very close the window, which was shattered and covered with black powder. He learned later that Derrick had been drinking rum for several hours prior to the attempt on his life, and borrowed the rifle used in the assault from Daniel Pelton's local store. Local law enforcement tracked down and arrested Derrick the next day. He was charged with attempted homicide, and placed on bail for $500 with a trial scheduled for May of 1806. The local community voiced support for the elderly Paine, and even the *New-York Commercial Advertiser*, a local Federalist publication, condemned Derrick for attempting to take the writer's life. "However mischievous have been the writings and conduct of Thomas Paine," the article read, "every honest man will join in execrating this diabolical transaction."[658]

Beyond the attempt on his life, it came to be known that Paine was owed $48 by Derrick for a stone bridge he intended to build. The trial was postponed for a time, but Paine ultimately refused to press charges against his attempted murderer. He left no writings indicating his reasoning, but it is likely he did not wish to relive the incident through testimony, or bring negative notoriety to himself within the local community. It is also possible Paine may have been repulsed by the fact that the trial may have resulted in the death penalty, which was practiced at the time in New York.

As someone opposed to the punishment for its application of violent revenge, Paine may have thought it best to prevent its association with his
name. A third reason may have been that he simply felt no longstanding
resentment toward Derrick, who had obviously behaved irrationally while
drunk. In any case, the gunshot at New Rochelle was yet another occasion
where Paine barely avoided an untimely death.

In his follow-up to an unresponsive Jefferson in early 1806, Paine restrained himself from revisiting his request for a financial grant from Congress. However, he did share his perspective on European military affairs,
especially as they related to France. Paine believed that Bonaparte, now
Emperor of the French, would initiate a continental peace with European
powers that did not include England, and possibly launch a naval invasion
of the island similar to the one he proposed in France. After boasting about
the merits of his "plan for a descent upon England by gunboats," he offered
his services to Jefferson to represent the administration as a diplomat in
the case of a European peace agreement. "I do this because I do not think
there is a person in the United States that can render so much service on
the business that will come on as myself," he wrote, highlighting his experience in "the greater matters that now occupy" European politics. As
he figured, Bonaparte would soon march into Vienna, proclaim an end to
continental hostilities, offer generous olive branches to his occupied kingdoms, and open trade on the high seas.[659]

For several reasons, the new request seemed absurd, and must have
perplexed Jefferson. Paine was in poor health, about to turn 69 years old,
and in no position to make another transatlantic voyage. Moreover, he totally misinterpreted the military situation in Europe, basing all of his
thoughts upon faulty assumptions. France's navy had just suffered a cataclysmic naval loss in the Battle of Trafalgar, which claimed the life of the
dazzling British admiral Horatio Nelson, but also destroyed the French naval fleet. Bonaparte was also in no position to force Europe into a peace,
and continental fighting between the Grand Armée and France's enemies
would continue for another decade.

Jefferson was polite, but direct, in his reply to his oblivious friend. The
United States had no current cause for discussions with France, he wrote,
and "full powers" had already been vested in American ambassadors to
negotiate with Britain and Spain. As a result, it was "not in contemplation

to look for any other hand." In regard to financial support from Virginia, Jefferson remarked that political matters "had now devolved on a younger race, few of whom were old enough to witness your services in the revolution, & who consequently know them only from the cold page of history." As such, it was unlikely Paine would find enough legislative support to grant his monetary request, even in the state governments.[660] The president's response came as a devastating blow, and appeared to affect Paine on an emotional level. From that point forward, he wrote little, save to a few close friends, and never again authored another political pamphlet. Defeated, he sank into a depression, and even abandoned self-care.

The spring of 1806 saw a ragged, disheveled Paine continue to disconnect from the world around him. When word of his despondency made its way to New York City, his old friend William Carver took a trip northward to visit him in New Rochelle. The blacksmith, who had known the polemicist since his days in Lewes, England, arrived to find his companion in utter disarray:

> I found you at a tavern in a most miserable situation. You appeared as if you had not been shaved for a fortnight, and as to a shirt, it could not be said that you had one on, it was only the remains of one, and this likewise appeared not to have been off for your back for a fortnight, and was nearly the color of tanned leather; and you had the most disagreeable smell possible, just like that of our poor beggars in England.

Carver was so aghast at his friend's squalor that he drew a bath, bathed Paine three times until he was clean, and shaved his fingernails, which were overgrown "like bird claws" and his toenails, which "exceeded half an inch in length, and others had grown round your toes." After the embarrassing ordeal, Carver took pity on Paine, and invited the writer to stay with him for a time at his home in New York City, where Carver could care for him more directly. Paine reluctantly agreed, and left once more for the bustle of the state's largest metropolis. In 1823, Carver wrote to Jefferson in memory of his friend. "Paine spread a light over the world," he wrote, while acknowledging the writer "like all others had his failings."

Specifically, he was "fond of ardent spirits," holder of "a sower disposition, and exceedingly dogmatical"—all characteristics that contributed to
his gloomy condition in 1806.[661]

By several accounts, the change in scenery seemed to have a positive
effect on the despondent elder. The city's busy streets, commerce, and energetic people seemed to raise his spirits, and Paine was rescued tempo-
rarily from the doldrums of depression. As one who thrived much more in
the city than the country, he continued to keep up with the news, and met
with continual visitors. Even though he felt discarded by his politically-
connected friends, Paine found ways to enjoy his surroundings. By the
summer of 1806, he had recovered enough to be put his pen to ink once
more, this time on the subject of communicable diseases. At the time, the
spread of yellow fever throughout the United States was a deadly threat.
In 1793, for instance, more than 4,000 Philadelphians succumbed to the
disease, approximately 10 percent of the city at the time.[662] By 1806, many
still suffered from its spread.

In *The Cause of the Yellow Fever*, Paine expressed that outbreaks were
largely concentrated to coastal cities where vessels arrived from the West
Indies. In addition, he observed that the affliction did not appear to be contagious and could not be carried through the air. Through a process of
elimination, he determined yellow fever was not "produced by the climate
naturally" and that the "low grounds on the shores of the rivers" of infected
cities were not affected. Paine concluded that yellow fever's origin was
likely "in the pernicious vapor" that emanated from the muddy bottoms of
the rivers, and that the large number of wharfs constructed in recent years
explained the epidemic. The best solution to the issue, he thought, was to
use arches to construct docks in such a way that tidewater could flow un-
derneath. He also noted the improved design would "render the wharfs
more productive than the present method" because it would save space.
The idea combined his engineering and scientific knowledge, and contrasted with his views from 1803 on the same topic. At that point, Paine
thought the disease may be transported in the cargo of ships, "especially
that part which is barreled up," and that when opened on the docks, "the
hot steaming air in contact with the ground imbibes the infection."[663]

Paine's pamphlet was distributed widely outside of New York, and
generated some praise even among antagonistic circles. According to one

account, Jefferson lauded his explanation as "one of the most sensible per-formances on that disease" brought to his attention.[664] After its publication, the country continued to be plagued for many years by yellow fever. For fear of contagion, some Americans stopped shaking hands with another, took strides to isolate the sick, avoided walking near graveyards, and even barricaded themselves in their homes. Some even ingested experimental remedies of their own design in hopes the affliction could be protected against. Despite Paine's creative approach to diagnosing the disease and articulating a possible solution, however, it was determined many years later that yellow fever was actually transmitted through mosquito bites. Though his analysis had yielded the wrong deduction and solution, he was right in his assertion that yellow fever was not contagious, did not pass through the air, and was mostly confined to coastal areas in the summer.

On July 4, Paine was lively enough to witness the spectacle that was New York City's annual celebration of American independence. The oc-casion must have been a joyous and emotional occasion for the aged au-thor, who had once opened the proverbial floodgates of independence from within the same city. His rehabilitated stature was soon threatened yet again, however, by yet another near-death experience. While climbing the stairs to his bed at Carver's residence, he felt as if he "had been shot through the head," suffering a stroke. He was thought to have suffered a fatal collapse, but the family nursed him back to health when they realized he was still living. "I got so very much hurt by the fall," he remarked, "that I have not been able to get in and out of bed since that day." After several weeks in a comatose state, Paine awakened and regained his senses. "My mental faculties have remained as perfect as I ever enjoyed them," he boasted to Andrew Dean, the newest renter of his home in New Rochelle. The recovering agitator considered the episode "as an experiment on dy-ing," and reported that he found "death has no terrors for me." The situa-tion only reinforced his lack of belief in Christian orthodoxy.[665]

During his period of recovery, Paine was visited by John Melish, a re-nowned Scottish mapmaker and fellow friend of Jefferson. Surrounded by a pile of newspapers, the writer and his visitor were drawn into a conver-sation on European affairs, and ultimately to the matter of England's fate in Europe. "The war must inevitably go on till the government of England fell," Paine said sternly, "for it was radically and systematically wrong, and altogether incompatible with the present state of society." To Melish's supposition that the country's new Whig administration sought to rectify many of the kingdom's shortcomings, Paine snapped back. All the dreamers that ever took power in the country, he exclaimed, were still hold hostage by its corrupt monarchical structure. No one "would ever be able to reform it," he insisted, for "the system was wrong, and it never would be set right without a revolution, which was as certain as fate, and at no great distance in time."[666] He was also seen frequently during this period by his admirer Grant Thorburn, the Presbyterian minister who had once been punished by his congregation for making acquaintance with the religious cynic. Even though the two had vastly different religious beliefs, they shared a cordial relationship. Thorburn admired Paine's wit, and was greatly impressed by the sharpness of his mind in old age.

Paine's stage of peace in recovery did not last long. According to Carver, Paine was a lousy houseguest. "After drinking a large portion of ardent spirits," he wrote, the writer frequently had to be lifted into his bed. Paine also complained about the size and condition of his room, which was the only one its owner could spare. For a time, Carver and his wife helped clean for him, feed him meals, and keep him warm during cold nights. When Paine feuded with Carver's wife over the specifics of cleaning his spaces, though, she arranged for his late friend Elihu Palmer's widow to attend to his daily needs. Despite this minor reprieve for the family, Paine continued to be a burden on the Carvers to the point that the task of moving him from place to place brought William physical discomfort. "I did so until it brought a pain in my side, that prevented me from sleeping after I got to bed myself," he agonized. Carver also accused his guest of refusing to provide for basic necessities for his own livelihood. "I expected so much money on your account," he wrote, "and received so little, that I could not go to any further expense."[667]

The issues between the two men got so serious that they had a complete falling out. Paine refused to pay Carver a sum of $150 in return for his lodgings and care. Astonished, the Englishman did not hesitate to respond with the same vociferous style that filled his political tirades. He had already paid the man four dollars each week he stayed for unexpected and subpar treatment, he claimed. "At your house I found my own bedding and the room I had was no other than a closet to the front room," and there was "no fire to come to when the weather grew cold," causing him to suffer "a great deal from the cold." Moreover, Paine's understanding was that Mrs. Palmer was to be paid not by himself, but by the Carvers as an attendant for the entire house. He also disputed that she was there for the full period of 12 weeks as William claimed, and grumbled that he had never been warned of "the particulars of the expenditure" until the recent demand for repayment. Paine alleged that Carver had also stolen his watch from a cupboard, and suspected him of stealing other belongings. "I did not like the treatment I received at your house," he griped. "In no case was it friendly, and it many cases not civil, especially from your wife." For being "such an unprincipled false-hearted man," Paine spitefully notified Carver that he had been removed from his will. He proposed to "settle the account" though mutual associates, after which point "all communication between you and me may cease."[668]

Carver responded in his own lengthy reply to Paine, which openly called his resident a liar and took aim at his integrity. The accusation he stole the author's watch was merely "one more of your lies," he countered, as he had only moved it for a time to keep it out of sight of Paine's visitors who may have wished to take it. He denied that Mrs. Palmer was employed to do work for the Carver family as a whole, and that his guest paid for all of the liquor he consumed in the evenings. Instead, he wrote, Paine "drank one quart of brandy per day" at his own expense. In a crude personal attack, he relayed the scandalous myth that Paine had been having an affair with Marguerite Bonneville. "I believe you have broken up the domestic tranquility of several families, with whom you have resided," he wrote, and Mrs. Bonneville "may have rendered you former and present secret services." Carver even went so far as to insinuate the three Bonneville children may even be his. "Whether the boys are yours, I leave you to judge." Paine failed to live up to his lofty virtues he wrote of so often, he alleged, and acted ungrateful toward family despite their assistance in his time of greatest need. "I think I have drawn a complete portrait of your character," which epitomized "hypocrisy and deception, under which you have acted in your political as well as moral capacity of life," Carver fumed.[669]

The dispute was so contentious that Paine recruited his friend John Fellows to serve as an intermediary between the two parties. He did so, negotiating a financial settlement with Carver and helping Paine plan for new boarding arrangements. In the same period, Paine ventured to New Rochelle to cast his vote in that year's state elections. When he arrived at the city post office, he received his tickets from the local electoral inspectors according to standard protocols in New York. Upon turning in each, the election supervisor Elisha Ward rebuffed him. "You are not an American citizen," he insisted. As Paine stood flabbergasted, the attendant explained that the scribe's citizenship was denied by his old nemesis Gouverneur Morris, who "would not reclaim you when you were imprisoned in the Luxembourg at Paris," and that the former president refused to assert otherwise as well. Paine aggressively protested the decision and explained that his citizenship was pressed by Monroe and confirmed by the French government in Paris. After making his case, he threatened to prosecute Ward for violating his voting rights. The supervisor then called for a local constable, promising to imprison the disenfranchised demagogue if he continued to object.[670]

Enraged, Paine left the polling station without further incident, but in a sour state. He eventually discovered that Ward was from a Tory family, and the deed was likely the result of longstanding animosity toward the most recognizable patriot spokesman of the era. Soon after the fiasco, he recruited legal services to bring forth a suit against the New York Board of Inspectors. He hired Richard Riker, then the district attorney of the region containing New York City, to represent him. Perhaps prompted by Riker, Paine drafted letters to James Madison, George Clinton, and his old friend Joel Barlow asking each for an attestation of his status as a citizen. Mrs. Bonneville wrote that Paine's case was argued before the New York Supreme Court, and that he lost the case. However, no court records exist that substantiate this, and it is unclear as to whether the suit was ever heard. In reply to Paine, Clinton confirmed that he had written and submitted the requested letter directly to Riker, but doubted it would be admissible into evidence.[671]

After Paine's feud with Carver, he ultimately settled in Manhattan at the end of 1806. At a boarding house on Church Street, he shared quarters with John Wesley Jarvis, a prominent artist. The previous year, the 26-

year-old Jarvis had painted a portrait of Paine that is now one of his most widely distributed likenesses. The unlikely pair became good friends, and shared a mutual respect for each other. According to the painter, Paine was "one of the most pleasant companions I have met with for an old man."[672] Jarvis' proximity to his elderly roommate kept him inescapably apprised of Paine's writing projects, which had shifted by this point back to religion once again.

In 1807, Paine edited and republished *An Essay on Dream*, a short essay that once saw distribution in France prior to his departure from the country. Its original title, "Extract from the M.S. Third Part of Thomas Paine's Age of Reason. Chapter the Second: Article, Dream," makes clear that it was intended to be part of the conclusion to his infamous saga on religion. The work emphasized the Bible's heavily dependence upon dreams and its audacity to "make them a foundation for religion." Paine observed that the prophecy of Jesus miraculous conception, instruction to Joseph and Mary to flee to Egypt, and other doctrinal commandments came through dreams. From this he deduced such visions were merely "childish stories" that could not be relied upon for truth. "Imagination cannot supply the place of real memory," he wrote, for "it has the wild faculty of counterfeiting memory." Christianity was therefore a "religion of dreams" that was so widely practiced despite "all the efforts that nature, reason, and conscience have made to awaken man from it."[673]

During his time with Jarvis in Manhattan, Paine made clear that he wished to remain undisturbed while he slept, and did not desire to see visitors at such times. Jarvis generally compiled with his request, but made an exception to the rule one day when he permitted an old woman he did not recognize to enter their quarters and speak with the sleeping essayist. "What do you want?" he asked in surprise. After confirming he was who she suspected, she launched into her purpose for coming. "Well then," she said, "I come from almighty God to tell you, that if you do not repent of your sins, and believe in our blessed savior Jesus Christ, you will be damned and—" Before she could continue, she was interrupted by a vexed Paine:

Poh, poh, it is not true, you were not sent with any such impertinent message; Jarvis, make her go away; pshaw! He would not send such a foolish ugly old woman about with his messages; go away, go back, shut the door.

The unknown old woman threw both of her hands up in the air in frustration and walked out without incident.[674] Paine's crude retort demonstrated his annoyance with evangelism and the propensity of strangers to invade his personal life.

Paine's season of relative comfort in the city was soon disrupted. In the time he spent with Jarvis, he suffered continual bouts physical discomfort. Jarvis was planning to take up a new residency, and the writer eventually decided upon the same course. In April, he packed up his belongings and brought them to Broome Street, at that time a new development in Lower Manhattan. For five dollars a month, he rented a room and adjoining parlor from the family of Zackarias Hitt, a banker. The urban sprawl in those days had not yet reached his new residence, and his distance from the rest of the city made keeping company difficult. Still, he devoted time to both personal correspondence and writings on religion. "What are you about?" he asked his old friend Joel Barlow, who had returned from France. Paine informed the American diplomat that his works had come under the fire "of the feds and priest." As he saw it, "the former do not attack my political publications; they rather try to keep them out of sight by silence," and the priests "act as if they would say, let us alone and we will let you alone."[675] Of course, the notorious penman never left any nemesis alone for long.

In 1807, Paine intended to continue writing articles for the *American Citizen*, as he had in the previous years, but was sidetracked from doing so by an editorial dispute. Paine completed the draft of an essay and delivered it to the publication's editor, James Cheetham, who promptly published it. When the writer first viewed his article, he realized his work had been "considerably altered," and in anger, approached its publisher. "I sir," he said, "never permit any one to alter any thing that I write, you have spoiled the whole sense that it was meant to convey on the subject." In response, Cheetham countered that much of Paine's language "was too harsh to appear in print." Paine responded bitterly that such an assessment "was not your business to determine," and insisted on the return of his manuscript. The incident was the catalyst for a permanent rift with Cheetham, and

Paine took his talents to the pro-Jeffersonian *New-York Public Advertiser* instead.[676]

Around the time of their schism, Cheetham's political allegiances turned away from the Republicans and toward their Federalist rivals. To get back at Paine for his disloyalty, the editorialist printed an explicit critique of the writer's character and accused him of stealing the political theories of John Locke and claiming them as is own. "I never read Locke nor ever had the work in my hand," Paine wrote in his fierce retort, "and by what I have heard of it from Horne Tooke, I had no inducement to read it." He added his view that Locke's written work was speculative and impractical, "and the style of it is heavy and tedious." In addition, Cheetham mocked Paine for sticking "correctly to his pen in a safe retreat, and never handled a musket offensively" during the War for Independence. Beyond defending himself, Paine also landed a reprisal against the publicist. Cheetham was "an ugly tempered man, and he carries the evidence of it in the vulgarity and forbiddingness of his countenance," he declared.[677]

The exchange spawned a new press war that resurrected the same tropes of the 1790s. In a second reprisal against Cheetham, "Farewell Reprimand to James Cheetham," Paine accused the man of "attempting to involve the United States in a quarrel with France for the benefit of England." The new foe was also guilty of abandoning representative government for despotism. "He is a disgrace to the republicans," he wrote, "whose principle is to live in peace and friendship with all nations, and not interfere in the domestic concerns of any." Furthermore, Cheetham's statement that the people of France languished under a military autocracy was "spoken exactly in the character of a stupid prejudiced John Bull, who, shut up in his island, and ignorant of the world, supposed all nations slaves but themselves." To the contrary, "of all people enslaved by their governments, none are so much so as the people of England," he maintained.[678]

Outside of his public scuffle with Cheetham, Paine contributed content on political issues, such as on the prospect of war with Britain. "For several years it has been the scheme of that government to terrify us, by acts of violence, into submission to her measures, and in the insane stupidity of tempting this, she has incensed us into war," he wrote. Even so, he assured his audience that "we neither fear nor care about England, otherwise than pitying the people who live under such a wretched system of government."

According to Paine, one of the kingdom's greatest weaknesses was that it relied too heavily on traditional naval ships of the line, in his mind outdated relics of the past. "The falsely imagined power of that navy ... prompted the ignorance of her government into insolence toward all foreign powers till England has not a friend left among nations," he claimed. Swift-moving gunboats of the type he proposed a decade earlier in his scheme for an amphibious invasion of the island were less costly, easier to maneuver, and harder for enemy shots to hit. In addition, their hulls offered the advantage of narrowing their susceptibility to enemy cannons because their own weapons faced forward.[679] Paine's warnings of British aggression on the high seas proved prophetic when, in matter of a few years, the country was pitted against the United States in the War of 1812.

By this time, it became clear that Paine would never publish the third volume of *The Age of Reason* in the same format he originally envisioned. The exact reasons why remain a bit unclear, given especially that he continued to print smaller pieces addressing the same topics. Some scholars have asserted that Jefferson advised him in 1802 not to publish the work in order to salvage his already-damaged reputation.[680] Regardless, his discourse with Samuel Adams and experiences writing for the *Prospect* showed that he had no hesitations about revisiting the same subjects. Another example of this came through *Examination on the Prophecies*, which he planned to use as the core of the third entry in *The Age of Reason*. Released in pamphlet form, it was his last work intended for public distribution.

In its introduction, Paine declared it was "the duty of every man, as far as his ability extends, to detect and expose delusion of error." A principal source of such errors, he wrote, was to be found in the "accounts and prophecies in the Old Testament about the coming of the person called Jesus Christ," as well as the "thousands of sermons" and "volumes written" to make man believe it. In the same vein of his other anti-religious diatribes, the penman denied prominent biblical prophecies—especially those pointing to the coming of Christ as a savior—on the basis that they referred to unrelated events. The prophecies Christians pointed to Christ fulfilling, then, were instead simply "circumstances the Jewish nation was in at the time." Paine believed the creator's true wisdom could be witnessed only by disregarding the fallacies of the Bible, and through the acceptance of "morality, justice, mercy and a benevolent disposition to all men and to all creatures." Only then, he explained, could mankind be given "a spirit of trust, confidence, and consolation in his creator, unshackled by the fables of books pretending to be the word of God."[681]

Paine's pamphlet was filled with refutations of popular prophecies and miracles. Christ's miraculous conception, presumed by Christians to be foretold of in Isaiah 7:14–17, could not refer to Christ, he argued, because the child referred to in the passage was said to cause the Jewish kings of Israel and Syria at the time to oppose him in battle. Because both monarchs were long dead by the time of the Christian savior's birth, then, he alleged the prophecy could not apply to Christ. The star guiding the wise men to Bethlehem, the place of Christ's birth, could be disregarded on account of "the absurdity of seeing and following a star in the day time." The forecast of Micah 5:2 that a savior would be born to Israel and bring peace to the land also could not be Christ, he wrote, because the fifth and sixth verse of the same chapter explicitly claimed the same man would defend the kingdom from an invasion of the Assyrians. "This is so evidently descriptive of a military chief that it cannot be applied to Christ without outraging the character they pretend to give us of him," he insisted. [682]

The assurance in Isaiah 53:4 that an unnamed male "hath borne our griefs and carried our sorrows" could not apply to the Christian martyr either, as Paine observed, because the reference was written in past tense. Likewise, he claimed Psalms 22:18's record of King David's reference to a group that "parted my garments among them, and upon my vesture did they cast lots" could not refer to the partition of Christ's clothing because the writer "is speaking of himself and his case, and not that of another." Beyond scriptural contradictions as he saw them, he purported that the ambiguous nature of the Old Testament prophets was such that biblical prophecies could be applied to a multitude of persons or situations. Isaiah in particular was, "upon the whole, a wild, disorderly writer" that "afforded so many opportunities to priestcraft … to impose those defects upon the world as prophecies of Jesus Christ," Paine remarked.[683]

The skeptic concluded his account with his bold assessment that the books of Matthew and Mark were contradictory doctrines. While Mark mandated a believer to believe in Christ and be baptized for salvation, he wrote, Matthew ignored the same requirements and encouraged followers only to partake in benevolent works to assist others in need. Within his narrow scope of reference, he deduced that the latter imposed none of the same guidelines as the former:

> Here is nothing about believing in Christ—nothing about that phantom of imagination called Faith. The works here spoken of are works of humanity and benevolence, or, in other words, an endeavor to make God's creation happy. Here is nothing about preaching and making long prayers, as if God must be dictated to by man; nor about building churches and meetings, nor hiring priests to pray and preach in them. Here is nothing about predestination, that lust which some men have for damning one another. Here is nothing about baptism, whether by sprinkling or plunging, nor about any of those ceremonies for which the Christian Church has been fighting, persecuting and burning each other ever since the Christian Church began.[684]

Rather than following biblical dogma, Paine supposed "those whose lives have been spent in doing good, and endeavoring to make their fellow-mortals happy ... will be happy hereafter," though the creator was under no obligation to preserve the "eternal existence" of individuals.

In sum, *Examination on the Prophecies* was by far Paine's most exhaustive dissection of biblical scripture, and relied on less overarching platitudes than the two volumes of *The Age of Reason*. Unique among his theistic writings, the tract was accessible both to religious theologians and the audience of commoners he typically reached. Still, he did not believe its contents would invite a torrent of refutations in the presses like some of his previous works had. "I do not believe that the priests will attack it," he wrote, "for it is not a book of opinions but of facts."[685]

When 1808 rolled around, Paine's impressive streak of writing the previous year was interrupted when Zackarias Hitt decided his rent would be increased from five to seven dollars a month. Struggling to make ends meet as he preserved most of his property for the Bonneville family, he wrote in desperation to the United States Senate for aid. According to Paine, the gigantic loan of six million livres he helped extract from France in 1781 was sufficient grounds for such a request. "As I never had a cent for this service, I feel myself entitled, as the country is now in a state of prosperity, to state the case to Congress," he asserted. Beyond his diplomatic exploits, he reasoned that his written contributions to the liberation of the United States from Britain was also worthy grounds for repayment. His political works "awakened America to a declaration of independence," and did much "to bring forward and establish the representation system of government." In his letter's conclusion, he depicted himself as the selfless champion for a better world who had been left unrewarded:

> I much question if an instance is to be found in ancient or modern times of a man who had no personal interest in the cause he took up … and who sought neither place nor office after it was established, that preserved in the same undeviating principles as I have done, and for more than thirty years, and that in spite of difficulties, dangerous, and inconveniences, of which I had my share.

As the appeal went unanswered, Paine made an attempt to resolve his immediate financial dilemma. After conferring with Mrs. Bonneville, he ultimately decided to sell his home and land in New Rochelle for $10,000, a sum that amounted to a small fortune at the time. However, the deal fell through when the buyer abruptly died, and out of sympathy, Paine reluctantly released the man's widow from the contract.[686]

In addition to his personal turmoil, the subject of congressional recognition weighed heavily on his conscience, and quickly became a matter of pride. Days after he turned 71 years old, Paine moved into the room above a small tavern at 63 Partition Street, where he drafted similar letters to the United States House of Representatives and the speaker of the body, Joseph Varnum. "It will be convenient to me to know what Congress will decide on," he remarked, "after so many years of generous services, and that in the most perilous times." In a moment of pettiness, Paine cautioned that the assembly's answer would determine whether he would "continue in this country, or offer my services to some other country."[687] Regardless of these bold words, his age and physical condition prevented him from offering his services to any country.

Paine remained persistent even while distraught at the continued lack of response. Repeated letters brought silence, however, caused him to hit rock bottom. According to Cheetham, "he had no care taken of him" in his desolate room above the tavern. "Drunk every day, he was neither washed nor shaved, nor shirted for weeks," a man "completely and notoriously nasty." The archenemy of Paine claimed to have sent a friend, "actuated by feelings of humanity," to visit the anguished writer. Upon his return, the man testified that Paine had stopped bathing, and had resigned himself to his miserable condition. "His crust of filth seemed to give him comfort," Cheetham wrote.[688]

Accounts from those close to Paine in his final years are sparse, but this representation clashes with the observations of those who remained friendly toward him. In addition to Jarvis and John Fellows, numerous other friends and acquaintances, along with "all the old inhabitants of New Rochelle," denied he was an alcoholic in his final years, and reported he drank sparingly if he was observed drinking at all. The owner of New York's City Hotel, where Paine spent time in his twilight years, reported that the author "drank less than any of his other boarders," and that "he did not, and could not, drink much." As biographer Gilbert Vale put it, his political and religious adversaries obsessively "sought to overwhelm the name of Paine by associating it with intoxication, for which there is not a particle of proof." Indeed, Cheetham and Carver held personal grudges toward him, and certainly had motives to falsify or embellish his drunkenness. Such insinuations—originally the design of the Tory and Federalist presses—aimed to damage his reputation, and were printed and reprinted for that purpose. By the testimony of Fellows, Cheetham in particular was willing "to fabricate any story calculated to throw obloquy" at Paine.[689]

Unanswered in his campaign to gain acknowledgement from Congress, Paine eventually broke down in a letter to Jefferson. He lamented that after many contacts, no official answer had been issued, even after he was told to expect such a reply from the speaker of the House. "I write this letter," he told his Virginian friend, "to request you to inform Mr. Holmes or the Committee of Claims have made any application to you on this subject." Jefferson hastily responded that David Holmes, the chairman of the committee in question, did in fact reach out to him for information regarding Paine's petition. He notified the struggling inquisitor that he had advised Holmes to search through the files of the Department of State to find the information requested, and had no doubt that the necessary records were obtained.[690] Notwithstanding Jefferson's affirmation, nothing came of Paine's request, and the subject was effectively ignored by Congress.

The body's silence may have been because of Paine's case being deprioritized in favor of other claims, because of the writer's loss of social standing, because he had already been granted financial compensation after the War for Independence, because many representatives were alienated by his political and religious views, or as a combination of several factors. A full year after Paine began his campaign to secure assistance from Congress, he received a letter of rejection. According to the note, his petition lacked sufficient evidence to prove his case, and argued that while he had joined Laurens in his mission to France, he travelled there as a private citizen and not as an officer of the government. As such, Congress held he was due no compensation. The letter complimented Paine for his contributions to America's transition to republicanism, but denied it had license to grant his request:

> That Mr. Paine rendered great and eminent services to the United States, during their struggle for liberty, cannot be doubted by any person acquainted with his labours in the cause, and attached to the principles of the contest. Whether he has been generously requited by his country for his meritorious exertions, is a question not submitted to your Committee, or within their province to decide.

The denial was an enormous letdown for Paine, who was "deeply grieved at this refusal," and his dejection "saw his means daily diminish."[691] America had forgotten the pen of its independence.

In light of his circumstances, two of Paine's friends in the area decided to help him. In order to fund better housing, they convinced him to sell seven acres of land and his home in Bordentown for $800. They then sought and obtained new housing for the writer in July of 1808. He and his meager belongings were taken to the home of Cornelius Ryder and his wife on the east side of Herring Street in Greenwich, then a small village removed from the heart of the city. The two-and-a-half story home was close in proximity to where Mrs. Bonneville and her three sons were living. The writer paid ten dollars a week to the Ryder family, who also provided meals and friendship. His residence there lasted ten months, a period which still saw Paine reading and writing.

In August, he submitted one last article to the *New-York Public Advertiser*. In "To the Federal Faction," he ridiculed Federalists within the United States for "continually abusing and blackguarding France and Bonaparte, and putting them in a fit disposition to cut short American commerce." Naval clashes with both the British and French had caused the Jefferson administration to institute the Embargo Act of 1807, which suppressed foreign trade. While keeping the country out of the wars of Europe for a time, the measure drew immense backlash, and destroyed the American maritime economy. Nevertheless, Paine believed strongly that keeping the United States out of overseas wars was a paramount objective, and accused Cheetham of being "an English impostor" for agitating to the contrary. "Our professed maxim is, 'to live in peace with all nations;' but this is an indecent violation of that principle," he warned.[692]

During his time in Greenwich, he also took a final shot at some of his Calvinist religious critics. Though not published for many years later, his "Predestination" essay criticized the cornerstone of the sect for alleging God had predetermined the fate of individual souls. This dogma was "presumption and nonsense" because the concept "pretends to know the private mind of God," he argued. One must deny "the justice of God" to believe the passages Calvinists cited in defense of their theory, he explained, because they denied the creator's "moral attributes." By likening God to a potter who molded humans out of clay, Paine believed Paul the Apostle tainted the deity's true vision for humanity by professing his intention "to make one vessel unto honor and another unto dishonor." According to the skeptic, the "impious doctrine of predestination ... would never have been thought of had it not been for some stupid passages in the Bible, which priestcraft at first, and ignorance since, have imposed upon mankind as revelation."[693]

In the last half of 1808, Paine's health broke down completely. Pain prevented him from walking, and he spent most of his time sitting a table, where he could read without having to hold a book in front of him. While he had few visitors in Greenwich, those who made the venture were greeted to pleasant conversation. One reported that "his appearance was that of a man of superior mind," and that "he was calm and gentleman-like, except when religion or party politics were mentioned." Another remarked that he "still retained his brilliance as a public figure," even in his broken condition. Even still, he could not keep his sadness completely hidden. Ryder noticed him suffer fits of crying several times, brought on by apparent loneliness. When he spoke of his grief, he complained only of his inability to walk without addressing other sources of agony at all.[694]

Realizing he was in his last days, Paine finalized his will on January 18, 1809. According to Mrs. Bonneville, he had drafted two previous wills, each time noting his revisions were the result of shifting sensibilities concerning who his true friends were. He left $1,500 of stock in the New York Phoenix Insurance Company, all of his "movable effects," and all money found on his possession at the time of his death to his friends Walter Morton and Thomas Addis Emmet. A portion of his land in New Rochelle was also to be placed in trust to the two men, who were to sell the north side. With the proceeds, Morton and Emmet were each to receive $200, and the widow of Elihu Palmer was to be given $100. The remaining sum was to be distributed evenly between Clio Rickman, his longtime friend who had returned to London, and Nicholas Bonneville, who was still living in Paris. The south side of his property in New Rochelle was to be held by Mrs. Bonneville and her three children, and used to the benefit of "their education and maintenance ... in order that she may bring them well up, give them good and useful learning, and instruct them in their duty to God, and the practice of morality."[695]

Paine was very clear about the specifications of his grave. "The place where I am buried," he wrote, was "to be a square of twelve feet, to be enclosed with rows of trees, and a stone or post and rail fence, with a headstone with my name and age engraved upon it, author of *Common Sense*." A permanent square marker with the same text was not placed upon his tomb until about 30 years after he was buried, but it is still visible at his New Rochelle farm today. In his will's close, the deteriorating author testified that he "lived an honest and useful life; my time has been spent in doing good, and I die in perfect composure and resignation to the will of my creator, God."[696]

Paine's will also conveyed his desire to be buried in the local Quaker burying grounds:

I know not if the Society of People called Quakers admit a person to be buried in their burying Ground, who does not belong to their Society, but if they do or will admit me, I would prefer being buried there my father belonged to that profession, and I was partly brought up in it.

If it was "not consistent with their rules to do this," Paine wished to be buried on his own farm in New Rochelle. For making the request, he was interviewed by a member of the local Quaker committee, Willet Hicks. Even though Paine volunteered to pay for the digging of his prospective grave, his request was denied as the result of his heretical religious beliefs, causing him to be "deeply moved" and respond that "their refusal was foolish." Hearing this, Mrs. Bonneville assured Paine he would be buried on his farm in accordance with his preferred contingency. He replied that he was satisfied with the plan, but worried his body would be displaced by its future owners. "They will dig my bones up before they be half rotten," he feared. When Mrs. Bonneville assured him his place of burial would never be disturbed, he was contented, and the subject was never addressed again.[697] At the time, Paine could not have known that his bones would be unearthed not by his farm's future owners, but by a fanatical devotee.

Paine's health declined immensely in early 1809. He suffered a fever in February of 1809, forcing him to be permanently bedridden. In March, he suffered immense pain. In his last months, Mrs. Bonneville visited him daily, and kept him company when she could. Doctor James Manley tended to him daily, and prescribed modifications of his medicines in attempt to subdue his anguish. With the Ryder family no longer equipped to care for him, Mrs. Bonneville eventually rented a small home on Columbia Street in May of 1809. To get inside the house, which was just steps away from the Ryders' home, Paine had to be carried in an armchair. Despite his physical torment, the change in scenery seemed to give him tranquility. He received friends in the afternoon, including the owner of New Rochelle's convenience store, Daniel Pelton, and also Jacob Frank, the editor of the *New-York Public Advertiser.* In his honor, the publication reprinted the last essay of *The Crisis,* which celebrated the final triumph of the states over British tyranny. Even Carver, who fought with Paine over unpaid debts and tactlessly disparaged his character, came to apologize to the dying writer.[698]

Some of his last words reflected bitterness, and sometimes manifested as unexpected outbursts. "I am very sorry that I ever returned to this country," he told Albert Gallatin, Jefferson and Madison's treasury secretary. Plagued by constant aching, he often groaned and cried out, "oh, Lord help me!"[699] Though fully privy to the specifics of Paine's theistic views, local religious evangelists had not yet given up on him. Out of genuine concern for his eternal standing, several endeavored to save his soul. In one case, two renowned Presbyterian ministers came to visit him, and approached the side of his bed. "Mr. Paine," one of them said, "we visit you as friends and neighbors: you have now a full view of death, you cannot live long, and whoever does not believe in Jesus Christ will assuredly be damned." The cynic would have nothing of it, and interrupted without hesitation. "Let me have none of your popish stuff," Paine shouted, "get away with you, good morning, good morning." The other minister made his own attempt, but was quickly rebuffed as well. The two were then hurried out the door by Mrs. Hedden, who served as his last housekeeper. According to Rickman, "he was completely unchanged in his theological sentiments."[700] His disposition was fully consistent with that which he relayed several years earlier to his former housemate, Jarvis.

Despite his well-known antipathy to the Bible, in his last month Mrs. Hedden read him passages daily to keep his mind engaged. Still, his mind wandered and he said little, except to ask who was in his room. Paine's continual cries for God to bring him solace led Manley to believe "that he had abandoned his former opinions" on religion. Mere hours before his life ended, he leaned over the bed to test his thesis:

> Mr. Paine, your opinions, by a large portion of the community, have been treated with deference: you have never been in the habit of mixing in your conversation, words of course: you have never indulged in the practice of profane swearing: you must be sensible that we are acquainted with your religious opinions as they are given to the world. What must we think of your present conduct? Why do you call upon Jesus Christ to help you? Do you believe that he can help you? Do you believe in the divinity of Jesus Christ? I want an answer as from the

lips of a dying man, for I verily believe that you will not live twenty-four hours.

Hearing no reply, Manley pushed the matter once more. "Mr. Paine ... do you believe that Jesus Christ is the son of God?" After a few minutes of silence, Paine answered slowly but audibly. "I have no wish to believe on that subject," he said.[701] The soft-spoken words were his last. The next morning, June 8, 1809, the most notorious radical of his age breathed his last breath, dying quietly in his sleep.

Chapter 9

Epilogue

In many ways, Paine's death signified the end of an age, and the great impression he made upon the world was universally recognized. "With heart-felt sorrow and poignant regret," the *New-York Public Advertiser* read the day of his death, "we are compelled to announce to the world that Mr. Thomas Paine is no more." According to the memorial, he was "the most distinguished philanthropist, whose life was devoted to the cause of humanity," and "if any man's memory deserved a place in the breast of freedman, it is that of the deceased." Clio Rickman, his lifetime friend, echoed this portrayal. "He was mild, unoffending, sincere, gentle, humble, and unassuming," he wrote, and "his talents were soaring, acute, profound, extensive, and original." However, he was not held in such high regard by everyone. According to the *New-York Evening Post*, "he had lived long, did some good and much harm."[702]

In the aftermath of Paine's passing, Marguerite Bonneville kept his wishes to the best of her ability. She arranged the transfer of his body from New York City to his New Rochelle farm, and also oversaw his funeral. Only six people attended the service, a group that included two black individuals who had likely been freed from slavery. "At his funeral was no pomp, no pageantry, no civic procession," and "no military display," abolitionist lawyer Robert Ingersoll wrote many years later.[703] No public officials attended, which has led many to conclude that Paine had been abandoned by all of his renowned friends. To the contrary, Paine's burial was speedily arranged for the day following his death, making it nearly impossible to spread word of the funeral in enough time to allow travelers to come from afar. It is true that he was held in far less esteem than he was in his brightest days, but he still commanded the respect and admiration of Thomas Jefferson, James Madison, James Monroe, various friends from New York City and New Rochelle, and others.

Even though William Carver endeavored to make amends with his estranged friend shortly before his death, he ultimately sold his fiery correspondence with Paine—which assailed the man's character in no uncertain terms—to James Cheetham, the writer's editorial nemesis. Cheetham hastily published the letters between Paine and Carver verbatim in his scathing 1809 biography of the writer. While Carver later withdrew his accusation that Paine was a raving alcoholic, as he alleged in his message to Paine, the original accusation has kickstarted what became—and is still—the favorite allegation of Paine's detractors. After seeing that Cheetham had printed lies about the paternity of her children in the same work, Mrs. Bonneville sued the polemicist. During the trial, Carver admitted he had "never seen the slightest indication of any meretricious or illicit commerce between Paine and Mrs. Bonneville," and his case collapsed. Despite the judge's open sympathy for Cheetham's book, which he praised for advancing "the cause of religion," Mrs. Bonneville won a $150 libel judgment.[704] Cheetham died in mysterious circumstances in 1810.

In stark contrast to Cheetham's narrative, Clio Rickman published his own account of Paine's life in 1819. His objective, contained within its preface, was to prove that "Mr. Paine died in the full conviction of the truth of the principles he held when living."[705] Paine's fortune served, as the writer intended, to the great benefit of the three Bonneville children. They all led fruitful lives, especially Benjamin Bonneville, who entered the United States Military Academy at West Point in 1813 and began a long and distinguished career as an officer. He served in both the Mexican-American War and the Civil War, where he commanded Benton Barracks, the union encampment in St. Louis, Missouri. After the exile of Napoleon Bonaparte in 1814, Nicholas Bonneville finally joined his wife and children in America. However, he returned to France in a matter of years, suffered immensely from mental illness, and died in 1828. Marguerite Bonneville served as the steward of Paine's written works, and lived until 1846.

A decade after Paine's death, William Cobbett, an English writer who had been imprisoned in his native country for seditious libel, concocted a grisly and bold plan. After moving to Long Island in 1817, he schemed to return Paine's bones to his native England, where they could be given, in his mind, a proper and honorable burial. "We will have a funeral worthy of the remains that are to be buried," he told a friend, "in a season when twenty wagon-loads of flowers can be brought to strew the road before the hearse."[706] The radical agitator, who had once been an outspoken Tory and adversary of Paine and his work, changed his mind about the writer after reading *The Decline and Fall of the English System of Finance*, the pamphleteer's assault upon the English financial system and championed bullion-based currency.

In September of 1819, Cobbett ventured in the dead of night to Paine's gravesite in New Rochelle with a group that included two black servants. He was horrified to find that the writer's place of rest, in "the corner of a rugged, barren field," was completely neglected. The group used shovels and pickaxes to dig up the coffin in its entirety, placed it in a wagon, and hauled it off to New York City. The local constable was alerted to their scheme, and attempted to assemble a party to pursue the graverobbers, but they could not procure horses in time. The coffin was shipped to England the next month, making the voyage alongside its thief. Nevertheless, Cobbett's plans for a grand memorial procession and mausoleum for the penman never came to fruition, and Paine's remains were still in his possession at the time of his death in 1835. His oldest son took possession over them as sole executor, and even inscribed Paine's name on the skull and several of the larger bones so that they would be identifiable. By 1845, the remains were in the possession of Benjamin Tilly, Cobbett's secretary.[707]

Instead of sympathizing with Cobbett's strange mission, most observers responded with horror, and the journalist was never able to raise the money he needed to give Paine the procession he envisioned. The famous English poet Lord Byron even made a mockery of the deed, which was captured in a widely-circulated epigram:

In digging up your bones, Tom Paine,
    Will Cobbett has done well;
You visit him on earth again;
    He'll visit you in hell.

Over the years, numerous legends have arisen to explain what became of them after that point. Conflicting stories allege the bones were destroyed, thrown into the River Thames, made into buttons, exhibited in a museum, sold as souvenirs, or given a secret burial.[708] For a man who proudly proclaimed "the world is my country," many of the accounts have his remains appropriately divided between several countries.

Conclusion

To generations of Americans young and old, Paine's ideas still resonate. So much so, in fact, that his prose has been adopted by prominent politicians of all kinds more than two centuries after they were written. For instance, Ronald Reagan relayed one of the writer's most famous phrases as he accepted the presidential nomination of the Republican Party in 1980. Americans of the time were "disturbed, but not dismayed," the Californian declared, as they were the "kind of men and women Tom Paine had in mind when he wrote, during the darkest days of the American Revolution, 'we have it in our power to begin the world over again.'" Likewise, Barack Obama concluded his 2009 inaugural address with words lifted directly from *The Crisis*. "Let it be told to the future world," he professed, "that in the depth of winter, when nothing but hope and virtue could survive, that the city and the country, alarmed at one common danger, came forth to meet [it]."[709] Without question, both sides of America's political paradigm have accepted Paine as their own.

Many biographers insist that their subject should be viewed in the context of their own age, but Paine was a man who far transcended his age. Never before had a single figure—let alone a commoner—so profoundly influenced the political development of two continents. Tellingly, this fact was even granted reluctantly by Paine's political rivals, who widely considered him too unhinged and radical. "I know not whether any man in the world has had more influence on its inhabitants or affairs for the last thirty years than Thomas Paine," wrote his philosophical foe John Adams. The penman's deeds had made the era "the Age of Paine," the former president admitted in bitterness.[710]

To be sure, the contemporary ramifications of Paine's ideas have been profound. The famed writer's groundbreaking opinions, sarcastic wit, and unapologetic tenacity are deeply entrenched in all regions of the United States. If *Common Sense* had been his only published work, he would have been a legend in his own right, but he left the world having done so much more. He was the rare, anti-aristocratic commoner who boldly injected himself into the most contentious political dispute of his time, serving as the catalyst for common people to oppose British tyranny and embrace secession from the crown. His brash and uncouth style so commonly fills informal conversations, and his defiant attitude remains ingrained into the American psyche. Whenever an individual ventures into controversial cultural or political territory and dares to speak the truth as it is, they are following the path Paine once paved.

But even then, Paine's contributions to American independence only scratched the surface of his life's accomplishments. He took on the most deeply-rooted institution of his day—hereditary monarchy—by exposing its follies, and making it entirely feasible for people to work against their existing impulses and customs to abolish the institution on two continents. Defying convention, he popularized fringe political positions even as cultural norms and institutions opposed him. Indeed, the groundbreaking success of *Common Sense* and *The Rights of Man* was enough to put an end to the aristocratic order in both America and France, and inspired much of the rest of the world to do the same in time. Even in Western nations that still feature a monarch, such as England and Spain, the occupant almost universally serves as a cultural figurehead rather than a political actor with tangible authority.

Paine perceptively blasted the government for printing worthless paper money and passing legal tender laws, which destroyed the purchasing power of the currency then and now. The inflationary crisis of the 1770s and 1780s was a disaster that challenged the early American republic, but its lessons have not always been heeded. As he put it, paper money policies "of any kind, operate to destroy morality, and to dissolve, by the pretense of law, what ought to be the principle of law to support, reciprocal justice between man and man." Despite Paine's warnings about the destructive potential of paper money, central banks rule the monetary system of nearly every country in the world, and fiat money is commonplace. Committees of well-connected political bankers manipulate interest rates and expand the money supply, greatly harming holders of personal savings. In a world where the United States dollar is worth approximately three percent of its original value when the Federal Reserve System was conceived in 1913, his trepidations on paper money seem timeless and prophetic.[711]

Long before Paine, the power of the written word was well known to the Western world, even among defenders of representative government. Long before he lived, the works of Cicero, Algernon Sidney, John Locke, and others challenged autocratic impulses and promoted republicanism. Still, the penman was more successful than any of his forerunners at translating complex principles into a format that was completely accessible to regular people. Even without fortune, fame, or the backing of a political party, Paine's ideas caught on like wildfire in a country that was barely ready to hear them. Ironically, the poor artisan from England, through his deft pen, was the one who most stirred everyday Americans to revolutionary action. Even without previous notoriety, his bearing on public discourse was felt through his artistic prose.

One of the factors that differentiated Paine from most of the eminent figures of his general was his abject poverty. He was born into England's modest artisan class, and his time as an excise officer in England gave him a meager living at best. Even after writing *Common Sense*—an unparalleled hit with all classes of Americans—a royalty dispute with its publisher left him with virtually nothing. Paine spent the next decade with almost no wealth to speak of, even as he emerged as one of the most notorious figures of his time. These experiences colored his perception of republicanism and led him to develop a system of economic egalitarianism a century before all the welfare states of the world were ever concocted. Indeed, his paltry experiences underscored many of the themes he later explored in his later writings.

One of the ways Paine's genuine concern for the poor manifested was through his plans to create an aid program for the least fortunate members of society. Paine's program to support the poor and the elderly, unprecedented in his day, called for annual payments to those naturally inclined to economic hardship. For the England's poor, his proposal would have nullified taxes, provided an annual stipend, and established a workfare system to cover basic living expenses. The elderly would have been divided into two general groups by age bracket, each of which were to receive a fixed disbursement from the treasury. In sum, Paine's fund for the elderly was the modern welfare state in germ. While his ideas in this area were completely ignored—even by his most radical friends—the system has been implemented almost universally in every part of the contemporary world.

In addition, the penman's novel aim in *Agrarian Justice*—to establish an annual payment to all individuals in society, supported by a tax on landowners—has also had lasting influence. In the contemporary, this form of wealth redistribution is now widely called "universal basic income" (UBI), and its precepts have been incorporated into several modern political campaigns. For instance, Switzerland held a referendum in 2016 to institute a universal income. It ultimately failed to secure the confidence of the Swiss electorate, but its characteristics were reminiscent of those Paine laid out in the 1790s. In 2008, China's special administration region of Macau launched its own UBI program, where all residents receive a disbursement yearly. In the United States, Democratic presidential contender Andrew Yang made UBI the centerpiece of his 2020 campaign and credited Paine with its inception. The "freedom dividend," as Yang branded his plan, was "a deeply American idea," he asserted. "Thomas Paine, one of our founding fathers, was for it at the beginning."[712] Here is yet another area, then, where Paine's ideas have profoundly influenced the present.

Despite its prevalence in the world, the modern welfare system has brought forth serious moral and financial challenges, and has evolved in ways Paine could never have imagined. Those who have succeeded in expanding the size and scope of the welfare state in nearly every country have largely resorted to substantial debt spending and higher taxes in order to do so. In contrast, Paine's proto-welfare program laid out in the second part of *The Rights of Man* relied upon sensible financial policy, a stable currency, and the repayment of national debts. For one generation to run "the next generation into debt," he wrote, would mean exploiting posterity "meanly and pitifully" in exchange for temporary expedience. At the end of his life, Paine commended the United States for greatly "reducing her public debts and taxes," and derided England for engaging in the "eccentric and wild" propensity to contract the same burdens.[713] His vision for a frugal government, then, is at direct odds with the contemporary United

States—a government averse to balanced budgets and more than $30 trillion in debt, with its paper currency routinely debased by its central bank. It remains doubtful Paine would have endeavored to alleviate poverty if it meant subjecting all Americans to the servitude of everlasting debt and inflation.

Paine was nothing if not an honest actor in the service of the United States, even though it once cost him his civil office. As secretary of the Committee of Foreign Affairs, he exposed to the American public the corruption of Silas Deane, who engaged in war profiteering at the expense of the young republic. By doing so, he invited a storm of vitriol from political adversaries who insisted his revelations would cost America its alliance with France and compromise the campaign from independence completely. Even so, Paine stressed that public openness was an integral element of republicanism, and reasoned that citizens deserved to know even the most intimate details of their government's inner workings. In an era where controversial figures like Edward Snowden and Julian Assange have disclosed closely-held governmental secrets to the general public, we look back at Paine as one of the originators of the same cause. As it turned out, he was America's first whistleblower.

Paine was also far ahead of his time when it came to his opposition to slavery, an institution he condemned as wicked and unjustifiable. At a time when it was most unpopular, he published a profoundly antislavery essay in the *Pennsylvania Magazine*, exposing his readers to the evils of the transatlantic slave trade and its moral shortcomings for the first time. His antislavery ideas served as the basis for a series of gradual manumission laws that took hold during the War of Independence, where slavery in several states was given a death sentence for the time in Western civilization. As a member of the Pennsylvania Abolition Society, he advocated emancipation and a more just future for the enslaved.

In 1790, Paine wrote from Paris of his great desire to achieve "an abolition of the infernal traffic in negroes" in America. "We must push that matter further on your side of the water," he told Benjamin Rush. While in London, he collaborated with Joseph Priestley on a pamphlet that lobbied for the passage of a radical slave abolition act in Parliament.[714] Paine's support for the revolution in Haiti, also, was built upon his moral resentment toward the longstanding bondage the country's inhabitants had been placed in. Without question, Paine helped lay the groundwork for American abolitionists to pick up the torch of manumission in the decades after his death, and eventually succeed in eradicating slavery from the United States through the 13th Amendment.

By all accounts, Paine's religious writings made him an absolute pariah. The citizenry of his day was not ready to accept his deistic views, especially as a great Protestant explosion transpired in America. Despite the widespread disapproval of his religious creed in his time, however, his influence on modern theistic scholarship has been momentous. Paine's life and ideas have inspired many atheist academics such as Christopher Hitchens, Susan Jacoby, and Sam Harris, who have cited him as an influence and channeled the writer's portrayal of orthodox religion as a net negative. Conversely, fundamentalist religious theorists such as Norman Geisler, Edward Feser, and Lee Strobel have made considerable efforts to refute notable allegations from *The Age of Reason*, such as its assertion that the Bible is full of contradictions, that divine revelation and miracles defied reason, and that institutional churches were created to enslave mankind.[715] Whatever side one takes on these matters, it cannot be denied that contemporary religious debates often revolve around the same claims Paine made two centuries ago.

As a steadfast advocate of religious liberty, Paine thought the history of state prosecution campaigns against religious dissidents was both a stain on the face of Western civilization and an innate characteristic of state-sponsored religion. He condemned England's kings for using the established church—whether Catholic or Anglican at the time—as instruments to force their subjects into compliance. "The adulterous connection of church and state" had done much evil, he wrote, by suppressing the free and open discussion of religious precepts and infringing upon each individual's freedom of conscience. Furthermore, in *The Rights of Man*, Paine made clear that the state and church should share no bond in a republican system. Within its pages, he glowingly pointed to America as a model of success for putting an end to religious oaths, ensuring the free exercise of religion, and prohibiting a central state church. Despite his own partiality against orthodox religion, then, he still believed unapologetically in of the right of each individual to commit themselves to any theistic doctrine. All free people possess "the same right to their belief as I have mine," he contended.[716]

If he had never dipped his pen in the ink that inspired two major revolutions, the world may better remember Paine as a brilliant architect. His iron bridge was one of the first of its kind, and even though he never actualized his dream of implementing it, his designs left humanity with a glimpse of the future. Iron bridges are now found in every part of the world, where they offer greater resilience at lower costs relative to alternatives, just as Paine claimed they would. Though his focus was often drawn away by political events, he stood at the brink of a new age in engineering, and his technical ingenuity went far beyond bridgebuilding. His plans for quick-moving gunboats and their potential for a grand amphibious assault were also way ahead of their time. The utility offered by Paine's model fleet is now widely accepted by military tacticians, and was put into actual use in the Allied invasion of Normandy on D-Day, June 6, 1944. Modern military convention conclusively vindicates Paine's radical naval theories.

Paine taught the world many important lessons, but perhaps none more crucial than the effectiveness of political radicalism. To be sure, the writer never relied upon the successes of a particular political party, on state bureaucracies to become more ethical, on law enforcement to stand down from enforcing divisive policies, or on the courts to weigh in on the right side of pressing controversies. Instead, he labored to convince the people as a whole—some of whom had no interest in politics before that point— to stand in defiance of governmental tyranny. By any measure, Paine was a dreadful politician and statesman. He had no political acumen to speak of, but possessed an uncanny ability to expose his readers to the oppression and hypocrisy of the state. Unquestionably, his work provided the spark that lit the fire of two revolutions, both of which culminated in the abandonment of monarchy and inauguration of republican government in the United States and France.

Beyond his philosophical principles, Paine's streak of radicalism was also seen in his strategy to attain a more just world. He made his impression on the American mind through his support of colonial secession from the British Empire, and the establishment of a new republican system that eschewed almost all the characteristics that defined the previous arrangement. In Britain, his comprehensive written treatise challenged the foundation of every prevailing political institution of the country, and succeeded in persuading subjects of the greatest empire the world had yet seen that their political framework was plagued by insufficiency and immorality. He tirelessly labored in France for the abolishment of the nation's archaic monarchical system, hereditary aristocracy, and political executions, and supported a broad extension of suffrage, bullion-based money, and a style of republicanism that elevated former subjects to their rightful standing as free citizens. In all three cases, he endeavored to alter society as a messenger and educator rather than as a politician, and inspired his audience to use push for political change through civil disobedience rather than through the ballot box. Rather than build legislative coalitions, he turned multitudes of loyal subjects into republican militants. Paine's approach, as he put it, "forced into action the mind that had been dormant."[717]

England's ruthless censorship campaign made Paine's work unlawful, forced him flee the country, and led to a conviction and death sentence for seditious libel. As government agents initiated a crusade to quash dissent against the English monarchy in response to *The Rights of Man*, he stood by his work nevertheless, and even reveled in the controversy. In doing so, he proved the value of notoriety and the power of ideas, which when employed by his hand proved sharper than swords. Despite the best efforts of William Pitt the Younger and his subordinates, Paine's works were too compelling for even the most powerful monarchy in the world to erase. While he never lived to see Britain's monarchy dissolved, the ultimate victor in the war between Paine and his censors is clear. Nearly everyone in the West acknowledges the pitfalls of state-imposed information suppression. In corners of the world where it was once illegal, airing grievances against those in power is now as typical an occurrence as the setting of the sun. All of this, then, is thanks in large part to Paine.

Despite Paine's drive to see France exude the same republican principles that America had, his vision was subverted on two major occasions, first by the Jacobins, who sought to punish alleged counterrevolutionary dissidents more than they sought to promote individual liberty, and second by Napoleon Bonaparte, whose personal ambitions for power displaced any semblance of representative government. His alignment with the Girondins and his opposition to the king's execution put him at odds with Robespierre, who with his allies imprisoned him during the Reign of Terror. After he narrowly escaped the fate of death that many of his friends fell prey to, he gained some short-lived patronage from the Directory. Regardless, political instability and the rise of military dictatorship undermined the principles he championed. By the end of his days in Paris, he was utterly disenchanted by the trajectory of the French Revolution. The years he spent there, however, proved unwavering commitment to his solemn belief that representative government was the universal gift from the creator to mankind—a condition any vigilant people could bring to fruition.

Today, the country that tried and convicted Paine for seditious libel universally celebrates his contributions to liberty. England honors the eminent writer in Thetford, where a statue of his likeness stands in the town square. One gilded bronze arm holds a quill pen, and the other a copy of *The Rights of Man*, his magnum opus. An engraving on the pedestal imparts some of his most famous prose to observers, who flock to the area to see it. The city of Lewes also celebrates Paine's presence through an annual festival, where jubilant masses congregate for both entertainment and intellectual conversation—just as the "citizen of the world" would have had it. Today, there are no public reminders whatsoever that the same son of England was a traitor to his country, and the publication that served as the catalyst for his conviction is widely considered the world's foremost treatise on classical liberalism.

Those across the sea revere Paine too, as was forecasted by his former commander Nathanael Greene. "Your fame for your writings, will be immortal," he wrote to the illustrious penman.[718] In the United States, Paine's name alone is synonymous with liberty, self-determination, and political radicalism. He is routinely mentioned alongside George Washington, Benjamin Franklin, Thomas Jefferson, and other intellectual giants of his time. The reverence that often accompanies his name stands in stark contrast to the man's ruthless foes. Neither his condemnation of Washington, nor his decision to propagate *The Age of Reason*, could ever rob him of the same prestige. His greatest detractors utterly failed to erase his memory from public consciousness, and his ideas are still invoked to represent untarnished liberty in a world that often rejects it.

Throughout his long and eventful life, Paine changed the political landscape on two continents, popularizing many beliefs we now take entirely for granted. Through unconventional means, he induced common people to revolutionary action in ways that far surpassed his more famous contemporaries, and his influence on the modern world has been enormous. As his friend Elihu Palmer wrote, "he reasons without logic, and convinces without argumentation; he strangles error by his first grasp, and develops truth with much simplicity, but with irresistible force."[719] Though William Cobbett succeeded in extracting his corpse from the ground, he never displaced Paine's imprint from the public psyche. After all, our modern heritage is the product of his most radical ideas.

Acknowledgements

Many people supported me as I worked on this project as I worked on it over the course of four years. During that time, much has changed. When I began the initial draft, I was single and living in Minnesota, and now I am married and in Tennessee. The governments I have lived under have subjected their citizens to immeasurable tyranny, just as they did in Paine's day. In homage to my subject, though, I am proud to say I have maintained my own streak of political radicalism throughout—even when it defied mainstream consensus. As I spent time writing and researching this work, correcting previous versions, revising the structure, and even doubting whether I would finish it, the below individuals provided crucial encouragement and helped me bring the project to fruition.

First, I profusely thank those who supported bringing this work to fruition in its current state. Jeff Deist, for giving my ideas credence, agreeing to read and endorse this work, and for allowing me to publish articles at the Mises Institute. To be sure, he is one of the most overlooked and underappreciated intellectuals in America today. Tom Woods, for agreeing to review and support this work, and for his brilliant historical, political, and economic insights. Tom is a walking encyclopedia of knowledge, and was immediately familiar with the Paine historiography when I told him of this project. Kevin Gutzman, for giving me much-needed professional writing advice, and also for creating some of the best works ever written on Thomas Jefferson, James Madison, and the founding era in general. Mike Maharrey, for his personal friendship, and also for remaining so dedicated to radical political decentralization for over a decade. I have spent more time discussing history with Mike than anyone else in my life, and we always seem to come to similar historical interpretations. Michael Boldin, working so assiduously to spread liberty in our time, and for citing my work in his amazing podcast. Aaron Harris, for doing an incredible job editing this work, and returning a far better manuscript than I originally gave him. Jeff Stewart, for designing a remarkable cover.

The Mises Institute, for its unapologetic embrace of Austrian economics and radical political methodology, and for remaining the greatest bastion of libertarian thought on the internet. The Tenth Amendment Center, for its dedication to nullification, and for using local activism to push back against the immoral, unconstitutional, and unpopular acts of the federal government. Murray Rothbard, Gordon Wood, Robert Middlekauff, and Simon Schama for their amazing narratives I referred to and cited often. Paine's biographers, especially Moncure Conway, John Keane, Philip Foner, and David Freeman Hawke, for writing fantastic material on the penman in times when research was infinitely more difficult than it is today. The Thomas Paine Historical Association, for keeping the memory of the renowned penman alive in the public consciousness.

As with all things in life, I could never have completed this book without friends that supported me throughout. Casey Sabol, Suzanne Sherman, Brion McClanahan, Bradley Birzer, Carl Jones, Amanda Bowers, Andrew Nappi, Scott Silvi, Devin Barras, Michael Heise, Joshua Smith, Marco Bassani, Nathan Coleman, Matt Wolf, Andrew Avery, Diane Rufino, Pete Hodgkins, Richard Walch, Alan Mosley, Caryn Ann Harlos, and many others unnamed were all instrumental in this way. I appreciate those who provided great suggestions, and urged me to continue writing and researching even when I questioned myself.

I also extend my earnest thanks to my heavenly father, the source of all life, liberty, and property. This project would never have been completed without my wife, who extended great patience as I dedicated countless hours to it. Finally, I would be totally remiss if I didn't thank Thomas Paine and the founding generation for their tireless devotion to liberty when the costs were highest.

About the Author

David Benner is the author of two books, *Compact of the Republic: The League of States and the Constitution*, and *The 14th Amendment and the Incorporation Doctrine*. He contributes content to the Tenth Amendment Center, Mises Institute, Abbeville Institute, and other publications. His areas of expertise include the American War for Independence, the United States Constitution and the ratification struggle, nullification, the history of tariffs and central banking in the United States, the antebellum United States Supreme Court, the late Roman Republic, and the American Civil War.

David considers himself an ardent Jeffersonian, apprehends the dangers of an overreaching centralized authority, and views the states as the "surest bulwarks against antirepublican tendencies." He is an opponent of perpetual debt, central banking, foreign wars of intervention, and fiat currency, and uses constitutional and moral arguments in support of these positions.

David was born in Knoxville, Tennessee, and has lived most of his life in Minnesota and Wisconsin. He has a Bachelor's Degree in History Education from the University of Wisconsin, River Falls. He currently resides in Nashville, Tennessee with his wife and dog.

Notes

INTRODUCTION

[1] Common Sense, in *The Writings of Thomas Paine*, Edited by Moncure Daniel Conway (New York: G.P. Putnam's Sons, 1894), I:118-119.

[2] Moncure Daniel Conway, *The Life of Thomas Paine: With a History of His Literary, Political, and Religious Career in America, France, and England* (2 Vols., New York: G.P. Putnam's Sons, 1909), I:64.

[3] Charles Lee to George Washington, January 24, 1776, in *The Papers of George Washington* (26 Vols., Charlottesville, VA: University Press of Virginia, 1988), Revolutionary War Series III:182-184; Quoted in John Eleazer Remsburg, *Thomas Paine, The Apostle of Religious and Political Liberty* (Boston: J.P. Mendum, 1881), 76; Quoted in Benson Lossing, *The Home of Washington* (Hartford: A.S. Hale & Company, 1871), 276; Samuel Adams to Thomas Paine, November 30, 1802, in *The Complete Writings of Thomas Paine*, Edited by Eric Foner (2 Vols., New York: The Citadel Press, 1945), II:1433; Thomas Jefferson to Francis Eppes Monticello, January 19, 1821, in *The Works of Thomas Jefferson,* Federal Edition, Edited by Paul Leicester Ford (12 Vols., New York: G.P. Putnam's Sons, 1904), XII:195; Benjamin Rush, *The Autobiography of Benjamin Rush* (London: Oxford University Press, 1948), 124-125; Benjamin Franklin to the Duke de La Rochefoucauld, April 15, 1787, in *The Writings of Benjamin Franklin*, Edited by Albert Henry Smyth (10 Vols., New York: The Macmillan Company, 1906), IX:565.

[4] Cato Letter III, in *Wartime Dissent in America: A History and Anthology*, Edited by Robert Mann (New York: Palgrave Macmillan, 2010), V:443-446; Cato Letter IV, in Ibid., V:514-517.

[5] Shall Louis XVI Have Respite?, in *The Writings of Thomas Paine*, III:125-127.

[6] Charles Inglis, *The True Interest of America*, in Gordon Wood, *The American Revolution: Writings from the Pamphlet Debate*, Edited by Gordon Wood (2 Vols., New York: Library of America, 2015), II:710.

[7] Common Sense, in *The Writings of Thomas Paine*, I:68.

[8] The Forester III, in *The Writings of Thomas Paine*, I:144.

[9] Moncure Daniel Conway, *The Life of Thomas Paine*, I:59.

[10] Thomas Paine to Andrew Deane, August 15, 1806, in *The Complete Writings of Thomas Paine*, II:1484.

[11] Letter Addressed to the Addressers on the Late Proclamation, in *The Writings of Thomas Paine*, III:67.

[12] Gordon Wood, *Revolutionary Characters: What Made the Founders Different* (New York: Penguin Press, 2006), 220; Christopher Hitchens, *Thomas Paine's Rights of Man: A Biography* (New York, NY: Grove Press, 2006), 142; Craig Nelson, *Thomas Paine: Enlightenment, Revolution, and the Birth of Modern Nations* (New York: Viking Penguin, 2006), 10; The Philosophy of Paine, in *The Diary and Sundry Observations*, Edited by Dagobert Runes (New York, NY: Greenwood Press, 1968).

[13] Letter Addressed to the Addressers on the Late Proclamation, in *The Writings of Thomas Paine*, III:67.

CHAPTER 1
HUMBLE BEGINNINGS

[14] See Moncure Daniel Conway, *The Life of Thomas* Paine, I:3-5. Some scholars have contended Paine was never baptized, but here Conway provides evidence to suggest that he almost certainly was.

[15] For Paine's comments on religion, see The Age of Reason, in *The Writings of Thomas Paine*, IV:65-66.

[16] "School History," Thetford Grammar School. https://www.thetfordgrammar.co.uk/43/school-history (accessed September 25, 2018).

[17] Quoted in Moncure Daniel Conway, *The Life of Thomas Paine*, I:11.

[18] The Age of Reason, in *The Writings of Thomas Paine*, IV:63, The Rights of Man, Part Second, in Ibid., II:462.

[19] The Rights of Man, Part Second, in Ibid., II:462-463. Paine incorrectly referred to Captain Menzies as "Captain Mendez."

[20] Ibid.

[21] The Age of Reason, in Ibid., IV:63.

[22] See Richard Platt, *Smuggling in the British Isles: A History* (Stroud: Tempus Publishing, 2007).

[23] For instance, rampant smuggling in the North American colonies during the 1760s, especially in Massachusetts, was largely welcomed by the local populace. This situation convinced the British government to set up admiralty courts to try offenders of the practice, a highly controversial decision.

[24] Quoted in Moncure Daniel Conway, *The Life of Thomas Paine*, I:17. The record of Paine's discharge from the Board of Excise was dated August 27, 1765.

[25] Ibid., I:18.

[26] "Thomas Paine Gets His Own Festival in Lewes," July 2, 2009, The Guardian. https://www.theguardian.com/books/2009/jul/02/thomas-paine-festival-lewes (accessed September 27, 2018); "Statue of Thomas Paine Unveiled in Lewes," BBC.com. https://www.bbc.com/news/10507823 (accessed September 27, 2018).

[27] Quoted in Moncure Daniel Conway, *The Life of Thomas Paine*, I:25. The account was penned by Thomas "Clio" Rickman, who maintained a friendly relationship with Paine in Lewes.

[28] Craig Nelson, *Thomas Paine: Enlightenment, Revolution, and the Birth of Modern Nations*, 40-41.

[29] The Case of the Officers of Excise, in *The Complete Writings of Thomas Paine*, II:3-15.

[30] Ibid., 10-11, 15.

[31] Moncure Daniel Conway, *The Life of Thomas Paine*, I:27-28, 49.

[32] Quoted in Ibid., I:29.

[33] A. J. Ayer, *Thomas Paine* (Chicago: The University of Chicago Press, 1988), 6. This claim was made by Thomas "Clio" Rickman.

[34] Craig Nelson, *Thomas Paine: Enlightenment, Revolution, and the Birth of Modern Nations*, 46.

[35] Mercy Otis Warren, *History of the Rise, Progress, and Termination of the American Revolution* (Indianapolis: Liberty Fund, 1989), I:68.

[36] Common Sense, in *The Writings of Thomas Paine*, I:90.

[37] Murray Rothbard, *Conceived in Liberty* (Auburn: The Mises Institute, 2011), 1043.

[38] George Washington to Bryan Fairfax, July 4, 1774, in *The Papers of George Washington*, Colonial Series X:109-110.

[39] Murray Rothbard, *Conceived in Liberty*, 1039.

[40] *The Parliamentary History of England, from the Earliest Period to the Year 1803*, Edited by John Wright (36 Vols., London: T.C. Hansard, 1813), XVII:1280-1281.

[41] Moncure Daniel Conway, *The Life of Thomas Paine*, I:36. Paine's interest in the subject can be found in his contributions to the *Pennsylvania Magazine*, where he served as editor the following year. As "Atlanticus," for example, he wrote an article concerning Franklin's electrical machine.

[42] Benjamin Franklin to Richard Bache, September 30, 1774, in *The Papers of Benjamin Franklin*, Edited by William Wilcox (42 Vols., New Haven, CT: Yale University Press, 1798), XXI:325-326.

[43] To Capt. Ayres, of the Ship Polly, on Voyage from London to Philadelphia, in *Ten Thousand Wonderful Things: Comprising the Marvellous and Rare, Odd, Curious, Quaint, Eccentric and Extraordinary in All Ages and Nations, in Art, Nature, and Science Including Many Wonders of the World* (London: Ward and Lock, 1859), 38-39.

[44] By 1770, most of the duties under the Townshend Acts were repealed by Parliament after rigorous protests from American colonists and British merchants, but taxes on tea remained.

[45] Ibid., XXI:515-518.

[46] Moncure Daniel Conway, *The Life of Thomas Paine*, I:42-43; Craig Nelson, *Thomas Paine: Enlightenment, Revolution, and the Birth of Modern Nations*, 61.

[47] A Summary View of the Rights of British America, in *The Works of Thomas Jefferson*, II:49-89.

[48] To the Inhabitants of Great Britain, in *Life and Correspondence of James Iredell*, Edited by Griffith McRee (New York: D. Appleton and Company, 1857), I:205-220.

[49] A Dialogue between General Wolfe and General Gage in a Wood Near Boston, in *The Writings of Thomas Paine*, I:10-12.

[50] Reflections on Titles, in Ibid., I:46-47.

[51] Duelling, in Ibid., I:40-45.

[52] African Slavery in America, in Ibid., I:4.

[53] Ibid., I:5-7.

[54] Ibid., I:7-9.

[55] Prefatory Note to Paine's First Essay, in Ibid., 1-3. Conway accordingly characterized Paine as "the first American abolitionist." Pennsylvania, New Hampshire, Connecticut, and Rhode Island passed gradual emancipation acts during 1776-1784. Through a 1781 opinion by the Massachusetts Supreme Court, *Commonwealth v. Jennison*, the Massachusetts state constitution was interpreted to produce a similar outcome. In addition, the independent Republic of Vermont outlawed nearly all slavery in its 1777 constitution.

[56] According to Benjamin Rush's account from several decades later, Paine confirmed that he was the author of the work. However, this account raises additional questions because Bush claimed Paine told him the essay was the first of his written in Philadelphia. Because the piece was not published until several months after Paine had published his first writings in the *Pennsylvania Magazine*, the publisher either delayed publication of the essay (likely because of its controversial content), or Rush was mistaken on the timing.

[57] A Serious Thought, in *The Writings of Thomas Paine*, I:65-66.

[58] Ibid., 65.

[59] Amartya Sen, *Poverty and Famines: An Essay on Entitlement and Deprivation* (Oxford: Oxford University Press, 1981), 39.

[60] A Serious Thought, in *The Writings of Thomas Paine*, I:65-66.

[61] Useful and Entertaining Hints, in Ibid., 20-25.

[62] An Occasional Letter on the Female Sex, in Ibid., 59.

[63] Ibid., 59-64.

[64] Reflections on Unhappy Marriages, in *The Writings of Thomas Paine*, I:51-54.

[65] Moncure Daniel Conway, *The Life of Thomas* Paine, I:47.

CHAPTER 2
BEGINNING THE WORLD OVER AGAIN

[66] Murray Rothbard, *Conceived in Liberty*, 1051-1054.

[67] Diary of John Adams, September 17, 1774, in *The Adams Papers*, Edited by Lyman Butterfield (40 Vols., Cambridge: Harvard University Press, 1961), II:134-135.

[68] Murray Rothbard, *Conceived in Liberty*, 1069-1075.

[69] Robert Middlekauff, *The Glorious Cause: The American Revolution, 1763-1789* (London: Oxford University Press, 2005), 268-270.

[70] George Washington to George Fairfax, May 31, 1775, in *The Papers of George Washington*, Colonial Series X:367-368; Joseph Warren, In Provincial Congress, Watertown, in *Journals of the American Congress from 1774-1788* (4 Vols., Washington: Way and Gideon, 1823), I:67; Common Sense; Moncure Daniel Conway, *The Life of Thomas Paine*, I:53.

[71] "The Charlotte Town Resolves; May 31, 1775," The Avalon Project: Documents in Law, History, and Diplomacy. https://avalon.law.yale.edu/18th_century/charlott.asp (accessed March 28, 2022); "Act of Renunciation, 1776," Rhode Island Department of State. https://www.sos.ri.gov/assets/downloads/documents/Act-of-Renunciation.pdf (accessed March 28, 2022).

[72] "Give me Liberty or Give me Death" The Avalon Project: Documents in Law, History, and Diplomacy. https://avalon.law.yale.edu/18th_century/patrick.asp (accessed March 28, 2022).

[73] Robert Middlekauff, *The Glorious Cause: The American Revolution, 1763-1789*, 287-298; Murray Rothbard, *Conceived in Liberty*, 1154-1156. For the account of Warren's mutilation, see Benjamin Hichborn to John Adams, November 25, 1775, in *The Adams Papers*, III:320-327.

[74] Craig Nelson, *Thomas Paine: Enlightenment, Revolution, and the Birth of Modern Nations*, 78.

[75] Richard Gimbel, *A Bibliographical Check List of Common Sense, With an Account of Its Publication* (New Haven, CT: Yale University Press, 1956), 17-21; Craig Nelson, *Thomas Paine: Enlightenment, Revolution, and the Birth of Modern Nations*, 89.

[76] Common Sense, in *The Writings of Thomas Paine*, I:67-68.

[77] Ibid., 69.

[78] Ibid., 70-71.

[79] Ibid., 71-72.

[80] Ibid., 72-73.

[81] Ibid., 74.

[82] Ibid., 75-76.

[83] Ibid., 76-79. For verses quoted, see 1 Samuel 8:11-18.

[84] Ibid., 80.

[85] Ibid., 79-81.

[86] Ibid., 82-83.

[87] Ibid., 75.

[88] Ibid., 83.

[89] Ibid., 84-85.

[90] Ibid.

[91] Ibid., 89-91.

[92] Ibid., 72.

[93] Ibid., 72-75.

[94] Speech on Conciliation with the Colonies, in *Select Works of Edmund Burke*, Edited by Francis Canavan (4 Vols., Liberty Fund: Indianapolis, 1999), 1:255.

[95] Ibid., 92.

[96] Ibid., 86-88.

[97] Ibid., 101.

[98] Ibid., 103-105.

[99] Ibid., 101, 106.

[100] Ibid., 99.

[101] Ibid., 97-98.

[102] Ibid., 98, 108-109.

[103] Ibid., 98.

[104] Ibid., 108.

[105] Ibid.

[106] Ibid., 99.

[107] Ibid., 91-92.

[108] Ibid. 91-93.

[109] Ibid., 111.

[110] Ibid., 68, A. J. Ayer, *Thomas Paine*, 35.

[111] Richard Gimbel, *A Biographical Check List of Common Sense, With an Account of its Publication* (New Haven, CT: Yale University Press, 1956), 21.

[112] A. J. Ayer, *Thomas Paine*, 35.

[113] The Forester I, in *The Writings of Thomas Paine*, I:135-136.

[114] Common Sense, in Ibid., I:122.

[115] Murray Rothbard, *Conceived in Liberty*, 1251.

[116] The Forester II, in *The Writings of Thomas Paine*, I:135-136; Autobiographical Sketch, January 14, 1779, in *The Life and Writings of Thomas Paine*, Edited by Daniel Edwin Wheeler (10 Vols., New York: Vincent Parke and Company, 1908), VIII:55. For the projection of 100,000 units, see The Rights of Man, in *The Writings of Thomas Paine*, II.463.

[117] Moncure Daniel Conway, *The Life of Thomas Paine,* I:69. For modern works that defend the 500,000 estimation, see *The Complete Writings of Thomas Paine*, I:xiv; Merrill Jensen, *Tracts of the American Revolution, 1763-1776* (Indianapolis: Bobbs-Merrill, 1967), lxvi-lxvii; Scott Liell, *46 Pages: Thomas Paine, Common Sense, and the Turning Point to American Independence* (Philadelphia: Running Press, 2003), 95. For the U.S. Census Bureau's projection for the North American population in 1776, see "The Fourth of July: 2016," Census.gov. https://www.census.gov/newsroom/facts-for-features/2016/cb16-ff13.html (accessed November 19, 2019).

[118] Cato Letter III, in *Wartime Dissent in America: A History and Anthology*, V: 443-446; Cato Letter IV, in Ibid., V:514-517.

[119] Charles Inglis, *The True Interest of America*, in Gordon Wood, *The American Revolution: Writings from the Pamphlet Debate*, II:709, 753, 763; To the Inhabitants of Philadelphia, in *American Archives: A Documentary History of the English Colonies in North America*, Edited by Peter Force (6 Vols, Washington: St. Clair Clarke and Peter Force, 1844), 802-804; Plain Truth, in *Wartime Dissent in America: A History and Anthology*, V:15-17; Autobiography, in *The Works of John Adams*, Edited by Charles Francis Adams (10 Vols., Boston: Charles C. Little and James Brown, 1850), II:507-508.

[120] The Forester I, in *The Writings of Thomas Paine*, I:131-133; The Forester II, in Ibid., I:133-137.

[121] The Forester II, in Ibid., I:139; The Forester III, in Ibid., I:146-147.

[122] Robert Parkinson, *The Common Cause: Creating Race and Nation in the American Revolution* (Chapel Hill: University of North Carolina Press, 2016), 205-206.

[123] George Washington to Joseph Reed, November 28, 1775, in *The Papers of George Washington*, Revolutionary War Series II:448-451.

[124] George Washington to Joseph Reed, April 1, 1776, in Ibid., Revolutionary War Series IV:9-13.; George Washington to Joseph Reed, January 31, 1776, in Ibid., Revolutionary War Series III:225-229.

[125] Benjamin Franklin to Charles Lee, February 19, 1776, in *The Works of Benjamin Franklin*, Edited by Jared Sparks (10 Vols., London: Benjamin Franklin Sievens, 1882), VIII:174; William Cushing to John Adams, in *Papers of John Adams*, Edited by Robert Taylor (18 Vols., Cambridge: Harvard University Press, 1979), IV:199-200; William Whipple to John Langdon, April 2, 1776, in *Letters of the Delegates to Congress* (24 Vols, Washington, D.C.: Library of Congress, 1979), III:479; Charles Lee to George Washington, January 24, 1776, in *The Papers of George Washington*, Edited by Philander Chase, Revolutionary War Series III:182-184.

[126] "Essex," The New York *Journal*, Mar. 17, 1776; The New London *Gazette*, Mar. 22, 1776; The *Pennsylvania Evening Post*, Feb. 13, 1776.

[127] John Winthrop to John Adams, April 1776, in Collections of the Massachusetts Historical Society (10 Vols., Boston: The Society, 1878), IV:298; Connecticut *Courant*, May 27, 1776; Benjamin Kent to John Adams, April 24, 1776, in *The Works of John Adams*, II:291.

[128] Benjamin Rush Quote; Joseph Ellis, *American Sphinx: The Character of Thomas Jefferson* (New York: Alfred A. Knopf, 1996), 49.

CHAPTER 3
THE CRISIS

[129] Joseph Hewes to Samuel Johnston, February 11, 1776, in *The Colonial Records of North Carolina*, Edited by William Saunders (26 Vols., Raleigh: Josephus Daniels, 1900), X:447; William Tudor to John Adams, February 29, 1776, in *The Adams Papers*, IV:41.

[130] John Adams to Charles Lee, February 19, 1776, in Ibid., IV:29-30; John Adams to James Warren, May 12, 1776, in Ibid., 181-183.

[131] Craig Nelson, *Thomas Paine: Enlightenment, Revolution, and the Birth of Modern Nations*, 90.

[132] Ibid.

[133] Murray Rothbard, *Conceived in Liberty*, 1208-1210; Robert Middlekauff, *The Glorious Cause: The American Revolution, 1763-1789*, 314-317.

[134] Murray Rothbard, *Conceived in Liberty*, 1371.

[135] John Adams to Timothy Pickering, August 6, 1822, in *The Works of John Adams*, II:512-514.

[136] Joseph Ellis, *American Sphinx: The Character of Thomas Jefferson*, 47-48, Dumas Malone, *Jefferson the Virginian* (Boston: Little, Brown and Company,

1948), 218; Kevin Gutzman, *Thomas Jefferson – Revolutionary: A Radical's Struggle to Remake America* (New York: St. Martin's Press, 2017), 25.

[137] David McCullough, *John Adams* (New York: Simon & Schuster, 2001), 125-129; Murray Rothbard, *Conceived in Liberty*, 1295-1298; Dumas Malone, *Jefferson the Virginian*, 220.

[138] Joseph Ellis, *American Sphinx: The Character of Thomas Jefferson*, 59.

[139] Notes of Proceedings in the Continental Congress, in *The Papers of Thomas Jefferson*, Edited by Julian Boyd (44 Vols., Princeton: Princeton University Press, 1950), I:314-315.

[140] Moncure Daniel Conway, *The Life of Thomas* Paine, I:81.

[141] For Jefferson's description of the document's purpose, see Thomas Jefferson to Henry Lee, May 8, 1825, in *The Works of Thomas Jefferson*, XII:408-409.

[142] Arthur Marks, "The Statue of King George II in New York and the Iconology of Regicide," *The American Art Journal* 13, No. 3 (1981):65; David McCullough, *1776* (New York: Simon & Schuster), 137-138.

[143] Robert Middlekauff, *The Glorious Cause: The American Revolution, 1763-1789*, 346-356; Murray Rothbard, *Conceived in Liberty*, 1301-1307.

[144] Craig Nelson, *Thomas Paine: Enlightenment, Revolution, and the Birth of Modern Nations*, 103.

[145] Robert Williams, "The State Constitutions of the Founding Decade: Pennsylvania's Radical 1776 Constitution and its Influences on American Constitutionalism, by Robert Williams," *Temple Law Review* 62, No. 541 (1989):554; Murray Rothbard, *Conceived in Liberty*, 1371-1372.

[146] David Benner, *Compact of the Republic: The League of States and the Constitution* (Minneapolis: Life & Liberty Publishing Group, 2015), 27-31.

[147] To the People, in *The Complete Writings of Thomas Paine*, II:270

[148] Thomas Mifflin, Mark Bird, Jonathan Potts, Edward Biddle, Samuel Potts, and James Wilson to Anthony Wayne, November 26, 1778, in *Life and Services of Gen. Anthony Wayne*, Edited by Horatio Moore (Philadelphia: Leary, Getz & Co, 1845), 72; Benjamin Rush to Anthony Wayne, May 19, 1777, in Letters of Benjamin Rush, Edited by Lyman Butterfield (2 Vols., Princeton: Princeton University Press, 1951), I:148.

[149] Thomas Paine to Messrs. Deane, Jay, and Gerard, September 14, 1779, in *The Writings of Thomas Paine*, I:444; George Washington to Samuel Washington, December 18, 1776, in *The Papers of George Washington*, Revolutionary War Series VII:369-372.

[150] A. J. Ayer, *Thomas Paine*, 44.

[151] The Crisis I, in *The Writings of Thomas Paine*, I:170.

[152] Ibid.

[153] Ibid., 173.

[154] Ibid., 174-176.

[155] Ibid., 176-177.

[156] Ibid., 177-178.

[157] Ibid., 178; Ron Chernow, *George Washington: A Life* (New York: Penguin Group, 2010), 270-271.

[158] Ibid., 271-276; Robert Middlekauff, *The Glorious Cause: The American Revolution, 1763-1789*, 365-367.

[159] The Crisis II, in *The Writings of Thomas Paine*, I:179-180.

[160] Ibid., 180, 184-185.

[161] Ibid., 188-189.

[162] The Crisis II, in *The Writings of Thomas Paine*, I:181.

[163] Ibid., 186-188; Moncure Daniel Conway, *The Life of Thomas Paine*, I:90-91.

[164] Gordon Wood, *The American Revolution* (New York: The Modern Library, 2002), 80.

[165] On the Question, Will There Be War?, in *The Complete Writings of Thomas Paine*, II:1013.

[166] The Crisis III, in *The Writings of Thomas Paine*, I:198.

[167] Ibid., 199-200.

[168] Robert Middlekauff, *The Glorious Cause: The American Revolution, 1763-1789*, 373-377; Gordon Wood, *The American Revolution*, 80.

[169] Richard Ketchum, *Saratoga: Turning Point of America's Revolutionary War* (New York: Henry Holt, 1997), 356.

[170] Ibid., 393-395; John Alden, *A History of the American Revolution* (New York: Da Capo Press, 1969), 297-298.

[171] The Crisis IV, in *The Writings of Thomas Paine*, I:229-231.

[172] Ibid., 231-232.

[173] Murray Rothbard, *Conceived in Liberty*, 1333-1335.

[174] Ibid.; Gordon Wood, *The American Revolution*, 80.

[175] Robert Middlekauff, *The Glorious Cause: The American Revolution, 1763-1789*, 387-391; Murray Rothbard, *Conceived in Liberty*, 1328-1330; John Alden, *A History of the American Revolution*, 325.

[176] Thomas Paine to Richard Henry Lee, October 30, 1777, quoted in Moncure Daniel Conway, *The Life of Thomas Paine*, I:95.

[177] John Alden, *A History of the American Revolution*, 326.

[178] George Washington to Henry Laurens, December 23, 1777, in *The Papers of George Washington*, Revolutionary War Series XII:683-687.

[179] John Alden, *A History of the American Revolution*, 300-301; Murray Rothbard, *Conceived in Liberty*, 1337.

[180] Moncure Daniel Conway, *The Life of Thomas Paine*, I:93-94.

[181] Murray Rothbard, *Conceived in Liberty*, 1336; George Clinton, *Public Papers of George Clinton, First Governor of New York*, Volume II (New York: Wynkoop Hallenbeck Crawford Co, 1900), 823, 866-867. Clinton arranged for 1700 additional barrels of salt pork to be sent a week later.

[182] John Alden, *A History of the American Revolution*, 384-385.

[183] The Crisis V, in *The Writings of Thomas Paine*, I:233-235, 245-246.

[184] Ibid., 246, 249.

[185] Murray Rothbard, *Conceived in Liberty*, 1342-1344; Robert Middlekauff, *The Glorious Cause: The American Revolution, 1763-1789*, 432-435.

[186] Coy Hilton James, *Silas Deane – Patriot or Traitor?* (Lansing: Michigan State University Press, 1975), 111-113; Quoted in Moncure Daniel Conway, *The Life of Thomas Paine*, I:123.

[187] A. J. Ayer, *Thomas Paine*, 46, Murray Rothbard, *Conceived in Liberty*, 1472-1473; To the Public on Mr. Deane's Affair, in *The Writings of Thomas Paine*, I:416-417; The Affair of Silas Deane, in Ibid., I:405; Diary, 1779, in *The Works of John Adams*, III:187.

[188] Charles Rappleye, *Robert Morris: Financier of the American Revolution* (New York: Simon & Schuster, 2010), 168-171; *The Pennsylvania Packet* (Philadelphia), January 12, 1779; Gordon Wood, *The Creation of the American Republic: 1776-1789* (Chapel Hill: University of North Carolina Press, 1969), 419-421.

[189] Craig Nelson, *Thomas Paine: Enlightenment, Revolution, and the Birth of Modern Nations*, 135-136.

[190] Moncure Daniel Conway, *The Life of Thomas Paine*, I:129-130.

[191] Ibid., 131-132. According to Conway, the letter was suppressed from Congress.

[192] Samuel Adams to Arthur Lee, August 1, 1799, in The Writings of Samuel Adams, Edited by Harry Alonzo Cushing (4 Vols., New York: G.P. Putnam's Sons, 1908), IV:156.

[193] Craig Nelson, *Thomas Paine: Enlightenment, Revolution, and the Birth of Modern Nations*, 140.

[194] Peace, and the Newfoundland Fisheries, First Letter, in *The Writings of Thomas Paine*, II:1-2.

[195] Ibid., 2-4.

[196] Ibid., 4-6.

[197] Ibid., 6-10.

[198] John Alden, *A History of the American Revolution*, 410-412.

[199] Moncure Daniel Conway, *The Life of Thomas Paine*, I:147-150.

[200] Edward Raymond Turner, "The Abolition of Slavery in Pennsylvania," *The Pennsylvania Magazine of History and Biography* 36, No. 2 (1912): 137.

[201] Emancipation of Slaves, Preamble to the Act Passed by the Pennsylvania Assembly, March 1, 1780, in *The Writings of Thomas Paine*, II:29-30; Moncure Daniel Conway, *The Life of Thomas Paine*, I:154.

[202] The Crisis VII, in *The Writings of Thomas Paine*, I:293.

[203] Ibid., 294-296.

[204] Robert Middlekauff, *The Glorious Cause: The American Revolution, 1763-1789*, 454-455; The Crisis IX, in *The Writings of Thomas Paine*, I:301.

[205] Public Good, in Ibid., II:32-33.

[206] Ibid., 36.

[207] Ibid., 37, 39, 46.

[208] Ibid., 60.

[209] Ibid., 59.

[210] Ibid., 60, 63.

[211] Ibid., 61.

[212] Ibid., 62-64. For calculation conversion of £4 million to the current value, see "Inflation Calculator," Bank of England. https://www.bankofengland.co.uk/monetary-policy/inflation/inflation-calculator (accessed June 23, 2020). For conversion to US dollars, see "Dollar to British Pound," Currency-Calc.com. https://www.currency-calc.com/USD_GBP (accessed June 23, 2020).

213 Thomas Jefferson to James Madison, March 24, 1782, in *The Works of Thomas Jefferson*, III:295-296; James Madison to Thomas Jefferson, April 23, 1782, in *The Writings of James Madison*, Edited by Gaillard Hunt (7 Vols., New York: G.P. Putnam's Sons, 1900), I:186-188.

214 Richard Henry Lee to Samuel Adams, September 10, 1780, in *The Letters of Richard Henry Lee* (2 Vols., New York: The Macmillan Company, 1914), II:200-201.

215 Response to an Accusation of Bribery, May 1, 1782, in *Thomas Paine: Collected Writings*, 318-324.

216 Eric Newman, *The Early Paper Money of America* (Iola: Krause Publications, 1997), 14-16.

217 The Crisis Extraordinary, in *The Writings of Thomas Paine*, I:306-323; Moncure Daniel Conway, *The Life of Thomas Paine*, I:161-162.

218 The Crisis Extraordinary, in *The Writings of Thomas Paine*, I:306-323; The Rights of Man, in Ibid., II:314.

219 For information on Arnold's court martial and defection, see William Sterne Randall, *Benedict Arnold: Patriot and Traitor* (New York: William Morrow & Co, 1990), 486-492, 511-512.

220 Murray Rothbard, *Conceived in Liberty*, 1435-1436.

221 Robert Middlekauff, *The Glorious Cause: The American Revolution, 1763-1789*, 468-482; Murray Rothbard, *Conceived in Liberty*, 1442-1445.

222 Moncure Daniel Conway, *The Life of Thomas Paine*, I:168-171; Craig Nelson, *Thomas Paine: Enlightenment, Revolution, and the Birth of Modern Nations*, 150.

223 "Thomas Paine to James Hutchinson, March 11, 1781," Thomas Paine National Historical Association. http://thomaspaine.org/letters/other/to-james-hutchinson-march-11th-1781.html (accessed June 26, 2020).

224 Walter Issacson, *Benjamin Franklin: An American Life* (New York: Simon & Schuster, 2003), 395-396.

225 Moncure Daniel Conway, *The Life of Thomas Paine*, I:168-172.

226 James Thomas Flexner, *Washington: The Indispensable Man* (New York: Back Bay Books, 1994), 150-151; Murray Rothbard, *Conceived in Liberty*, 1397.

227 "George Washington to Nathanael Greene, February 2, 1781," Founders Online, National Archives. https://founders.archives.gov/documents/Washington/99-01-02-04731 (accessed June 28, 2020); "George Washington to Robert Livingston, January 31, 1781," Ibid., https://founders.archives.gov/documents/Washington/99-01-02-04710 (accessed March 28, 2022).

228 Murray Rothbard, *Conceived in Liberty*, 1459-1462; John Alden, *A History of the American Revolution*, 474.

229 The Crisis X, in *The Writings of Thomas Paine*, I:323-324.

230 Nathaniel Wraxall, *Historical Memoirs of My Own Time* (2 Vols., London: T. Cadell and W. Davies, 1815), II:102-103, 107-108.

231 Murray Rothbard, *Conceived in Liberty*, 1466-1468.

232 Ibid., 1470-1478.

233 Bernard Bailyn, *The Ideological Origins of the American Revolution* (Cambridge, MA: Belknap Press, 1992), xi; Gordon Wood, *The Radicalism of the American Revolution* (New York: Alfred A. Knopf, 1992), 3.

CHAPTER 4
CROSSROADS OF THE REPUBLIC

234 John Keane, *Tom Paine: A Political Life* (Boston: Little, Brown and Company, 1995), 213-214.

235 "Thomas Paine to George Washington, November 30, 1781," Founders Online, National Archives. https://founders.archives.gov/documents/Washington/99-01-02-07467 (accessed July 18, 1781).

236 Pelatiah Webster, *Political Essays on the Nature and Operation of Money, Public Finances, and Other Subjects* (Philadelphia: Joseph Crukshank, 1791), 116-117.

237 Thomas Paine to Jonathan Williams, November 26, 1781, in Moncure Daniel Conway, *The Life of Thomas Paine*, I:175-176; "Thomas Paine to George Washington, November 30, 1781," Founders Online, National Archives. https://founders.archives.gov/documents/Washington/99-01-02-07467 (accessed July 18, 2020).

238 Murray Rothbard, *Conceived in Liberty*, 1502-1505.

239 The Continentalist No. I, in *Alexander Hamilton: Writings* (New York: Library of America, 2001), 101-106.

240 Murray Rothbard, *Conceived in Liberty*, 1505-1506.

241 The King's Speech on Opening the Session, November 27, 1781, in *The Parliamentary History of England* (36 Vols., London: T.C. Hansard, 1814), XXII:635-637.

242 Ibid., 636-637.

243 The Crisis X, in *The Writings of Thomas Paine*, I:324, 326.

244 Ibid., 324-325.

245 Ibid., 325-326.

246 Ibid., 326-330.

247 Motion on Impost, in *The Papers of James Madison*, Edited by William Hutchinson and William Rachal (17 Vols., Chicago: The University of Chicago Press, 1962), II:303-304.

248 Thomas Paine to Robert Morris, March 1782, in *The Complete Writings of Thomas Paine*, II:1211.

249 To the People in America, in *The Writings of Thomas Paine*, I:332-338.

250 Ibid., 339-343.

251 Ibid., 342-342.

252 The Necessity of Taxation, April 4, 1782, in *Thomas Paine: Collected Writings*, 312-313.

253 Ibid., 314-316.

254 Murray Rothbard, *Conceived in Liberty*, 1514-1516.

255 Ibid., 1516-1517.

256 Six Letters to Rhode Island, Letter I, in *The Complete Writings of Thomas Paine*, II:336.

257 Ibid., 336-337.

258 Letter III, in Ibid., 350-351.

[259] Letter V, in Ibid., 358.

[260] Ibid., 359.

[261] Ibid., 360-361.

[262] Letter III, in Ibid., 352.

[263] Thomas Paine to Robert Morris, November 20, 1782, in *The Complete Writings of Thomas Paine*, II:1213-1215.

[264] Murray Rothbard, *Conceived in Liberty*, 1514-1517.

[265] Abbé Raynal, *The Revolution of America* (London: Lockyer Davis, 1781), 32-33.

[266] Ibid., 36-37.

[267] Ibid., 14-17.

[268] Ibid., 27, 78-79, 81, 86-87.

[269] Ibid., 42, 44-45.

[270] Letter to the Abbé Raynal, on the Affairs of North America, in *The Writings of Thomas Paine*, II:71; Abbé Raynal, *The Revolution of America*, 126-127.

[271] Letter to the Abbé Raynal, on the Affairs of North America, in *The Writings of Thomas Paine*, II:73-75.

[272] Ibid.

[273] Ibid., 92-93; John Alden, *A History of the American Revolution*, 387.

[274] Letter to the Abbé Raynal, on the Affairs of North America, in *The Writings of Thomas Paine*, II:106-107.

[275] Ibid., 107.

[276] Ibid., 115.

[277] Ibid., 79-83.

[278] John Keane, *Tom Paine: A Political Life*, 251.

[279] Ibid., 251-252.

[280] Ibid., 252.

[281] Ibid., 252-253.

[282] Ibid., 206. Despite a push by Dr. James Hutchinson to include Paine, the writer was denied membership in 1781.

[283] Alexander Hamilton to James Duane, September 3, 1780, in The Papers of Alexander Hamilton, Edited by Harold Syrett (27 Vols., New York: Columbia University Press, 1961), II:402; Quoted in Gordon Wood, *The Creation of the American Republic: 1776-1789*, 471.

[284] Murray Rothbard, *Conceived in Liberty, Volume V: The New Republic, 1784-1971* (Auburn: The Mises Institute, 2019), 130.

[285] John DeWitt II, in The Complete Anti-Federalist (7 Vols., Chicago: University of Chicago Press, 1981), IV:20.

[286] George Washington to Benjamin Harrison, January 18, 1784, in *The Papers of George Washington*, Confederation Series I:56-57.

[287] Dissertations on Government, The Affairs of the Bank, and Paper Money, in *The Writings of Thomas Paine*, II:132.

[288] Ibid., 133-137.

[289] Ibid., 177-179.

[290] Ibid., 181.

[291] Murray Rothbard, *Conceived in Liberty, Volume V: The New Republic, 1784-1971*, 54-56.

[292] Dissertations on Government, The Affairs of the Bank, and Paper Money, in *The Writings of Thomas Paine*, II:182.

[293] Moncure Daniel Conway, *The Life of Thomas Paine*, I:242; John Keane, *Tom Paine: A Political Life*, 267.

[294] John Keane, *Tom Paine: A Political* Life, 269.

[295] Ibid., 269-270.

[296] Ibid., 270.

[297] James Warren to John Adams, October 22, 1786, in The Papers of John Adams, Edited by Gregg Lint, Sara Martin, C. James Taylor, Sara Georgini, Hobson Woodward, Sara Sikes, and Amanda Norton (18 Vols., Cambridge: Belknap Press, 2016), XVIII:430.

[298] Ira Stoll, *Samuel Adams: A Life* (New York: Free Press, 2008), 223-224.

[299] Thomas Jefferson to James Madison, January 30, 1787, in *The Papers of Thomas Jefferson*, XI:92-97; Thomas Jefferson to William Stephens Smith, November 13, 1787, in Ibid., XII:355-357.

[300] Moncure Daniel Conway, *The Life of Thomas Paine*, I:226.

[301] Ibid.

[302] Jefferson's Observations on DéMeunier's Manuscript, 22 June 1786, in *The Papers of Thomas Jefferson*, X:58.

[303] James Madison to Thomas Jefferson, October 24, 1787, in The Papers of James Madison, X:163-165; Robert Yates, *Notes of the Secret Debates of the Federal Convention of 1787* (Hawthorne: Omni, 1986), 145-147.

[304] Jonathan Elliot, ed., *The Debates in the Several State Conventions on the Adoption of the Federal Constitution* (5 Vols., Washington: Taylor & Maury, 1861), III: 522; Ibid., IV:315-316; The Federalist No. 45, Alexander Hamilton, James Madison, and John Jay, *The Federalist*, ed. Jacob E. Cooke (Middletown: Wesleyan University, 1961), 313; *The Debates in the Several State Conventions on the Adoption of the Federal Constitution*, IV:202.

[305] "Thomas Paine to George Washington, July 30, 1796," Thomas Paine National Historical Association. https://thomaspaine.org/major-works/letter-to-george-washington.html (accessed May 22, 2021).

[306] Ibid.

[307]

[308] Thomas Jefferson to Thomas Paine, December 23, 1788, in *The Papers of Thomas Jefferson*, XIV:372-377.

[309]

[310] Prospects on the Rubicon, in *The Writings of Thomas Paine*, II:191-192.

[311] For example, see "Thomas Paine to George Washington, July 30, 1796," Thomas Paine National Historical Association. https://thomaspaine.org/major-works/letter-to-george-washington.html (accessed May 22, 2021); Thomas Jefferson to James Madison, December 20, 1787, in *The Papers of Thomas Jefferson*, XII:438-443.

[312] John Keane, *Tom Paine: A Political* Life, 275.

313 Thomas Clio Rickman, *The Life of Thomas Paine* (London: Thomas Clio Rickman, 1819), XV (Preface); John Keane, *Tom Paine: A Political* Life, 275.

314 Craig Nelson, *Thomas Paine: Enlightenment, Revolution, and the Birth of Modern Nations*, 176.

315 Thomas Paine to Edmund Burke, August 7, 1788, in Ibid., 179-180.

316 Specification of Thomas Paine, A.D. 1788 No 1667, Constructing Arches, Vaulted Roofs, and Ceilings, in *The Writings of Thomas Paine*, II:227-228; Thomas Jefferson to Joseph Willard, March 24, 1789, in *The Papers of Thomas Jefferson*, XIV:697-699.

CHAPTER 5
THE RIGHTS OF MAN

317 Simon Schama, *Citizens: A Chronicle of the French Revolution* (New York: Alfred A. Knopf, 1989), 238-245.

318 Thomas Paine to Thomas Jefferson, February 16, 1789, in *The Papers of Thomas Jefferson*, XIV:564.

319 The Rights of Man, in *The Writings of Thomas Paine*, II:345.

320 Ibid., II:289.

321 Thomas Paine to George Washington, October 16, 1789, in *The Papers of George Washington*, Presidential Series IV:196-198.

322 Thomas Paine to Benjamin Rush, March 16, 1789, in *The Theological Works of Thomas Paine*, (Boston: J.P. Mendum, 1859), 36. See Miscellaneous Letters section.

323 Simon Schama, *Citizens: A Chronicle of the French Revolution*, 458.

324 John Keane, *Tom Paine: A Political* Life, 278-279.

325 "Thomas Paine to John Hall, November 25, 1791," Thomas Paine National Historical Association. https://thomaspaine.org/letters/other/to-john-hall-november-25-1791.html (accessed June 4, 2022).

326 Edmund Burke to Lord Charlemont, August 9, 1789, in *The Correspondence of Edmund Burke*, Edited by Thomas Copeland (10 Vols., Cambridge: University Press, 1968), VI:10; Edmund Burke to William Windham, September 27, 1789, in *Selected Letters of Edmund Burke*, Edited by Harvey Mansfield (Chicago: University of Chicago Press, 1984), 252.

327 *The General Evening Post* (London), March 8, 1790.

328 Thomas Paine to George Washington, May 1, 1790

329 Edmund Burke, *Reflections on the Revolution in France* (London: Oxford University Press, 2009), 284.

330 A Discourse on the Love of our Country, in *Richard Price: Political Writings*, Edited by D.O. Thomas (New York: Cambridge University Press, 1991), 190; Meeting of the Revolution Society, November 4, 1790, in *The Spirit of the Times: Containing an Account of the English Commemoration of the First Anniversary of the French Revolution*, Edited by Simon Search (London: H. Gardner, Strand; J. Evans, Paternoster-Row; and J. Axtell, Royal-Exchange 1790), 183.

331 Edmund Burke, *Reflections on the Revolution in France*, 294.

[332] Ibid., 295-296.
[333] Ibid., 368.
[334] Ibid., 314-325.
[335] Ibid., 359-360.
[336] Ibid., 312-313.
[337] Ibid., 489
[338] Ibid., 362.
[339] Bradley Birzer, *Reflections on Reflections: A Close Reading of Edmund Burke* (Hillsdale: Spirit of Cecilia Books, 2018), 26.
[340] Thomas Jefferson to Benjamin Vaughan, May 11, 1791, in *The Papers of Thomas Jefferson*, X:391-392.
[341] John Keane, *Tom Paine: A Political* Life, 289.
[342] Mary Wollstonecraft, *A Vindication of the Rights of Men, in a Letter to the Right Honourable Edmund Burke, Occasioned by His Reflections on the Revolution in France* (London: J. Johnson, 1790), iv, 9, 22-23.
[343] The Rights of Man, in *The Writings of Thomas Paine*, II:267.
[344] Ibid., 269, 275.
[345] Ibid., 277-278, 281.
[346] Ibid., 279-280.
[347] Ibid., 282, 385.
[348] Ibid., 411-412.
[349] Ibid., 304-305.
[350] Ibid., 304-305.
[351] Ibid., 283-284.
[352] Ibid., 283-284.
[353] Ibid., 285-286.
[354] Ibid., 293-295.
[355] Ibid., 293-294.
[356] Ibid., 296.
[357] Ibid., 290-294; Simon Schama, *Citizens: A Chronicle of the French Revolution*, 373-377.
[358] The Rights of Man, in *The Writings of Thomas Paine*, II:309-310.
[359] Ibid., 310, 437.
[360] Ibid., 311. For more on Paine's critique of the English Constitution and its susceptibility to government malignment, see Common Sense, in Ibid., I:71-72.
[361] The Rights of Man, in Ibid., II:312-313.
[362] Ibid., 313-314. For more information on quarrels over hunting in England, see the Grand Remonstrance of 1641, which charged King Charles I with interpreting royal charters to expand public lands and suppress game rights.
[363] Ibid., 315.
[364] Ibid., 315.
[365] Ibid., 316, 512, 270.
[366] Ibid., 316-317.
[367] Ibid., 319-320.

[368] Ibid., 319-321. For more information on the elimination of primogeniture in Virginia in 1785, see Kevin Gutzman, *Thomas Jefferson – Revolutionary: A Radical's Struggle to Remake America* (New York, NY: St. Martin's Press, 2017), 4.

[369] Ibid., 327-328.

[370] Ibid., 363, 357-358.

[371] Ibid., 365.

[372] Ibid., 382, 363.

[373] Ibid., 367.

[374] John Keane, *Tom Paine: A Political* Life, 304.

[375] David Freeman Hawke, *Paine* (New York, NY: Harper & Row, 1974), 223. For currency conversion figures, see "Currency Converter: 1270-2017," National Archives. https://www.nationalarchives.gov.uk/currency-converter/ (accessed October 3, 2021).

[376] John Keane, *Tom Paine: A Political* Life, 308.

[377] Charles James Fox, Quoted in Joseph Moreau, *Testimonials to the Merits of Thomas Paine* (Burlington, NJ: F.L. Taylor, 1861), 17; Thomas Campbell, Quoted in Sir James Mackintosh, *The Life of the Right Honourable Sir James Mackintosh* (London: Edward Moxon, 1836), 59; Richard Henry Lee, Quoted in Benjamin Lossing, *The Home of Washington and its Associations, Historical, Biographical, and Pictorial* (New York, NY: W.A. Townsend, 1866), 262; James Monroe, Address to the French National Convention, August 15, 1794, in *The Papers of James Monroe* (Westport, CT: Greenwood, 2009), III:30-31; Madame Roland, Quoted in Joseph Moreau, *Testimonials to the Merits of Thomas Paine*, 26.

[378] Thomas Jefferson to Jonathan Smith, April 26, 1791, in *The Papers of Thomas Jefferson*, XX:290; Thomas Jefferson to Thomas Paine, June 19, 1792, in Ibid., XX:312-313.

[379] London *Monthly Review*, May 1791, Appendix E3; Brooke Boothby, *Observations on the Appeal from the New to the Old Whigs, and on Mr. Paine's Rights of Man* (London: J. Stockdale, 1792), 86; Samuel Romilly, Memoirs of the Life of Samuel Romilly (London: John Murray, 1840), I:317-318.

[380] John Keane, *Tom Paine: A Political* Life, 307; Total figures per Appleton's Cyclopedia of American Biography, Quoted in John Remburg, *Thomas Paine* (New York, NY: The Truth Seeker Co, 1920), 54.

[381] Pitt's sentiments are according to the account to Lady Hester Stanhope, Quoted in Ibid., 60.

[382] John Keane, *Tom Paine: A Political* Life, 296.

[383] Letter Addressed to the Addressers on the Late Proclamation, in *The Writings of Thomas Paine*, III:65.

[384] *The Diary and Letters of Gouverneur Morris*, Edited by Anne Cary Morris (2 Vols., New York: Charles Scribner's Sons, 1888), I:400. Based on the style of his journal, it is unlikely that Morris shared his opinion on Paine's pamphlet with the author himself.

[385] George Washington to Thomas Paine, May 6, 1792, in *The Papers of George Washington*, X:357-358; David Freeman Hawke, *Paine*, 236.

[386] Thomas Clio Rickman, *The Life of Thomas Paine*, 84.

387 Moncure Daniel Conway, *The Life of Thomas Paine*, I:308.

388 Edmund Burke, *Reflections on the Revolution in France* (London: Oxford University Press, 2009), 344.

389 Monro Price, *The Fall of the French Monarchy* (London: Macmillan, 2002), 193-194.

390 Simon Schama, *Citizens: A Chronicle of the French Revolution*, 554-555.

391 Ibid., 560. Maximilien Robespierre, for example, favored such a system of constitutional monarchy.

392 The Republican Proclamation, in *The Writings of Thomas Paine*, III:1-3.

393 For Paine and Paine and Châtelet's plans to spread republicanism through France, see Introduction in Ibid., III:vi-vii.

394 To the Abbe Sieyès, in Ibid., III:9-10.

395 The Republican Proclamation, in Ibid., III:2-3.

396 John Keane, *Tom Paine: A Political* Life, 320-321.

397 To the Abbe Sieyès, in *The Writings of Thomas Paine*, III:10; Address and Declaration, in *The Theological Works of Thomas Paine* (3 Vols., Boston: J.P Mendum, 1859) III:65.

398 Edmund Burke, *Appeal from the New, to the Old Whigs* (London: J. Dodsley, 1791) 51, 131, 21. Title VII of the French Constitution of 1791 stated that "The National Constituent Assembly declares that the nation has the imprescriptible right to change its Constitution."

399 "Thomas Paine to William Short, November 2, 1791," Thomas Paine National Historical Association. https://thomaspaine.org/works/letters/other/to-william-short-november-2-1791.html (accessed October 26, 2021).

400 Ibid.

401 "Thomas Paine to John Hall, November 25, 1791," Thomas Paine National Historical Association. https://thomaspaine.org/letters/other/to-john-hall-november-25-1791.html (accessed October 26, 2021). Paine noted that he favored the low pricing scheme "because it will alarm the wise mad folks at St. James."

402 John Keane, *Tom Paine: A Political* Life, 324-326.

403 Ibid., 326-327.

404 Ibid., 327.

405 To the Abbe Sieyès, in *The Writings of Thomas Paine*, III:10.

406 The Rights of Man, Part Second, in Ibid., II:392.

407 Ibid., 394-395.

408 Ibid. 397-398.

409 Ibid., 398.

410 Ibid., 399-400.

411 Ibid., 401-402, 407.

412 Ibid., 410.

413 Ibid., 411-414.

414 Ibid., 403-404, 409.

415 Ibid., 418.

416 Ibid., 415-417.

417 Ibid., 418-419.

418 Ibid., 420-421, 423-424.

[419] Ibid., 428, 432

[420] Ibid. 429-431.

[421] Ibid., 432-435.

[422] Ibid., 435-436.

[423] Ibid., 436-437, 454-455.

[424] Ibid., 465.

[425] Ibid., 440-442.

[426] Ibid., 496-500.

[427] Ibid., 444-446.

[428] Ibid., 454-458, 488. In 1797, Paine built upon these ideas in *Agrarian Justice*.

[429] Ibid., 462-487.

[430] Ibid., 486-487, 490. For Paine's commentary on public schools, see footnote 36.

[431] Ibid., 487-489.

[432] Ibid., 491-493.

[433] Ibid., 490-491.

[434] Ibid., 495-498.

[435] *The Diary and Letters of Gouverneur Morris*, I:515.

[436] John Keane, *Tom Paine: A Political* Life, 327-329; Quoted in E.P. Thompson, *The Making of the English Working Class* (New York: Random House, 1964), 110.

[437] John Keane, *Tom Paine: A Political* Life, 331.

[438] Ibid., 307, 332-333. Total figures in England are from Appleton's Cyclopedia of American Biography, Quoted in John Remburg, *Thomas Paine*, 54.

[439] John Keane, *Tom Paine: A Political* Life, 334-335.

[440] Ibid., 335-336.

[441] "The Rights of Man, or Tommy Paine, the Little American Taylor, Taking Measure of the Crown, for a New Pair of Revolution Breeches," The British Museum, Museum Number 1868,0808.6057. https://www.britishmuseum.org/collection/object/P_1868-0808-6057 (accessed November 3, 2021); "Intercepted Correspondence, from Satan to Citizen Paine," The British Museum, Museum Number 1868,0808.6327. https://www.britishmuseum.org/collection/object/P_1868-0808-6327 (accessed November 3, 2021); Frank Peel, *Spen Valley: Past and Present* (Heckmondwike, Senior and Co., 1893), 307-308.

[442] Letter Adressed to the Addressers on the Late Proclamation, in *The Writings of Thomas Paine*, III:65-66.

[443] David Freeman Hawke, *Paine*, 248-249; To Mr. Secretary Dundas, in *The Writings of Thomas Paine*, III:15-29.

[444] To the Attorney General, in Ibid., III:11-13.

[445] Ibid., 14; The Rights of Man, Part Second, in Ibid., II:417; Steven Blakemore, *Intertextual War: Edmund Burke and the French Revolution in the Writings of Mary Wollstonecraft, Thomas Paine, and James Mackintosh* (London: Associated University Press, 1997), 85-89.

[446] Moncure Daniel Conway, *The Life of Thomas Paine*, I:346.

[447] Letters to Onslow Cranley, First Letter, in To the Attorney General, in *The Writings of Thomas Paine*, III:30-33.

[448] As to the claim that William Blake urged Paine to depart from England, see G.E. Bentley, *Blake Records* (Oxford: Clarendon, 1969), 530. For one prominent rebuttal to the tale, see Niall McDevitt, "Revolting Romantics," April 14, 2021. https://www.historytoday.com/miscellanies/revolting-romantics (accessed November 5, 2021). For Paine's account of the incident at the York Hotel in Dover, see To Mr. Secretary Dundas, in *The Writings of Thomas Paine*, III:41-44.

[449] Ibid., 41. The letter from Calais is quoted in David Freeman Hawke, *Paine*, 252.

[450] To Mr. Secretary Dundas, in *The Writings of Thomas Paine*, III:41-44.

[451] *The London Chronicle*, September 19, 1792.

CHAPTER 6
THE AGE OF REASON

[452] Moncure Daniel Conway, *The Life of Thomas Paine*, I:347, 353-354.

[453] Ibid., I:356.

[454] Address to the People of France, in *The Writings of Thomas Paine*, III:97-100.

[455] For Paine's opinion on the war, see "Thomas Paine to Benjamin Mosley, October 1, 1792," Thomas Paine National Historical Association. https://thomaspaine.org/letters/other/to-benjamin-mosley-october-1-1792.html (accessed November 8, 2021).

[456] Anti-monarchal Essay, For the Use of New Republicans, in *The Writings of Thomas Paine*, III:101-104

[457] Ibid., 107-108.

[458] Address to the People of France, in Ibid., III:100.

[459] Ibid., III:98.

[460] Address to the People of France, in Ibid., III:100.

[461] *The Diary and Letters of Gouverneur Morris*, II:2, 7.

[462] Anti-monarchal Essay, For the Use of New Republicans, in *The Writings of Thomas Paine*, III:102.

[463] Simon Schama, *Citizens: A Chronicle of the French Revolution*, 650-651.

[464] The English translation of Saint-Just's speech is quoted in Eugene Newton Curtis, *Saint-Just, Colleague of Robespierre* (New York: Octagon Books, 1973), 38.

[465] On the Propriety of Bringing Louis XVI to Trial, in *The Writings of Thomas Paine*, III:114-118.

[466] Simon Schama, *Citizens: A Chronicle of the French Revolution*, 651-652. For Robespierre's famous quote in support of executing Louis XVI, see "Robespierre (3 December 1792)," Liberté, Égalité, Fraternité: Exploring the French Revolution. https://revolution.chnm.org/items/show/526 (accessed November 13, 2021).

[467] Reasons for Preserving the Life of Louis Capet, in *The Writings of Thomas Paine*, III:119-122.

[468] Ibid., 121-124.

[469] Shall Louis XVI Have Respite?, in Ibid., III:125.

[470] Ibid., 126-127. In footnote 1, Moncure Conway cites a primary source to substantiate Marat's strategy to undermine him.

[471] "The Whole Proceedings on the Trial of an Information Exhibited Ex Officio by the King's Attorney-General Against Thomas Paine: For a Libel Upon the Revolution and Settlement of the Crown and Regal Government as by Law Established, Tried by a Special Jury in the Court of King's Bench, Guildhall, on Tuesday, the 18th of December, 1792," Eighteenth Century Collections Online. https://quod.lib.umich.edu/e/ecco/004809449.0001.000/1:2?rgn=div1;view=fulltext (accessed November 16, 2021).

[472] Speech for Thomas Paine, in *Speeches of Thomas Lord Erskine*, Edited by Edward Walford (2 Vols., London: Reeves & Turner, 1870), 305-309, 337.

[473] Ibid., 309-317.

[474] Mark Crosby, "The Voice of Flattery vs Sober Truth: William Godwin, Thomas Paine and the 1792 Trial of Thomas Paine for Sedition," *The Review of English Studies* 62, No. 253 (2011):92.

[475] "Thomas Paine to Doctor James O'Fallon February the 17, 1793," Thomas Paine National Historical Association. https://thomaspaine.org/letters/other/to-doctor-james-o-fallon-february-the-17-1793.html (accessed November 17, 2021).

[476] Moncure Daniel Conway, *The Life of Thomas Paine*, I:379-380. This quote is according to the recollections of John King, a friend of Paine.

[477] Ibid.

[478] Declaration of Rights, in *The Writings of Thomas Paine*, III:128-131.

[479] Forgetfulness, in Ibid., 317-318; Private Letters to Jefferson, April 20, 1793, in Ibid., 132.

[480] Thomas Clio Rickman, *The Life of Thomas Paine*, 129-130.

[481] Ibid., 134-135.

[482] Earl Higgins, *The French Revolution as Told by* Contemporaries (New York: Houghton Mifflin Company, 1938), 284.

[483] Private Letters to Jefferson, April 20, 1793, in *The Writings of Thomas Paine*, III:133.

[484] John Keane, *Tom Paine: A Political* Life, 250-251.

[485] Letter to Danton, May 6, 1793, in *The Writings of Thomas Paine*, III:135-138.

[486] Ibid., 138. For information on Paine's letter to Marat, see Ibid., 135, footnote 1, and John Keane, *Tom Paine: A Political* Life, 378.

[487]

[488] *The Diary and Letters of Gouverneur Morris*, II:48.

[489] "Thomas Paine to Citizen Barrere, September 5, 1793," Thomas Paine National Historical Association. https://thomaspaine.org/letters/other/to-citizen-barrere-september-5-1793.html (accessed November 24, 2021).

[490] For instance, see John Keane, *Tom Paine: A Political* Life, 386. Keane alleged Paine's failure to set sail was prompted by his fear of being perceived as a traitor.

[491] The verbal condemnation of Paine is quoted in Moncure Daniel Conway, *The Life of Thomas Paine*, II:94.

[492] Thomas Paine to Thomas Jefferson, October 20, 1793, in *The Writings of Thomas Paine*, III:134.

[493] Forgetfulness, in Ibid., III:318-319; John Keane, *Tom Paine: A Political* Life, 389-390.

[494] Autobiography, in *The Works of John Adams*, II:508.

[495] Moncure Daniel Conway, *The Life of Thomas Paine*, II:104-106.

[496] Ibid., 106-107.

[497] Addenda 5, in *The Writings of Thomas Paine*, III:212; Gouverneur Morris to Thomas Jefferson, March 6, 1794, in *The Life and Correspondence of Gouverneur Morris*, Edited by Jared Sparks (3 Vols., Boston: Gray & Bowen, 1832), II:409; Gouverneur Morris to Thomas Jefferson, January 21, 1794, in Ibid., 393.

[498] Prison conditions are described in John Keane, *Tom Paine: A Political* Life, 403; Craig Nelson, *Thomas Paine: Enlightenment, Revolution, and the Birth of Modern Nations*, 274-275.

[499] Gouverneur Morris to François Deforgues, in *The Writings of Thomas Paine*, III:159-160. For English translations, see footnote 1 on page 160; Gouverneur Morris to Thomas Jefferson, January 21, 1794, in *The Life and Correspondence of Gouverneur Morris*, 393.

[500] Paine to Gouverneur Morris, February 14, 1793, in Ibid., 181. See footnote 1.

[501] Thomas Paine to James Monroe, September 10, 1794, in *The Writings of Thomas Paine*, III:180.

[502]Ibid., 221-222; "Thomas Paine to James Monroe, October 4, 1794," Thomas Paine National Historical Association. https://thomaspaine.org/letters/james-monroe/to-james-monroe-october-4-1794.html (accessed November 30, 2021).

[503] Moncure Daniel Conway, *The Life of Thomas Paine*, II:107-109.

[504] The petition's reception was described by the account of Paine's friend Thomas Griffith, quoted in *My Scrap-Book of the French Revolution*, Edited by Elizabeth Latimer (Chicago: A.C. McClurg and Company, 1898), 51; Moncure Daniel Conway, *The Life of Thomas Paine*, II:109-110.

[505] Thomas Paine to James Monroe, August 17, 1794, in *The Writings of Thomas Paine*, III:164-166.

[506] Letter to Danton, May 6, 1793, in Ibid., III:135. See footnote 1.

[507] Simon Schama, *Citizens: A Chronicle of the French Revolution*, 834-836.

[508] For casualties of the Reign of Terror, see Hugh Gough, *The Terror in the French Revolution* (New York: Red Globe Press, 2010), 109, and Donald Greer, *The Incidence of the Terror during the French Revolution: A Statistical Interpretation*, (Cambridge: Harvard University Press, 1935). This figure includes the official court record of 16,594 sentenced to death, those that were executed without trial, and those that died in prison.

[509] Quoted in Adam Black and Charles Black, "France," *Encyclopaedia Britannica, or Dictionary of Arts, Sciences, and General Literature* (21 Vols, Edinburgh: Adam and Charles Black, 1842), X:90.

[510] John Keane, *Tom Paine: A Political* Life, 412-413; Letter III, Letters to American Citizens, in *The Writings of Thomas Paine*, III:395; General Introduction, in Ibid., IV:xiv-xv.

[511] Ibid., 395-397; Thomas Clio Rickman, *The Life of Thomas Paine*, 26.

[512] Appeal to the Convention, in *The Writings of Thomas Paine*, III:147-148.

[513] Ibid., 148-149.

[514] Thomas Clio Rickman, *The Life of Thomas Paine*, 261. It is unclear why the communication never reached the National Convention, as by this time the prohibition on correspondence had been lifted in Luxembourg prison.

[515] "Thomas Paine to James Monroe, August 16, 1794," Thomas Paine National Historical Association. https://thomaspaine.org/letters/james-monroe/to-james-monroe-august-16-1794.html (accessed November 30, 2021); "Thomas Paine to James Monroe, August 18, 1794," Ibid., https://thomaspaine.org/letters/james-monroe/to-james-monroe-august-18-1794.html (accessed November 30, 2021).

[516] "Thomas Paine to James Monroe, August 25, 1794," Thomas Paine National Historical Association. https://thomaspaine.org/letters/james-monroe/to-james-monroe-august-25-1794.html (accessed November 30, 1794); "Thomas Paine to James Monroe, October 13, 1794," Ibid., https://thomaspaine.org/letters/james-monroe/to-james-monroe-october-13-1794.html (accessed November 30, 2021).

[517] The Memorial to Monroe, in *The Writings of Thomas Paine*, III:207-211.

[518] To the Committee of General Security, in *The Writings of James Monroe*, II:96-98.

[519] James Monroe to Edmund Randolph, November 7, 1794, in Ibid., II:106-108; James Monroe to James Madison, January 20, 1796, in Ibid., II:440-441.

[520] Paine noted the unavailability of candles in Memorial to Monroe, *The Writings of Thomas Paine*, III:193.

[521] The Age of Reason, in Ibid., IV:21-22.

[522] Ibid., 22.

[523] Ibid.

[524] Ibid., 23-24.

[525] Ibid., 26-27.

[526] Ibid., 28-30.

[527] Ibid., 47, 68-73.

[528] Ibid., 75-80,

[529] Ibid., 81-82.

[530] Ibid., 65-66, 83.

[531] Ibid., 83-84.

[532] For David Hume's probable influence on Paine, see Caroline Robbins, "The Lifelong Education of Thomas Paine," *Proceedings of the American Philosophical Society* 127, No. 3 (1983):135-142; The Rights of Man, Part Second, in *The Writings of Thomas Paine*, II:508; The Age of Reason, in Ibid., IV:65.

[533] Ibid., 32; Ibid., II:508; John Keane, *Tom Paine: A Political* Life, 39; Eric Foner, *Tom Paine and Revolutionary America* (London: Oxford University Press, 1976), 270.

[534] For Washington's stern letter to Carleton, see "George Washington to Guy Carleton, May 6, 1783," Founders Archive, National Archives. https://founders.archives.gov/documents/Washington/99-01-02-11218 (accessed March 28, 2022). Article VII of the 1783 Treaty of Paris stipulated that Britain was to, "with all convenient speed, and without causing any Destruction, or carrying away any Negroes or other Property of the American inhabitants, withdraw all his Armies, Garrisons & Fleets from the said United States."

[535] "Thomas Paine to Samuel Adams, March 6, 1795," Thomas Paine National Historical Association. https://thomaspaine.org/letters/other/to-samuel-adams-march-6-1795.html (accessed December 2, 2021); Paine's Seventh Letter, in *The Writings of Thomas Paine*, III:420-421.

[536] The Age of Reason, Part Second, in Ibid., IV:88.

CHAPTER 7
DIRECTORY TO DICTATORSHIP

[537] James Monroe to Edmund Randolph, January 13, 1795, in *The Writings of James Monroe*, II:167-168; John Keane, *Tom Paine: A Political* Life, 421.

[538] Descriptions for the of the two houses are from the English translation of the quote from Boissy d'Anglas in "The Constitutional Novelties of the Year III," Open Edition Books. https://books.openedition.org/pur/19748?lang=fr (accessed December 3, 2021).

[539] The Eighteenth Fructidor, in *The Writings of Thomas Paine*, III:345-349.

[540] Ibid., 349.

[541] Dissertation on the First Principles of Government, in Ibid., 260-261, 265.

[542] The Constitution of 1795, in Ibid., 279-285.

[543] "Thomas Paine to James Madison, September 24, 1795," Thomas Paine National Historical Association. https://thomaspaine.org/letters/other/to-james-madison-september-24-1795.html (accessed December 4, 2021); The Philadelphia *Aurora General Advertiser*, January 14, 1796.

[544] The Age of Reason, Part Second, in *The Writings of Thomas Paine*, IV:90.

[545] Ibid., 91-92.

[546] Ibid., 93-94, 96; Peter Enns, *The Evolution of Adam: What the Bible Does and Doesn't Say about Human Origins* (Grand Rapids: Brazos Press, 2012), 17.

[547] The Age of Reason, Part Second, in *The Writings of Thomas Paine*, IV:152-156, 158-159. The biblical account of the saints arising from their graves is found in Matthew 27:52.

[548] Ibid., 190-194.

[549] Ibid., 184-185.

[550] Joseph Priestley, *An Answer to Mr. Paine's Age of Reason, being a Continuation of Letters to the Philosophers and Politicians of France on the Subject of Religion and of the Letters to a Philosophical Unbeliever* (London: J. Johnson, 1794), 83-85.

[551] Richard Watson, *An Apology for the Bible, in a Series of Letters* (New York: T. & J. Swords, 1796), 78.

[552] Agrarian Justice, in *The Writings of Thomas Paine*, III:322-324, 327.

[553] Ibid., 382-331.

[554] John Locke, The Two Treatises of Government (London: A. Millar, 1689), 216-217.

[555] Agrarian Justice, in *The Writings of Thomas Paine*, III:331-332, 338. The calculation of £15 in 1795 to United States dollars in 2021, figuring for inflation,

according to "CPI Inflation Calculator," https://www.in2013dollars.com/uk/infla-tion/2020?amount=1895 (accessed December 5, 2021).

[556] Agrarian Justice, in *The Writings of Thomas Paine*, III:331-334.

[557] Ibid., 322.

[558] The Decline and Fall of the English System of Finance, in Ibid., III:287-299.

[559] Ibid., 300-301, 312.

[560] John Keane, *Tom Paine: A Political* Life, 427-428.

[561] "Thomas Paine to Thomas Jefferson, April 1, 1797," Thomas Paine National Historical Association. https://thomaspaine.org/letters/thomas-jefferson/to-thomas-jefferson-april-1-1797.html (accessed December 7, 2021).

[562] George Washington to Timothy Pickering, September 23, 1795, in *The Papers of George Washington*, Presidential Series XVIII:726-728.

[563] Thomas Paine, Paris, February 22, 1795, in *The Writings of Thomas Paine*, III:230-231. This letter was never sent to Washington.

[564] Ibid., 232-235.

[565] Thomas Paine to George Washington, September 20, 1795, in Ibid., 229-230.

[566] Ibid.

[567] James Monroe to James Madison, July 5, 1796, in *The Writings of James Monroe*, III:20-21.

[568] Letter to George Washington, in *The Writings of Thomas Paine*, III:213-214.

[569] Ibid., 215.

[570] Ibid., 217-218.

[571] Ibid., 247-252.

[572] Details of Monroe's letter are covered in Harry Ammon, *James Monroe: The Quest for National Identity* (Charlottesville: University Press of Virginia), 151-152; Ron Chernow, *Washington: A Life* (New York: Penguin Books, 2010), 744.

[573] The *Columbian Centinel*, January 18, 1797; Patrick Kennedy, *An Answer to Paine's Letter to General Washington* (Philadelphia: William Cobbett, Opposite Christ Church, 1798), Introduction; An American Citizen, In Whose Heart the Amor Patriae Holds the Highest Place, *A Letter to Thomas Paine, in Answer to His Scurrilous Epistle Addressed to Our Late Worthy President Washington* (New York: John Bull, No. 115 Cherry Street, 1787), 1, 14, 23.

[574] "George Washington to David Stuart, January 8, 1797," in *The Papers of George Washington*, Retirement Series II:37-38; William Cobbett, *Porcupine's Political Censor, for December, 1796* (Philadelphia: William Cobbett, Opposite Christ Church, 1797), 2, 17-18. Despite Cobbett's "strong and coarse expressions," Washington depicted the work as "not a bad thing."

[575] "Thomas Paine to James Madison, April 27, 1787," Thomas Paine National Historical Association. https://thomaspaine.org/letters/other/to-james-madison-april-27-1797.html (accessed December 30, 2021

[576] The Eighteenth Fructidor, in *The Writings of Thomas Paine*, III:356-357.

[577] For the resolution granting Washington extraordinary power, see *Journals of the Continental Congress, 1774-1789*, Edited by Worthington Ford (34 Vols., Washington, D.C.: Library of Congress, 1906), VI:1027; The Eighteenth Fructidor, in *The Writings of Thomas Paine*, III:357-358.

[578] Ibid., 359.

[579] The Recall of Monroe, in *The Writings of Thomas Paine*, III:369-370.

[580] Alfred Owen Aldridge, "Thomas Paine's Plan for a Descent on England," *The William and Mary Quarterly* 127, No. 1 (January, 1957):75, 80. *Observations on the Construction and Operation of Navies with a Plan for an Invasion of England and the Final Overthrow of the English Government* was published for the first time in this article.

[581] Ibid., 81-83.

[582] Thomas Paine to The Council of Five Hundred, in *Thomas Paine: Collected Writings*, II:1403.

[583] Moncure Daniel Conway, *The Life of Thomas Paine*, II:275-276; Thomas Clio Rickman, *The Life of Thomas Paine*, 164; "Thomas Paine to Thomas Jefferson, January 30, 1806," Thomas Paine National Historical Association. https://thomaspaine.org/letters/thomas-jefferson/to-thomas-jefferson-january-30-1806.html (accessed January 10, 2022). The particulars of Bonaparte's proposed provisional republic for England is found in Bernard Vincent, *Thomas Paine ou la religion de la liberté* (Paris: Aubier 1987), 343.

[584] Henry Readhead Yorke, *France in Eighteen Hundred and Two: Described in a Series of Contemporary Letters*, Edited by J.A.C. Sykes (London: William Heinemann, 1906), 241-242.

[585] Ibid., 242. It is unknown why Paine suggested a peace with Britain while in the company of Napoleon's military council. The decision was erratic for Paine, who continued to hope France would invade his homeland and abolish its monarchical system.

[586] Ibid.

[587] Christian Cherfils, *Bonaparte et l'islam d'après les documents français & arabes* (Paris: A. Pedone, 1914), 127.

[588] John Keane, *Tom Paine: A Political* Life, 442-443.

[589] Robert Asprey, *The Rise of Napoleon Bonaparte* (New York: Basic Books, 2000), 312.

[590] Ibid., 321-323.

[591] Ibid., 336-338.

[592] Ibid., 388; Andrew Roberts, *Napoleon: A Life* (New York: Penguin, 2014), 223-225.

[593] John Keane, *Tom Paine: A Political* Life, 443-444.

[594] Ibid., 444.

[595] Thomas Paine to Anonymous, 12 Thermidor, Year 8, in *Thomas Paine: Collected Writings*, II:1406.

[596] Henry Readhead Yorke, *France in Eighteen Hundred and Two: Described in a Series of Contemporary Letters*, 242.

[597] For the Federalist prosecution campaign, see Wendell Bird, Criminal Dissent: Prosecutions under the Alien and Sedition Acts of 1798 (Cambridge: Harvard University Press, 2020). For the Sedition Act Crisis, see Dave Benner, David Benner, *Compact of the Republic: The League of States and the Constitution* (Minneapolis: Life & Liberty Publishing Group, 2015), 147-175. For Jefferson's description, see Thomas Jefferson to John Taylor, June 4, 1798, in *The Papers of Thomas Jefferson*, XXX:387-390.

[598] Thomas Paine to Thomas Jefferson, June 9, 1801, in *Thomas Paine: Collected Writings*, II:1419. For Jefferson's presidential platform, see "Thomas Jefferson's First Inaugural Address, March 4, 1801," The Avalon Project: Documents in Law, History, and Diplomacy. https://avalon.law.yale.edu/19th_century/jefinau1.asp (accessed January 23, 2022).

[599] Thomas Paine to Thomas Jefferson, October 1, 1800, in *Thomas Paine: Collected Writings*, II:1411-1412.

[600] Moncure Daniel Conway, *The Life of Thomas Paine,* II:284.

[601] For the controversy over the proposition to bring Paine back to American on board a public vessel, see Ibid., II:296-299.

[602] Thomas Paine to Consul Roth, July 8, 1802, in *Thomas Paine: Collected Writings*, II:1429.

[603] Thomas Clio Rickman, *The Life of Thomas Paine*, 171-172.

CHAPTER 8
RETURN TO AMERICA

[604] Thomas Jefferson to George Washington, September 9, 1792, in *The Papers of Thomas Jefferson*, XXIV:351-360.

[605] For the report of Paine and Jefferson's meetings, see Chapter XLII, in *The Life and Correspondence of Gouverneur Morris*, II:427. For Paine's description of his reception, see Thomas Paine to Clio Rickman, March 8, 1803, in *Thomas Paine: Collected Writings*, II:1439-1440.

[606] *The Baltimore Republic, or The Anti-Democrat*, October 18, 1802; Port Folio, July 18, 1801; Introduction, in *Thomas Paine: Collected Writings*, I:xlii; *Gazette of the United States, and Daily Advertiser,* July 21; Ibid., September 28, 1801.

[607] *National Intelligencer*, November 3, 1802; Ibid., November 10, 1802.

[608] *New-York Evening Post*, November 3, 1802.

[609] John Keane, *Tom Paine: A Political* Life, 459-460; *Richmond Recorder*, December 8, 1802.

[610] Ibid.; Thomas Paine to Elihu Palmer, February 21, 1802, in *Thomas Paine: Collected Writings*, 1426.

[611] Thomas Jefferson to Ezra Stiles Ely, in *The Papers of Thomas Jefferson*, XIV:470-471; Thomas Jefferson, *The Life and Morals of Jesus of Nazareth* (New York: N.D. Thompson Publishing Co., 1902).

[612] Proposal that Louisiana Be Purchased, in *The Writings of Thomas Paine*, III:379-380.

[613] Livingston's quote

[614] Timothy Pickering to Richard Peters, in Henry Adams, *Documents Relating to New-England Federalism*, 1800-1815 (Boston: Little Brown, 1877), Claude Bowers, Jefferson in Power: *The Death Struggle of the Federalists* (Boston: Riverside Press, 1936), 235.

[615] Thomas Jefferson to John Dickinson, August 9, 1803, in *The Papers of Thomas Jefferson*, XLI:169-171.

[616] To the Citizens of the United States, in *The Complete Writings of Thomas Paine*, II:909-912.

[617] Ibid., 913-915, 936.

[618] Ibid., 918-923.

[619] Ibid., 929-931.

[620] Samuel Adams to Thomas Paine, November 30, 1802, in Ibid., II:1433.

[621] Thomas Paine to Samuel Adams, January 1, 1803, in Ibid., II:1434-1438.

[622] Ibid., 1438.

[623] Thomas Paine to Thomas Jefferson, January 12, 1803, in Ibid., II:1439.

[624] Thomas Jefferson to Thomas Paine, January 13, 1803, in *The Papers of Thomas Jefferson*, XXXIX:331; The Construction of Iron Bridges, in *The Complete Writings of Thomas Paine*, II:1051.

[625] The Philadelphia *Aurora General Advertiser*, February 17, 1803; John Keane, *Tom Paine: A Political* Life, 478-479.

[626] Ibid., 479.

[627] Moncure Daniel Conway, *The Life of Thomas Paine*, II:472. This was taken from an entry in Hall's diary for April 19, 1803.

[628] Ibid., II:327.

[629] John Keane, *Tom Paine: A Political* Life, 480-482; The New York *American Citizen,* March 16, 1803; James Cheetham, *The Life of Thomas Paine* (London: A. Maxwell, Bell Yard, Temple Bar, 1817), 145.

[630] Louisiana, in *The Complete Writings of Thomas Paine*, II:1502-1503.

[631] Moncure Daniel Conway, *The Life of Thomas Paine*, II:447.

[632] The Construction of Iron Bridges, in *The Writings of Thomas Paine*, IV:445-449. In regard to internal improvements, one of the key aspects of Henry Clay's "American System" called for the construction of roads, bridges, and canals by the general government. The first major battle of this issue culminated in James Madison's veto of such a plan in 1817.

[633] Thomas Paine to Thomas Jefferson, September 23, 1803, in *The Complete Writings of Thomas Paine*, II:1447-1448

[634] Ibid., 1460, 1462.

[635] "Paine, Thomas (1737-1809) to Anthony Taylor," The Gilder Lehrman Institute of American History. https://www.gilderlehrman.org/collection/glc04281 (accessed March 3, 2022); Thomas Paine to Mr. Hyer, March 24, 1804, in *The Complete Writings of Thomas Paine*, II:1451-1452.

[636] To the People of England, in *The Writings of Thomas Paine*, IV:451-456.

[637] Ibid.; Robert Asprey, *The Rise of Napoleon Bonaparte*, 500-511.

[638] To the French Inhabitants of Louisiana, in *The Complete Writings of Thomas Paine*, II:964-967.

[639] Ibid., 965, 968.

[640] Elihu Palmer, *Principles of Nature; or a Development of the Moral Causes of Happiness and Misery among the Human Species* (London: John Cahuac, 1819), 95.

[641] Prospect Papers, in *The Complete Writings of Thomas Paine*, II:789-790, 794-795.

[642] Ibid., 801.

[643] "Thomas Paine to Elisha Babcock, August 8, 1804," Thomas Paine National Historical Association. https://thomaspaine.org/letters/to-elisha-babcock-1804-08-27.html (accessed March 9, 2022); To the Citizens of the United States, in *The Complete Writings of Thomas Paine*, II:947-948.

[644] Ibid., 957.

[645] Constitutions, Governments, and Charters, in *The Complete Writings of Thomas Paine*, II:989-990.

[646] Ibid., 987, 991.

[647] Another Callender – Thomas Turner of Virginia, in *The Complete Writings of Thomas Paine*, II:980-983.

[648] Ibid., 983-985.

[649] Constitutional Reform, in Ibid., II:992-994.

[650] Ibid., 999-1002.

[651] Ibid., 1001-1005.

[652] Ibid., 1007.

[653] David Freeman Hawke, *Paine*, 372.

[654] Thomas Paine to John Fellows, July 31, 1805, in *The Complete Writings of Thomas Paine*, II:1471.

[655] Thomas Paine to Thomas Jefferson, September 30, 1805, in *The Complete Writings of Thomas Paine*, II:1472-1473.

[656] "Thomas Paine to Thomas Jefferson, November 14, 1805" Library of Congress. https://www.loc.gov/item/mtjbib015289/ (accessed March 11, 2022).

[657] Marian Touba, "Paine's Misfortunes in New Rochelle: Some Matters of Chronology," *Bulletin of Thomas Paine Friends*, Vol 10, No. 4 (Winter 2009-2010):4. Many biographers place the date of the incident on Christmas Eve of 1804 rather than 1805. However, various newspaper accounts and corroborating court dates for Derrick's trial reveal that the attempt on Paine's life actually took place in 1805. Paine's letter to Carver with a January 16, 1805 date can be explained as a mistake on the part of the writer, who likely wrote in the old year out of habit.

[658] Thomas Paine to William Carver, January 16, 1805, in *The Complete Writings of Thomas Paine*, II:1455-1456; The New-York *Commercial Advertiser*, January 31, 1806.

[659] Thomas Paine to Thomas Jefferson, January 30, 1806, in *The Complete Writings of Thomas Paine*, II:1473-1476, 1478.

[660] "Thomas Jefferson to Thomas Paine, March 25, 1806," Founders Online, National Archives. https://founders.archives.gov/documents/Jefferson/99-01-02-3477 (accessed March 14, 2022); "Thomas Jefferson to Thomas Paine, February 21, 1806," Founders Online, National Archives. https://founders.archives.gov/documents/Jefferson/99-01-02-3276 (accessed March 14, 2022).

[661] William Carver to Thomas Paine, December 2, 1806, quoted in James Cheetham, *The Life of Thomas Paine*, 138-139; "William Carver to Thomas Jefferson, November 25, 1823," Founders Online, National Archives. https://founders.archives.gov/documents/Jefferson/98-01-02-3884 (accessed March 15, 2022).

[662] "Philadelphia Under Siege: The Yellow Fever of 1793," Pennsylvania Center for the Book. https://www.pabook.libraries.psu.edu/literary-cultural-heritage-

map-pa/feature-articles/philadelphia-under-siege-yellow-fever-1793   (accessed March 16, 2022.

[663] The Cause of the Yellow Fever, and the Means of Preventing it in Places Not Yet Infected With It, in *The Complete Writings of Thomas Paine*, II:1060-1061, 1065-1066; Thomas Paine to Thomas Jefferson, September 23, 1803, in Ibid., 1450.

[664] Quoted in John Keane, *Tom Paine: A Political* Life, 517. From the account of John Melish, a Scottish-born mapmaker who befriended Jefferson.

[665] Thomas Paine to Andrew Dean, August 15, 1806, in *The Complete Writings of Thomas Paine*, II:1483-1485.

[666] John Melish, *Travels in the United States of America, in the Years 1806 & 1807, and 1809, 1810, & 1811* (London: Reprinted for the Author, 1818), 61-62.

[667] William Carver to Thomas Paine, December 2, 1806, in James Cheetham, *The Life of Thomas Paine*, 133-141.

[668] Thomas Paine to William Carver, November 25, 1806, in Ibid., 131-133.

[669] William Carver to Thomas Paine, December 2, 1806, in Ibid., 133-141.

[670] Thomas Jefferson to James Madison, May 3, 1807, in *The Complete Writings of Thomas Paine*, II:1486-1487; Thomas Jefferson to George Clinton, May 4, 1807, in Ibid., 1487-1488; Thomas Jefferson to Joel Barlow, May 4, 1807, in Ibid., 1488-1489.

[671] Thomas Scoble, "Thomas Paine's Citizenship Record," Thomas Paine National Historical Association. http://thomaspaine.org/aboutpaine/thomas-paine-s-citizenship-record.html (accessed March 21, 2022).

[672] Harold Dickson, "The Jarvis Portrait of Thomas Paine," *The New-York Historical Society Quarterly* 34, No. 1 (1950):9.

[673] An Essay on Dream, in *The Complete Writings of Thomas Paine*, II:841-848.

[674] Thomas Clio Rickman, *The Life of Thomas Paine*, 182-183.

[675] Thomas Paine to Joel Barlow, May 4, 1807, in *The Complete Writings of Thomas Paine*, II:1488-1489.

[676] Alfred Albridge, *Man of Reason: The Life of Thomas Paine* (Philadelphia: Lippincott, 1959), 308.

[677] Ibid., 308-309.

[678] Cheetham and his Tory Paper, in *The Complete Writings of Thomas Paine*, II:1017-1018.

[679] Will There be War?, in Ibid., II:1012-1017; Of Gun-boats, in Ibid., 1067-1072.

[680] For comments on Jefferson's supposed advice, see Examination of the Prophecies, in *The Complete Writings of Thomas Paine*, II:848. Foner states that Jefferson "advised and requested him" not to publish the work, but leaves no citation for the quotes, which do not appear in any volume of Jefferson's writings. Other scholars have repeated this claim, apparently on the basis of Foner's note, such as in Edward Davidson and William Scheick, *Paine, Scripture, and Authority: The Age of Reason as Religious and Political Idea* (Bethlehem, PA: Lehigh University Press, 1994), 103-106.

[681] Examination of the Prophecies, in *The Complete Writings of Thomas Paine*, II:848-850.

[682] Ibid., 852-854.

[683] Ibid., 859-861, 870.

[684] Ibid., 891-892. Paine's opinion conflicts with Matthew when considered in its entirety. For instance, Matthew 21:22 and 6:9-13 instructs Christ's followers to engage in prayer and to have faith in his power, Matthew 28:19-20 encourages disciples to baptize others in his name and engage in evangelism, and Matthew 26:26-28 instituted the Lord's Supper as a ritual for believers.

[685] Thomas Paine to Joel Barlow, May 4, 1807, in *The Complete Writings of Thomas Paine*, II:1489.

[686] To the Honorable Senate of the United States, January 21, 1808, in Ibid., II:1489-1492; John Keane, *Tom Paine: A Political* Life, 509.

[687] To the Honorable Senate of the United States, January 21, 1808, in Ibid., II:1492-1495.

[688] James Cheetham, *The Life of Thomas Paine*, 148.

[689] Gilbert Vale, *The Life of Thomas Paine* (New York: The Author, 1841), 159-164. Vale personally interviewed the array of men denying the prevailing accusations, many of which knew Paine intimately. To the contrary of their testimony, Cheetham's allegations greatly influenced most subsequent biographies, such as those by Francis Oldys, Howard Fast, John Keane, which generally repeated the same claims without subjecting them to scrutiny.

[690] Thomas Paine to Thomas Jefferson, July 8, 1808, in *The Complete Writings of Thomas Paine*, II:1496-1497; "Thomas Jefferson to Thomas Paine, July 17, 1808," National Archives. https://founders.archives.gov/documents/Jefferson/99-01-02-8350 (accessed March 24, 2022).

[691] Paine's response recorded in The Cobbett Papers, in Moncure Daniel Conway, *The Life of Thomas* Paine, II:450. These observations according to Marguerite Bonneville, who intended to publish a biography of Paine. A decade after his death, she sold the manuscript to William Cobbett.

[692] To the Federal Faction, in *The Political Writings of Thomas Paine* (2 Vols., Boston: J.P Mendum, 1870), II:507-508.

[693] Predestination, in *The Complete Writings of Thomas Paine*, II:894-897.

[694] T. Adams, in *Democracy Unveiled; in a Letter to Sir Francis Burdett* (London: W. McDowall, 1811), 292-294; John Keane, *Tom Paine: A Political* Life, 531-532.

[695] The Cobbett Papers, in Moncure Daniel Conway, *The Life of Thomas* Paine, II:450-451; The Will of Thomas Paine, in *The Complete Writings of Thomas Paine*, II:1498-1501.

[696] Ibid., 1500. Information on Paine's grave from The Cobbett Papers, in Moncure Daniel Conway, *The Life of Thomas* Paine, II:455, and James Feron, "Paine Tombstone Uncovered Upstate Revives Mystery About Pamphleteer," *The New York Times*, July 19, 1796. https://www.nytimes.com/1976/07/19/archives/paine-tombstone-uncovered-upstate-revives-mystery-about-pamphleteer.html (accessed March 26, 2022). In the immediate years after his death, pilgrims broke off pieces of the original gravestone.

[697] Ibid., 1500; The Cobbett Papers, in Moncure Daniel Conway, *The Life of Thomas* Paine, II:451.

[698] Information regarding visitors in Paine's last days courtesy of John Keane, *Tom Paine: A Political* Life, 533-535.

[699] The Cobbett Papers, in Moncure Daniel Conway, *The Life of Thomas* Paine, II:453-454.

[700] Thomas Clio Rickman, *The Life of Thomas Paine*, 183-185.

[701] James Manley to James Cheetham, October 2, 1809, in James Cheetham, *The Life of Thomas Paine*, 158-159.

CHAPTER 9
EPILOGUE

[702] The New York *Public Advertiser*, June 9, 1809; Thomas Clio Rickman, *The Life of Thomas Paine*, 207; The New-York *Evening Post,* June 10, 1809.

[703] Robert Ingersoll, "Thomas Paine," *North American Review*, August (1892).

[704] A. J. Ayer, *Thomas Paine*, 125-126, 172; Moncure Daniel Conway, *The Life of Thomas* Paine, II:401.

[705] Thomas Clio Rickman, *The Life of Thomas Paine*, X (Preface).

[706] For Cobbett's plan to give the writer a proper burial, see William Cobbett, "Brief History of the Remains of Thomas Paine," Thomas Paine National Historical Association. https://thomaspaine.org/aboutpaine/brief-history-of-the-remains-of-thomas-paine.html (accessed March 26, 2022).

[707] Ibid.; "Paine's First Grave," The *New-York Daily Tribune*, May 4, 1902.

[708] Ibid.; "Heather Thomas, "The Bones of Thomas Paine," Library of Congress, April 2, 2019. https://blogs.loc.gov/headlinesandheroes/2019/04/the-bones-of-thomas-paine/ (accessed March 27, 2022).

CONCLUSION

[709] "Obama's Vindication of Thomas Paine," The Nation. https://www.thenation.com/article/archive/obamas-vindication-thomas-paine/ (accessed March 9, 2022).

[710] "John Adams to Benjamin Waterhouse, October 29, 1805," Founders Online, National Archives. https://founders.archives.gov/documents/Adams/99-02-02-5107 (accessed November 3, 2021).

[711] Dissertations on Government, The Affairs of the Bank, and Paper Money, in *The Writings of Thomas Paine*, II:180. For the value of the United States dollar in 1913 compared to 2022, figuring for inflation, see "CPI Inflation Calculator," https://www.officialdata.org/us/inflation/1913?amount=1 (accessed February 1, 2022).

[712] For the Swiss universal basic income referendum, see "Switzerland's Voters Reject Basic Income Plan," BBC News, https://www.bbc.com/news/world-europe-36454060 (accessed February 3, 2022). For Macau's system, see "Macau's Residents Each Get 9,000 Pataca Handout, but Critics not Satisfied," South China Morning Post, https://www.scmp.com/news/china/article/1354764/macaus-residents-each-get-9000-pataca-handout-critics-not-satisfied (accessed February 3,

2022). For Andrew Yang's promotion of his universal basic income scheme, see "Democratic Presidential Candidate Andrew Yang Draws Hundreds in Cambridge Common Rally," The Harvard Crimson, https://www.thecrimson.com/article/2019/9/17/yang-rally-cambridge/ (accessed February 3, 2020).

[713] Common Sense, in *The Writings of Thomas Paine*, I:89; To the People of England, in Ibid., IV:451.

[714] Thomas Paine to Benjamin Rush, March 16, 1790, in *The Complete Writings of Thomas Paine*, II:1286. For Paine's antislavery tract, see "What was Thomas Paine's Stance on Slavery?," Thomas Paine National Historical Association. https://thomaspaine.org/aboutpaine/what-was-thomas-paine-s-stance-on-slavery.html (accessed February 6, 2022)

[715] For Paine's influence on modern atheism, see Christopher Hitchens, *Thomas Paine's Rights of Man: A Biography*, 123-134, and Susan Jacoby, *Freethinkers: A History of American Secularism* (New York: Henry Holt and Company, 2004), 41-65, and more generally, Sam Harris, *The End of Faith: Religion, Terror, and the Future of Reason* (New York: W. W. Norton & Company, 2004). For modern refutations of Paine's religious ideas, see Norman Geisler and William Roach, *Defending Inerrancy: Affirming the Accuracy of Scripture for a New Generation* (Grand Rapids, Baker Books, 2011), Edward Feser, *The Last Superstition: A Refutation of the New Atheism* (South Bend: St. Augustine's Press, 2010), and Lee Strobel, *The Case for Christ: A Journalist's Personal Investigation of the Evidence for Jesus* (Grand Rapids: Zondervan, 1998).

[716] The Age of Reason, in *The Writings of Thomas Paine*, IV:22.

[717] To the Citizens of the United States, in *The Complete Writings of Thomas Paine*, II:926.

[718] Nathanael Greene to Thomas Paine, November 18, 1782, quoted in Moncure Daniel Conway, *The Life of Thomas* Paine, II:437.

[719] Elihu Palmer, *Principles of Nature; or a Development of the Moral Causes of Happiness and Misery among the Human Species*, 95.

Index